THE LIFE AND TIMES OF
Vuk Stefanović KARADŽIĆ
1787-1864

THE LIFE AND TIMES OF
VUK STEFANOVIĆ KARADŽIĆ

1. THE YOUNG VUK, c. 1816

THE LIFE AND TIMES OF
VUK STEFANOVIĆ KARADŽIĆ
1787–1864

LITERACY, LITERATURE, AND
NATIONAL INDEPENDENCE IN SERBIA

DUNCAN WILSON

καὶ φθέγμα καὶ ἀνεμόεν
φρόνημα καὶ ἀστυνόμους
ὀργὰς ἐδιδάξατο . . .

Ann Arbor

Copyright © 1986 by the University of Michigan
All rights reserved.

Offset from the edition published in 1970
by Oxford University Press by permission.

Library of Congress Cataloging-in-Publication Data
Wilson, Duncan, Sir.
   The life and times of Vuk Stefanović Karadžić, 1787-1864.

   Reprint. Originally published: Oxford : Clarendon Press, 1970.
   Includes bibliographies and index.
   1. Karadžić, Vuk Stefanović, 1787-1864. 2. Slavists-Yugoslavia--Serbia--Biography. 3. Philologists--Yugoslavia--Serbia--Biography. 4. Serbia--Biography.
5. Serbia--History--1804-1918. I. Title.
PG13.M46 no. 27 [PG1217.K3] 398.2'092'4 [B] 86-18194
ISBN 0- 930042-63-8

Michigan Slavic Publications
Department of Slavic Languages and Literatures
The University of Michigan
Ann Arbor, Michigan 48109

TO
BETTY, CATHERINE, DAVID
AND
ELIZABETH
IN MEMORY OF OUR DAYS
IN YUGOSLAVIA

PREFACE

THIS book is not based on primary sources. Vuk's manuscript remains in Belgrade are now being studied in detail by Yugoslav scholars, and the relevant archives in Vienna have been exhaustively used already; it is unlikely that many pickings here or elsewhere remain for a foreign biographer. In any case, as a working diplomat, I could not have found the time necessary for original research. I have therefore confined myself to secondary sources, and in case of need can say with the singers of Serbian tales:

> Niti lažem, nit' istinu kažem,
> Onaj laže koji mene kaže.

(If I do not tell the truth, yet I do not lie. The liar is he who told me.)

As a spare-time author, I have needed much help. It is my first and most agreeable duty to acknowledge the extreme generosity with which this has been given by many Yugoslav friends. My greatest debt is to Dr. Djuro Gavela, Director of the Vuk and Dositej Museum, Belgrade, who from 1964 onwards made available to me the resources of his library and guided me in the use of them. I could not have begun or completed my task without his constant interest and encouragement. Miss Jelena Šaulić of the staff of the Museum was also constantly helpful; I am particularly grateful to her for reading the book in draft and for valuable comments. Professor Nikola Banašević, formerly of Belgrade University, read part of the draft and allowed me to profit from his great knowledge and enthusiasm. At Belgrade University I was also fortunate to be able to discuss certain points with Professor Miodrag Popović, author of the latest (centenary) life of Vuk; and Professor Rela Novaković took much trouble in finding suitable maps. The late Mr. M. Panić-Surep and Mr. S. Milosavljević of the National Library of Serbia were most helpful in providing me with books. Mrs. Nada Čurčija-Prodanović, herself an accomplished translator from Serbo-Croat into English, was kind enough to read the translations in Appendix A, and to make some most valuable comments and corrections. I am indebted to Mr. Buda Milenković (of Vuk's Tršić), Mr. Dimitrije Stefanović, and Mr. V. M. Vukomirović for sending me interesting material. Nor can I leave unmentioned a longer-term debt, to Mr. Rade Stojanović for teaching me over many years something of the Serbo-Croat language and for his company on many journeys in Serbia.

I must record my gratitude to the staff of the French Embassy in Belgrade, particularly to Mr. Gérard Amanrich, for making available some very useful French books.

In England also I have found much help and encouragement. Mr. Rohan Butler, Mr. Peter Calvocoressi, and Professor Hugh Seton-Watson were good enough to read all or most of the book in draft. I am grateful to the latter for expert comments on Chapter IX; and this chapter could not have been drafted originally without the unfailing kindness and detailed researches of Mr. Alexander Elkin. Professor Elizabeth Hill made valuable comments on the early chapters. Mr. and Mrs. Richard Kindersley gave me much support from the first, and organized my first visit to Vuk's birthplace, Tršić. My son, Mr. David Wilson, helped me greatly with the drafting of Chapter I. I have been much encouraged by the interest shown on various points by Mr. Michael Balfour, Sir Maurice Bowra, Mr. F. W. D. Deakin, Lady Garvey, Mr. H. Koeppler, Sir Fitzroy Maclean, and Mr. Stephen Stewart. I acknowledge gratefully the help given by Wilma Hodge, Ann Hudson, Eileen Endruweit, Isobel Duncan, Jean Martin, and Pat Flanagan in typing successive stages of my draft.

Finally I must thank my wife for her constant interest and encouragement and for enabling me to spend an inordinate proportion of my spare time on the preparation of this book.

CONTENTS

LIST OF PLATES	xi
LIST OF MAPS	xi
PRONUNCIATION OF SERBO-CROAT	xiii
MONETARY TABLE	xv
I. SURVEY OF VUK'S LIFE AND WORK	1
II. EARLY YEARS AND BACKGROUND: 1787–1804	11
III. THE SERBIAN UPRISING: 1804–5	28
IV. FURTHER EDUCATION IN KARLOVCI AND BELGRADE	45
V. BUDA, 1810: SERBIA, 1810–13	63
VI. KOPITAR AND FIRST YEARS IN VIENNA	79
VII. GRAMMAR AND 'POPULAR SONGS'	98
VIII. DICTIONARY AND MARRIAGE	114
IX. JOURNEY TO RUSSIA, 1819	131
X. VUK AND MILOŠ OBRENOVIĆ	150
XI. GERMANY, 1823–4	172
XII. 'NATIONAL POETRY' AND ROMANTIC EUROPE	190
XIII. HISTORICAL WRITING	208
XIV. SERBIA, 1828–32: VUK AND MILOŠ	230
XV. VUK BREAKS WITH MILOŠ OBRENOVIĆ	249
XVI. VUK AND THE RULERS OF SERBIA, 1832–45	272

CONTENTS

XVII. LINGUISTIC DEBATES AND THE 'ILLYRIAN' MOVEMENT   294

XVIII. VUK AS EDITOR AND ARTIST   314

XIX. PUBLICATION OF NEW TESTAMENT AND REVISED DICTIONARY   325

XX. FAMILY LIFE AND LAST YEARS   334

XXI. CONCLUSION   349

APPENDIXES

A. Translations   361
B. The Slavonic and Serb Alphabets   386
C. Forms of the Southern Slavonic Language   388
D. Review by Jakob Grimm of Book III of Vuk's Leipzig Collection of Serb 'Popular Songs', 1823   390
E. Vuk's introduction to Book I of his Leipzig Collection of Serb 'Popular Songs', 1824   395
F. Vuk's writings on Montenegro   401

BIBLIOGRAPHY   403

INDEX   407

LIST OF PLATES

1. The young Vuk, c. 1816 — *Frontispiece*
2. Mina Karadžić-Vukomanović — *facing p.* 336
3. Vuk's house at Tršić, as restored — ,, 340
4. View of Belgrade, 1849 — ,, 341
5. Vuk and his wife in old age — ,, 352

LIST OF MAPS

MAP 1 Serbia and adjacent districts or countries — 406

MAP 2 Serbia — 407

PRONUNCIATION OF SERBO-CROAT

a somewhere between *a* in *father* and *u* in *luck*.

c as *ts* in *rats* (Cer = 'Tser').

ć a soft 'tch', or as *tu* in *picture* (Bihać = 'Bihatch').

č a rather harder 'tch', or as *ch* in *church* (Čačak = 'Tchatchak').

i as *ee* in *been*, but rather shorter.

j as 'y' (Kragujevac = 'Kraguyevats'); after *a*, *j* is used to produce the sound *ie* in English *tie* (Kajmak = 'Kiemak').

lj, nj: except at the end of words, *j* softens *l* or *n* audibly, and is pronounced together with the consonant (Ljuba = 'lyuba', the 'lyu' being sounded as in the English pronunciation of *lieu*; Njegoš = 'Nyegosh', the 'nye' being sounded much as *gne* in the French *insigne*, but rather more firmly). At the end of words, the *j* only very slightly softens *l* or *n*; again the French *gne* is the nearest equivalent.

š as 'sh' (Šabac = 'Shabats').

zh as *j* in French *jour*, or *si* in English *vision*.

h: something like Scottish *ch* in *loch*, but rather softer, and thus often omitted at the beginning of Serbo-Croat words ('Ajduk' for 'Hajduk').

u: as *oo* in *moon*, but rather shorter.

MONETARY TABLE

THE following is a rough table of equivalents, showing the values of the various forms of currency mentioned in this book. These values and their interrelations changed considerably during the period which it covers; the figures shown below apply to the period 1827–35:

    40 para   = 1 groš
    5 groš   = 1 florin (forint)
    60 kreuzer = 1 florin
    2 florins = 1 taler
    5 florins = 1 ducat
    4 florins = 1 rubl
    10 florins = £1 sterling

For a comprehensive treatment of this subject and some discussion of the purchasing power of money in Serbia in the late eighteenth and early nineteenth centuries, see Vuk Vinaver, article in *Zbornik museja prvog srpskog ustanka* ('Collections of the Museum of the First Serb Uprising'), ii, Belgrade, 1960, and Danica Milić, *Trgovina Srbije* ('Trade of Serbia') *1815–1839*, Nolit, Belgrade, 1959.

I

SURVEY OF VUK'S LIFE AND WORK

1

IN the late summer of 1813, while the energies of the Russian and Austrian Governments were concentrated on the final struggle with Napoleon, a tragedy, small only by the measure of the Napoleonic wars, was enacted in Eastern Europe. The people of Serbia, who had fought successfully for their independence in 1804, were overwhelmed by Turkish troops and became once more subjects of the Ottoman Empire. A Turkish Governor was again seated in Belgrade, and tens of thousands of Serbians crossed the rivers Sava and Danube northwards into the lands of the Austrian Empire; here they found many of their kinsmen whose ancestors had made the same journey in preceding centuries.

Among the newcomers was a young man from a West Serbian village, Vuk Stefanović (son of Stephen), who only afterwards adopted the Montenegrin clan name Karadžić. One disability and one talent distinguished him from the mass of his fellow refugees. He was lame, and in order to walk he needed both a crutch and a wooden attachment to his left leg, which was withered at the knee. This disability had at least enabled him to survive the campaign against the Turks, in which so many of his contemporaries had fallen.

Equally important for his own future and for that of his country the young Vuk Stefanović could read. This was a rare accomplishment in Serbia under the Turkish rule which had prevailed over the whole country for the past four hundred years. Vuk (as he is known without further title in Yugoslavia today) was precluded as a delicate child from more active occupations and had received more schooling than most of his contemporaries. What he had learned from the local monks had been supplemented by a year at school among the young Serbs in Karlovci, the principal town of the Serbian Srem province of the Austrian Empire, and later he had spent some months among young Serb intellectuals in

Budapest. In newly independent Serbia, under the rule of Karadjordje (Black George, leader of the revolt of 1804), Vuk as a young man of education had to exercise his talents in important clerical and administrative positions; neither Karadjordje nor his principal warrior chiefs had any book-learning, and years afterwards Vuk tried in vain to persuade one of the latter, Miloš Obrenovič, by then Prince of Serbia, that reading was an accomplishment of some value for the execution of his duties. He was thus a young man of some experience by the time that he reached Vienna.

In another and not so obvious way Vuk was outstanding among his contemporaries. When he entered Austrian territory he could truly have told the immigration authorities that he had nothing to declare but his memory. This proved to be a remarkable instrument. Vuk carried in it a store of detailed knowledge about the customs, language, and oral traditions of the ordinary Serb village, and above all a stock of those narrative 'popular songs' which served the unlettered people of Serbia[1] in the office of history books, to keep alive their national consciousness; of newspapers, to inform them about current events; and of satiric entertainment about local affairs.

Vuk had begun to take a conscious interest in these subjects while he was still in Serbia, but he was not fully aware of what could be made of the knowledge which he had acquired. The crucial point in his life was his meeting, soon after arrival in Vienna, with the Imperial censor dealing with Slavonic (or 'Illyrian') subjects, Jernej Kopitar. A Slovene by birth and only three years older than Vuk, Kopitar was in 1813 a much better-educated and sophisticated man. He was a fine linguist and had embarked on a detailed study of Slavonic languages; above all he had absorbed Herder's ideas about the importance, political as well as linguistic, of the 'popular' as opposed to the literary form of language, and about 'popular' literature and art as the most profound expression of the national spirit. Moreover Kopitar strongly backed the policy, already quite well established, of encouraging the Slav populations of the Austrian Empire to develop their national personalities further, so to speak, within the Austrian

---

[1] Before the Turkish occupation, there had been a medieval Serbian literature, derived from Byzantine models, but with original characteristics. This had been written in an 'old Serbian' language (Church Slavonic considerably modified by popular speech).

SURVEY OF VUK'S LIFE AND WORK 3

framework and thus immunizing them against the influence of Russia.

So far as these views concerned the Serb population of the Austrian Empire, Vuk seemed to Kopitar to have very useful qualifications, and he himself was enthused by many of Kopitar's ideas. It was in fact principally Kopitar's literary programme that Vuk carried out from 1814 until his death fifty years later, quite consciously, although he never specifically subscribed to Kopitar's 'Austro-Slav' views and was often acting against them. The literary programme, as expounded in one of Kopitar's letters to Vuk, comprised a Grammar and Dictionary of the 'popular' Serb language —the former to illustrate the rules of popular speech, the latter to illustrate popular usage by copious examples; also the collection and publication of the 'popular songs' which were to bring Vuk much fame abroad even during his lifetime, and of folk-tales and proverbs. Not less important was the idea, pursued separately by Kopitar, of a translation of the New Testament from the old Slavonic–Serb form currently used into popular speech.

By 1864 Vuk had completed the tasks laid down for him by Kopitar. He had also done a great deal more, particularly in the way of critical, ethnographic, and historical writing. For there were two very important factors affecting Vuk's life and work, with which neither Kopitar nor he reckoned sufficiently in 1814. The first and more predictable of these was the bitter antagonism raised among the authorities of the Serbian Orthodox Church and the Serbs of the Austrian Empire by Vuk's attempts at linguistic reform. Virtually no one disputed the idea that a form of popular language should be used in Serb literature. But the Orthodox Church authorities wanted a form of popular language a good deal beautified, and near to the 'classical' Slavonicized style affected both in writing and in speech by the better-educated Serbs of the Austrian Empire. Vuk's primary aim was, on the contrary, to make the Serb language as spoken by the ordinary peasant under Turkish rule into the literary norm. Thus, between the proponents of a 'classical-popular' and a 'vulgar' language, there was bound to be the sort of dispute familiar in the history of sixteenth-century Italian and nineteenth-century Greek literature.

Vuk's secondary object was to establish a uniform orthography which would further his primary aim, and this in turn involved simplifying and revising the alphabet, and superseding a number of the Old Slavonic letters used in Serbian 'Classical' literature. Only thus, in Vuk's view, could a standard literary language be evolved. The religious and literary authorities among the Austrian Serbs would hardly have taken kindly to such a programme at best; and Vuk in fact pressed his reforms polemically, in a highly combative and provocative style. He was accused from the first of acting as an Austrian and Catholic agent to break the linguistic and cultural links between the Serb and Russian Orthodox Churches, and from the first some of the charges against him stuck; the result was that he could never count on an adequate public for his literary work among the Serbs of the Austrian Empire.

This failure forced him to seek for patronage and financial help outside the Austrian Empire. The most important and distant of his journeys was to Russia in 1819. Here he was successful in interesting a number of eminent Academicians in his qualifications as a collector of old Serb manuscripts and antiquities. He was awarded a pension by the Tsar in 1826, and later on his house at Vienna became a regular meeting-place for Slavists from Russia.

More than once Vuk sought to take up a regular career in the service of Russia, but always in vain. For his livelihood he had to look increasingly to the possibilities of work, administrative as well as literary, in his native Serbia. These proved to be very much greater than Kopitar and he had foreseen in 1814—and this was their second original miscalculation. The Ottoman Empire in Europe was in fact weaker than they had thought at that time. In the spring of 1815, Miloš Obrenović, who alone of Karadjordje's principal captains had elected to stay in Serbia and collaborate with the Turks, led another revolt against them. He was successful but chose not to press his luck. Instead he embarked on a shrewd long-term policy of working under the Turkish authorities, and gradually edging them (and any Serbian rivals of his own) out of positions of real power. He would neither directly challenge the Turks himself, nor back others openly (for instance the Greeks) when they did so. By 1820 it looked already as if Miloš's unheroic policy was working out well, and by the end of 1830 it had been proved completely successful.

Naturally as a good Serb patriot Vuk wished to do what he could for his native country either by working for Miloš on the spot, or by making Western European readers familiar with Serbian

SURVEY OF VUK'S LIFE AND WORK

achievements and the Serb way of life (Vuk was resentful of the publicity achieved by the Greeks in the years following 1821). In consequence he devoted much time to the writing of contemporary Serb history, which, if judiciously compiled, would be pleasant to the ruler of Serbia. He also collaborated in a very happy partnership with the young Ranke, providing him with the material for his book, *The Serbian Revolution*, published in 1828. The desire to spread abroad the fame of Serbia and its heroic history was also one of the motives which had induced Vuk to travel to Germany in 1823, where he interested both Jakob Grimm and Goethe in the translation and publication of his new collections of Serb 'popular songs'.

Within Serbia itself Vuk hoped to combine duty with reasonable profit by taking some prominent part in Miloš's new administration. His favourite dream had been to organize a system of public education. This was soon proved to be impracticable, but during his second principal stay at Miloš's Serbian court, from 1829 to 1832, he became successively President of a committee for drafting a Constitution and President of the Belgrade Magistrates' Court. These were well-paid positions, but he could not stand the primitive conditions of Miloš's court, the intrigues of his principal favourites, or the very arbitrary nature of Miloš's personal rule. In 1832, not without danger and difficulty, Vuk returned to Vienna, a bitterly disappointed man. He had moreover suffered a severe literary set-back when the Orthodox Church authorities induced Miloš to ban the circulation in Serbia of works printed in his new alphabet. In fact the principal monument to his work in Serbia was the simple but detailed and damning indictment of the Prince's tyranny contained in the *Letter to Miloš Obrenović*, which is his best-known original work.

For the last thirty years of his life too Vuk's fate was closely intertwined with that of the Obrenović family, whether they held power in Belgrade, or (from 1842 to 1859) lived in exile (mainly in Vienna). His long battle of wits with Miloš, in turn or simultaneously a far-sighted diplomat, a cruel and vicious tyrant, and a skilful financial operator, and always a vital human being, is a fascinating study in itself. From 1844 onwards, Miloš's son, Prince Mihail, gave Vuk at last the financial security for which he had struggled so long. But for some time after 1832 Serbia was virtually barred to Vuk. It was in these years that he started to travel widely in Croatia, Dalmatia, and Montenegro, in search of new folkloristic and historical material. His linguistic theories too began to be adapted in the light of his wider travels, and it was at this time that Vuk became closely connected with the 'Illyrian' agitation centred in Zagreb. As a political movement for increased Slav independence within the Austrian Empire, this was swept aside by the centralization which followed the revolutionary uprisings of 1848; but as a cultural movement it was important in bringing closer together Serbs, Croats, and Dalmatians. Vuk himself did much to minimize the linguistic differences between Serbs and Croats and thus to prepare the way for the foundation of a Yugoslav state.

It was during the period of his enforced absence from Serbia that Vuk's house at Vienna became a centre of pilgrimage not only for Russian Slavists but for young intellectuals from Serbia, the Serb community in the Austrian Empire and Croatia. Vuk had continued untiringly his polemics against the old spelling and for the 'popular' language, and a new generation—some of them better equipped than himself as etymologists, grammarians, or creative writers—was arising to fight his battles. With the restoration of the Obrenović dynasty in 1859, Vuk was able to return to Serbia, and soon afterwards the ban on the circulation of his works there was lifted. His literary programme of 1814 had meanwhile been completed, and by the time of his death in 1864 the victory of his linguistic theories on a wide front was assured, if not finally won.

2

Vuk's was thus an extraordinary achievement. At the end of his life, after fifty years of single-minded (in two senses of the words) and almost single-handed work, he had not only accomplished the task imposed on himself at the start of his career, but had also— led on by compelling circumstances—done a good deal more than he had intended. All this too in spite of the handicaps of constant ill health and, until well after his fiftieth year, constant financial difficulties. It is a remarkable record of intellectual and physical energy. In what ways however can such a record concern the reader of general history, with no special knowledge of Eastern Europe or Slav languages?

The short answer is that many incidents, if not the main lines of Vuk's career, are of great general interest; but this answer needs to be expanded.

The various branches of Vuk's work were all undertaken with the one aim in view, of reviving the Serb popular language for the greater use and glory of the Serb nation. But, bearing this constantly in mind, it is still reasonable to distinguish between Vuk the innovator and Vuk the conservative; in other words between his linguistic controversies and propaganda for his new alphabet on the one hand, and on the other his collection of popular songs, tales, and proverbs, and his descriptions of the life and customs of Serbian peasant society.

It is Vuk the reformer who is naturally best remembered in his native country. The stock reaction to the word 'Vuk' in present-day Yugoslavia would be the quotation which he adopted himself to justify his reformed alphabet: 'Write as you speak.' Outside Yugoslavia it is unfortunately only experts in Slavonic languages who can easily grasp more than the most general principles at issue in Vuk's linguistic and orthographical debates; and even they may be repelled by the repetitions and dusty details of verbal battles more than a century old. The foreign biographer of Vuk is thus liable to distort the pattern of his life by insufficient emphasis on the reforming element. Fortunately however the incidental circumstances and results of Vuk's linguistic controversies are often of considerable interest to the general historian even outside Yugoslavia. For example, an important battle in Vuk's campaign to establish the Serb popular language as a respectable literary medium centred about the publication of his translation of the New Testament. Here a large number of factors outside Serbian literary politics affected the issue—for example, the relations of the Serb Orthodox Church authorities in the Austrian Empire with the Austrian Government, the Holy Synod in Moscow, and Miloš Obrenović in Serbia itself; or the missionary activities of the St. Petersburg and London Bible Societies—it was the latter which after nearly thirty years provided the money that enabled Vuk to print his version.

Moreover it was not only Vuk who kept constantly in mind the national aims of his linguistic campaigns. Something has been said already about the relevance of his linguistic work to the 'Illyrian' movement within the Austrian Empire, and about the part which he played in creating the cultural basis for co-operation between Serbs and Croats. Within the wider 'Pan-Slav' context as well, Vuk's work in reviving the popular Serb language and thus helping the re-emergence of Serb national consciousness had its importance. Vuk was an honoured figure, and no more ineffective than other Austrian Slavs, at the famous Slav Congress at Prague in 1848.

Even more important in this context was Vuk's 'conservative' aspect—his effort to collect and publicize the popular literary heritage of Serbia. This can be considered as part of a much wider, if hardly co-ordinated, movement throughout Eastern Europe to arouse the national consciousness of the Slav peoples. And the importance of Vuk's work in this direction is comparatively easy for a Western European to appreciate.

Of particular interest at the time of their publication were Vuk's collections of the 'popular songs' of Serbia. As will be explained in more detail in Chapter XII, there was in the early nineteenth century a special market for such poetry, the 'heroic songs' in particular. They had the right romantic and exotic flavour to suit the fashionable literary taste of the time; much of Vuk's collections was translated into German, French, and English during the 1820s and the vogue was such as to inspire one of the most famous literary hoaxes of all time—Prosper Mérimée's bogus collection of Dalmatian ballads, some of which were translated into Russian by Pushkin himself. The literary vogue of the Serbian 'popular songs' was short-lived, but they had also inspired more serious and lasting interest among scholars. Jakob Grimm in particular considered the 'heroic songs' in the context of his previous studies of early epic poetry, and awarded them his highest praise.

It is in the same sort of context that scholars of comparative epic poetry, and particularly of Homer, have re-examined in our own times Vuk's work of collecting and editing Serb heroic songs. There is a large specialist literature on this aspect, and it would be presumptuous to try to contribute anything to this in a general survey of Vuk's life and work. But Vuk's own introductions and notes to his collections of 'popular songs' have not been translated, and are much less familiar to scholars in the field of comparative epic than the 'songs' themselves. They include vivid portraits of some of his 'singers', and much interesting material about the oral transmission of the Serb songs, as well as about his own problems in collecting and editing them. Much of this will be found in the main text or appendixes of this book.

SURVEY OF VUK'S LIFE AND WORK

A large number of the 'heroic songs' recorded by Vuk cover his own times, and the events of the Serbian revolt of 1804 which he afterwards recorded in his prose histories. These themselves have some of the qualities of primitive epic. They are not skilfully constructed narratives, and the absence of dates makes them often confusing to read, but their faults are more than compensated by the absence of pomposity, pathos, and generalities, the use of first-hand sources, the shrewd eye for characteristic and detailed incident, and the convincing reproduction of the very tone of the heroes' speech. I have quoted extensively in Chapter V from Vuk's portrait of his favourite hero, Hajduk Veljko, and have tried to convey the effect of a historical style utterly foreign to the normal and formal classicism of the time; it is as if Walter Scott had narrated 'Tales of a Grandfather' in the style of Wandering Willie. One would give much for more details of the collaboration between Vuk and Ranke.

So far as content is concerned, Vuk's historical narratives throw a good deal of light on the realities of 'liberation wars', anti-heroic as well as heroic, and Vuk is by no means unfair to his Turkish adversaries. Perhaps even more revealing of the state of south-eastern Europe during the decline of the Ottoman Empire are the general descriptions of social relations, for instance between Turkish landowners and Serbian peasants, in Vuk's essays on the life and customs of the Serb people. And most enlightening of all about the state of Serbia in the late eighteenth and early nineteenth centuries are some of the little anecdotes of village life with which Vuk illustrates entries in his Dictionary of the popular Serb language. Here he was describing from inside knowledge a society which was already being completely reshaped by war and new economic forces; he gives an incomparably vivid mosaic picture of a rural civilization which had been, so to speak, fossilized under long Turkish rule; from his miscellaneous writings the reader can learn of the myths, stories, and songs current in eighteenth-century (and probably in fifteenth-century) Serbia, as well as of village ritual, customs, and superstitions. Vuk is of great importance and interest as an ethnographer, not least when he is not deliberately trying to act as such. Particularly in the early chapters of this book, I have tried to give some idea of Vuk's work in this field, without diverging too far from the main narrative, and have supplemented the scanty specific data about his early life with material from his writings which has some autobiographical interest, either direct or indirect.

The historian of international politics in the early nineteenth century may not find much directly to interest him in Vuk's writings, apart from his account of the Serbian revolt against the Turks. The course of Vuk's life however was largely determined by decisions of the Austrian, the Serbian, and to a lesser extent of the Russian Governments, referring directly to him but taken on very broad foreign policy grounds. Thus in 1823 he was driven to publish his revised collection of songs in Germany because Metternich would not permit the printing in Austria of material likely to be considered subversive by the Turkish Government (typically the circulation in Austria of the copies printed in Leipzig was then allowed without objection). Again in 1832 it was at the specific request of Miloš Obrenović to the Austrian Government that Vuk, regarded by Miloš at the time as a dangerous revolutionary, was allowed to travel back from Zemun on the Austro-Serbian border, to Vienna, where Metternich's police had previously suspected him of being a dangerous Russian or Serbian agent. Thus Vuk's career often illustrates how the combinations of international policy worked out in terms of one usually unfortunate individual, and from this aspect too has its special interest.

Finally, and in the last analysis most important, Vuk was not only determined and combative—so much stands out obviously from his achievements; he was also highly articulate, and developed a direct and vivid style particularly in his correspondence, of which seven large volumes have been published. I have tried so far as possible to let him tell his own story himself, as he recorded it at the time largely in letters to Kopitar. Vuk was no conventional hero—he had far too much peasant common sense for the heroic role, and his human failings as well as his clarity of thought and energy of expression earn him much sympathy. His achievement however was heroic, and with his 'industrious valour' he had done much to prepare for the day when, after the ruin of 'a great work of time', Yugoslavia could emerge as a new country from the mould of the Austrian Empire.

II

EARLY YEARS AND BACKGROUND
1787-1804

I

VUK STEFANOVIĆ KARADŽIĆ was born on 26 October 1787, at Tršić, a typical Serbian hill village about 70 miles west-south-west of Belgrade, not far from the border of Serbia and Bosnia. Little is known of his parents, about whom he was very reticent, or of his childhood. His first biographer, I. I. Sreznevski, a Russian professor of Slav languages and history, had long conversations with Vuk over fifty years later in Vienna.[1] From these Sreznevski compiled what purports to be an autobiographical account by Vuk of his early years. It sounds authentic enough and remains the best source, but it is brief. Apart from this, there are a number of scattered autobiographical references in Vuk's own *Dictionary* and critical writings; and from his later general descriptions of Serb village life and customs a good deal may be deduced about his own early experience. The very scarcity of material about Vuk himself has led me in this chapter to attempt a general picture of conditions in rural Serbia at the end of the eighteenth century as much as a continuous narrative of Vuk's childhood.

Vuk's own parents, Stefan Joksimović and his wife Jegda, were themselves the descendants of immigrants to the district. The Austro-Turkish wars of the late seventeenth and eighteenth centuries caused large movements of population. From 1718 to 1739 the Austrians occupied the city and province of Belgrade. In the war against the Turks which started in 1737, Austrian armies had penetrated much further, into south Serbia and to the borders of Montenegro and Albania. They had been accompanied by large numbers of Serb soldiers, and when they retreated again before Turkish counter-attacks and surrendered Belgrade, the Serb auxiliaries together with their families had good reason to fly from

[1] Sreznevski was Professor of Slavonic Philology at the Universities of Kharkov and, later, St. Petersburg. His principal conversations with Vuk took place in 1842. In 1846 he published a biography of Vuk, and in 1876 added to it a supplement covering the years 1843-64.

the vengeance of the Turks. It was this pattern that had originally led to the great migration of the Serbs to Hungary, under their Patriarch, Arsenije Čarnojović, in 1690; and in 1739 a number of inhabitants of Hercegovina, who had served with the Austrians, retreated northwards with them, and settled near the confluence of the Drina and Sava rivers. This was one of the typical countercurrents within the main ebb of Turkish power from Eastern Europe. Vuk himself wrote later: 'As there are few people in the Srem whose fathers or grandfathers did not settle there from Serbia, so there are few in Serbia whose ancestors did not immigrate from Hercegovina.'

Of Vuk's parents, Sreznevski records: 'There [i.e. at Tršić] they found empty sites among old settlements, and moved into them, near the hills, as was the Serb custom—the nearer they were to the hills and mountains, the nearer also to the woods and the further from the Turks. They brought with them families and kinsmen too.' Among the forty immigrant families were some belonging to the clan Karadžić from Drobnjak in Montenegro.

Vuk's father, Stefan Joksimović, was a comparatively well-to-do peasant farmer, and this was about the highest status that could be attained by a Serb. The Turkish overlords occupied the towns, and left the countryside to the infidel Serb peasantry (or *raja*),only paying occasional visits to their estates. Thus the Serb farmer could live an independent life, if the local Turkish landowners (spahis) were moderate, as many were, in their assessment and exaction of taxes. As a merchant, the Serb might prosper more; but if his business brought him to the towns, he would have to live there as a second-class citizen, exposed to more frequent danger from the Turks.

Vuk's parents had had five children before he was born, but none of them survived infancy. His name, which means wolf, was given to him as a protection. The previous children were thought, in accordance with a common superstition, to have been eaten by witches; these would not dare, however, to touch a wolf. Like other Serbian children of his time, he was for many years known simply by his christian name and patronymic, Vuk Stefanović. It was only later that he found this Homeric style inconvenient and began to use the clan name Karadžić[1] as a surname. The clan

---

[1] The change of name can still cause some confusion to foreign researchers, and it is wise to look for references to Vuk under 'Stefanović' as well as under 'Karadžić'.

EARLY YEARS AND BACKGROUND: 1787–1804

names, as Vuk later noted, were originally used in Montenegro, as a result of the institution of blood feuding, 'to ensure that anyone who was thinking of killing someone else should know with whom he would have to feud, and to whom he would owe blood. So when anyone is mentioned in those parts, he is given not only his first name and patronymic, but also the name of his clan and of the branch concerned.' In Serbia, Vuk explained, blood feuds did not exist, and old surnames might attract unwelcome attention from the Turks: 'When the Turks were levying poll-tax, everyone called himself by his father's or mother's name; and in other cases it was seldom that anyone's name was asked, let alone written down. Thus it has been the custom with us (in Serbia) to this day for people to call themselves by their christian name rather than by any surname.'[1]

Of Vuk's family and group surroundings in his early years we know little, but in later writings he gave a good general picture of the sort of Serbian village in which he grew up.

In Serbia there are big villages with about 100 houses, and others with about 15; but most of them have from 30 to 50. In hilly country the houses are so far scattered that a village of 40 houses may cover more ground than Vienna;[2] for example there will be a few houses by one stream and then (perhaps half-an-hour's or a full hour's walk away) a few more by another, but the whole will be called one village, so long as its land continues—and the limits of this are very well known (thus people from two villages can be neighbours).

On the plains there will be a good number of houses in the villages not arranged regularly, as for example in the Srem and in Germany, but scattered about the fields, as in Turkish towns.[3]

Under Turkish rule people could move from one village to another as they liked, without telling the spahi from whose village they moved, nor the one to whose village they went. They could sell or knock down their houses, and come back to harvest their orchards and vineyards every year, giving a tithe to the spahi. In the village to which a man migrated, he could build a house wherever he liked on waste ground,

---

[1] The habit of calling people by christian name and patronymic alone was discouraged earlier among the Serbs of the Austrian Empire, since it led to duplication of names and caused difficulties for the Imperial census officials.

[2] This is one of the passages directly echoed in Ranke, *The Serbian Revolution*, 1828.

[3] To this day the villages of the Vojvodina, with regularly spaced houses facing sideways on to a single long street, contrast visibly with the haphazard layout of the villages in old Serbia.

clear fields and meadows, and plant orchards and vineyards as he wanted. When the spahi arrived in the village to collect 'poll-tax' and began (through his clerk) to call up the villagers by name, they would say to him 'This one's gone away' or 'This one's come'. In the plains, particularly in rocky parts, the houses are very poor. Usually roofs are of thatch or straw. But in the hilly districts there are some good solid houses; many are built of stone and they usually have wooden roofs. The houses are not everywhere divided into rooms; most often people warm themselves in winter at the fire, but sleep in outhouses, or as they may in the house. Chimneys practically don't exist in the villages. As a result in some houses one's eyes nearly fall out of one's head for the smoke. In Serbia it is only around Soko that the Turks settled in some villages;[1] elsewhere only Serbs live in the villages and the Turks are in the towns; but in Bosnia there are both Turkish and Christian villages.[2]

At Tršić today can be seen a skilful reconstruction, complete with contemporary furniture, of the sort of house in which Vuk was born and brought up. His father's original house was burnt by the Turks, but the site of the hearth was known and it is around this that the present house has been constructed.

The village society of eighteenth-century Serbia was patriarchal in form, and a single household would comprise various branches and two or three generations of the same family, sharing central rooms. These group households (or *Zadruga*) were a convenient means of concentrating labour, and also of minimizing the taxes due to the Turks. Vuk described such households as follows:

> Serbs generally live in a common group. In some households there are 4 or 5 married couples, and few single households exist. There are outside sheds around the house for each married couple; in the house itself they eat together around the fire and the old men and women sleep there; the rest sleep with wives and children each in his outhouse without fires, summer and winter. Around some of the bigger landowners' houses the outhouses and other buildings (e.g. granaries . . .) stand like a small village.
> In every household there is an 'elder' who governs and manages the house and all the property. He gives orders to the children and young men, where each is to go and what each is to do. He deals with the Turks and goes to village and district meetings and discussions. With

---

[1] Soko (now Soko Banja) is in a district of eastern Serbia, where exceptionally the main landlords belonged to a Serbian family, the Karapandjas.
[2] 'Christian' is here used loosely to mean 'Serb'. No Turks were Christians, but then as now many Serbs in Bosnia were Moslems.

EARLY YEARS AND BACKGROUND: 1787-1804

the consent of the members of the household he sells what there is to sell and buys what must be bought. He keeps the money chest and has the worry of how to pay the various taxes. He has to speak first and last when there are prayers. When there are guests in the house (and in the big houses a day seldom goes by without guests), he talks with them and dines and sups with them—in the big houses where there are many people, the elder and the guests are served first at one table, then at another the boys and young men who work outside, and after that the women and children eat. The 'elder' is not always the eldest in the house by years. When the father gets old, he hands over the office of elder to the cleverest son (or brother or nephew) even if he is the youngest. If it happens that an elder does not manage the house well, then the inmates choose another. In these 'group' houses, each woman spins, weaves and makes garments for herself, her husband and children; they take it in turns, a week at a time, to cook the common meal.

Vuk was here describing the type of a patriarchal community which became obsolescent in his own lifetime, as the Serbian economy was diversified under the rule of Miloš Obrenović; but some features of it (e.g. the serving of the head of the household and his guests at a separate table) may still be found in Serb villages today.

2

So far as education was concerned, Vuk's parents tried to give him the best available at the time and place. Vuk was a keen pupil, but the process of learning was not easy. It was recorded by Sreznevski as remembered by Vuk some forty years later:

His first teacher was his kinsman Jefto Savić; Jefto mixed some powder with water, took a piece of cartridge-paper, then began to write down letters and make Vuk learn them. Only much later was Jefto able to get for his young kinsman a book of letters—perhaps one from Russia—with pictures; the one that interested Vuk most was of a magic bird. He was very fond of this book. As he went about the village or on the road and read it, he would seldom miss the chance of asking anyone who could be expected to give him an answer whether or not he was reading it right. As soon as he saw such a man—merchant or priest or monk, only so long as it was not a Turk (and that could easily be told by his dress)[1], he would take off his cap to the stranger, kiss his hand, and put the book

---

[1] Serbs were forbidden to wear certain types and colours of dress (especially the sacred green). The leaders of the 1804 revolt adopted Turkish dress to make evident their victory.

of letters in front of him. Then it was 'Please, good master' (in the case of a merchant) or 'Your reverence' (for a monk), 'please tell me . . .'; then he'd kiss the man's hand once more, say 'thank you' and get back again to his book. Often enough it would happen, particularly with merchants, that in reply to his question Vuk would get no better answer than: 'God help us, sonny, I know no better than you!'

In 1795, when Vuk was eight years old, a small school was opened in the local town of Loznica, some five miles off, and Stefan sent his son to it. Vuk rubbed up his alphabet, began to study the *Book of Hours*, which contained suitable prayers for all times and occasions, and had just qualified to read it when the plague broke out in Loznica, and he had to go home again. Stefan waited two months, then sent Vuk to another school at the monastery of Tronoša.[1]

The monasteries of Serbia had played an enormously important part in preserving national pride and consciousness among the Serbs during over four hundred years of Turkish occupation. Vuk in later life fiercely and not without cause castigated the prelates of the Orthodox Church, but he also stated more simply and vividly than anyone what the monasteries had meant to the average Serb peasant:

There is at least one monastery in each district, and in some as many as three or four. Serbian monasteries are all in wooded places or by streams.[2] Not only are the churches themselves finely built of stone (they usually have domes), but many have walls all around them, like small towns. Up to this time they have been the only true pillars and guardians of the Christian faith and of the Serb name. It is not only that people go there to make confession, receive pardon, and hear the holy services; they also assemble there often on holidays (for example at Easter, Trinity, etc.) as at a fair. At some monasteries, when the weather is fine, several thousand people are gathered. The merchants sell their various wares; inn-keepers pour out wine and rakija; butchers

[1] The restored monastery of Tronoša now contains an excellent small museum, illustrating the sort of school which Vuk must have attended.
[2] The finely preserved monastery of Studenica in Serbia, still inhabited by monks, perfectly illustrates Vuk's description. It stands beneath high wooded slopes, just above a stream running eastwards into the Ibar river, and the churches and monks' quarters are enclosed by a high wall. The passage quoted here comes from Vuk's *Dictionary* of 1818. Some of the other descriptions in this chapter are quoted from the survey of Serbia printed in his *Day-star* of 1827; others from the *Life and Customs of the Serb People* (1867), compiled from Vuk's notes and published after his death.

EARLY YEARS AND BACKGROUND: 1787-1804

roast lambs, sheep, goats, and pigs, and sell the meat; blind men strike up on the *gusle*[1] and sing heroic songs, old and new; the young men eye the girls (the girls usually go there at the feast of flowers [Whitsun] and the young brides at Easter); gossips, friends, and acquaintances meet and talk about this and that; sometimes the elders of the people (chiefs and headmen) meet and confer. Such meetings are held also in the church, but not so regularly as at the monasteries.

When people go to the church or monastery they dress and deck themselves out as finely as they can. Those who live near set out in the morning, but many, especially from distant villages, arrive on the eve of the holiday and stay the night. Usually people go to the nearest monastery; but they may go further, sometimes for several days' journey—for example, rich people from the whole of Serbia and from Bosnia and Hercegovina go to Studenica for Trinity.

Apart from fields, vineyards, and plum orchards (which their own villagers work for them), monasteries in Serbia have their own labourers in other villages whom they can call up as for a *moba*.[2] Apart from all this, monasteries used to live mainly from contributions and from 'writing'.[3] In some places, the monks would be almost like visitors in the monasteries, and would be always on the move (throughout the Serb-speaking Turkish area). They would earn gifts by 'writing' (money, livestock, grain, drink, linen, etc.). What they couldn't bring with them or drive back to the monastery, they would sell and turn into money on the spot, and many people would of their own accord bring charitable gifts to the monastery on holidays. Some of the bigger monasteries used to send monks . . . even as far as Russia to collect gifts, and there the rulers sometimes decreed that yearly sums should be given to them, which are still paid if the monasteries have not been deserted.[4]

The monastery of Tronoša played an important part in the life of Tršić, particularly at the end of the eighteenth century under the leadership of its Archimandrite, Stefan Jovanović. In return

---

[1] The *gusle* was a one-stringed instrument, shaped more like a lute than a violin, held in something like the violoncello position, and played by bowing. It provided the traditional accompaniment for narrative songs.

[2] In certain villages labourers, known as *prnjavori*, were bound to work for the monasteries. The *moba* was a collective harvesting, performed for land-owners by labourers not owing them service, in return for food and drink (a sort of 'harvest-home' feast), on Saints' days when it was a sin for them to work on their own behalf.

[3] 'Writing', mainly done by itinerant monks, was the listing, in return for suitable gifts, of names to be remembered in prayers.

[4] It was during Karadjordje's administration of Serbia (1804-13) that 'writing' was first forbidden.

for the work put in by the local villagers on the monastery's land, the Archimandrite paid their taxes, on a fixed assessment, to the Turkish landowners; he also exercised judicial authority in all except the most important cases—again a considerable protection for the villagers. Stefan Jovanović himself seems to have been a formidable personality. In 1789 he had led an armed force in support of the Austrian troops against the Turks, and after some time in Vienna (from 1791 onwards) returned to his own country to resume charge of his monastery, until in 1799 the Turks trapped and poisoned him. Vuk himself was later to write a short life of him and praised highly his courage and charitable ways.[1]

As a boy of 9, however, Vuk could not appreciate the historical role of the Serbian monasteries, or the courage of Stefan Jovanović; and clearly the education offered to him at Tronoša was not impressive. His opinion of it can again be deduced from a later and generalized description of schooling in Serbia before Karadjordje's uprising:

> In Serbia down to 1804 there was not so much as one school to a hundred villages; those who intended to become priests or monks learned in the monasteries with the monks or in the villages with the priests. In every monastery there were some pupils. The younger ones in summer kept the goats, sheep, lambs, and pigs, sowed and weeded onions, walked by the plough, gathered hay and plums, and so on; the older ones went with the monks on their 'writing'. In winter after every one had brought in wood in the morning, the older ones watered the monks' horses, and the younger ones cleaned their rooms; then they all gathered in one room, and some monk or deacon would teach them to read, or each would learn with his own 'spiritual adviser'. Many would forget in summer what they had learnt in winter, and so there were some boys who had been learning for four or five years and still didn't know how to read. The village priests usually had one or two pupils each, who also kept their livestock, did all the work in the house and carried water in the villages. If any school existed or was founded in the district, people from the villages around would bring their children to the 'magister' and pay him by the month for teaching them in school. Children had to sit and learn from morning to night (except that they would go out for dinner). When they were learning and reading, they

[1] Vuk's short biography was in his series, modelled on Plutarch, *Lives of the Serbian Marshals* (extended to cover other notables). Stefan Jovanović during his exile in Vienna tried to persuade the Austrians to provide arms for Serbia, and only returned to Tronoša, in Vuk's words, 'when he got tired of begging to no purpose, and the Austrians of hearing his requests and reproaches'.

EARLY YEARS AND BACKGROUND: 1787–1804   19

had to shout as loud as they could (as each read out his piece) so that it was impossible to make out anything. In the schools they taught a little writing (as much as the teacher himself knew), but otherwise the lessons were all the same as in the monasteries. As in the monasteries and with the priests, so in the schools, children began to read from handwriting (there were no spelling books); for example, the teacher would write down what the child had to learn that day, then when he'd learnt that, the teacher would write something else and so on. When a pupil had in this way learned the alphabet, he would go on to the Book of Hours; and when he'd mastered that and recited it a few times, he'd go on to the Book of Psalms. Anyone who'd mastered and recited the psalms had 'learned his books'; he could then be, if he wanted, priest, monk, teacher, head-priest or archimandrite; or, if he had enough money, a bishop.[1]

Just as a teacher could open a school at will, so he could close it as and when he liked, and go to another place or take up some completely different work.

A good deal of bitter personal experience can be read between the lines of this general description, and Vuk's only particular reminiscence of Tronoša is not a happy one.

In 1855 he had returned for a visit to Loznica and was offered wine at supper. 'Add a little water', he said, 'I don't drink it unmixed', and then continued:

When I was at the monastery of Tronoša, I worked as pupil for a monk and served him at table. The monk would himself pour wine into his cup, and then shout at me: 'Child, add a little water; I don't drink it unmixed.' So I would hurry to pour some water in, but the holy man's cup was so full of wine that it couldn't hold more than a drop or two of water. When the cup was thus over-full and brimmed over, the monk would scold me, and beat me too, God help me!

Vuk was evidently one of those younger pupils at Tronoša who was employed to mind the monks' livestock. His father, according to Sreznevski's account, was not amused at having to pay for a herdsman himself while Vuk watched the monastery goats. So Vuk walked back over the hills from Tronoša to Tršić, along the path which has now been made into a sort of pilgrim's way, marked at

[1] A story told by Prota Matija Nenadović in his autobiographical memoirs well illustrates the common uses of literacy in eighteenth-century Serbia. Matija's mother was congratulated by a neighbour on having such a learned son, who could read the calendar and point out to her the very numerous saints' days on which it would be sinful for her to work.

intervals by wooden boards inscribed with a biography of Vuk and with suitable texts from his works. Stefan then kept Vuk at home 'though much against his will; for he saw his son as an "open-minded child", wanted him in time to become a merchant or a priest, and with this in view wished to give him a fitting education'.

Vuk was capable of an objective view about the role of the monasteries in the life of the normal Serb peasant, and he had sincere respect for the Church's part in the history of the Serbian nation; but even before he had become entangled with the Orthodox hierarchy in controversies over language and literature, he was always ready to laugh or snarl at the less worthy monks or priests of his time, barely literate, often pretentious and greedy.

The second half of the eighteenth century was indeed a particularly difficult time for the Orthodox Church in Serbia. Previously the Church had enjoyed a real autonomy; the existence of a separate Serb Patriarchate at Peć had provided a centre for ecclesiastical discipline as well as a focus for the loyalty of monks and priests of the Serbian people as a whole. After the retreat of the Austrians in 1739, the Turks first took care to put their own nominee in the Serbian Patriarchate, and in 1766 it was abolished. Authority was transferred to the Greek (Phanariot)[1] Patriarch at Constantinople; Phanariots were appointed also, usually after payment of a suitable fee, to the Serbian Bishoprics. They had to make good their initial expenses, and became notorious among the Serbs for their exactions and worldly way of life; moreover it became known that any bright or ambitious Serb who wished to make a career as a priest or a monk would have a better chance across the Sava, in the Serbian community in Hungary. It is not surprising that in the late eighteenth century the standard of living, learning, and discipline of the Orthodox Church in Serbia sank to a low level.

Vuk's later writings, and not least the first edition of his *Dictionary*, contain a number of stories about the failings of priests and monks which fairly reflect the general attitude. There is for example the tale illustrating the word *pustenica* (a loose branch, or divorced wife). A priest and his pupil were riding along a woodland path. The boy was ahead and turned at one point to say: 'Look out,

---

[1] The Phanariots were originally patrician Greek families from the Phanar district of Istanbul, who provided many prominent officials for the Ottoman administration.

father, there's a loose one in the way—I'll hold her back.' The priest, whose mind was set on worldly things, replied, 'Nay, my son, suffer her to come unto me if she be young', and so received the branch smack in the face. There is a similar imputation in the entry under which Vuk describes how the Serb peasants distinguished two types of dove by setting words to their respective calls. One was meant to say (at the right time of year): 'Sow leeks! Sow leeks!'; the other, more verbosely: 'What are you up to, dirty old parson, with someone else's good wife or daughter?'

The villagers might be sincere enough in their Christianity and their reverence for the Church in general, but were unlikely to take individual monks or priests too seriously.

3

Vuk left the monastery of Tronoša in 1798 and spent the next six years in and around his father's home at Tršić. Very little is recorded of his life and occupation during these years. All that is known for certain is that Vuk's father tried to continue his education as best he could by procuring for him some books evidently of a strictly edifying character. The most specific titles which Vuk later mentioned to Sreznjevski were *The Life of the Righteous Aleksej* and *The Sacrifice of Abraham*. These are typical of the very scanty and almost entirely ecclesiastical literature then available in Serbia—and not very widely available even for the few who could read.

His years of village life proved however to be a much more valuable education for Vuk than any formal schooling or booklearning that was available to him. In the first place, he took his part as an alert and sensitive boy in the ritual of the Serbian peasant, virtually unchanged for hundreds of years. Priests and monasteries took their place here alongside a mass of pagan superstitions and customs, of which Vuk later recorded a rich selection in the pages of his *Dictionary*. They read more like the notebook of some Serbian Thomas Hardy than the scientific account of a trained modern anthropologist, and are correspondingly vivid and entertaining. There are the rainmakers, with their special songs and dances, there are elaborate marriage and mourning customs, and the spells by which young girls try to conjure up the vision of their destined husband. There is a rich variety of witches and evil spirits (the plague, for instance, was personalized and envisaged as an outcast woman wandering from village to village—her entry could be prevented by the appropriate ritual).[1] There are vampires, and rules for putting an end to their activities.[2] There are folk tales, fanciful and humorous, and traditional funny stories from the villagers. A small selection of this material, which provides a lively picture of late-eighteenth-century Serbia, is translated in Appendix A. To some of the entries in his *Dictionary* Vuk gave an autobiographical reference, recording how he himself participated as a boy in various ceremonies of village life. A good instance is his description of an ordeal by boiling water to detect thieves.

Up to recently in Serbia, they would sometimes 'pull out the iron'; that is when anyone was accused of stealing something and said that he hadn't, they would boil a cauldron or big kettle full of water, and then put into the boiling water a piece of white-hot iron (or a stone); the man accused of theft rolls up his sleeves and then with both hands takes the iron out of the water. If he hasn't stolen what they say he has, he won't be burnt at all; and if he has stolen it, his hands will be burnt. I know of no one who pulled out the stone without getting his hands hurt, but of two I know that their hands were burnt—Panta Stanović from the village of Tršić in Jadar and Mitar Tufekčija from Radjevina in the village of Mujković.

The unsparing detail of the last sentence is typical of Vuk's realistic method in dealing with what might be considered romantic subjects.

In his later writings, Vuk also records some of the stories current at Tršić during his childhood. One of the most vivid is about the outlaw Pecirep, who had lost a hand, but could still shoot with the best marksmen by sitting down and propping the barrel of his gun on his foot. The Turks captured him and led him off to be impaled without bothering to tie his one effective arm; but Pecirep managed to kill two of his incautious escort before finally being overpowered and executed. The heroic and tragic tone is typical. Another

[1] For the personalized spirit of the plague, see also Robert Curzon, *Visits to Monasteries in the Levant*, chapter xxii., apropos of the plague ranging in the Phanar district of Istanbul, 1837: 'Some people are said to have seen the plague, its appearance being that of an old woman, tall, thin and ghastly, and dressed sometimes in black, sometimes in white. . . .'

[2] The scene of the activities of Bret Harte's Dracula was Transylvania. The name 'Drakulić' is current in Serbia today.

EARLY YEARS AND BACKGROUND: 1787-1804

curious passage in Vuk's writings shows the bitterness of the Serbian peasant's struggle for existence, even apart from Turkish oppression. 'Over there' (i.e. in Serbia; he was usually writing in Vienna) 'people often die in this way; when someone is travelling in mountain country particularly and is caught by a blizzard, he won't be able to see anything for the snow and wind, and not recognizing the country under snow will lose his way and die of cold.'

To return to more direct autobiography, Vuk in another later note describes how in his childhood his father explained to him a local legend:

At the monastery of Tronoša, a naked man was carved on the right of the door, with snakes around him who were biting him and sucking his breasts. Parents have the habit of explaining to their children the various pictures and images in churches and monasteries, and my father would tell me that the old man was called Gavan the Rich; with all his overgreat riches he was very hard and uncompassionate, and it was for this that God punished him in such a way (this agrees fairly well with the songs and tales about Gavan current in the Western districts of Serbia).

Here is the first reference to a song theme, and there can be little doubt that, like other Serbian children of his own and previous generations, Vuk's main source of education both about past history and about current affairs lay in the songs which he heard at the family fireside. About these, he left a good deal of information, scattered among the introductions and notes to the various collections of Serb songs which he published between 1814 and 1845. So far as songs were concerned, the young Vuk was in a favoured position. 'I was born and brought up', he wrote, 'in a house where sometimes my grandfather and uncle, sometimes various men from Hercegovina (who would come almost every year to spend the winter with us), would sing and recite songs the whole winter through'; and again: 'I knew from childhood God's plenty of songs; I understood them all well, as the people understand them, and they were dear to me as to all the others.' Vuk's father, 'as a serious and God-fearing man gave little attention to songs' but some he 'remembered almost against his will from his own father Joksim and his brother Toma, who not only knew a lot of songs and liked singing and reciting them, but also composed songs themselves'. Grandfather Joksim in particular seems to have been an accomplished singer, with a predilection for comic themes (not least in parody of tragic songs); some fragments of his songs were later printed by Vuk in his collections.

Heroic songs in particular were a well-known feature of Serbian village life at the end of the eighteenth century. They were circulated mainly, Vuk wrote,

by blind men, travellers and *hajduks* (outlaws). The blind men go begging from house to house right round the country.[1] In front of every house they sing a song, and then ask for something to be given to them; when something is offered they will sing more. On holidays they go to the monasteries and churches for the services and sing the whole day long. Again when a traveller arrives at a house for lodging, it is usual to ask him to sing to the *gusle*, so that travellers sing and listen in the evening. Then the *hajduks* in winter ... drink and sing to the *gusle* all night, mainly songs about *hajduks*.

In village life songs had a varied and important part. The traditional songs, for instance the famous 'cycle' about the defeat of Tsar Lazar by the Turks at Kosovo in 1389, were substitutes for history books; this in the circumstances of Turkish rule was a vital role in itself. Vuk's later reminiscences show that some of the new songs were also a substitute for news-sheets. He relates for example how he saw his uncle Toma in 1803 at work in the fields, 'muttering to himself as he composed a ballad about the death of Smailbeg Begzadić, who had been killed only four or five days before. When Toma sat down for a rest, he called me to him and began to recite the ballad. I wrote down as much as I could remember of it in 1814.'

More common in the natural course of things was the composition of comic and satirical songs on current village themes, which were likely to be ephemeral. It was not hard to compose these, the normal metre being as near to the rhythm of common Serb speech as that of 'Hiawatha' is to the rhythm of spoken English. 'Anyone who knows fifty songs', says Vuk (implying that this was no rarity), 'can easily compose a new one.' The main themes of comic songs were likely to be 'weddings, for instance when the bridegroom's friends quarrel and someone has his head broken or is beaten on the back with a stick (if anyone fell down dead, a comic song would not be fitting), or when the bride runs away, or particu-

---

[1] For the tradition of blind singers see Chapter VII, p. 111, n. 1.

EARLY YEARS AND BACKGROUND: 1787–1804

larly if a marriage falls through or if there is a vain attempt at abduction'.[1]

In a later essay (fully quoted at Appendix E), Vuk gave a full account of the genesis of such a comic song:

> There was a young bride in Tršić, from the family Kujundjić in Klubac, who had a pretty sister still living as a maiden with her mother. One day she said by way of a joke to a man called Mitar Mijailović that she'd give the girl to him and they began to call each other 'brother-in-law' and 'sister-in-law'. After a good time of this 'in-lawing', there was a corn-husking in the village, at which Mitar began to call Mrs. Živan 'sister-in-law'. Now whether she was in a bad temper anyhow, or was ashamed at hearing herself (who came from one honest family and had married into another) called 'sister-in-law' before all the village by Mitar (who had the reputation of stealing—especially pigs and lambs), she did not take this well but let herself go, telling him not to call her by that name in future, for she would never let him have her sister. She gave him such a scolding that he ran away for shame and began to threaten that he would abduct her sister. But given that the Kujundjićes lived in a common household, and that the men of Klubac had a name for sticking together, none of the lads of any note in Tršić were willing to join him in the abduction, which thus went no further than an empty boast and threat. Here was a theme for a ballad! After a few weeks the young men all around Tršić began to sing of how Mitar had set out to abduct the girl and couldn't do it.

Vuk proceeds to give the story of the ballad, and to quote some fragments. One of these may be translated (roughly in the metre of the original), to illustrate the ease with which the local bard adapted the high heroic style:

> Milica the maid once dreamed a dream,
> Milica, sister of Ban Kujundjić,
> She whose sister wed Živan the furrier.
> Thus she told her dreams unto her mother:
> 'God protect us, mother, my old mother,
> I have had this night a wondrous vision,
> How towards us drove a dense white cloud,
> Came from Tršić, that most evil village,
> And above the cloud swans were flying.'

The end of the story was that, after a mock-heroic siege of the

[1] For a translation of Vuk's account of the habit of abduction in Serbia, see Appendix A, no. 9.

Kujundjić house, the family pretended to surrender, and hid their daughter while pretending to prepare the bridal gifts; 'thus Mitar was left as a laughing-stock'.[1]

'I have only told this', said Vuk, 'that it may be more easily understood how our heroic songs took form and are still composed today. Just as the more humorous old men and youngsters make up such comic songs, so others compose historical ones about wars and other important happenings.'

From 1804 onwards, the life of Vuk Stefanović was conditioned more directly by the great events of his time, and the tide of them was to sweep him far from Tršić, Loznica, and Tronoša. The picture of him as a boy which can be reconstructed from his later writings, directly or indirectly autobiographical, is in one respect more than others incomplete. There is absolutely no information about his health. His addiction to books and learning may in itself be taken as evidence that he was not regarded as fit for more obviously manly occupations, and simply from his subsequent sufferings and illnesses it may be deduced that from the first he was delicate. Heredity may have been against him: five brothers and sisters had been born to his parents and predeceased him. When he married himself only two out of his thirteen children survived infancy or childhood; but nothing definite is known of any childhood illness of the young Vuk himself. He was evidently of far from heroic stature. The only recorded remark of his mother Jegda is an allusion to his size: 'A ducat is a small coin, but worth more than a thaler.'

We may imagine him then on the threshold of his active career as a rather small and weakly boy, with a store of inner vitality. Of formal education he had little, but no less than his contemporaries in Serbia under the Turks. He was at least peculiarly anxious to learn, and had taught himself enough to make it possible for him to become a monk or a priest, had he so wished, or a merchant in some nearby town. He was recognized as a learned clerk in his own district, and it seems from some incidental remarks in his later controversial writings that he had already started to do occasional work as 'writer' or clerk for the local

---

[1] Mitar later returned to the district to become a high Turkish official at Šabac. There has been some speculation whether Vuk himself was the writer of the comic song quoted; but the evidence in favour does not weigh much against his reiterated statement that he was no poet himself.

merchants or Turkish spahis. No doubt he was thought, and thought himself, more remarkable in and around Tršić for this degree of book-learning than for what he had absorbed of local myth and story and of the songs, heard in his father's house. All this was the common heritage of his country; he had not yet proved that he was peculiarly receptive to it, much less that he could so reproduce it as to make the name of Serbia famous in Europe.

III

THE SERBIAN UPRISING
1804-1805

I

THE regaining of Serbian independence and the history of Serbia as the nucleus of modern Yugoslavia began with the revolt led by Karadjordje (Black George) against the Turks in 1804. It was the first of the great nationalist movements of the nineteenth century. It resulted from and intensified a deep crisis in the administration of the Ottoman Empire. This was at least in part a reaction to the series of defeats suffered by the Turks at the hands of the Austrians and Russians in the second half of the eighteenth century; and in consequence the Serb revolt of 1804 is too often considered in its international context simply as a phase of the 'Eastern Question', and of Austro-Russo-Turkish relations. It did not look at all like that to the men on the spot at the time, of whom Vuk was one, a young but shrewd observer. For him and other Serbs, the revolt was against a new form of Turkish oppression, not against the Sultan, nor necessarily against the highest nominal Turkish authorities in Serbia (the Pashas), nor against the local Turkish landlords, but against an irresponsible soldiery, who reacted violently against attempts from Constantinople to curb their power. The new oppression was all the more resented by the Serb population in that for ten years before they had enjoyed benefits from a sort of Turkish 'New Order'.

To see Turkish-Serb relations in perspective, it is necessary to go back a little way in history, and to look at the general picture in the second half of the eighteenth century, so far as possible through the eyes of Vuk himself, as historian and sociologist. At this time, Turks and Serbs co-existed in Serbia under a sort of *apartheid* system. The Turks lived in the towns, the Serbs in the countryside. The backbone of the Turkish system in Serbia was for a long time the spahis, who were landowners under a sort of feudal tenure.

THE SERBIAN UPRISING: 1804-1805

They had to provide military service for the Turkish Government, and in return they managed their own fiefs, keeping the taxes themselves. The land was generally worked by Serb peasants who owned it and could bequeath or inherit it; but it usually included some estates owned by the spahi himself, and worked by the peasants for him. The spahis' fiefs were theoretically not hereditary; in practice they usually were, and this fact was conducive to the growth of local autonomy. Vuk himself admitted that the spahi system often worked well, and that, where Turkish rule was not oppressive, there was no thought of revolt. The spahis generally went around their villages themselves in autumn and winter to collect grain-tax and poll-tax (which was meant to excuse the villagers from military service).[1] Some of the spahis in Serbia, and most of them in Bosnia, were of Serbian race themselves, and Vuk paints an almost idyllic picture of a typical spahi visitation:

When the spahi comes to a village, he dismounts at some landowner's place where there is a sizeable house, and all the villagers give him what he needs to eat. There are but few spahis who make the round of the village themselves or inspect what harvest the peasants have brought in. Normally, they just ask: 'Well, Radojica, how much maize have you harvested this year?' If Radojica says that he has brought in 20 loads, the spahi will ask his neighbour if that is the truth. If the neighbour says that it is, the spahi will say: 'Swear it on your soul, man!' If Radojica answers that he sowed late and frost killed his maize, or that it was flooded or laid by hail, and so he got nothing in, the spahi will say (by way of comfort to Radojica and himself), 'Well, God will grant better next year'.

The spahi system was however only the bottom layer, so to speak, of Turkish rule. A system which grew in the eighteenth century was the *Čitluk-* (or *chiftlik-*) *Sahibija* under which the Turkish landowner became something like a resident and hereditary proprietor of Serbian serf labour. The lord of a *čitluk* village offered his protection (often necessary) against oppressive neighbours; in return he regarded the village land as his and demanded a heavy tax and service in his own fields.[2] He would normally allow

---

[1] Sometimes administration was simplified by the conversion of tithe, poll-tax, and other taxes into one yearly payment; this was the case at Vuk's native Tršić, for which the monastery of Tronoša made the yearly payment.

[2] *Čitluk* service was normally demanded on Sundays. Vuk notes that on such occasions the landlord usually fed his labourers well and that the young therefore often liked them.

village families to remain on their own land, but if any family died out, the land reverted to his private estate. The *čitluk* system was, in Vuk's own view, the worst of any Turkish institutions in Serbia, and by the end of the eighteenth century was spreading fast. It was fostered by the increasingly unsettled social condition of the Ottoman Empire in Europe. There was a general labour surplus and as a result an increasing amount of brigandage; 'private armies' were formed to conduct forays into the country, or to defend established landlords against such forays. Turkish landowners would induce some villagers to become their serfs by getting them condemned for some crime, and offering to remit punishment; once the Turks had a foothold in the village concerned, they could put pressure on the other villagers to join, for instance by driving off their stock.

Landlords apart, the Serb population was exposed to arbitrary rule from Turkish governors and judges at district level and above. As the authority of the Ottoman Emperor and his financial strength declined, appointments involving tax perquisites were sold for ready money, and the buyers tended to recoup their expenses in the shortest possible time from taxes and fines in their districts. Vuk describes vividly some of their excesses under the heading of *globa* or 'blood-tax':

When a man was killed, search for the culprit was half-hearted; what was looked for was the blood-tax, first of all from the place where the crime was committed and afterwards, to increase the takings, from nearby places too. The blood-tax would be at least a thousand *groš*, and it was due not only in cases of murder, but also if a man fell from a tree or a horse and was killed, or if he was drowned or died of cold—or however it might be, provided that there was a corpse. There was also a tax as heavy as blood-money when it happened that an unmarried girl bore a child. In the nature of the case, this usually amounted to blood-money since such children were usually found dead; but in the end no one asked whether the child was dead or alive—these were regarded as fixed taxes, and were paid communally. There was also no end to the fines paid individually, as for example if someone were accused of having offended against the Turks or had spoken ill of them—such impositions were usually levied on people who were known or thought by the Turks to be rich. When such a man was accused, arrested, and imprisoned, they would tell him right away either that he'd be killed or given so and so many strokes if he didn't pay such and such a sum; or they'd simply say that he'd be killed, and then he'd have to get ransom for himself from his relations; or they would put him in a cell with chains round his neck and his feet in a block—perhaps pouring water under him as well, and then, when he'd had enough of this, he would promise ransom from his kinsmen and look for means of getting himself out.

Vuk's picture of the good side of Turkish rule is favourable enough to guarantee his credibility when he speaks, as above, of its completely arbitrary aspect.

On the Serb side of the relationship, some degree of self-government was allowed. This was exercised by the chiefs (*knezovi*) in various districts, who operated through the headman (*kmetovi*) in the villages. In each district (*nahija*) there would be a number of sub-districts (*kneževine*), and usually one senior chief (*oborknez*). The system was applied mainly for the raising of taxes, fixed by the Turkish governors for the various districts and then raised by the chiefs, who divided the total between their own sub-districts; each in his own sub-district operated through the village headmen. The chiefs also had certain minor judicial rights (though the villagers could always appeal to the Turks over their heads), and had the duty of presenting any grievances of the population to the Turkish Vizir. 'Such chiefs', wrote Vuk, 'were all villagers themselves, and in their home life were not to be distinguished from the other villagers.' Nor were their powers to be distinguished very clearly from those of the headmen, who also could judge minor cases of law, if called in by the disputants, and could on occasion present petitions to the minor Turkish authorities. The office or title of headman was not elective or hereditary (as that of the chief often was). 'Anyone', wrote Vuk, 'who was prominent among the villagers for honesty or intelligence, or particularly for a ready tongue, became an elder.'

Even under Turkish occupation, the Serbs thus had some machinery for self-government at village level, and for dividing among themselves the burdens imposed by the Turks. The replacement of the Serbian Patriarch and Serbian bishops by Phanariot churchmen deprived the Serbian people of one means of representing their grievances to the alien authorities; but by the last five years of the eighteenth century, they were allowed to choose their own chiefs, rather than to have them nominated by the Turks, and an attempt was made to fix in advance the amount of tax to be imposed on each district. Self-government was thus on the way to becoming a reality at district level.

The Serbian villager, particularly in hilly or wooded country, did not need to rely only on passive resistance or formal petitions through his village headmen to record his opinion of Turkish rule. When this became too oppressive, he could vote with his feet, take to the woods and become an outlaw or *hajduk*, as his ancestors had done before him for generations. At least by the mid-eighteenth century, the *hajduks* were a mixed lot—some patriotic opponents of Turkish occupation, some Robin Hoods who carried out a redistribution of wealth at the expense of rich merchants, whatever their nationality, some plain brigands, the majority perhaps a mixture of the three types. Vuk's own account of the *hajduk*—almost the peculiar institution of Serbia—can hardly be bettered:

Our people think and sing in their songs that men became *hajduks* in Serbia as the result of Turkish terror and misrule. It should be said that some went off to be *hajduks* without being forced to it, in order to wear what clothes and carry what weapons they liked[1] or to take revenge on someone; but the full truth is that the milder was the Turkish Government, the less *hajduks* there were in the land, and the worse and more arbitrary it was, the more *hajduks* there were. Thus among the *hajduks* there were at times some most honourable men—at the beginning of Turkish rule a very great many of them came from among the first lords and nobles. The truth is that many became *hajduks* without thought of doing evil; but when men, and particularly simple folk, are once cut off from human society and take their leave of all authority, they begin—especially when banded together—to do wrong. So the *hajduks* do wrong to their own people who still love and pity them in comparison with the Turks; and even now it is the greatest shame and reproach for a *hajduk* to be called a thief and 'scourge of women'.

In the old times, as is sung in the songs, the *hajduks* liked best to lie in wait for the Turks when they were carrying tax-money. That has rarely happened in our time; they lie in wait rather for merchants and other travellers, and sometimes attack the houses of people who are thought to have money or fine clothes and weapons. When they attack a house and do not find money, but think that there is some, they find a son or brother of the owner, take him off and keep him with them until the ransom is paid. A proper *hajduk* will never kill a man who has done him no harm, unless he is persuaded to it by some friend or 'fence'.

Even if there are only two *hajduks*, it is still known which of the two

[1] The *raja* or Serb subject-population was not allowed either to carry weapons, or to wear clothes of certain forms or colours.

is the captain or elder. In the summer, *hajduks* live in the woods and come to the 'fences' who feed them—for example they will come in the evening, and the 'fence' will give them food to take away in baskets, enough to feed them till the next evening. Sometimes the 'fence' will instal them somewhere in the woods, and bring them dinner and supper himself. When winter comes, they part company, and go off each to his own friends for winter quarters, after having agreed how and where to meet in the spring. In winter quarters, some of them lie up for the day in cellars or other buildings, and at night they feast and sing to the *gusle*; others dress in ordinary clothes and keep stock for people as servants. If anyone fails to come at the appointed time to the place agreed, the company go to look for him. If it happens that a 'fence' has betrayed or killed a *hajduk* in winter quarters, all the others will look to their revenge even for fifty years afterwards.

The *hajduks* of our time in Serbia usually wore bright blue cloth trousers, with stockings and soft shoes on their feet, a cloth waistcoat and sleeved jacket on top, and sometimes a blue or green jacket, with an ordinary cloak over all. On their head they would wear either a high cap or fez, or a silken embroidered cap from which silken tassels would hang down on one side over their chest—these were worn by few except *hajduks*. They particularly liked to wear silver discs on their breast, and those who could not yet afford them, would sew on heavy silver coins. For weapons they would carry a long gun and two knives, a large and a small.

While the Turks ruled in Serbia, there was in practically every sub-district one commander with a number of guards, among whom there were Serbs as well as Turks. They hunted the *hajduks*, and sometimes, when many *hajduks* had appeared and there was much killing and robbing, the Turks would gather the whole population for a 'drive'. Then, although some people would find *hajduks*, march them along in their own ranks or hide them in their houses or in the woods, sometimes *hajduks* were caught and killed. When the guards killed anyone, they would cut off his head, take it into the town and put it on a pole on the ramparts. Anyone who fell into the hands of the Turks alive would be impaled. When not even a 'drive' had any effect on the *hajduks*, the Turks would go out on a *teftish*—that is to say some high Turkish officer would go among the people with a good number of young men, and by imprisonment, terror, and fines would drive the headmen and everyone in the *hajduks*' native village to find out the 'fences' and to capture the *hajduks* (but except for the *teftishes* against the *hajduks*' village, no one harmed their wives and children, if they had any, and these lived at peace in their homes). *Teftishes* occurred most often after the wars when for fear of the Turks many ran off to become *hajduks*.

When a man had had his fill of being a *hajduk*, or had been talked over into giving it up, he would surrender himself and ask the headman to produce a guarantee for him from the Pasha; he could then go around again among the people and after that no one would dare to remind him of what he had done in his time as a *hajduk*. Surrendered *hajduks* usually become official guards, because they have become unused to doing normal work; but a former *hajduk* cannot become a chief.

Hajduks keep to their faith, fast and pray like other people, and when they are being taken to be impaled and the Turks offer to spare their lives if they will become converts, they curse Mohammed, saying 'As if I wasn't going to die some time anyhow!' *Hajduks* all regard themselves as great heroes, and it is rare that any dares to join them who is not self-reliant.

When they are caught and taken to be impaled, they usually sing at the top of their voice, to show that they care not at all for their lives. Even a surrendered *hajduk* is always bolder-mannered and bluffer than other people; he will allow no liberties to be taken with him, and all are rather afraid of him.[1]

2

Such was the general pattern of relations between Serbs and Turks in Serbia down to the last decade of the 18th century. In 1789 however—a crucial date for the history of Eastern as well as Western Europe—the reforming Sultan, Selim III, succeeded to the Turkish throne. In 1791 he signed the Peace Treaty of Sistovo with the Austrians, regaining control of Serbia.[2] Drawing the consequences from a series of wars in which the local population was always against the Turks, and from the need to restore the Imperial finances, Selim issued in 1792 and 1793 a series of decrees radically reforming the provincial administration of the Ottoman Empire, including Serbia. An important object of the new regulations was to break the power of the janissaries. In the great days of the Ottoman Empire these had been an élite corps, specially recruited and strictly disciplined. By the end of the seventeenth century, they had become a hereditary caste and were allowed to

---

[1] Vuk ends his essay on *hajduks* with a reminiscence of his native district, which shows them as common brigands who could be frightened off by firm resistance.

[2] In return, Leopold II of Austria gained an area of the Banat, immediately north of the Iron Gates on the Danube. The Serbs gained nothing by the Treaty except the promise of an amnesty, and felt badly let down by the Austrians.

engage in trade or plunder.[1] At the end of the eighteenth century, they were largely out of control of Constantinople, and had become a lawless and rapacious body of mercenaries, ready to support the highest bidders for their services. Moreover a new type of such bidders had emerged—the virtually independent rulers who exercised power in outlying districts of the Ottoman Empire, particularly in Albania and Rumelia (now Rumania and Bulgaria).

It was important for Selim to build up a well and regularly paid body of troops in order to re-establish the central power, and to secure for himself the support of the local populations of his empire. As a means to these ends, he increased the scope of Serbian local self-government and took measures to limit the rapacity of Turkish officials by various means; the amount of taxes to be raised in each district was formally fixed, and Turks were forbidden to settle outside the towns or to extend the system of *Čitluk-Sahibija*. Serbian national consciousness was actively fostered, in that the Serbs were allowed once more to build monasteries and churches, and to sound bells in them. Above all, there was an amnesty—and of more than a nominal nature—for the Serbs who had fought in *Freikorps* (volunteer regiments) with the Austrian army in Serbia during the recent war, and Serbs were formally allowed to retain arms.

Such measures were designed in part to forestall the possibility of further Serbian uprisings fostered by the Austrians (it was one such uprising that had grown into the Austro-Turkish war of 1789). The reforming Sultan's main need in Serbia was to strengthen the hand of his own Pasha in Belgrade by securing for him local support against the janissaries. In 1793 the appointment of Hadji Mustapha Pasha as governor of the Belgrade province marked an important stage in the new Turkish policy. The janissaries were forbidden to remain within the province of Belgrade, and in effect Mustapha Pasha promoted an alliance between Serbian peasants, loyal Turkish troops, and spahis against the janissaries. Vital steps along this road were taken in 1797, when for the first time the Serb chiefs were allowed to raise

---

[1] As early as 1568 Selim II was forced to grant the janissaries the privilege of enrolling their sons in the Corps. By 1717, when Lady Mary Wortley Montagu travelled through Serbia on her way to Istanbul, she noted their arbitrary and uncontrolled behaviour.

their own troops instead of paying extra taxes to help Mustapha Pasha, and in 1798, when they were given the right to maintain their own guards against brigands.

The policy of moderation was however halted half-way. At a time of increasing international tension, there were naturally conservative advisers at the Porte who were doubtful about the wisdom or indeed of the legality under Moslem law of arming the Serbs. Moreover to the east of Serbia, at Vidin in 'Rumelia', the local pasha, Pazvan Oglu, had set up his own power in 1796, and shown himself increasingly independent of the Porte. The newly armed Serbs might, it was thought, join forces with him to gain their independence.

Osman Pazvan Oglu was an important and typical figure in the decline of the Ottoman Empire at this time. Born in 1758, he had distinguished himself in the Austro-Turkish wars of 1788–91 as leader of a troop of volunteer cavalry. When the Treaty of Sistovo was signed in 1791, he retained his own force to take possession of the estates at Vidin from which his father (with his own help) had been expelled. Once installed at Vidin, Pazvan Oglu attracted to his service first some irregular bands of soldiers, known as the *krdjalije*, who had been dismissed from the Sultan's service in the course of his reform of the Turkish army, and had since been living off plunder in Macedonia and south-eastern Serbia; and thereafter the dissident janissaries who had been expelled from the province of Belgrade. Pazvan Oglu was liberal at the same time with promises of greater freedom to Christians, in order to attract support against Selim. Essentially however he was opposed to any meaningful reform of the Ottoman Empire, unlike his neighbour, Constantine Ypsilanti, the *hospodar* of Wallachia, who wished to see it transformed into something like a confederation of principalities.

Pazvan Oglu occupied an important strategic position on the borders of Serbia, the Turkish-controlled part of Rumania and Wallachia. The Turkish Government decided that their first priority must be to reduce his power, and in order to attract forces away from him, Mustapha Pasha was made to go into reverse, welcome the janissaries back to Serbia (1799) and impose new and heavy taxes on the Serbs. From this time on, Serbian relations with the Turkish authorities went steadily downhill. The janissaries soon began to pick quarrels, first with the Serbian chiefs and then

THE SERBIAN UPRISING: 1804-1805   37

with Mustapha Pasha himself, who was murdered in 1801.[1] The real power now rested in the hands of four *Dahijas*,[2] representatives of the janissaries, and the new Vizir Hasan Pasha was a tool in their hands. Turkish spahis and Serb chiefs and merchants all suffered alike from the excesses of the new Turkish authorities in Belgrade. By 1802, the spahis were organizing their own revolt, but one of them betrayed his companions. The *Dahijas* in the meantime were recruiting their private armies; they struck the first blow and executed numbers of the spahis themselves and of their prominent Serb supporters.

By this time Serbs and moderate Turks had little to lose by rebellion. They were encouraged by the temporary success of an expedition from the Porte against Pazvan Oglu in Rumelia, which deprived the *Dahijas* of some probable support. From mid-1803 onwards, the Serb leaders were making preparations for a rising, including an attempt to get munitions from the Austrian authorities; they maintained links with Peter I, the Prince-Bishop of Montenegro, who was himself in touch with the Russians,[3] with a view to co-ordinating a 'war of liberation' against the Turks.

In the meantime an increasing number of the Serbian population took to the woods. As Vuk wrote later:

However poor was the reputation of the *hajduks* in Serbia under the wise and just rule of Mustapha Pasha, now as the result of so much force and terror, a tenth of the population became *hajduks*; in nearly all sub-districts there would be one *hajduk* captain with at least ten comrades, and apart from that there were five times as many people who had not turned completely into *hajduks* but kept a wary eye on the Turks, and hid themselves either in the woods or in other villages with their friends.

The Serb population complained directly to the Sultan about the rule of the *Dahijas*, and in communicating with the latter, the Sultan made the scarcely veiled threat that he would arm the Serbs against them. It was this that determined the *Dahijas* to take further preventive action,[4] which in turn finally precipitated the

[1] In his *First Year of the War against the Dahijas* (1828) Vuk wrote of Mustapha Pasha: 'He so tended and cherished the Serbs that down to this day they mourn his memory and say that he was a mother to Serbia.'
[2] The more familiar anglicized form of *Dahija* is *Dey* (as of Algiers).
[3] In 1803 Peter I of Montenegro sent his envoy, Arsenije Gagović, to ask for Russian armed support against the Turks.
[4] The *Dahijas* decided, on receipt of the Sultan's *ferman*, to execute all

Serb revolt of 1804. The crucial point, in Vuk's account, was the failure of the Turkish attempt to capture and kill Karadjordje (Black George) of Topola, a notable *hajduk*.

Karadjordje was the most notable military leader and the most forceful personality of the Serbian Revolt. He was born in the mid-1760s, and in 1787, when an Austrian invasion of Serbia seemed imminent, he crossed the Sava to join the Austrian army. According to a story current by 1804, he killed his father at the river-crossing rather than let him stay behind in Serbia as he wished to do; this story shows at least that Karadjordje gained very early a reputation for single-minded ruthlessness and the aura of a great tragic hero.[1] He served with the Austrian army as a sergeant in the Serbian *Freikorps* and after the peace of Sistovo remained for a short time as forester at the monastery of Krušedol, just below the southern slopes of the Fruška Gora hills near Novi Sad. When Mustapha became Pasha of Belgrade province, Karadjordje decided that he had nothing to fear from the Turks, and returned to his land at Topola, some fifty miles south of Belgrade, where he became a prosperous pig merchant. He was one of those who had most to lose by the unhindered imposition of the *Dahijas'* rule, and Vuk pictures him in 1804 talking thus to his fellow conspirators:

> The Turks have devised all sorts of violence, and now their intent is to cut us all down and kill us. The only salvation is for us to defend ourselves, and to kill them. If we are otherwise going to be bound and die like women at the hands of their horsemen, it's better to die like heroes and men, to make them pay for our lives and to avenge our brothers. We may lose our wives and children and houses, but we're not masters of them as it is.

Such words, Vuk continues, were very much to the taste of the *hajduks* and of those whose relations had been killed by the Turks, and the others could say nothing against Karadjordje.

Now therefore, to open people's eyes, all that was necessary was to kill one single Turk at sight; and a start was made in the village of Šibnic in the Belgrade district. Now it was the whole people that was involved against the Turks; if up to that point anyone had thought that the Turks picked and chose, executed only the chiefs and prominent people, and

potential Serb leaders. Among their victims was Aleksa, brother of Jakob, and father of Prota Matija Nenadović, who in his *Memoirs* movingly describes his father's last hours.

[1] The Russian A. I. Turgenev heard this story as early as 1804.

THE SERBIAN UPRISING: 1804-1805 39

would not turn against the whole *raja* population, now it was plain that they would kill and burn and enslave all alike.

Karadjordje had in fact made sure that his revolt was a 'people's war', whether the people liked it or not.[1] Vuk's account of how Karadjordje was finally chosen as leader is a further good example of his powers of realism. He described the debate among the various captains. One notable *hajduk* felt that normally law-abiding men would never follow him. A prominent chief was pressed to take on the job but looked ahead warily at the possibility of a Turkish victory, in which case he could protect the people by blaming the revolt on the *hajduks*. The best thing was for Karadjordje to become leader:

'The Turks know him as a *hajduk* anyhow. Then if a Turkish army comes into Serbia and the Turks rule again, he can run off to the woods with his *hajduks* and we can appear before the Turks and throw all the blame on him and the rest of them, and afterwards we can easily get a special guarantee for him and hand him over as a *hajduk*. If things go the other way and the present state of affairs continues, we'll continue to rule and give orders, the people are in our hands anyhow.' Then everyone pressed Karadjordje to become leader, and he began to excuse himself saying that he didn't know how to rule, and that he was wild and ill-tempered, that he just wanted to go out and fight right away, and so on. But Chief Teodosija said to him: 'What you don't know, we'll teach you. And as for being wild and the rest of it, that's just the sort of man who is needed now.' So Karadjordje took on the leadership.[2]

---

[1] According to Vuk, the directive was for all able men to take arms and join the warrior bands (*čete*—hence the familiar *četnik* of the Second World War), while women and children should take to the woods. 'As the bands increased in size, they began a drive against those who would not join the revolt, to burn their houses and to use violence against them as against the Turks.'

[2] An early description by a non-Serb source of Karadjordje the supreme commander was given by the Russian Marshal Diebitsch, who was on an official mission to Serbia, 1810-11: '... we must admit that he has a mind of a masculine and commanding order. The imputation of ... bloodthirstiness appears to be unjust; when the country was without the shadow of a constitution, and when he commanded an unorganized and uncultivated nation, he was compelled to be severe; he dared not oscillate, or relax his discipline; but now there are courts of law and legal forms, he hands every case over to the regular tribunals. He has very little to say for himself, and is rude in his manners; but his judgments on civil affairs are promptly and soundly formed and to great address he joins unwearied industry. As a soldier, there is but one opinion of his talents, bravery and enduring firmness.' (Quoted by Andrew Archibald Paton in *Servia, the Youngest Member of the European Family*, 1845.) An interesting account of the Serbian army under Karadjordje is contained in an article 'Einiges über

3

This is not the place to give a connected narrative of the first Serbian uprising. So far as concerns Vuk's own minor part in the events of 1804, two points should be re-emphasized. Firstly, the uprising started as a revolt against Turks whom the Turkish authorities themselves regarded as usurpers, and against a soldiery which the Sultan himself and Mustapha Pasha had recently sought to suppress with Serbian aid. Whatever the inmost thoughts and intentions of the Serb leaders, they could reasonably and probably with truth say that they were rising not against Turkish rule as such, but against the *Dahijas* who were themselves rebels against the Sultan; what they were asking for in the first place was the restoration of the rights granted them under Mustapha Pasha.

Even more important was the fact that, although Karadjordje was recognized as supreme commander, his powers were ill-defined and limited. There were other local leaders (particularly Jakob Nenadović in Western Serbia) who enjoyed a good deal of independence; and they too found great difficulty in disciplining *hajduk* leaders in their own areas. Action was thus likely to be on a local basis, and the personality and interests of the local leader concerned counted much more than any general idea of freedom and nationality. The local chiefs started very soon to quarrel about the division of spoil and the exercise of political influence. The history of Highland Scotland in the 1745 rebellion and of the Greek war of liberation in 1821 would furnish some instructive parallels.

Vuk himself saw the beginnings of the Serbian revolt from a vantage point of special interest. His native village of Tršić lay on the eastern edge of the Mačva Plain, immediately south of the Sava and the Srem province of the Austrian Empire. The Mačva Plain is bordered to the west by the river Drina, which runs into the Sava northwards near the town of Šabac; and west of the Drina lay the Turkish province of Bosnia—not the less firmly on the Turkish side because its inhabitants, including many of the most powerful men, were largely Serbs who had adopted the Moslem religion. The Mačva Plain is the obvious route for troops attempting to

Serbien . . .' by an anonymous author in *Streffleurs Militärische Zeitschrift* (Vienna), 1808. This was drawn to my attention by Professor Rela Novaković of Belgrade University.

THE SERBIAN UPRISING: 1804-1805

advance from Bosnia to Belgrade (it was near Tršić that the Austrian army was heavily defeated in 1914 at the Cer Mountain, visible on a clear evening from the western suburbs of Belgrade). Tršić was thus within easy reach of Turkish forces coming from Bosnia to succour Belgrade, Šabac, or the local small town of Loznica. On the Serbian side, it lay to the north-east of Valjevo, where Jakob Nenadović, one of the principal Serbian leaders, had his command, and to the south-west of the home area of a formidable *hajduk* leader, Djordje Čurčija, whose headquarters were in the woods of Cer.

The experience of the local population in 1804-5 was, not surprisingly, bloody and confused. Vuk himself was conscripted during the early months of the revolt to serve as clerk to the *hajduk* leader Čurčija, in his own native district. His service gave him some direct acquaintance with the realities of the heroic life pictured in the songs and stories which he afterwards collected; and the small corner of the war which Vuk himself experienced is worth a brief description, because it was typical of the fighting as a whole.

The revolt in the Šumadija (the wooded district of central Serbia) began in February. While the main forces of Karadjordje had considerable success there, further westwards Jakob Nenadović advanced in mid-March to lay siege to Šabac; Čurčija came out to help him, operating in fact independently and with no fixed plan. Together with Nenadović, Čurčija went in mid-April to counter a Turkish expedition that was coming from Bosnia to relieve Šabac, but found that Nenadović had held back much of his strength at Šabac. This was done for good reasons, but Čurčija thought that the object was to leave all the fighting to his own troops, and he retired sulking to Cer.[1] When Šabac was surrendered

---

[1] The details recorded here about Čurčija's campaigns are taken from Vuk's *First Year of the War against the Dahijas* (1828). A parallel account in verse was given in one of the narrative 'popular songs' of the blind poet, Philip Višnjić who recorded Čurčija's speech to Jakob Nenadović in some famous lines:

> Now, Jakob, you Serbian commander,
> Will you bring more troops to the battle?
> If you bring no more troops to the battle,
> I shall not be first to fight the Turks.
> For I am no willow by the river
> To grow new shoots if they cut me down
> And to be again as once I was.
> I am Čurčija, the great hill captain,
> When they cut me down, I'll grow no more.

by the Turks shortly afterwards, Čurčija again went with Nenadović to join Karadjordje's main force; but he soon quarrelled with Karadjordje too over the division of booty and Karadjordje's violent attempt to discipline one of his own men. He returned to Šabac and the Mačva, replaced with his own men those whom Nenadović had appointed as local authorities, and proceeded in July to the district of Jadar (in which Tršić and Loznica lay), in order to raise new forces and clear the district of the Turks. It was almost certainly at this stage that Vuk was recruited as a 'writer' or clerk by Čurčija. No doubt it was he himself who drafted the appeal to the Turkish authorities of Loznica to abandon the town (it is improbable that anyone else in Čurčija's entourage could write);[1] and he stayed for some weeks afterwards in Čurčija's encampment on the Drina.

Čurčija's army must have been an incalculable force. Vuk described it later with his usual frankness: 'One man would take a cauldron or something similar as booty, and go off home with it; someone else would capture a cow or mare from the Turks, and take that home; another would buy some of the booty and go away to sell it; yet another would get bored at just sitting with nothing to do, and go off home to reap the corn or look after the rest of the harvesting.' Čurčija had to resort to strange methods in order to maintain discipline. Vuk describes one of these in an entry under the word *Koviljača* (a place-name)[2] in his *Dictionary*:

In the year 1804, our camp was just under Koviljača. One morning Čurčija, who was then commander in Jadar, ordered all his men to parade, then came out in front of them and began to speak; 'Do you see that hill, men? I've heard in Germany[3] that this was once a bigger town than Šabac or Zvornik; and just before the Turks came to rule over the land, people crammed together here a store of rifles and guns and powder and shot and sabres and knives and all sorts of weapons. Then they covered it all with earth, and bushes have grown up over it. And now we have nothing to do, so let's bring billhooks and spades and dig it up. Then we shall have a town and weapons and guns. You can see

[1] The appeal was typical of Serbian propaganda tactics of the time. It said that the Serbs were attacking only the *Čitluk* owners and others who did not obey the Sultan's orders; they had no quarrel with the other Turks who had 'lived peacefully and decently among them'.

[2] Today Koviljača Banja, a sulphur-spring resort about 30 miles west of Belgrade. It was the sulphurous taste of the water which Čurčija explained by the story about hidden stores of powder.

[3] 'Germany' in common Serb parlance of the time usually meant 'Austria'. Austrians were often known as *Shvobs* (*Schwaben*).

THE SERBIAN UPRISING: 1804-1805

this water here smells of powder, and that's because it has passed under the town and must somewhere have flowed through the powder!' So his officers went to the village to get billhooks and axes and spades, and for two or three days they set about clearing and digging up the hill, starting at the top. But in the meantime the Turks attacked, the camp was broken up and transferred, and Koviljača remains just as it was. On the whole I think that Čurčija only wanted to dig it up in order to prevent his soldiers deserting and going home from the camp.

In any case Čurčija's army was scattered and defeated late in the summer of 1804 by the Turkish counter-attack from Bosnia. The Turks penetrated to Loznica and up to Šabac, then retired again across the Drina, causing much destruction and taking much booty with them, before the forces sent up by Karadjordje from Valjevo could intercept them. Inevitably Nenadović blamed Čurčija for this disaster and spread the rumour that it was caused by his treachery. He obtained the consent of Karadjordje to have Čurčija killed, and our last sight of the *hajduk* leader is in Vuk's narrative:[1]

> When he saw that his wound would not let him retreat further, he drew his pistol and, sitting in a hut, drove off his attackers. After he had fired a few shots at the men who were shooting at him from all around, his wounds overpowered him and he fell to the ground. The men ran up to him from the side, clubbed him with the butts of their rifles, and pulled off his clothes and grabbed his weapon from him even before he was dead.

New chiefs were appointed by Nenadović to look after the Jadar district, including Vuk's own cousin Jefto Savić from Tršić. With the agreement of Karadjordje and Nenadović, they made their own terms with the Turkish authorities in Bosnia, while Karadjordje in the Belgrade province had to fight and negotiate for more than a year before he could take Belgrade and secure his position as chief of a virtually independent principality.

Vuk's experience of war had been typical and unhappy. The army with which he served had been easily scattered and defeated, and its leader killed. He had seen plenty of intrigue and disunity on the Serbian side. And he returned to Tršić to find his father's house burned to the ground. His father may still have wanted him

[1] Much of Vuk's narrative about Čurčija is reproduced in Ranke's *The Serbian Revolution* (see Chapter II, p. 13, n. 2; and Chapter XIII).

to become a merchant or a priest, but his own mind was evidently made up. He urged his father to let him go north of the Sava to continue his education, and threatened otherwise to run off with the *hajduks*. Faced with this threat, his father did not hesitate to let him go.

IV

FURTHER EDUCATION IN KARLOVCI AND BELGRADE; SERBIA DURING THE REVOLT AGAINST THE TURKS

1

PROBABLY in March 1805,[1] Vuk crossed the river Sava into the Syrmien (Srem) province of the Austrian Empire and went to school in Sremski Karlovci until some time in 1805. Sremski Karlovci (or Karlovci as it will henceforth be called) was the metropolitan town, and the main cultural centre of the Serb community. Still conspicuous for its church towers, it lies just off the highroad to Novi Sad some fifty miles from Belgrade, between the north-eastern slopes of the wooded Fruška Gora hills and the Danube. In the eighteenth century it was the central town for the close network of monasteries in the Fruška Gora, many of which had been established in the sixteenth century, well before the main migration of the Serb community to the Srem province.

Evidence of how Vuk spent his time at Karlovci, what he learnt, and exactly where he learned it, is scanty and contradictory. It seems that he was a boarder in the free 'Alumneum' (students' house) established by the Metropolitan of the time, Stefan Stratimirović; there he would take a preliminary course for the 'Gymnasium' founded for Serb students in 1791. When Vuk came to Karlovci, it is recorded that he had previously 'learned to read *The Book of Hours* in Serbian, knew how to write a little and to add, subtract, and multiply'. When he left, he is said 'to have learnt to read Serb and German well, to have finished Slavonic grammar, the whole of arithmetic and the catechism'. In 1806, Vuk was reckoned either to be too old for admittance to the 'Gymnasium', or not to have learned enough German to qualify for attendance in

---

[1] Vuk's own evidence on the date is contradictory, but his most considered statement favours 1805 (see *Kovčežić*, iii, p. 176).

anything but the lowest class—a humble position indeed for a boy of 19. He left Sremski Karlovci to try his luck elsewhere.

This is the bare and uncertain record of one and a half years which were probably frustrating for the young Vuk. First there was the shock of finding—to his great discomfort, as he afterwards recorded—that all knowledge was not comprised in *The Book of Hours* and the *Psalter*. He was older than most of his fellow pupils and the discipline of a boarding school is not likely to have been congenial to a boy who had known the freedom and comradeship (if also the squalor and dangers) of the *hajduks'* camp. He must have felt anxiety about his parents, his native village, and the course of the fighting in Serbia. And finally it was made insultingly clear to him that further learning would be a waste of time; his teachers told him, according to Sreznevski, that he had 'had enough training for Serbia, he could become whatever he liked there—priest, teacher, or clerk'.

Once again, as in Tršić, the indirect education which Vuk received from observation of his environment at Karlovci was much more important for his subsequent career than anything which he learnt at school there. It was at Karlovci that he first became aware of the great power exercised over the Austrian Serb community by those Orthodox Church dignitaries who later opposed most vigorously his life work, and also of some of those currents of secular thought which were already undermining their influence.

Early in the eighteenth century the Serb community in the Srem province were oppressed by their immediate neighbours (the Hungarians) and denied the political rights which they had been promised by the Emperor Leopold I. The Austrian Government came to regard the Serbs, like the Slavs settled in the military zone on the Croatian-Bosnian border, mainly as useful soldiers.[1] The Serbs themselves came to depend no less than their kinsmen under Turkish rule on the Orthodox Church. It was the only autonomous institution which they were allowed, and its assemblies were the principal means of conveying their wishes to

---

[1] The frontiersman (*graničari*) from the Croatian-Bosnian border played a large role in the Imperial army. In 1740, out of 113,000 troops inherited by Maria Theresia from Karl VI, over 45,000 were *graničari*, and in the time of the French Revolution they numbered 100,000. (Jovan Skerlić, *Srpska Knjizhevnost u XVIII Veku*, Belgrade, 1923, p. 19.) Avoidance of military service was frequent among the Serbs of the Srem. They either retreated into already overcrowded monasteries, or migrated to Russia (see § 4).

KARLOVCI AND BELGRADE 47

the Austrian authorities. From 1710 onwards the Austrian Government weakened the link between the Church authorities in their territory and the Serbian Patriarchate at Peć, in Turkish-occupied Serbia, and encouraged Catholic proselytizing activity, but this had the opposite effect to that intended; the Orthodox Church was universally regarded as standing for Serbian nationality and culture against Austrian and Hungarian influence. The cultural and political restrictions imposed on the Serbs in the Srem had one further result which was most unwelcome to the Austrian Government. The Orthodox Church authorities turned increasingly to Moscow for help, particularly in the establishment of an educational system. The results were not large, but served to increase the prestige both of the Church and of Russia.

In the last two decades of the eighteenth century, the authority and prestige of the Orthodox Church was affected by the reforms of Joseph II in Austria as a whole and by the particular actions taken to implement these reforms among the Serb community. The main instrument of implementation was the 'Illyrian Court Chancellery', established at Vienna in 1745. Many of Joseph's reforms were welcome to the Orthodox Church, especially the 'Toleranz-Patent' of 1781 which gave it a status equal to that of the Catholics. From 1781 onwards the Serbs were at last allowed to build their own churches, with bells (1787) and doors facing on to the main street (1789);[1] in 1790 it was forbidden to call the Serbs 'schismatics'—the worst that could be said of them were that they were 'non-uniti'. All this weakened the position of the Catholics in the Austrian Empire and strengthened that of the Serbs particularly *vis-à-vis* the Hungarians (this was of course Joseph's primary intention); it also strengthened the position of the Orthodox Church among the Serbs. Yet the general tendency was towards the spread of a rationalist spirit and the secularization of Serb society. In 1791 Leopold II allowed the establishment of the first Serb 'Gymnasium' at Karlovci, and allowed the Serbs to have their own press (with Cyrillic lettering) in Buda (rather than in Vienna, where printing of Serb books in Cyrillic had begun in 1771). Here from 1792 to 1796 newspapers in the Serb language

---

[1] See Chapter II, p. 13, n. 3. It seems to have been thought that if the main entrances faced the street, people would be more likely to indulge in gossip and even in unlawful assembly; many houses in the villages of the Vojvodina to-day have special bow- or box-windows facing the street, to facilitate conversation.

were printed twice weekly. This all added up to a substantial inroad on the Orthodox Church's monopoly of learning and education. The measures were designed or allowed by the Austrians in order to foster Serbian national spirit and to secure the backing of the Serbian community for a forward Austrian policy in the Balkans; to improve the image of Austria as protector of the Serbs (including the Orthodox Church) in their own area of influence; and consequently to counter the tendency of the Orthodox Church and educated Serbs as a whole to look to Russia alone for spiritual and cultural affinities. From 1785 Serbian national groups were formed to support the Josephine reforms, and under the influence of Dositej Obradović (of whom more later in this chapter) a considerable pro-Josephine literature, full of rationalist doctrine, began to appear.

There was also however strong opposition among the Serbs to the 'reformist' tendencies and not only from the most conservative elements of the Orthodox hierarchy. The great majority of the Serbs in the Austrian Empire still looked on the Orthodox Church, with all its weaknesses and abuses, as the protector of Serbian nationhood and religion against the Austrians, and treasured the link of the Serbian Church with the Russian Church (though in fact this was becoming less and less important).[1] The Austrian Government, however 'enlightened' the Emperor, remained suspect of trying indirectly to impose Catholicism on their subjects, or to facilitate its spread; and Joseph's own centralizing tendencies aroused much opposition. Moreover even when the Austrian Government adopted a liberal policy in the sphere of education, some of their first steps had been so inept that the memory of them could not easily be erased by later changes. Thus the first regulations allowing the Serbs to build their own schools (1770) were accompanied by a stipulation (afterwards revoked) that Serb children who could not attend them must go to Catholic

[1] The most important link in the chain had been an educational mission sent by the Moscow Synod to Karlovci in 1727, under their own translator, Maksim Terentevich Suvorov, which stayed for over ten years. Suvorov and his teachers had a considerable influence on the Orthodox educational system in the Srem province, but neither he nor his Serb hosts enjoyed the process of doctrinal co-existence. The Serb monks were reported to have said: 'What's all this about "mine", "yours", and "his"? We know that much without any grammar.' Suvorov himself wrote to his Metropolitan that, while he had once had his doubts about purgatory, he now believed in it and moreover knew exactly where it was. See also Chapter VII, § 1 and Appendix C.

schools. This looked to the Serbs like the prelude to a further Catholic propaganda effort. Finally, apart from these more or less reasonable suspicions on the part of the more educated Serbs, the conservative peasants much disliked various rationalist reforms which had little to do with religious doctrine and much with their traditional way of life, such as the abolition of many of the numerous holidays for Saints' days.

For all these reasons the power of the Orthodox Church in the face of rationalist reforms remained very considerable. Moreover it was in nearly all cases the Church which in fact controlled the operation of the new machinery of public education. The Church institutions still absorbed a large proportion of the educated population, and were bound to play a large part in the development of the school system organized or encouraged by the Austrians from 1776 onwards.[1] And the Orthodox Church under the Metropolitan Stratimirović exercised censorship over the productions—whether books or newspapers—of the new Serb press at Budapest.

In Karlovci particularly the influence of the Orthodox Church was very important at the time of Vuk's stay. It was the metropolitan town, and the Metropolitan himself was a strong and forceful character, with an important part to play in the history of Serbia as a whole, and in Vuk's own subsequent life. Stefan Stratimirović was a great lord of the Church, at home with the great lords of Austria, and a Privy Counsellor of the Austrian court. He was a learned man who procured books from a wide range of correspondents in many languages—Latin, Church Slavonic, Russian, Magyar, French, and German. His extensive reading included Kant, Ossian, and something of the French encyclopaedists (the writings of Voltaire and Rousseau were only banned from his diocese by Imperial decree in 1804). He was interested in linguistics and had himself announced the intention of compiling a Serbian or 'Slavonic-Serbian' dictionary. He was also actively interested in politics, and backed the Serbian revolt of 1804, exchanging gifts with its leaders (his own included a silken tent for outdoor church services). His longer-term political plans included one, secretly communicated to the Tsar, for a

---

[1] By 1780 there were 110 Serb primary schools in the Srem province and Slavonia (the most easterly part of Croatia). The first Serb secondary school was the 'Gymnasium' of Karlovci, founded in 1791; and the first theological school was founded, also at Karlovci, in 1794.

single autonomous Serb state, under Russian protection, but still paying taxes to the Turks and affording special status to them. Vuk quarrelled with Stratimirović later on, and was a good hater. He thus tended to suppress memories of early kindness from Stratimirović, which he certainly received along with criticism early in his literary career, and perhaps even in his first student days at Karlovci.

A humbler but still important Church dignitary, Lukian Mušicki, was in 1805 a professor of classical literature at the 'Gymnasium'. He was already known as a man of learning and a poet.[1] It is doubtful whether Vuk made his acquaintance as a student, but for some years after 1814, Mušicki was his close friend and keen supporter. He was keenly interested in Serbian popular poetry. In the introduction to his first book of Serbian 'popular songs' (quoted in full in Chapter VI) Vuk describes how Mušicki encouraged the schoolboys at Karlovci to write down Serbian songs, and how he himself hesitated for fear of being mocked. The passage has been much discussed in relation to the part played by Mušicki in stimulating Vuk's literary interests, and more will be said of it later in this work. Perhaps the only safe conclusion from it is that Vuk, the over-age schoolboy who had served with a *hajduk* chief, was in 1805-6 a very prickly subject for any professor.

2

A much more powerful influence on Vuk, as upon most others of his generation, was the other Grand Old Man of Serbian literature—its grandfather, if Vuk himself may be called its father —Dositej Obradović, who was then at the height of his fame. Stratimirović was the powerful representative of the Orthodox Church, the preserver of the old Serbian culture. Dositej represented

[1] Lukian Mušicki (1777-1837) had studied philosophy, law, and theology, and in addition had a wide knowledge of ancient and modern languages. From 1812 to 1822 he was Archimandrite of the monastery of Šišatovac, in the wooded hills of the Fruška Gora, some fifty miles north-west of Belgrade. Here he did much to help Vuk. He was a prominent poet of his time, affecting a classical style, and modelling himself on Horace and Klopstock. Subsequent chapters record some details of his correspondence with Vuk. In 1822, Mušicki was suspended from his Archimandrite's office, partly because of his friendship with Vuk; but in 1824 he began to devote himself again to Church affairs, in a new position. He became a Bishop in 1828 and for the last ten years of his life he and Vuk were progressively estranged.

KARLOVCI AND BELGRADE 51

the 'Enlightenment' of the eighteenth century, and the longer-term influence of Joseph II's anti-Catholic reforms. This strange and attractive figure needs some longer introduction if the intellectual world in which Vuk operated is to be understood. Born in 1742 or 1743 in a small Serbo-Rumanian town, Obradović made his way to Hopovo monastery[1] in 1757 and became a monk in 1758, taking the name of Dositej. At first his zeal for godly learning, piety, and asceticism were famous, but two or three years of Hopovo bred some scepticism and a desire to extend his knowledge beyond the narrowly limited literature of the monastery library. The laziness and worldly behaviour of the Hopovo monks (with some honourable exceptions) made a deep impression on him (though only golden memories are recorded in his *Autobiography*), and in 1760 he ran away. As teacher, tutor, preacher, and priest, he travelled widely in Dalmatia, Montenegro, and Greece, learning Italian and literary Greek and going as far as Smyrna in 1766. In 1771 he reached Vienna and stayed there five years as a language teacher—himself acquiring a good knowledge of German and French. By the end of the 1770s he was travelling widely again as a tutor,[2] and in 1782 went to Halle University in Germany to study philosophy. It was at this time that he determined to start writing himself in order to further education in Serbia, and his first books were produced at Leipzig in 1783-4.

Dositej was, so to speak, a small scale Encyclopedist. His aim was less to write original books than to reflect the light of 'philosophy' (or useful learning of any kind), then shining in Germany, France, and England, on to his own compatriots in Austrian or Turkish-occupied Serbia, and to introduce European culture to them. He continued to travel widely—France 1784, England 1784-5, White Russia and the Baltic States 1788-9. And he continued to translate into Serbian and publish the ideas of his favourite German, French,

[1] Hopovo monastery was one of those not totally destroyed in the Second World War and is (1968) in process of restoration. It lies in the woods of the Fruška Gora, directly under the main excursion point, Iriški Venac, about forty miles north-west of Belgrade.
[2] Dositej went in 1779 to Trieste and Italy as tutor to a Russian Archimandrite, Varlaam; and thence as a teacher to Chios, Istanbul, and Jassy. His entertaining autobiography was translated and published, with a commentary and notes, by Professor G. R. Noyes, *The Life and Adventures of Dimitrije Obradović, Who as a Monk was Given the Name Dositej*, University of California Press, 1953.

and English authors. Dositej provided the mental and spiritual background for the reforms of Joseph II. He was highly eclectic in his own tastes and ideas, and retained some loyalty to Church institutions. In French, for example, his favourite author was Fénélon,[1] and he never translated Voltaire or Rousseau. English was his favourite language and culture and his works included many elegant extracts from Addison (the *Spectator* was a particular love), Pope, Swift, Defoe, Chesterfield,[2] Richardson, and Johnson. From German he translated passages of Lessing, the philosopher Christian Wolf, and many lesser-known Protestant preachers.

This is a miscellaneous list, but there is no doubt of the general tendency of Dositej's work. He had a passionate hatred of superstition, and thought that man should serve God with all his mind, as well as with all his heart and soul—man's mental powers too were God-given. Dositej's own writings provide a number of instances to show how necessary his own work of enlightenment was, and how desperately backward were the monks who were meant to educate the Serb community in the Austrian Empire. He described some of the pagan habits still prevalent there and wrote of them, without any of the romantic enthusiasm which Vuk later devoted to the description of folk customs, as 'phenomena of dark magic and lack of intelligence'. Dositej quoted, for example, the popular verdict on a reforming bishop: 'The bishop is worse than the Turks: he won't let us dance the *koledo* [a pagan dance] or dig up vampires.' He was much more a pious Protestant than a learned agnostic, but the net effect of his teaching was anti-conservative and thus in the climate of the eighteenth-century Serbian provinces anti-clerical. 'Books', he said, 'were more important than bells.' He backed the rationalist Joseph II over cutting down Church holidays and enforcing for instance sensible sanitary regulations, to replace the traditional, long-drawn-out, and insanitary funeral ceremonies. He preached universal moral standards, in a tone very different to that of the narrow-minded

---

[1] Fénélon's moral tale *Télémaque*, a sort of continuation of the Odyssey, provided an image of a Utopian society and was often translated in eighteenth-century Russia. See James H. Billington, *The Ikon and the Axe*, Weidenfeld and Nicolson, London, 1966, p. 218. It also inspired high-minded Serbs after Dositej.

[2] Dositej's translations from Chesterfield and others helped to make fashionable a would-be classical prose style which is very ill suited to the genius of the Serb language.

confessional literature favoured by the Austrian-Serb clergy of the eighteenth century. At the same time he was a strong Serbian patriot, recognizing that 'faith can be changed, but race and tongue never'. Dositej had no detailed linguistic theories, and made no systematical attempt at reform of the Serbian language, but he was concerned that his works should be read as widely as possible, and made a serious effort to write them in the popular Serbian language (this again did not endear him to the Orthodox Church authorities). He had great influence on the movement to end the separation of the 'literary' from the 'popular' style. His patriotism also took more concrete forms as occasion arose. In 1804 he was staying in Trieste and raised money for the Serbian revolt against the Turks, which he regarded as the first part of a movement to free all Serbs from foreign domination. By the end of 1806, Dositej was travelling among the Serb communities in Austria and Moldavia, with a view to crossing the Sava or Danube into the newly liberated territory. He thus had those qualities of mental energy and patriotism most likely of all to appeal to young Serbs at this time, and there can be little doubt that Vuk during his stay at Karlovci fell under the influence of Dositej's work and personality—though he did not meet him until a year or two later in Belgrade.

3

By the autumn of 1806 it was made clear to Vuk that there was little hope of further education for him at Karlovci. He made his way north-eastwards to Petrinj on the Wallachian border. Here there was a German-language 'Gymnasium', frequented by the sons of Serb officers in the Austrian army, who hoped to follow in their fathers' footsteps. If little is known for certain about Vuk's stay in Karlovci, all that can be said about his few months at Petrinj is that he was miserably poor, that poverty hindered his education, and that 'he hoped to continue his German studies there, but in fact walked more than he learned'.

Soon, probably in the summer of 1807, Vuk crossed the Sava again to Belgrade (which had been captured by Karadjordje's troops in the previous year) and made his way back to his own native district. For a few weeks he acted as clerk once more to the local commander—but this time it was Jakob Nenadović, a grim disciplinarian, rather than the heroic *hajduk* Čurčija, and Vuk was working in an office rather than in a military camp. Some time later in 1807 he returned to Belgrade and settled there for over a year.

Whatever the deficiencies of Vuk's education, there was no lack of work in Karadjordje's Serbia for someone even of his modest clerical and literary attainments. By 1807, after the capture of Belgrade, Karadjordje had in effect a small independent country to govern, and one which was the centre and object of some very intricate diplomatic manœuvres. Karadjordje ruled with the aid of, or in spite of the intrigues of, a Council of elected notables (established on Russian advice) which had in the autumn of 1807 just been transferred from Smederevo (some thirty miles eastwards on the Danube) to Belgrade. Vuk's cousin, Jefto Savić, who had been Serb chief for the district of Zvornik on the Drina when it was still under the Turks in 1805, represented the same district (now part of an independent Serbia) in Karadjordje's Council.[1] Savić procured for Vuk an appointment as a clerk to the Council, and took him to live in his house. Nor was Vuk's education neglected. The Secretary of the Council, Ivan Jugović, former professor of classical languages at the Karlovci 'Gymnasium', was a man of learning, and at Vuk's request he too was lodged in Savić's house. From Jugović Vuk clearly learned a good deal, and later wrote about the process as follows:

> As I was buying and procuring what was needed for the house, I went on one occasion to a shop . . . and found there a great heap of books. I hastened eagerly to look at them, and found that there was not a single one in Serb; they were all in German or Latin. So I asked the shopkeeper to let me take them home. When Jugović looked them over, he said of one: 'I'll take that for myself', and another he handed to me and said: 'You take that one, and you can read it aloud to me to learn German.' My book was called *Eduard Rosenthal, an Adventure Story*; I read it aloud to him, and he would show me where I had not understood. The book Jugović chose for himself was *History of All Peoples from the Beginning of the World to Christ*, and he started immediately to translate this into Serbian. Every morning I'd bring him a glass of rose-liqueur or plum brandy from Jadar, which he would sip as he translated until by noon he had drunk the lot. What he had translated

---

[1] Savić had previously been arrested by Karadjordje for collaboration with the Turks, but was released and promoted at the instance of Jakob Nenadović.

in the morning he would read to me afterwards, especially in the evening, and ask me whether I understood; then if there was anything that I did not understand, he would explain it. Jugović never told me why he was translating this book, but when he had finished it he said that he was going to open the High School; at the recommendation of Mladen (Milovanović) the Council and Karadjordje had laid down that he should receive 1500 *groš* a year.

This High School—the last stage of Vuk's formal education—was opened at the end of August 1808 in Jefto Savić's house (one of the very few buildings of this period still left in Belgrade). There was one class only, in which about twenty boys were enrolled; probably there were not many more literate boys available in Serbia to profit from the instruction. The class included the sons of some of the most prominent leaders of the Serbian revolt—Karadjordje and Jakob Nenadović among others. There were no benches, desks, or books, and only one professor, Jugović himself, who taught history, geography, arithmetic, and German. He was a skilled as well as universal lecturer who, as Vuk later said, 'could penetrate even a wooden head'. At this crucial time and place in Serbian history, the Greek and Roman classics in particular proved to be very stimulating. One of Vuk's fellow pupils recorded that the boys 'could never without great excitement talk of the Athenians Aristides, Themistocles, the enlightened Socrates, and Solon, the lawgiver of Athens'. Their heroes were such patriots as Mucius Scaevola, who 'lived only to sacrifice themselves for their fatherland and race'.

No doubt this account is embellished by a selective memory. But there is no doubt either that, when education was such a rarity, it was highly prized. Vuk himself, in the preface to his spelling-book of 1826, gives a simple but emphatic view of the excellence and profit of literacy:

Whatever men may have invented in this world, nothing can be compared with writing. . . . The biggest difference between a wise man and a simpleton is that the wise man is always writing and striving to learn or find out something better, so that he may be wiser than his ancestors, and his children than him; while the simpleton remains happy that he is just as his fathers were, and his children just like himself.

The High School was temporarily dissolved in June 1809, when the Turks had again advanced into Serbia and defeated the

Serbian army at Kamenica;[1] by the time that it reopened in 1810, Vuk was no longer in Belgrade. In any case, as at Tršić and Karlovci, his main education during his stay in Belgrade must have taken place outside his school hours. As a clerk of Karadjordje's Council he saw the very unedifying behaviour of Serbia's new masters, and stored memories for the history of those years which he was later to write. Karadjordje's captains were a rough lot, and had no intention of forgoing the spoils of office. The worst of all was the President of the Council, Mladen Milovanović, and the rest were not far behind. They took the best of Turkish possessions and property for themselves, and as Vuk wrote, 'behaved like the *Dahijas*, destroying and burning as the mood took them'. They kept their private bands of young guards, and Vuk later recounted how he saw some of Karadjordje's bully-boys drag a man from his horse and beat him almost to death for failing to greet them with sufficient humility. Outside Belgrade too the Turkish authorities were replaced by men equally oppressive and anxious to make what they might while the going was good: 'There was no freedom', wrote Vuk, 'to sell bread, meat, wine spirits and so on. Only a few people got this right for themselves and sold to others, while the poor, who were normally able to help themselves by selling these things, suffered and everything became dearer in consequence.'

4

Vuk must also have witnessed at close quarters, not least through his acquaintance with Jugović, something of the international intrigues centred around Serbia and Belgrade. Serbo-Turkish relations were in themselves complex enough. In 1806 the Porte had to judge, after the first limited successes of the Serbian revolt and the capture of Belgrade by Karadjordje, whether the interests and stability of the Turkish Empire and the tranquillity of its other subject races were best served by crushing the Serb rebels (at the risk of getting involved in more active war with Russia) or by re-establishing a sovereign–subject relationship on the basis originally introduced by Mustapha Pasha in 1793, which involved more autonomy for the Serbs and more co-operation between Turkish and Serb authorities.

---

[1] It was after the battle of Kamenica that the Turkish commander beheaded his Serb prisoners, and had their skulls built into the 'Tower of Skulls', still advertised as one of the main tourist attractions of Niš.

KARLOVCI AND BELGRADE

By the summer of 1807 however this was no longer an open question. Whatever the inclination of Sultan Selim III himself (and he favoured a generally moderate policy), he was faced with strong conservative opposition in Constantinople and throughout the Ottoman homelands from those who thought it not only bad policy but heresy to allow the *raja* so much freedom—including the freedom to bear arms and fight against Moslems. Selim misjudged his own strength, and his attempts in 1807 finally to break the power of the janissaries and of Pazvan Oglu of Vidin miscarried. Later in the same year he was deposed; his successors had no intention of making any more than tactical accommodations with Karadjordje's Serbia, and the Serbs themselves were well aware of this.

Turkey could not however isolate her dealings with Serbia from the general European context. Her moves were watched anxiously by Austria, Russia, and France, each of them with important interests at stake. Austria from 1804 to 1810 had little energy to spare from campaigns against Napoleon and their aftermath, but was deeply interested in the fortunes of the Serbian revolt. The Austrian Government, by virtue of the million or so Serbs in the Vojvodina, had some title to protect the Serbs in Serbia proper. Moreover they had the means of supporting or hindering the Serbian revolt, according to whether they encouraged or hindered the flow of volunteers, arms, and other supplies across the Sava. They did not like the idea of national insurgence against established governments. They were doubtful whether the establishment of a truly independent Serbia was possible, and whether they could at this time afford to protect a new client state. Above all however they feared that if an aggressively minded Russian Government were to replace the Turkish administration in Serbia, or to establish a puppet state there, their own frontiers might become more vulnerable. For commercial reasons also the Austrians were inclined to prefer a fairly weak Turkey to a strong Russia as their neighbour. Their trade with Turkey had grown considerably in the latter half of the eighteenth century, and particularly since their Commercial Treaty of 1780. All in all therefore the Austrians, quite apart from preoccupations with Napoleon, tended to be cautious in support of the Serbian revolt, and to encourage a Serbian accommodation with the Turks by their diplomacy at the Porte.

Russia, like Austria, was in 1804-5 preoccupied with Napoleon, but by mid-1807 had much greater freedom of action (after Napoleon and Tsar Alexander I had signed the Treaty of Tilsit). Her interest in Serbia was to some extent the counterpart or reverse of Austria's. The Russians were anxious to retain some client state between the Austrians and themselves, and could not be absolutely sure of their own power and influence in a totally independent Serbia. The optimum solution for them might be a dependent principality of Serbia; but the next best state of affairs was a nominal Turkish rule, under cover of which they could ensure their own influence. And at the end of the eighteenth century they were reasonably well placed to secure this. The Treaty of Kutchuk Kainardji in 1774 had given them a vaguely defined right of religious protection over the Orthodox subjects of the Ottoman Empire. In 1787, as the result of a further war against the Turks, they had secured a dominant position in Moldavia and Wallachia, the districts of present-day Rumania adjoining the north-eastern corner of Serbia.[1] With the Serbs themselves, they had long-standing religious, cultural, and personal links. In particular, from about 1750 onwards, there had been a large-scale migration of Serbs to southern Russia, and many of them had risen to prominent positions in the Russian official service. The Russians too had the sentimental advantage over the Austrians of not having let the Serbs down, as the Austrian army had done more than once—most recently in 1791, when it retreated from Serbia and left the inhabitants to the mercy of the Turks.

Of the three great powers on the European continent, France was the most dynamic and unaccountable. The pre-revolutionary tradition of French diplomacy was to support the Turks against the Austrians and Russians. In his general aim of rebuilding and reforming the Ottoman Empire, Selim had received strong diplomatic support and above all military aid from the revolutionary Government of France;[2] but by the time of the Serbian revolt

---

[1] These provinces were given back to the Porte under the Russo-Turkish Treaty of Jassy, 1792; but a Turkish decree of 1802 provided that the *Hospodars* of Moldavia and Wallachia should normally rule for seven years, and should not be deposed without the consent of the Tsar. The alleged non-observance of this condition was the occasion of the Russo-Turkish war of 1806.

[2] From 1785 onwards there was a strong French military mission at Istanbul. Its importance increased with the accession of Selim III, and it did much to reform the Turkish infantry, artillery, and fortifications.

KARLOVCI AND BELGRADE 59

Franco-Turkish relations had become complicated by the accession of Napoleon. His campaign in Egypt and Syria involved him in at least nominal hostilities with Turkey, and, if it suited them to do so, the French Government were well qualified ideologically to back liberation movements at the expense of the Turkish Government. By 1804 however Napoleon's Middle Eastern adventure had been wound up and he was anxious to resume the traditional Franco-Turkish alliance, not least in order to establish French influence in the Adriatic. On their side, the Turks were anxious to profit from Napoleon's victories in Europe, and after the battle of Austerlitz (1805), French military assistance to Turkey was resumed.[1] In 1806, further encouraged by Napoleon's success at Jena, the Turks declared war against the Russians.

It was at this point that the fortunes of Serbia were directly and favourably affected by the general conjuncture of European affairs. To counter Turkish moves, the Russians sent troops into the north-eastern province of Serbia, and gave active encouragement to the Montenegrins to attack the Turks. Karadjordje's position *vis-à-vis* the Turks was moreover essentially strengthened when at the Peace of Tilsit in 1807 Napoleon reversed his alliances and was temporarily reconciled with Tsar Alexander I. Admittedly, at the end of 1807 the Russians signed an armistice with the Turks which did not include special provisions in favour of the Serbs; but in order to secure Russian co-operation in his 'continental system' against England, Napoleon was willing to allow the annexation of Moldavia and Wallachia by the Russians, and encouraged them to make further territorial gains at Turkish expense, reviving the old schemes of the 1770s for the partition of the Ottoman Empire in Europe.

In these circumstances it is at first sight surprising that Karadjordje was at all hesitant in his attachment to the Russian alliance. It was however important for him not to tie himself so closely to the Russians that in the event of any Russo-Austrian clash the Austrians would sever his connections with the Serbs in the Srem and cut off the supplies of arms, ammunition, and volunteers which reached him from across the Sava and Danube. If the worst

[1] French assistance was opposed by conservative Moslems and stimulated hostile action by the British and Russian Governments. A British naval squadron was sent to Istanbul and repulsed in 1806. The French hold on the Dalmatian coast was disputed by the Montenegrins, inspired and supported by the Russians.

came to the worst, he could not be sure of timely Russian support (and in fact their troops only came to his rescue at the last moment when the Turks advanced far into Serbia in 1809). Karadjordje was moreover very suspicious of the role of the Russian diplomatic mission, sent to Belgrade at the end of 1807. Its chief task was to persuade him to rely on Russian protection and negotiate with the Turks rather than appealing for Austrian aid. The leader of the mission, Rodofinikin, was a Phanariot Greek in close relations with the unpopular Phanariot Metropolitan of Serbia, Leontije, and thus doubly suspect to most Serbs; he intrigued openly with members of the Serbian Council with the object of weakening Karadjordje's position and securing leadership which would be more pliable to Russian pressure. Karadjordje in consequence was in touch with the Austrian Government in 1808 and 1809 and put forward proposals, which were seriously considered in Vienna, both for the incorporation of Serbia in Austria and for establishing it as a sort of Austrian protectorate under Turkish suzerainty. The Austrians were very cautious about involving themselves in difficulties with Russia at this stage; and more open Russian support for Karadjordje in 1809–10 put an end to this scheme for reinsurance.

5

Karadjordje's own hesitations and divided allegiance between the Russian and Austrian Governments were reflected in the formation of pro-Russian and pro-Austrian groups among the Serb population of Belgrade. Vuk must have heard a good deal at first hand about the political conflict between them. His patron and kinsman, Jefto Savić, was an Austrophil (as were most of the Serb merchants, who had the Austrian market in mind). So was Ivan Jugović—the more so as he had been removed from his job as Secretary to the council by Russophil influence. And in general the behaviour of the senior members of the Council, known to enjoy Rodofinikin's support, did little to endear them and the cause of the Russian alliance to patriotic Serbs. The opposition between the two parties took a violent form, particularly when, in the summer of 1809, it looked as if the Turks might re-occupy Serbia without any effective Russian intervention.[1] Rodofinikin fled and his mistress and her mother were assassinated.

[1] It was at this stage, in August 1809, that Karadjordje made his first appeal

At the other end of the scale—and here we return to the literary scene—there was an exchange of epigrams and scurrilous verses (no newspapers then existed in Belgrade) in which both Jugović and the famous Dositej Obradović were involved. Dositej was the greatest ornament of the pro-Russian party, and it seems to have been at this period that Vuk first lost enthusiasm for him and his works. The clash between them might well have come in any case —Dositej was a man of the Enlightenment, Vuk in some ways a romantic conservative; but there may also have been more personal reasons for the very hostile attitude which Vuk for the rest of his life adopted towards Dositej. In a review dated 1820, which remained unpublished, Vuk told a story which is almost certainly autobiographical. It concerns a young man from Serbian Austria who called reverently on Dositej in Belgrade to ask his advice on a literary career, and was turned abruptly from his door. Afterwards the same young man, clothed in Serbian dress and armed with a laudatory article about Dositej, had no difficulty in securing entry to the great man, who was overjoyed at the gross flattery of the article. The story could apply very easily to Vuk himself. He might well have tried to call on Dositej immediately after leaving Karlovci, where he had become enthusiastic about Dositej's work; it would be typical of the cunning and persistence which he afterwards showed throughout his active life to gain entrance to Dositej's house by flattery; and it must be added that the subsequent and rancorous article about Dositej is also typical of the least agreeable side of Vuk's character.[1]

Vuk's schooling, direct and indirect, came to an end in the last months of 1808, when illness forced him to leave Belgrade and go first to his native Tršić. He began to suffer severe rheumatic pains in his hands and feet. By the spring of 1809 the pain in his knee made it impossible for him to stand on his left foot. As the Serbs

to Napoleon for protection, offering to foster revolts of the Serbs in Hungary and Slavonia (France was still at war with Austria). Napoleon gave very cautious encouragement through the French consul at Bucharest. Karadjordje made a further appeal for protection and supplies early in 1810, with no more concrete result.

[1] In the same article Vuk attacked Dositej for laziness and money-grubbing after his return to Serbia in 1806. It would have been better for Dositej's reputation, he said, to have stayed in Austria, where words were enough, and not to have come to Serbia where something had to be done. What was the use of all Dositej's writing about the superstitions of the Orthodox Church? There is something comic about Vuk posing as Defender of the Faith.

prepared once more for active warfare against the Turks, Vuk lay helpless in his parents' house. An episode of this time was recorded by Sreznevski from Vuk's table-talk. Sreznevski had asked him how it came about that he was neither married nor in love by the time that he reached Vienna in 1813. Vuk replied:

No, I wasn't married, and I wasn't even in love. I might indeed have married, and perhaps fallen in love too. Your question reminds me of Ruža Todorović. Her parents and mine were neighbours and lived in friendship. Ruža's mother was the most beautiful woman in our village and the dressiest, and could get herself up tastefully; and Ruža was sweet, both as a child and as a girl. We grew up together, I liked her, I must say, and maybe she liked me; it was just the most common sort of country friendship. But our parents thought otherwise. Ruža's father said to me, 'I'll give you the girl', and though I was angry on hearing this, it looks as if our parents had already agreed the matter. From 1804 when I set off for Karlovci[1] I didn't see her till 1809 when I came back home, sick. One day Ruža came to our house, I don't know why, and I wanted to see her. At my wish she came from the kitchen to the room where I was lying. She kissed my hand. I took her by the hand, and asked: 'Well, are you a grown-up girl now?' 'You can see', she said, 'I'm grown-up' and then she went on: 'And where in the wide world have you been, pushing off and leaving your father and mother? If sickness hadn't driven you, you'd never have come home on your own!' With something like these words our talk ended. I didn't get better at home, and as you know went off to the waters. In 1812 I was in Belgrade when one day a man came up to me from Ruža's father and said, 'They're courting Ruža.' He reminded me of the agreement reached by our parents long ago, according to which I was betrothed to Ruža; and it appeared that even now, when someone else was asking for her hand, the parents wouldn't give it until they knew what I would say. I told the messenger that I wasn't thinking then of taking a wife. She should marry, and God grant her happiness. That was the answer which the messenger took back to Tršić.

[1] Vuk probably meant 1805. See p. 45, n. 1.

V

BUDA, 1810 : SERBIA, 1810–1813

I

VUK's pains were not cured by lying at Tršić, and the village lay all too much in the way of any Turkish advance from Bosnia across the Drina. He made his way to the sulphur spa of Mehadjia in the Banat province north of the Danube, and from there in the winter of 1809 to the hospital at Novi Sad. The doctors and surgeons were not clear about the nature of Vuk's illness. His left leg was withering from the knee down, and the joint of the knee was ossifying. To judge by the prescriptions made for him, the doctors seem to have suspected a kind of hereditary syphilitic arthritis. Medical opinion today is inclined to diagnose rheumatoid polyarthritis, rather than anything connected with syphilis, or the hereditary tuberculosis suspected by Vuk's most authoritative biographer, Ljubomir Stojanović.[1] At all events his sufferings could only be relieved, not cured. He emerged from hospital at Novi Sad lame, unfit as it seemed for any kind of active life and embittered: 'That was the time', he later wrote, 'at which all my friends and benefactors scorned and deserted me—all those who, while I was in health and could be of use to them, had made much of me and promised me mountains of gold.'

This reads like an exaggeration in the fashionable manner of the 'man of feeling', though it may contain a covert reference to Vuk's kinsman, Jefto Savić, who seems to have neglected him at this time. In fact, though the lonely winter months in the hospital at Novi Sad may reasonably have embittered Vuk, a benefactor was at hand. A rich Serb woman from a merchant family, Marija Stanisavljević,[2] satisfied her maternal instincts in charitable deeds and gave Vuk—'a most wretched man whom up to then she had

---

[1] There is an exhaustive analysis of the medical data available by Olga Srdanović-Barać in *Kovčežić*, ii, pp. 89 seq.

[2] The full name was 'ot Stanisavljević'. This was a style adopted by some Serb families in the Austrian Empire, who wished to imitate the German 'von'.

never seen or heard of'—150 *forints* to take him for a further cure to Budapest. She earned an unthought-of fame within 4 years in the dedication of Vuk's first collection of songs. This merits further quotation as an example of Vuk's peasant sharpness cutting through the language of romantic sensibility:

O rare signs of charity and of a heart compassionate towards the poor! A man of little experience might say: 'Well, she had plenty and so gave of it.' No, no, that is not the question! It is not just those who have the means that do good, but those who feel joy in doing it. I have presented petitions, like that which I presented to you, breathing the very depths of poverty, to people who with their yearly income alone could have bought up your property, and yet . . .

And so in the summer of 1810 Vuk went to the springs of Buda for a further cure. It was not fully successful, and he returned within a few months, equipped with the wooden attachment to his left leg and the crutch which had to support him for the rest of his life, and became his distinguishing property. In the meantime he had gained other and spiritual supports. He had made friendships with educated young Serbs, who had their own unconventional ideas about literature and many other matters; and these were friends that lasted Vuk well.

There was in Buda a Serb community, mainly of merchants, established since well before the Serb migration of 1690, and flourishing considerably in the eighteenth century. This was a cultured community—in the eparchy of Buda alone there were at this time over fifty Serb primary schools—and it provided the greater part of the public which was interested in the work of Dositej Obradović and could look beyond the intellectual limits imposed by the Orthodox Church.

By the beginning of the nineteenth century, the Church had performed its essential and literally conservative task of preserving the Serb community from being assimilated by Austrians or Hungarians. Serbian nationalism was finding other means of expressing itself. The 'Protestant' Dositej had widened the horizons of literate Serbs and introduced them to various currents of European thought of his own and earlier times. The younger generation of Serbs growing up in Vienna and Buda were not content however just to receive and absorb literature and philosophy from abroad in Dositej's translations. They wanted to make their own literature and to write it in their own language. In this mood they inevitably turned against the conservative traditions of the Orthodox Church, and particularly against its adherence to a type of Church Slavonic alphabet and language. This subject is discussed more fully in Chapter VII and Appendix B. Here it is enough to say that the alphabet used by the Church was inefficient at reproducing the sound of the spoken language. Grammar and syntax were not properly articulated, and allowed too great a variety of usage. Most important, the Church Slavonic language bore little relation to the current speech of the Serb people, nor was it a suitable vehicle for conveying either everyday or sophisticated thoughts.

The desire to evolve an efficient and truly national language, natural enough in itself, was stimulated by the romantic concepts familiarized by Herder about the supreme value of national culture and the importance of national or 'folk' language as the purest expression of this culture. Thus the question of alphabetical and linguistic reform was one to arouse the passions not only of philologists and grammarians but also of young and patriotic intellectuals. It was bound up not only with a revolt against the conservatism of the Orthodox Church but also with a more positive assertion of Serbian nationalism against Turks, Austrians, and Russians alike.

Such was the climate of opinion among many of the young Serb students at Buda. Vuk was himself by no means obviously of their intellectual calibre, but he had news-value for them. The young generation of Serbs (and of Hungarians too) were very much interested and excited by Karadjordje's revolt against the Turks, and Vuk as a genuine Serb from south of the Sava had first-hand reports to give. He seems soon to have made the acquaintance of an intellectually active set, many of them like himself not born or brought up in Hungary. Notable among these were Dimitrije Frušić and Dimitrije Davidović, who figured prominently in Vuk's later life; also Luka Milovanov and Sava Mrkalj, who were both active at this time in the linguistic field.

Milovanov was a grammarian and critic, and in 1810 he had published a work in which he demanded the introduction of a 'popular' language and literature. 'If any son of a Serb mother', he wrote, 'wants to write in his mother tongue, he had better first publish a handbook of his own language.' In the same year, when Vuk was in Buda, Sava Mrkalj was engaged in the publication of a much more direct attack on the Church Slavonic alphabet, symbolized by one of its letters, the 'hard sign', which had no obvious function in the Serbian language,[1] but constituted a visible orthographic link between that and the Russian ecclesiastical languages, and was correspondingly treasured by the Russophil Orthodox clergy. Mrkalj's book was written in a much simplified alphabet, and caused a great outcry among the Orthodox hierarchy.

Thus Vuk's short stay in Buda was of vital importance for the rest of his career. It introduced him to literary aims which were of revolutionary importance in the Serbian provinces of his time, however modest they may appear now. No doubt it gave him some idea of the scandal which would be caused by the attempt to promote these aims, and of the opposition to be expected from the Orthodox Church. And from 1810 on he must gradually have come to realize that, with his own knowledge and experience of current Serbian speech and poetry from his village days, he had much to contribute towards the reformation of the Serbian language, and consequently (in the logic of the time at least) towards the re-establishment of the Serbian nation.

2

Some time in the autumn of 1810, Vuk returned to Belgrade, where he was appointed to teach in a new primary school. 'I was not the sort of teacher that I would have liked to be,' he told Sreznevski later, 'but even at that time my friends—most of them Serbs from Hungary—had noticed my knowledge of the people's language, and called me an expert in the Serbian tongue.' He had picked up unorthodox ideas, not only in the linguistic field, from the young Serbs in Budapest. One of his friends wrote later that at this time in Belgrade he was regarded as an 'atheist because of his rudeness and foolish behaviour'. And he was beginning to evolve some literary plans, also as the result of his stay in Buda. By the spring of 1811, Vuk and another young teacher in the Belgrade school, Sima Milutinović,[2] were thinking of a joint

[1] The Serb consonant is normally hard, and softening is marked by the addition of *j* or the vowel 'и' (*i*) after the consonant. See Appendix B.

[2] Sima (Simeon) Milutinović (1791–1847) probably became acquainted with Vuk at Karlovci in 1805. The friendship between them was deep and lasting, although it had its ups and downs, and Sima was on linguistic matters never a 'Vukist'.

history of Karadjordje's uprising, Sima's contribution to be in verse and Vuk's in prose.

Vuk was however not left long to teach at his school, or to write books. At that time any Serb who had attained his degree of literacy was desperately needed for the administration of his own new country. Early in 1811, Karadjordje carried out a major reorganization of his government. Some of the other principal Serb leaders had been acutely jealous of his powers, and intrigued against him with the Russian military commanders. At the end of 1810 however Karadjordje convinced the Russian General Kamenski that he should be *de facto* as well as in name Commander-in-Chief and leader of Serbia. The Council, which had been the centre of opposition to him, was reformed and could no longer provide a suitable cover for the activity of the other main chieftains of Serbia; and the district commanders were made directly responsible to Karadjordje as Commander-in-Chief. As a result of these constitutional changes, Karadjordje had removed the previous military leaders in the district of Brza Palanka in Eastern Serbia for intrigues against him, and was looking for his own nominees who would owe personal loyalty to him. Vuk's kinsman, Jefto Savić, was appointed 'to be in command' at Brza Palanka and Vuk himself was sent shortly afterwards to manage the customs office at Kladovo, on the Danube opposite Turnu Severin. Here he was responsible for a large surrounding district. This was in itself an important administrative post. The East Serbian district of Krajina had for long preserved a *de facto* independence from Turkish rule and had begun to enjoy a considerable direct and transit trade in agricultural products, livestock, and wine with Austria. This in turn had brought benefits to Serbia proper in the shape of payments to customs posts for transit trade; but as the result of the fighting in Serbia, other transit routes had been sought. Karadjordje was anxious to restore trade to the original routes and to adapt Serbian customs policy to this purpose. Vuk evidently was instructed to take various actions in this sense. He arranged, for example, that goods sent by river from 'Rumelia' to Croatia should pay customs dues only once, so long as they kept to the Serbian or southern bank of the Danube. The same sort of regulations applied to Austrian merchants trading through Serbia with Turkey. The work involved Vuk in much travelling, including a journey to conduct negotiations with the independent Turkish commander of

Vidin, Mula Pasha, successor to the famous Pazvan Oglu; and Vuk soon found that travel in hard conditions was too much of a strain for his lame leg and generally weakened health. He twice applied to Belgrade for a change of post, but was put off with fair words and requests for patience. His 'tender concern and loyalty to his country' were well known; the authorities would in time commend him to Karadjordje and then he would have the chance to serve his country even better. He should be patient for a time 'until we find some occasion of contenting you too'.

For two years Vuk was occupied with this administrative work. It probably required a high degree of adaptability, since it is by no means clear how the state administration fitted in with the privileges granted or sold to local chiefs and leaders. For example the customs rights in the district of Negotin were bought in 1812 by the most renowned warrior in that area, Hajduk Veljko—of whom more later in this chapter; and Jefto Savić himself is said to have bought the tax-rights in Kladovo, as the local elder. Probably the services of the State revenue officer were regarded as part of the bargain when the tax rights were sold, and in any conflict of competencies under the conditions of the time the local leader, with his own force immediately available, would come off better than the Government in Belgrade. It also seems likely that, under the patronage of the local leader, the revenue officers and other administrators could engage in profitable trade themselves. Vuk himself must have done something to line his own pockets at this period. He had sufficient financial resources to keep him alive for some time in Vienna a year or two later, when his literary earnings were at a minimum; and it is clear from his correspondence that by the autumn of 1813, when he had to leave his district, he had made a number of loans to his friends. The source of his short-lived prosperity was most probably the salt trade. Salt was one of the few commodities which had to be imported by the peasants of Serbia; under the benevolent rule of Mustapha Pasha their subsequent leader, Miloš Obrenović, had done good trade in salt amongst other things between central Serbia and the Dalmatian coast, and was later to secure a monopoly in the salt trade with North-Eastern Serbia and the adjoining parts of Moldavia and Wallachia.

The local customs officer may have had good and reasonably legitimate opportunities for private gain, but he also had to be ready to turn his hand to any administrative work. Theoretically there were in Karadjordje's Serbia commanders, magistrates, and customs officers operating separately in each district. Not surprisingly in the absence of trained men, anyone engaged in one branch of administration would in fact find himself employed indiscriminately in the others.

In another respect too the position of the civilian administrator was bound to be difficult. It was the war commanders who had the real power and used it as ruthlessly against the subjects (*raja*) in their districts as had the Turks before them. Civilian administrators had no prestige either with these leaders or with their subjects. They were to the former simply necessary instruments, to the latter the known devil, preferable only to the unknown military devils. There is no obvious sign of Vuk resenting this position, but it may be that the warmth of his affection and admiration for Hajduk Veljko was due in part to the fact that with Veljko alone of the commanders that he met Vuk was able to establish a personal relationship.

Some others among his enduring friendships dated from this time in Eastern Serbia. The most important figures for Vuk's later development were Stevan Živković, who had married his second cousin Savka, and would discuss together with Vuk his translation of Fénélon's *Télémaque*;[1] Todor Tirka, a merchant, who afterwards migrated to Vienna and helped Vuk to publish his *Dictionary*; and Sara, widow of Mihail Karapandja, the hereditary chieftain of the Krajina district, who found Vuk sympathetic to her views about the new Serb masters of the Karapandja domain (she regarded them as wild barbarians).

Vuk's correspondence and later writings contain a few passages to illustrate his life as an official in Kladovo and Brza Palanka. Sima Milutinović suggested (in a letter to a mutual friend) that Vuk lived as well as any of the new Serb lords of the district, with two maids 'to serve him day and night like spirits. They dress and undress him, make his bed and bring his meals.'

Vuk was also beginning to develop his interest in the national language—it would indeed be surprising if he had not done so after his contact with Milovanov and Mrkalj in Buda. He told

---

[1] Stefan Vasiljević Živković was an 'Austrian Serb' who migrated to Karadjordje's Serbia in 1805. He was attached to the Russian mission in Serbia from 1808 to 1812, and acted as provisioner for them.

Sreznevski how his new friends' regard for him as a connoisseur of the Serbian language stimulated his vanity:

... I neglected no occasion for justifying their good opinion, and listened with great attention to the people's speech, carefully writing down everything in it which seemed to me interesting. Particularly useful to me was the time which I spent in summer 1813 as judge in Brza Palanka. There I listened attentively to the villagers as they gave evidence, and every word which was new to me I would note straight away on paper. This with no idea of book-making—I didn't even dream of it at the time—but just for its own sake.

Again, in an early draft for the preface of the first book of the Leipzig edition of his Serbian songs (1823) Vuk shows that he was noting songs as well as words during his time in Eastern Serbia. 'In 1812', he wrote, 'a Greek from Brza Palanka asked for the hand of a Christian girl from Kladovo. The match was then spoiled, and nothing came of it. There was a boy about 25 years of age in service with us at the time, Arsenije Stanojević from the Mačva, who composed such a comic ballad against the Greek that anyone who knew the people concerned would have burst with laughter, and those who didn't know them would have said that it was some ballad about God knows what ancient time and its heroes. I heard Arsenije sing it a few times; he was good at singing to the *gusle* and I had bought him one, so he would often sing to us at lunch or dinner; I didn't learn it all by heart, but know only how it began.' The lines remembered by Vuk are quoted in translation at Appendix A. They describe the wooing by Bazerdjan Sterija of a maiden in Kladovo, and his choice of three envoys to press his suit.

3

Vuk's request in 1813 for a less exacting job had met with a temporizing answer; in fact when orders for a transfer arrived it was to a more active and responsible post. At the end of April, Karadjordje ordered Jefto Savić to proceed on a diplomatic mission to Sofia, and Vuk assumed command at Brza Palanka. This was no sinecure, but an important post at a crucial time. Karadjordje was doing what he could to prepare himself against a further Turkish attack, and the North-Eastern corner of Serbia was likely to be immediately in the path of one of the main Turkish armies.

The new state of Serbia could by now expect little military or even diplomatic support against the Turks. So far as external relations were concerned, 1811 had been the most prosperous year for Karadjordje. By this time, the Serbian armies had recovered from their defeat at Kamenica (1809), while the Russian armies had resumed war against the Turks (interrupted by the armistice of 1807), crossed the Danube and cleared all Turkish troops from Serbia in 1810, and gained further victories over the Turks in 1811. But in 1812 the French invasion forced the Russians to concentrate their strength in their own country. They signed the Treaty of Bucharest with the Turks in June, and this contained no adequate provision for the protection of the Serbs against their enemies. Important concessions were forced on the Serbs—they had to restore to the Turks fortified centres that had existed before 1804, and to destroy those established since that time. They had to admit liability to pay taxation to the Sultan (no limits were specified for the amount), and were to be allowed only the right to collect the taxes themselves, and some other limited forms of autonomy. The exact terms of their relations with the Turks were to be worked out in direct negotiations with the Sultan.[1] Negotiations were indeed started: Karadjordje tried to spin them out and was probably ready to accept fairly stiff terms so long as these provided for full local self-government and a special position for himself as *Oborknez* or senior chief. The Turks however realized clearly that the Russians would give the Serbs no further military support, and that any diplomatic efforts on behalf of the Serbs would be half-hearted. They had strong reasons for imposing their own full conditions and teaching the rebels a military lesson while the Russians and Austrians were fully occupied in the struggle against Napoleon. By 1813 there was no support in Constantinople for the moderate policies once pursued by Selim III (deposed in 1807), and no one to recommend a 'soft' policy towards the Serbs as a means of securing their co-operation and thus ultimately strengthening the Ottoman Empire. The final Serbian demands, that they should be allowed to carry firearms and that the janissaries who had served in Serbia should not be allowed to return, were refused.

[1] The crucial article of the Treaty of Bucharest (1812) was No. VIII. The provisions on taxation and autonomy were drafted in very general terms, and the Serbs were refused the right to carry arms.

Karadjordje had missed his last chance of entering into a diplomatic combination when he failed to give active support to Mula Pasha, the independent commander of 'Rumelia', and allowed Vidin to fall into the hands of the Sultan's commanders. By the summer of 1813 it was clear that the Turks were preparing a final settlement of accounts with Karadjordje by means of an armed attack.

The prospects of an adequate Serb defence were poor in any case, and made even worse by the continual and bitter dissension among their rulers. Karadjordje had formally strengthened his position by dismissing or demoting some of his immediate subordinates, but their lack of goodwill was bound to weaken him when it came to further fighting. One can sympathize with Karadjordje's desire for some tighter control at a time of almost perpetual military and diplomatic crisis and of continuous intrigue against his authority in the Council. With the expulsion of Milenko Stojković and Petar Dobrnjac in 1811, and the removal of Hajduk Veljko (his most effective rival as a fighting soldier) from Belgrade, Karadjordje had ensured that he himself would not have to face active political opposition in his own capital; but outside Belgrade the presence in the provinces of leaders with strong local forces and bitter grudges against him made his command less effective. Vuk's own summary verdict on Karadjordje's political strategy (in his later history of these years in Serbia) was as follows:

Thus Karadjordje freed himself from his adversaries and became unhindered lord; but by doing so he cleared the way for the Turks to conquer the country more easily and drive him out. If Milenko (Stojković) had been in command on the Danube in 1813, the Turks would certainly not have had such an easy time in that region; and so long as their shipping could not pass up the Danube to the Morava, the Turkish army from Deligrad would never have been able to establish itself on the Morava, even if it had got so far. Similarly if Petar (Dobrnjac) had been defending Deligrad, he would have held up the Turks on that point much better than his successor. . . .

It seems in fact very doubtful whether without a much stronger central command, better communications, and more support from outside Serbia could have stood up to the Turkish attack in 1813. Vuk himself elsewhere makes it clear that the plan of campaign —such as would have been forced on Karadjordje by any of his local commanders—was far too ambitious. The only hope of salvation for the Serbs (and Vuk could claim to have foreseen this) was to retreat before the Turks and fight in the hills inland. It is unlikely that any of the local commanders available, whatever their relations with Karadjordje, would have been ready to adopt this policy, which involved giving up their own local privileges, property, and tax-rights.

As civilian commander of Brza Palanka at a time when the Serbs were desperately preparing their defences on the frontier, Vuk was mainly engaged in trying to secure from Belgrade the necessary munitions and supplies for the local military commander, Hajduk Veljko. He was convinced that Veljko's die-hard strategy was wrong, and also that of Karadjordje's Council, who wished the commander to stay in Negotin, near the frontier, and withstand the siege of the Turkish army when it advanced. Vuk did not hesitate to send Karadjordje's Secretariat sound military advice. This took the indirect form of a translation by Sava Tekelija[1] of what he described as the work of an English author, Watson, *The Romans in Spain*;[2] the moral was that, against an army superior in numbers and training, guerrilla warfare offered the best opportunities. It is typical of Vuk and his time that such advice should take a literary-historical form. The Austrians would not have allowed the printing in Budapest of a work directly advising the Serbs on how to fight the Turks; and in any case a military parallel carried more weight than personal advice by any civilian. Even so, it is curious to reflect that the lesson had to be drawn from Spain of the first century B.C. rather than from contemporary Spain, where guerrilla resistance to Napoleon's armies had created the preconditions for the decisive campaigns of Wellington, taking place at this very time.

Veljko himself Vuk regarded with much sympathy and admiration.

[1] Sava Tekelija (1761–1842) was a Serb-Hungarian nobleman, a dilettante and traveller, and the author of grammatical, political, legal, and literary works, including an interesting volume of memoirs. He hoped to serve under Karadjordje in 1804, and/or to become Prince of an independent Serbia himself; but these plans fell through, and his principal 'war work' consisted of an attempt to gain Napoleon's support for the constitution of a greater Illyrian buffer-state, and the printing of maps of Serbia which he sent to Karadjordje.

[2] I have been unable to trace the original, in spite of kind assistance from Professor Sir Ronald Syme, and the Secretary of the London Library. Possibly 'Watson' was an invention, to lend an appearance of authority to Tekelija's own work.

His views can be conveyed best in words, taken from his own brief life of Veljko:

> For courage and physical heroism Veljko was the first not only in Serbia but one may fairly say in all Europe during this time of war. In the days of Achilles or Miloš Obilić,[1] he would certainly have been their companion, but God knows whether they would have compared with him in his own time. But this great prowess of his was not properly employed in those last years by Karadjordje and Mladen (Milovanović). Negotin or any other town could have been defended better by someone who was less of a hero and more of an administrator; but in the open field at the head of some chosen horsemen Veljko was worth a thousand others. Apart from that, he always needed a good adviser to tell him what to do; he admitted this himself and used to say that of all the Serbian elders who had served with him he most liked to consult Vujica and the chief Miloje Teodorović (of Mladen [Milovanović] he said openly that he was not for the army, and that wherever Mladen was in command the Serbs would suffer misfortune and defeat). Like many other great men, he knew his own worth, and would often be angry that other lesser leaders, who had got their commands by purchase or lying rather than by valour, . . . had the same honour and reputation as himself. Often he would say: 'God grant that the Serbs never make peace with the Turks while I am alive, for as soon as the Turks strike at us, people begin to see the difference between me and these poultry farmers, but if there is peace with the Turks, even the women start to give judgement on me. And when I'm dead God grant them all peace that they never have to go to war again!' The truth was that Karadjordje feared him almost more than he feared Karadjordje; but Veljko obeyed orders pretty well, especially when he had been transferred to Negotin. He was a real *hajduk*, and gloried and took pride in the name to the day of his death. As a true hero, he found it impossible to lie, even when he should have done. He was so simple and straightforward that he could never be entrusted with any secret. Perhaps the most uncharacteristic thing which he ever did was to betray Milenko (Stojković) and Petar (Dobrnjac) in Belgrade.[2] On

---

[1] On Miloš Obilić, see p. 190, n. 1 and Appendix A, no. 5.

[2] Milenko Stojković and Petar Dobrnjac were two of Karadjordje's most famous captains, both strongly pro-Russian. They were exiled in 1811 for intrigues against their leader, and settled in Bessarabia after the Treaty of Bucharest in 1812; in 1821 they served with Ypsilanti's armies in the Wallachian revolt against the Turks. Stojković learned to read in Russia, after the failure of previous attempts, by a method which Vuk tried to introduce in Serbia. It involved calling the letters of the alphabet as far as possible by their sound ('ah', 'bay', etc.) rather than by special nonsense words ('az', buki', etc.). Vuk

campaigns he was quick to seize money or any kind of booty, but he was correspondingly careless of such things when he had them, and made generous presents not only to his own soldiers but to all sorts of other people. 'When I have anything,' he would say, 'anyone who has need should come and I'll give to him, but when I'm in want I shall take from anyone whom I know to be rich.' He was exceedingly fond of the Russians and adopted many customs from them, e.g. eating at table, cutting his hair, wearing a scarf around his neck, drinking punch, and playing cards. Only he did not adopt from them the custom of seating his wife with him at table. She and her sisters had to pour water for the guests for washing, serve the food, and change the plates. He was so convinced of Russian invincibility that he could never believe the French to have entered Moscow, nor would anyone dare to mention this to him until they had retreated. When in 1812 it was announced that under the terms of the Treaty of Bucharest the Serbs had to hand their weapons over to the Turks, he said that he would go over to Russia with his men. . . .

One official document survives about Vuk's relations as civilian district commander with this notable *hajduk* hero. On June 17, Karadjordje's secretary, who was on an inspection tour, wrote to Vuk from Negotin, telling him to provide one hundred men for the fortifications now to be erected there, and as reinforcements for two hundred men of Veljko's soldiery: 'I have thought it good that the captain Jefto [Savić] should take command of the fortification with these three hundred men, and you are to command them until he comes. And see that you build the trench as well and strongly as possible. General Veljko will come to measure where and how the fortification should be put up. . . .'

At the end of June, Vuk went to Negotin to take counsel with Veljko, and in mid-July left him for Belgrade, in order to organize provisions and munitions. In his life of Veljko, he gave an account of the last conversations between the general and a 'friend'— almost certainly himself. Veljko had already sent his wife and relations away from Negotin to Poreć (up the river), when 'the friend' visited him in his house.

Seeing about the room various silver trappings for horses and other similar precious things, he asked Veljko that evening why he hadn't sent these with his wife to Poreć. Veljko answered: 'Let the women take

himself met Dobrnjac in Russia in 1819 and was amazed by his skill at dictating to a clerk, although he had never learned to read.

and keep their shifts and stockings and linen and spindles; what you see here are a hero's belongings, which I won with the sword and must now defend with the sword. He who cannot keep and fight for them with the sword, is not worthy to possess them. It would be shame for me if the Turks came to my house, and for all my great honour and repute found nothing in it!' Veljko's friend proposed to go to Belgrade, but Veljko kept him back saying: 'We have had some merry days here together. Stay here now and let us beat Kapetan Pasha' (it was reported that he was coming with his army to attack Negotin) 'and then we can share the glory too.' His friend asked him how he thought he could defeat the Turks, and he replied: 'How? Why, I'll lead my soldiers and gunners out to meet them and then I'll * * * *[1] their mothers properly. At that time he had no more than 3,000 men under his command, and those not all in Negotin, while it was known that the Turks were coming against Negotin with more than 15,000 men. So his friend said to him: 'But this time it's not only the provincial generals who will attack you but the Sultan's army, bringing its great cannons. Perhaps it would be better if you did not shut yourself up in Negotin, but made another small fort somewhere in the hills and took with you only enough footsoldiers to defend the trenches, and appointed good officers over them. Then when the Turks attack Timok, you can go out and wait for them with your gunners and soldiers. If you beat them, then you can come back to Negotin, and if the Turks beat you, then you can go off into the hills with all your cavalry and the rest of your army which cannot be fitted into the fortification. With 1,000 men in the hills, the Turks will fear you more than if they shut you up here with 10,000.' At that he roared with laughter and answered: 'There, you're frightened of the Turks. Just you pray to God that the Turks attack, then when my cossacks come from Timok and say "there are the Turks", I shall gird on my sword and go out to meet them. You ask Petar the porter to bring you a jug of spirits. Then you sit here and drink, and take the field-glasses and watch how I'll * * * *[1] them.' So in a few days his friend went off safely to Poreć and from there to Belgrade, while he stayed on in Negotin as before.

Vuk's fears for Veljko were justified. He was closely besieged by a superior Turkish army in Negotin. When he himself was shot dead by a Turkish sniper, his men soon lost heart. By the time that Vuk had set out again from Belgrade on 21 August, it was too late. Negotin had fallen, and the Turks were advancing in irresistible force. Karadjordje himself fled to Austria, from which he was subsequently deported to Russia. There was no one who could

---

[1] The asterisks are Vuk's.

rally the Serb forces in his place, and as many as 100,000 Serbs fled before the advancing Turks to Austrian or Russian territory. The Turks reoccupied Belgrade and Serbia, and Serbian independence had to be regained by a more subtle and gradual policy. Vuk himself crossed the Danube to Austria without returning to Belgrade. Like other immigrants he had to endure a three-week period of quarantine near Pančevo. At the end of September he was pronounced fit and free to proceed 'together with his family' (probably his father and a cousin). Leaving them at Karlovci, Vuk joined Stefan Živković and his wife, and set out for Buda and Vienna. At the end of October 1813 the party reached Vienna, which was to be Vuk's main home for the remaining 50 years of his life.

His life's work of linguistic reform and collecting folk-lore and songs was now to begin. The stereotype of Vuk is the figure of a totally unlearned peasant-boy with preternaturally quick wits which enabled him to make up for lost time in ten years and to become in that interval a worthy intellectual consort for Grimm, Ranke, and Goethe. It would certainly be wrong to underrate Vuk's native intellectual power, but the conventional picture is rather misleading. It took form partly because Vuk was careful in early publications to guard against criticism by portraying himself as a simple country boy, and mainly as the result of propaganda by his enemies in later linguistic controversies about the total ignorance of this 'lame goatherd' (and many other and more offensive words to the same effect).

There was enough truth in such attacks for Vuk to resent them deeply; and envy was mixed with his scorn for the conventional learning of the Serb Orthodox dignitaries. In fact however by the autumn of 1813, the twenty-seven-year old Vuk had acquired a certain amount of education—as much as was possible for a Serb in Turkish-occupied Serbia. He had read what there was for him to read; he had met some of the most prominent of the new generation of the Serb intelligentsia in Budapest and was well aware of their interests. Of course he had not the polyglot learning of Dositej Obradović or Stefan Stratimirović; but he was no illiterate. His main talent however, which was in the long run to do so much for his own career and for the development of Serbian literature and education, was not yet fully developed, nor was he himself fully aware of it. This lay in the almost instinctive knowledge of village lore and sayings and of popular poetry which he was already beginning deliberately to cultivate and which none of his learned contemporaries could equal.

Vuk had other assets of temperament and character which were to be of inestimable use to Serbian literature. In days when the ideas of the 'heroic' and of 'national character' were very much the fashion in the more cultivated capitals of Europe, Vuk had an unromantically close knowledge of how they were likely to work out in practice. He knew the more squalid side of village life, and he knew what the 'wars of liberation' of that time looked like from the inside. He had lived as a peasant and if he had not himself lived as a hero of song, he had been very close to one, in the shape of Veljko. He greatly admired Veljko, but was under no illusions about the obverse qualities of this hero of his own time and area. Since such heroes' tasks and character had changed little with the centuries, this meant that Vuk had an incomparably deep understanding of the epic literary material with which he was to deal for the rest of his life. The material itself may often have been conventionally romantic, but Vuk was himself in many ways ruthlessly realistic. Nevertheless he did not allow his realism to obscure his ideals. He was ready to adopt and appropriate Herder's doctrine that the essence of a nation's life is to be found in the uncorrupted speech and poetry of its people. Vuk did more perhaps than any single man to uncover the traditional speech and literature of the Serbs, and thus to prepare the way for a modern system of education in Serbia, and to provide the linguistic basis for the ultimate union of the Southern Slavs. These were not simply the ultimate by-products of his life's work. They were deliberate aims, consciously pursued. It was the good fortune of his country that Vuk who realized such lofty ideals kept his feet so firmly on the ground of his native soil, and his ear so close to the true speech of his people. For that his early experience was responsible.

VI

KOPITAR AND FIRST YEARS IN VIENNA

1

ARRIVING in Vienna in November 1813, Vuk settled together with his travelling companions, Stefan and Savka Živković, in the Landstrasse suburb (Rochusgasse), where there was growing up a lively community of émigrés from South-Eastern Europe. It seems likely that Vuk and Živković turned their thoughts from the first to literary activity among the Serb community. There was not a wide choice of profession for them, and both had developed literary aspirations. Živković was finally to publish in 1814 his version of Fénélon's *Télémaque* which for the rest of his life was to provide him with a nickname (Stefan Živković-Telemak). Vuk represented himself later as entirely disoriented when he arrived in Vienna, and without any specific intention except that of learning German (which in truth he never mastered very thoroughly). The fact is that immediately after arrival, Vuk called on the editors of the newly established Serb newspaper in Vienna *Srpske Novine* (Serbian News), Dimitrije Davidović and Dimitrije Frušić, known to him already as young students of philosophy from his days in Budapest, 1810. For them he wrote a 'booklet' in the form of a letter to Karadjordje, about the fall of Serbia and the personalities of the Serbian uprising (it was not printed and the manuscript has never been found). The editors submitted it, as in duty bound, to the Imperial censor for Slavonic languages, Jernej Kopitar, and Kopitar, enthusiastic about the article, sought out Vuk. This was the beginning of a warm and very unsordid friendship, and also of a collaboration of the utmost importance for the history of the Serbian language and literature.

Kopitar was a most remarkable man, of great energy, imagination, and versatility. Born in Repnja, a Slovenian village, in 1779 (seven years before Vuk), he like Vuk was a country child. He was originally educated for the Catholic priesthood and as a result of his training acquired a strong distaste for priests—there is some similarity here with Dositej Obradović. Before his training for the priesthood was finished, Kopitar became tutor and personal secretary in the family of a rich Maecenas of Slovene culture, Baron Zois. Here he was encouraged to take an active interest in Slavonic languages and met a number of young Slovene writers. He also began to come into contact with French culture and personalities. From 1805 the French had been in occupation of Slovene lands,[1] and in 1806 a senior officer in the army of occupation, General de Bellegarde, found that neither his daughter nor her governess could understand his Slovene cook, with resulting difficulties for his household.[2] He talked over his troubles with Baron Zois, at whose suggestion Kopitar became tutor to the young Eugénie-Lucie-Adelaide de Bellegarde. He had no grammar of the Slovenian or 'Krainisch' language to hand, so composed one in French as the lessons proceeded. Kopitar referred later to Baron Zois's role in one of his letters to the literary historian Šafarik,[3] and said in his own typically mixed language: 'Selbst ich trieb Slavica auf Seine Anregung und gab Krainischen Unterricht der Comtesse Bellegarde auf seine Einladung—et haec fuit origo meae Gramm.' ('I too pursued Slavonic studies at his instance, and gave Slovene lessons to the Countess Bellegarde on his invitation—and this was the origin of my grammar'.)

In October 1808, before his major work on Slovene grammar was

[1] At the Peace of Pressburg (concluded after his victory at Austerlitz in 1805) Napoleon acquired from Austria the districts of Carniola, Western Carinthia, Goricia, and Istria (i.e. much of present-day Slovenia), together with part of Croatia, Dalmatia, and Ragusa (Dubrovnik). These were incorporated into the French Empire in 1809 under the Treaty of Vienna as the 'Illyrian provinces' and were administered first by Marshal Marmont, Duke of Ragusa. The territories were re-ceded in 1814–15, Istria, Carinthia, Carniola, and Goricia forming the 'Kingdom of Illyria' under Austria, Dalmatia and Ragusa coming separately under Austrian sovereignty, and Croatia and Slavonia being incorporated in Hungary.

[2] Mademoiselle de Bellegarde's vanity seems to have been involved. She was told that 'lepše bi bilo' (it would be nicer) if she could speak Slovenian; she misunderstood this to mean that 'she would be even prettier ('lepša bi bila') if she could do so.

[3] Josif Pavle Šafařík (1795–1862), a notable man of letters, was of Slovak origin and became the first director of the Serb 'gymnasium' at Novi Sad. His *History of Slavonic literatures* was published in 1826. Šafařík approved Vuk's ideas about popular language and spelling reform but not his tactics in propagating them.

finally printed at Ljubljana, Kopitar made his way to Vienna where he spent the rest of his life. He made some pretence of embarking on legal studies, but these were never serious. He earned a little money at first by lecturing on Slav subjects, and from the end of 1809 his articles began to appear in the learned papers of Vienna. After refusing the chair of Czech language at Vienna University, he accepted in August 1810 the post of official censor of Slav books, and in December a post in the Imperial library, which he retained until his death. From this vantage point, Kopitar built up a large network of correspondence on linguistic and philological questions with the most eminent Slavonic experts within and, where possible, outside the Austrian Empire. He was in particular the favourite pupil and correspondent of the Abbé Dobrovski, the greatest authority of his time on 'Slavistic' questions and author of the first scientific grammar of old Slavonic.[1]

Kopitar's interests were by no means entirely philological. His work and his human interests led him to frequent the society of a large group of refugees or travellers from South-Eastern Europe— Serbs, Slovenes, Greeks, Rumanians, and Albanians—who assembled regularly at the Weisser Wolf inn in the Fleischmarkt in Vienna.[2] Kopitar's first object in the company of these foreign priests, merchants, and students was to collect linguistic and ethnographical information, but he was led step by step to sympathize with the political aspirations which were often the *raison d'être* of their literary interests. He learned modern Greek and had particularly close relations with the Greek patriots, among them Adamantinos Koraes,[3] who regarded a purified modern

[1] Josif Dobrovski (1753-1829), a Czech scholar, has been called the 'father of Slav studies'. Besides his grammar of old Slavonic (*Institutiones linguae Slavicae*) he wrote a grammar and history of the Czech languages.

[2] Kopitar and the 'Weisser Wolf' were celebrated by Hoffmann von Fallersleben (author of *Deutschland über alles*), who was a frequent member of its polyglot clientele. Of Kopitar he wrote:
> Sein Nam ist weit und breit geehrt
> Und lebt in aller Munde,
> So lange Treu' und Wahrheit währt
> Von Laibach bis zum Sunde;
> Am liebsten und am besten
> Ist er bekannt den Gästen
> Im Wolfen.

[3] Adamantinos Koraes, or Korais (1748-1833), was born in Chios, but spent most of his life in Paris. He was a friend of many French Encyclopedists and corresponded with Thomas Jefferson on constitutional matters. His literary and

Greek language as a necessary condition of Greek political independence, and enjoyed Kopitar's ardent support.

Indeed Kopitar himself, while concerned first to discover the culture of the Slav peoples of Austria-Hungary and to make them conscious of their own inheritance, had developed wide-ranging ideas about the political role which they should play. He was in fact the first prominent Austro-Slav. His principal aim was to transform Vienna into the main centre of Slav culture, and to ensure that the Slav populations of Austria were educated to enjoy the equal political rights which they should be given in a re-fashioned Austrian Empire. Only in this way, Kopitar thought, could the Slavs of central and Eastern Europe be attracted away from the influence of Russia, which he regarded as essentially backward and barbaric (in his attitude towards Russia at least, Kopitar was a good Austrian Catholic of his time). His viewpoint was well summarized in a report which he wrote in July 1818 to Austrian police headquarters about Vuk's activity: 'A time will come when the South Slavs of Austria, politically happy and scientifically educated, will look down with justified national pride on the Russians to whom they now look enviously as higher and more fortunate beings.' By education too the Slavs could develop their full potentialities, to constitute the most important national element of Austria—for Kopitar was an Austrian patriot with no great admiration for the German element of his country. He would have agreed with a phrase of his Czech correspondent, Dobrovski: 'Teutscher Verstand ist nicht zu Verachten aber Unserm von Nicht gleich zu setzen. Französischer Esprit verraucht zu leicht, und lässt sich kaum fest Halten.'[1] ('German brains are not to be despised, but by no means to be compared with ours. French wit blows away too easily, and can hardly be pinned down.')

political interests were closely connected. He wished to establish the continuity of Romaic with ancient Greek and to set a literary and educational standard which would facilitate the establishment of political unity in Greece. Koraes advocated a compromise between those who wished to impose a return to classical Greek, and those who wanted to make the popular language of folk-tales and poetry (the 'Koiné') into the language of all kinds of literature. His aim was to evolve a 'mixed language', the 'Katharevousa' or 'puristic', which would essentially be the vernacular adapted to the forms of ancient Greek, and with new coinages derived from it. Many parallels could be drawn with Vuk's later ideas and work.

[1] Letter to Kopitar from Dobrovski of 7 May 1815.

Kopitar was never drawn to the idea of an independent Illyria under French patronage, nor did he think that the experiment begun by Napoleon in 1805 would be lasting. He was however a Slovene patriot, and rejoiced to see any revival of Slovene national spirit. He was also intensely interested in the mechanics, so to speak, of national education, and watched keenly the efforts of the French occupation authorities to evolve a 'national language' and an alphabet which could combine the advantages of the Latin and Cyrillic scripts. He admired the way in which they organized schools (a successful beginning was made under Marshal Marmont) and produced the basic books required for any comprehensive educational system—particularly a grammar and a dictionary. He did not agree with the French choices either of a dialect (Dubrovnik rather than Slovene) for the 'national' language of Illyria, nor of a writer (Vodnik rather than himself) for the proposed grammar; but he could not but approve the general line of their policy.

Such being his general philosophy, it followed that to Kopitar, the intellectual advancement of the Serb community settled in the Austrian Empire was a very important matter. He was interested in the institution of Serbian language higher schools, and the appointment by the Austrians (1810) of an official Serb inspector to raise the standard of education gave him much pleasure, even if it was little more than a reaction to the forward policy of the French in 'Illyria'. Personally Kopitar did a good deal to secure better printing facilities for the Serb community. In 1812 a type-founder, Schade, came to Vienna from Berlin, and Kopitar persuaded him to produce Cyrillic as well as Greek letters. Soon afterwards he was disputing, in correspondence with the Metropolitan Stratimirović, the monopoly rights of the Buda press to print Serbian books in Austria and Hungary. He had in mind from the start the foundation of a Serbian newspaper in Vienna, and his first success came when permission was given in 1813 for the foundation of *Serbian News*. It was not long before the Cyrillic press in Vienna began to extend its scope to books as well as newspapers.

Naturally Kopitar had tried soon after his arrival in Vienna to establish links with the Serb intellectual leaders and to inform himself about their culture. His first contacts seem to have been made in Vienna through a certain Ranković, son of a Serb officer in the Austrian army, who had lived in Sremski Karlovci. In June 1812 he had addressed himself to the Metropolitan Stratimirović explaining his interests and desire to find learned correspondents in every Slav land. He was referred to Lukian Mušicki, formerly professor of classical languages at the 'Gymnasium' at Karlovci, and now Archimandrite of the monastery of Šišatovac in the Fruška Gora hills. Their correspondence was infrequent and Kopitar established various other contacts—with Pavle Solarić, a pupil of Dositej Obradović, who managed a Serb language press in Venice;[1] with Uros Neštorović, the new Inspector of Serb schools; and with Frušić and Davidović among the younger generation (then in Budapest and soon to migrate to Vienna).

Kopitar was starting from scratch, so far as Serbian studies and literature were concerned. This is hardly surprising since published books were not easy to come by and a good deal of early Serbian literature had been circulated simply in manuscript from author to author. One of his first inquiries from Mušicki, for example, was for news of Orphelin[2] (author of the first famous Serbian *Book of Letters*), who had died thirty years before. He was from the first keenly interested in the work of Dositej Obradović, to whom his attention had been directed in 1809 by Dobrovski. It was Obradović's efforts to 'enlighten' his own people by introducing them to European ideas, and above all his attempt to use their own popular language in doing so, that particularly endeared him both to Dobrovski and to Kopitar. The latter described him in a phrase typical of the time and himself as 'the Serbian Anacharsis,[3] who spoke to them [the Serbs] in the new Serbian tongue words from England about the love of freedom and fatherland and from Fénélon about the love of lofty virtue'. From 1810 onwards, Kopitar was publishing in the learned papers of Vienna articles

---

[1] The Serbian language press in Venice was founded in 1758 and printed mainly Russian ecclesiastical literature, with type sent from Moscow, for circulation among the Orthodox Serbs.

[2] Zaharija Stefanović 'Orphelin' (1726–85) was a man of many parts. His literary work alone covered history, poetry, theology, nature study, and school books. Nearly as important for the development of Serb literature as Dositej Obradović, he was also concerned to introduce the 'popular language' into literature, and in 1762 published in 'popular language' his poem 'How the Serbs and the Turks fought at Kosovo'.

[3] Anacharsis was, according to Herodotus, a Scythian sage, who travelled widely in the sixth century B.C. According to Plutarch, he made the acquaintance of Solon at Athens, and Lucian composed a dialogue between the two. Anacharsis became for the philosophers of the Enlightenment a symbol of new wisdom from afar; a particularly well-known work was the Abbé Barthélémy's *Voyage du jeune Anacharsis en Grèce*, 1790.

on Dositej and extracts from his autobiographical writings. And it was Dositej's ideas about popular language which led Kopitar warmly to greet, in another review article, Sava Mrkalj's essay on alphabetical reform, *The Hardness of the Hard Sign* (cf. Chapter V above). He was no doubt unaware at the time of how much he might offend his correspondent, the Metropolitan Stratimirović, by so doing.

Kopitar's ideas about 'national language' at this stage, before he met Vuk, can be summarized as follows:

(i) The language of literature should be that of the people.
(ii) In any national language there should be 'equal rights' for all dialects.
(iii) Dialects should not be artificially mixed to form a literary language (this practice he called 'makaronism'). Still less should old and new forms of language be deliberately mixed.
(iv) There must be a common Slav alphabet for the Slav races of Austria-Hungary. The Cyrillic script was more suitable for this purpose than the Latin. The motto must be that of the German philologist and grammarian Adelung: 'Write as you speak.'
(v) Grammar should not be an *a priori* construction but a set of rules derived from popular linguistic practice.
(vi) To illustrate popular speech and the way of life of any people, it was important to collect and publish their national poetry, stories, etc.

The last point leads to Kopitar's early interest in the collection of South Slav popular poetry. This was established well before he met Vuk. Since the publication of Ossian and the collection of Herder, national or 'popular' poetry had been very much in vogue (this subject is treated at some length in Chapter XII), and no doubt Kopitar, apart from his genuine linguistic interests, wanted to make the most of the current literary fashion. He had read what little 'popular' poetry had been published in the Serbian language; he had also noted down some Serbian specimens himself and tried to collect others through his correspondents. It was probably Kopitar who inspired Vrhovac, the Bishop of Zagreb, to circularize the priests of his diocese, asking them to collect specimens of popular language together with provincial and national songs. In a long review of the state of Serbian literature written in 1811, he demanded the publication of 'more of those national songs in which the Serbs and Croats are so rich. It is wonderful how they stir the reader.'

Kopitar was thus by 1813 actively interested in the subjects which Vuk was to make his own, but interested on a broad comparative basis and without knowledge in depth. Vuk himself was also prepared for his meeting with Kopitar, by his first-hand knowledge of Serbian popular songs and popular language. He was at least well aware of the discussions about the need for a more rational alphabet; and he had taken part, as best he could, in the Karadjordje administration of the free Serbian principality, including its first attempts at instituting a system of national education. If anyone was fitted to appreciate the link, or potential link, between literary and political reforms, it was he.

2

Vuk's own accounts of his first contacts with Kopitar date from some thirty years after the event. The least polemical of them occurs in Sreznevski's biography of Vuk, dating from 1842, and runs as follows:

One evening, at that unforgettable time when Vuk and I used to spend most evenings together, we were talking about contemporary Serbian literature. Passing from one thing to another, I asked him how he originally became a writer. Vuk smiled, pondered, smiled again blinking with his bright eyes, and answered: 'Well, it's like this. Without this crutch here, and without my good wife, and without the excellent Kopitar, I'd never have become a writer; it has helped, too, that I have liked travelling....' Vuk went on to explain that if he hadn't been lame, he would have been caught up in the Serbian wars against the Turks and very possibly killed; as for his wife, she was a good Viennese and persuaded him to stay in Vienna where he had to earn his living from literature. 'But the main cause for my being a writer will always remain Kopitar. In that respect I owe him, if not everything, at least a great deal, a very great deal. You have to know that really excellent man as well as I have got to know him in order to respect him as he deserves—both as an expert and as a man. . . .[1] The fact is, it's Kopitar alone that I have to thank for becoming a writer and for being such a writer as I am. In 1813 I left Serbia at the same time as Black

[1] Vuk was talking to Sreznevski, a Russian, and the Russians, probably aware of Kopitar's views about their culture, tended to dislike him.

KOPITAR AND FIRST YEARS IN VIENNA 87

George (Karadjordje), and came to Vienna without knowing or having any idea of what would become of me. Kopitar, young as he was at that time, was already a censor. Amongst other things he had to act as censor for the *Serbian News*, published in Vienna at the time by Frušić and Davidović. Kopitar used to urge the editors to write pure grammatical Serbian, and told them that the language which they wrote could not possibly be pure Serbian. They didn't reject his suggestion, but for all that they knew no other form of language except that in which they wrote and talked. The ordinary people's language they regarded as something for shepherds and swineherds. . . . When this [Vuk's article about the fall of Serbia] came into Kopitar's hands, it attracted his attention by its unusual language. Kopitar wanted to see me, and we became friends. In the course of our talks, the subject of Serbian popular songs[1] came up. Kopitar saw that I knew a lot of them, and began to urge me to write them down—the more the better—and then, in God's name, to get them printed. Well, what was I to do—it interested me, and there I was writing down the songs. What I didn't know myself, I asked my kinsman, the wife of Stevan Živković, with whom I'd come to Vienna. We put together a fair-sized batch of them and it came out under the name of "A small book of simple popular Serb-Slavonic songs".'

(The immediately following paragraphs deal with Kopitar's share in inspiring Vuk's Serb grammar and dictionary; they are quoted separately and in full at the appropriate points later in this narrative).

'After Kopitar had put me on my feet . . . I got to know my business gradually, and now you all know how much joy I get from my work as a writer. I don't look for fame or put myself out to earn the praise of the multitude. But I'd like it if after my death someone who knew his business could be convinced, on reading my books, that I had faithfully reproduced what I know. Whatever I have written, I've always had in mind what Kopitar or Grimm[2] would say about it, and have cared nothing for the rest. Let them say what they want, nobody can please the whole world.'

Vuk's account of his debt to Kopitar is important, but not to be

[1] I have throughout translated the Serb *narodne pesme* as 'popular songs'. In spite of the overtones of the English words, this seems to be the least objectionable version. For Vuk the word *narodni* implied 'coming from among the people' (a song could be the undoubted work of an individual author and still be 'popular'), 'addressed to a popular audience', and 'in popular language'.

[2] Jakob Grimm (1785–1863), the famous German philologist and collector of *Grimm's Fairy Tales*. An almost exact contemporary, he helped Vuk's literary career to an enormous extent.

taken at all points quite literally—it was written or spoken thirty years after the event and at a time when Vuk was (or had recently been) concerned to meet accusations that other Serbs had inspired the activity for which he was alleged to be claiming the exclusive credit.[1] So far as the first impact of the two personalities is concerned, Vuk probably remembered one or two points with advantages. It has already been remarked for example that he can hardly have arrived in Vienna without at least some idea of a literary career. It is also rather doubtful whether Kopitar was attracted primarily, as Vuk says, by the language and style of the lost article on the fall of Serbia. Certainly in a letter of February 1814 Kopitar referred to Vuk as a man who 'writes wonderful Serbian'. In fact however, to judge by his first preserved writings, Vuk's prose was at this time by no means free from the influence of the literary Slavonicized language favoured by the Church, and was far from the true popular style which he later evolved. Moreover Kopitar was at this time no connoisseur of Serbian style; he could applaud the intentions of Dositej without knowing how far Dositej (or Vuk) had succeeded in writing the true language of the people. It is probable that Kopitar was attracted to Vuk by a number of other qualities likely to have been present (to judge by all his other writings) in this first historical essay—Vuk's peasant clarity of thought, his confident opinions, and not least his patriotism. To judge again by the historical writings which have been preserved, Vuk is likely to have spoken strongly against the eventual reliance of Karadjordje on the Russians, and bitterly against the way in which the Russians had let the Serbs down by signing the Treaty of Bucharest (1812) with the Turks. Anti-Russian sentiments would naturally be welcome to Kopitar, with his broad concept of building up Austria against Russia as a centre of Slav culture and civilization; and all the more welcome at a time when the general sentiment of the Serbs in Austria was hardening against the Austrian Government.[2]

Whatever the exact reasons that originally excited Kopitar's

---

[1] Vuk's most detailed defence was made in an article of 1842, 'The true cause of my beginning to collect popular poetry', which is more polemical and gives even more exclusive credit to Kopitar than his account (of about the same time) to Sreznevski.

[2] It was widely resented that the Austrian Government, having given no support to the Serbs against the Turks, would not even permit the publication of political news about Serbia in the Vienna *Serbian News*.

interest in Vuk, it was confirmed by their meeting, and mutual interest soon ripened into a warm and deep friendship. It is possible that there was a special psychological sympathy between two men who each suffered from a physical disability. Vuk was lame and debarred from the normal forms of active life; Kopitar was notoriously ugly, so much so that he would never allow his portrait to be painted, even in those pre-photographic days when portraiture was a routine affair. But without going into deep psychological speculations it is easy to find good reasons for the mutual attraction between the two men. Though Catholic enough in the face of 'Russian barbarism', Kopitar was a true child of the Enlightenment, and this again was a point of sympathetic contact with Vuk. Kopitar's intellectual scepticism accorded well with Vuk's peasant common sense. Vuk's views on the common run of orthodox priests have been illustrated in Chapter II—they were to be strongly reinforced by his subsequent experience in trying to push through linguistic reforms. Kopitar's views on priests in general were recorded after his death by Vuk (in 1852): 'He cared for the Pope of Rome just as little as for the Patriarch of Constantinople and no more than for the Turkish Mufti. In conversation, he would often say that priests and monks, especially the senior ones, were alike at all places and times in trying to keep the people as far as possible in ignorance, so that they could live the better and richer from this ignorance. Therefore except in emergency one should never undertake anything in common with them—but one has to pay one's respects to them.'

Above all however both Kopitar and Vuk were essentially propagandists in the most favourable sense of the word. Each believed or came to believe deeply in certain ideas, and would not rest content till he had tried to convert others to them. Vuk's proselytizing tendencies will be amply illustrated throughout this book. Kopitar's are well expressed in a letter answering the charge that in a review he had indulged in 'proselytism which is always hateful': he wrote: 'What is the meaning of the text: "Go forth into the whole world and preach the gospel to all mankind" but basically a charge to proselytize? And what would we all have been without such proselytizing work which was so hateful to our polytheist forefathers? And *what is all writing of books but proselytizing?* So you see the idea and the aim is natural and psychologically necessary—nobody is defending dishonest means.'

Most of Kopitar's proselytizing was done in national and literary causes; he immediately saw how useful Vuk could be to him, and proceeded to his most fruitful act of conversion. What Kopitar wanted first from Vuk was help in producing a Serbian grammar, and in collecting Serb national songs—a dictionary was also in his mind, but that was obviously longer-term work. Vuk was little prepared by previous experience for collaboration on such a broad front, but seems to have been to some extent swept away by the range and fire of Kopitar's enthusiasms He naturally needed most convincing about the comparatively technical work of a grammar. The songs were a different matter. He knew plenty by heart himself, and he had Savka Živković, his cousin, to dictate to him some other 'women's' songs. As is apparent from the preface quoted immediately below, he knew something of a previous collection of popular songs edited and in most cases substantially adapted by a certain Kačić, and of the popularity which it had attained; he had also brought with him to Vienna a collection of Russian folk-songs.[1] Moreover there was a special stimulus. Kopitar was able to show him Herder's *Stimmen der Völker*, the collection of German and other folk-songs which by now was famous all over Europe, and Vuk as well as Kopitar came to realize that there was a European fashion for such literature, apart from what he considered as a national need to record it. He brought to the work his own memory and energy, and by the end of January 1814 a small volume of Serbian songs was ready for printing.

3

Vuk prefaced this volume with an introduction which is a key document in his life, both for what it says, and for the manner in which he says it. Some of the material in it has already been used for the story of his earlier years, but at the cost of some duplication it should be given in full at this stage:

---

[1] Among those who accused Vuk in 1842 of taking the credit for other men's work was Sava Tekelija, who said that, on return from Russia in 1811, he brought with him a book of Russian songs which pleased him greatly; he gave this book to others, with the recommendation that they should collect similar Serbian material for printing. Tekelija's chronology is confused, but he showed the songs to Živković and Mušicki (it may well have been Kirsha Danilov's collection of 1804) and conceivably it is this book which Vuk brought with him to Vienna in 1813. See article by N. Banašević, *Kovčežić*, i, pp. 48 et seq.

Eight years ago I was at Sremski Karlovci—a place where I found myself along with a number of other Serbs from Serbia in the charitable institution of the father and protector of the Serbian Muses [the Metropolitan Stefan Stratimirović]; and where I learned to my great and unforgettable sorrow that there is more knowledge in the world than is contained in our *Psalter* and *Book of Hours*. It was there that Master Lukian Mušicki, the present Archimandrite, requested that we should write down for him any simple Serbian songs known to any of us. At that time indeed I had in my memory songs of various kinds, five times as many and ten times as clear as now; but I did not dare to write down even one of them and hand it in, for I was convinced that Mušicki was using this as a means to mock us, lads who had grown up in the woods, among pigs, goats, and sheep.

Afterwards when sheer poverty forced me to give up learning (an object which was then the most precious to my heart and which I still prefer to all inventions and delights of this world), and drove me back to my native land, I found there a great volume of songs (Kačić's) written in Latin letters; as soon as I laid my hands on it and saw that these were songs, and just such songs as our Serbs sing to the *gusle*, sitting by the fire, I began to suspect that Master Mušicki had after all not been playing a joke on us; and when I had read through Kačić's song book, I began to guess his true intention.

Now unhappily I have had to cross over again from Serbia and come here to Vienna (in the hope that out of all my trials I might at least learn a little German). With me I brought a big Russian song-book, and when I read various songs from it, it came into my head to ask: 'Is it the Russians alone who have a book of this kind and size? Or do other nations have the same, and is it only we Serbs who lack it?' When I came on German song-books, I was clearly convinced that the latter and not the former was the case. Then I began to ponder further on this question. 'Did our people never have its national songs? Or did it once have them and does it possess them still, but without anyone who would take the trouble to collect and write them down, so that it has rejected and forgotten them, as it has much else (particularly of our own)?' I concluded that things must stand in one or other of these ways and that there was no clear sign pointing in one or other direction. But on thinking again I could hardly affirm that we never had our songs, for various signs told me that even now they exist among our people. So the true case must be as stated in my second question.

Pondering on this regretfully for a few days and passing from one thought to another, I came upon an Ode of Master Mušicki; in which the following lines increased my sorrow yet more: 'Full many of you in tongue and custom have been borne down by your neighbour

Tyranny, to be as turban-bearers, wolves to your nation, as sons of Árpád, a strange folk.' True, these are only four lines to look at, but as happens in poems, a weighty judgement is here spoken, and if it were to be expounded clearly and in detail, in truth our writers would have some work to do. But Master Mušicki will perhaps allow me, a Serb from Serbia and a small man, not to be compared with him in any way except for tenderness and love towards my race, to discuss this question a little further.

That we have been borne down among the turban-bearers, is the truth, but it was the bitterest and greatest need that drove us to this, as it still oppresses us and holds us down. Yet for all this it is those Serbs from Serbia, in their state of slavery, who up to this day have maintained the national spirit better than those on this side of the Sava in their free and enlightened empire, where they have liberty to put up churches and build schools for their own language, and where nothing is forbidden them which may serve for the enlightenment of a people. And for all this they are distinguished from the Serbs of Serbia only in that they have grown away from their native land—not in anything else. Those very same subjects which were taught in the Serb tongue at the time of the most blessed Patriarch Arsenije Čarnojević [1690] at monasteries and in some places at schools in Serbia and Hercegovina, these are still taught today there in the same way as here.

The fact that there are Serbs here who have had the chance of taking courses in a foreign tongue and learning it, cannot in my opinion be called a step forward in the enlightenment of our people. And the fact that there are many who, after learning in this way and achieving something, are sorry to be Serbs and ashamed of that name, want to be called something else and scorn their own race and language, that is too much. Truly it is hard to accustom a child to love the woman who is only said by others to be its mother more than her from whose breasts it has sucked milk and conscious life.

Now if any one were to ask me: Well, in what part can those Serbs be found who have till now best preserved their national spirit? And where do they talk the purest Serbian? I would answer him as follows: The hearth and home of the Serbian race and of the purest language may be found today between the Drina and the Morava, and more particularly some way away from the Danube and Sava, as for example in the districts of Kragujevac, Karanovac, Rudnik, Užice, Kruševac, and further over from Novi Pazar in Herzegovina proper. But when you cross the Drina from the Mačva into Bosnia, many have adopted Turkish customs and use more Turkish words. It is the same beyond the Morava; once you pass through Resava and the district of Požarevac to Timok, the people are mixed with the Vlachs [Rumanians]. But in the districts first mentioned and in Resava, the Serbs are still like their forefathers, and among them you will still hear the good Serbian-Slavonic names . . . not all sorts of Jewish and Greek names and God knows what as in other places.*

In the consideration of this material, Master Milovan Vidaković deserves particular gratitude from his race, not only for enlightening them and enlarging their taste in his books, but also particularly for his use of Serbian-Slavonic names in his books and for mentioning those places through which we could remind ourselves that we too have been a power in the world.

Such and similar thoughts and meditations gave me the impulse to publish to the world this small collection of simple popular songs. Here there is no single song which has been composed according to the laws of poetry by any educated spirit, enriched by much reading; they are all such as are sung by simple innocent hearts naturally and without artifice. I am no singer myself, but I memorized these songs when, twelve years ago, in the happiest condition known to mortals, I kept sheep and goats.

Thus, since I heard this quantity of songs and without any deliberate intention memorized them in the place of my birth (the village of Tršić, in the district of Jadar), it stands to reason that, if any one took the trouble, he could collect a great book of songs, as big as the Russian song-book. I am publishing these; someone else could perhaps work to collect similar songs in the Srem; and others still in Bačka, the Banat, Slavonia, Croatia, and Dalmatia; and if fate so wills, someone could collect further songs in Serbia, Bosnia, Hercegovina, and Montenegro. And then perhaps a man will be found, whom God has endowed with gifts of poetry and who has had the chance of learning its rules in the Latin or German tongue; he may try to sift all these collections, and write some poems himself according to the taste and manner of his race, and thus out of all these small collections create one big whole.

I hope that this small song-book of mine will be to the taste of every Serb who loves the national spirit of his race. If there are those who despise me, what of it? That would not astonish me. It is sufficient comfort to me that I am publishing this work with good intent and out of my burning love for the Serb race, and that there will be found people among the Serbs who will recognize this and approve it.

Criticism, from which nothing in this world is free, will doubtless not

* [*Vuk's Note*: 'No one should judge from this that I like some Serbs only and am prejudiced against others. All Serbs from the Adriatic to the Black Sea, of whatever faith, all are equally near and dear to my heart; and I wish that they may love and respect each other as sensible and honourable brothers. I have only raised this matter in order to explain better the abovementioned lines of Master Mušicki.']

leave this song-book of mine untouched. As regards the songs in it, I may be criticized by some simple women from Serbia or Sarajevo, but I hope that they too will pardon me if they find something in the wrong form, as they think, or left out. For I, as I have said, am no singer myself, and another point—it is so long since I heard these songs that I might have forgotten my own name in the interval. As regards language and spelling, everyone may criticize me as they like, I have written these songs down as I have heard them sung. For the rest I have not been able to decide which line to follow; for not only do no two people approve each other's ways and write alike, but also no single man writes consistently—today it will be one way and tomorrow another. And so it will be without cease, until our learned men (and especially those whose duty demands it and calls them to it) can agree among themselves and in co-operation write a Serbian Grammar and a single dictionary. Then that man will have to blush who has not the knowledge or desire to confine himself to their rules. But till then each will write according to his own lights and desire; and in the same way each will criticize the other, for neither author nor critic has any other rules; each thinks that on every subject that particular style is best and most correct which he, according to his own judgement, thinks good and right.

Apart from tender love-songs for women's voices, there are a few songs here, especially at the end of the book, to be sung by men's voices, in the well-known Serbian style, to the *gusle*, and some whose contents form a kind of narrative. Of such songs I could add more, but I fear that what is here may be too much, and that some Serb of the new type may say of me: 'What has come into his head to publish these blind men's songs?' Yet it seems to me that it is such songs which have preserved and still preserve among the common people the name and essence of the Serbia of former times.

4

Vuk's preface is an extremely interesting document. No allowances have to be made by the reader for hindsight, as is necessary for instance in the interpretation of Vuk's reminiscences, already quoted, about his debt to Kopitar. But it must be recognized that Vuk is to some extent bowing to current literary fashions. He deliberately presents himself as an innocent child of nature, projected by pure chance into the literary world. This picture was likely to be welcome to a romantically inclined public, and was to some extent defensively designed to forestall criticism from the

KOPITAR AND FIRST YEARS IN VIENNA 95

learned; but it was essentially false and Vuk was in danger of involving himself in some contradiction by passionately defending, later on in the same preface, the claim of the Serbian swineherds to be the true preservers of the national language. There is also some rhetoric in his questions about the existence or survival of Serbian national songs in quantity, when (as he admits later in his preface) he only had to appeal to his own memory and common sense to find an answer. Again in his references to Kačić, Vuk seems to be pandering to popular conceptions against his own better judgement. No doubt with longer experience as a collector, Vuk grew to be much quicker at recognizing the essential qualities of real folk-poetry; but he is likely fairly early to have had some idea that most of the poems in Kačić's collection, popular as they were in one sense, were not an entirely natural growth. So far as the numbers of popular songs were concerned, Vuk with his experience of the genesis of ballads both in his native Tršić and in Brza Palanka (Chapters II and V), knew well enough that there was plenty of poetry left to collect; so far as quantity was concerned, he had not had time to forget much— it was not all that long since he had left Tršić. The whole passage recording the dialogue in his mind is rather defensive, besides being pleasantly modish and artificial.

One or two other passages probably reflect hastily digested discussions with Kopitar. The idea of some later artist making one great poem out of the songs collected from the various parts of Serbia may well be an indirect reference to current theories of Homeric scholarship,[1] with which he could have become acquainted through Kopitar.

These are comparatively minor points. What is much more interesting and important is the decisiveness with which Vuk had adopted Kopitar's main ideas, and the passion with which he already expounds them in this preface. They both enthusiastically subscribed to Herder's doctrine of the people's language and the people's artistic achievements constituting the essence of a

[1] Particularly the thesis of F. A. Wolf's *Prolegomena ad Homerum* (1795), that the *Iliad* and *Odyssey* were concatenations of separate lays. As late as 1845, Jakob Grimm asked Vuk whether it might not be possible to construct an epic poem on Prince Marko, by joining together various songs. Vuk was well aware of the difficulties (e.g. the contradictions between the various single poems) and neglected the suggestion. See N. Banašević, 'Ranija i novija nauka i Vukovi pogledi na narodnu epiku', in *Prilozi*, xxx, nos. 3–4, 1964.

nation—Vuk partially restates it in the last sentence of his preface. Moreover Vuk lays down firmly that there will always be disputes about what constitutes the popular language of Serbia until an authoritative grammar and dictionary are available. In other words, he had by the end of January 1814 been persuaded of the need for the carrying out of Kopitar's linguistic programme, though he had not yet finally determined to carry it out himself.

Incidentally the language and orthography of his preface show that his ideas on these subjects and on how to write in truly popular style were very far from clearly formed. It is difficult or impossible to convey in translation the fact that Vuk's spelling and vocabulary is here little different from the old Slavonicized style favoured by the Church authorities, and later so sharply attacked by Vuk himself; it is in any case quite unlike the style which he came to adopt by 1818. It is theoretically conceivable that Vuk might have pulled his punches on this question and written in a slightly artificial style in contradiction to his own distinct ideas about spelling and language, in order to ease the reception of his book by the Serb communities of the Austrian Empire and by the Orthodox Church authorities themselves. It is however much more likely that his language and spelling were simply the traditional best that he knew at the time.

It seems indeed that Vuk had little idea of the storm which his ideas might raise among his Orthodox readers. The most surprising points in his preface, and the most personal ones, are the claims that it was the Serbs in Turkish-occupied Serbia, not the Serb community in the Austrian Empire, who had done most to uphold the Serbian idea; and that the purest Serbian was that spoken in Hercegovina and the heartland of Turkish-occupied Serbia. These claims were moreover linked with what reads, in spite of an apologetic note, rather like an attack on the priest–poet Mušicki and very much like an attack on the Austrian Serbs in general. The effect of Vuk's outburst is heightened by the long list of true Serbian names—a sort of Homeric catalogue—which is omitted from the translation; and by the sharp phrase at the end of the list, contrasting them with 'Jewish and Greek names, and God knows what'. Mušicki's own Christian name had been Luka and was changed to Lukian, when he became a monk.

It is perhaps surprising that Kopitar let this passage pass. There is no explanation of it other than as a spontaneous expression of

Vuk's own deepest feelings. His was a very strong personality, and, as already remarked, he could not write an advertisement or a formal dedication without letting something of himself appear through the routine phrases. In his preface Vuk was talking about subjects on which he felt strongly. Some of his argument is formal and modish, but there is no doubt of the sincerity of his last sentence in which he says that the songs have preserved 'the name and essence of the Serbia of former times'—the good old Serbia. Nor need his conviction be doubted that the Serbs in Serbia proper, where they were oppressed as a subject race by the Turks, but separated from them, had remained truer to themselves than in the Austrian Empire, where they were by the beginning of the nineteenth century treated comparatively well, but correspondingly exposed to outside influences of culture and religion. Vuk's sense of this contrast was of course heightened by his memories of the recent history of Karadjordje's short-lived principality of Serbia, where his countrymen had fought however vainly to preserve their liberties; while the Austrian Empire, including the Serbs there, had been, so it appeared, cautious in giving any help. Finally, though Vuk may at times have enjoyed posing as a 'child of nature', he was and always remained sensitive to the charge, so often made against him later by learned priests and their protagonists, that he was no more than a half-educated goatherd. There is a touch of venom as well as of patriotic warmth in Vuk's writing here, which not only typifies the man, but also gives a foretaste of many and prolonged controversies in the future. Vuk's preface is partly a manifesto and partly a declaration of war against the Serbs of the Austrian Empire, who thought themselves educated and were in Vuk's opinion ignorant of the essentials of their own language and national character.

VII

GRAMMAR AND 'POPULAR SONGS'

I

IN March 1814 Vuk left Vienna for a stay in Buda. His motives were mixed. One of them was no doubt to cut down his own expenses. Four months' living in Vienna had made large inroads into whatever money he had been able to bring with him or collect from his debtors in Serbia; he was living on a tiny margin—a situation that became all too familiar to him over the next twenty years. Vuk was also rather embarrassed at this time by Kopitar's concern with his lameness. It appears from one of his first letters to Kopitar (and from the time of his stay in Budapest these letters are a new and invaluable source of information) that a doctor to whom Kopitar had introduced him had recommended an operation. Vuk wrote (20 May 1814):

As for what you write about my taking fright at that young doctor and slipping away from Vienna to avoid being driven into hospital, you mustn't think that. It is quite different reasons which have made me move, and these I could only explain to you orally. If I haven't followed your kindly meant advice about going to hospital, the reason is as follows. I am sincerely convinced that no mortal skill or means can cure me—it would need Jesus Christ with all the power ascribed to him in the gospels.

Warm as is the tone of their correspondence, it appears from this letter that Vuk had not felt the need to keep Kopitar informed in any detail about his movements. This is the more interesting in that, by the time of his departure from Vienna, he was deeply engaged in, possibly almost hypnotized by, Kopitar's plans for providing a solid base for the revival of the Serbian language.

'The Serbs are still awaiting their Hercules–Korais,' Kopitar wrote in the *Serbian News*, 20 March 1814, 'who can clear out this Augean stable, and secure proper rights both for the dead language of the church and for the living language of the people. And that

Hercules will appear.' Vuk was to be Kopitar's Hercules, and his first labour was to be the writing of a Serbian grammar. He was at first reluctant, as he records in the autobiographical talk to Sreznevski already quoted:

... I heard Kopitar talk about a grammar, and, not knowing how to set about it, I proposed to Frušić and Davidović that we should write a Serbian grammar together, they helping me with their learning and I them with my knowledge of the Serbian language. 'Get on with you and your nonsense', they replied, and the matter stopped there. But as I learned more and more in talking with Kopitar and felt more and more the need of a Serbian grammar for my own purposes, I decided to write one myself. This pitiful attempt at a Serbian grammar, of which today I must be ashamed, was printed in 1814. Kopitar did not hide the little book's faults from me, but he was glad to see it printed, if only for the reason that he could now work on my pride—in the sense that I couldn't be content to stop at such a beginning. So he persuaded me to work on, and advised me to prepare myself for the grammarian's profession by other subsidiary work.

It seems that by March 1814 Vuk was convinced of his mission —even down to the grammar—and his main reason for going to Buda was probably to seek the company and help of Luka Milovanov, a friend from the time of his first stay in Buda, 1810. Milovanov was well educated—he knew Latin, German, and Hungarian as well as Serbian. His treatise on Serbian versification[1] —the publication of which had been banned by the Orthodox Church authorities—contained much material on the Serbian language, and he was as well qualified as anyone to offer useful advice on the composition of a Serbian grammar.

Little need be said about this work on which they jointly engaged. In Vuk's introduction to it he mentioned the works of Friedrich Adelung, the famous German grammarian, disclaiming any merit equal to theirs, but implying that he had seen them; no doubt Kopitar had shown them to him. Kopitar's own Slovene

[1] Luka Milovanov wrote his work on Serb rhyme and prosody in 1810. His father had migrated from Bosnia to Buda, after service in the Austrian army with the Serbian volunteers (*Freikorps*), and he himself became a teacher of the Serbian language there. Vuk later wrote an Aubreyesque 'Short Life' of him, describing how he became totally deaf by catching cold when on his way to teach mathematics to some Russian singers, and took to drink. The Serb group of Buda employed him as a translator, giving him a minimum monthly salary, clothes, and as much food and wine as necessary—'for he couldn't do a thing when sober, and didn't care for spirits'. He died in utter poverty in 1828.

grammar is not mentioned—nor, indeed, is there any acknowledgement of his help—another sign that Vuk was cautious about advertising this connection to the Serb community at large. His chief model, as he later told Sreznevski, was the Slavonic-Serbian grammar of Avram Mrazović, originally published in the eighteenth century.[1] Kopitar told Vuk that all he had to do was to substitute true Serbian forms for the Slavonic-Serbian ones in this book, and no doubt it was this encouragement which led him to undertake a work for which he had been so little trained. Vuk himself said that in general he provided the examples, while Milovanov advised him on the general rules.

As regards the merits of the work, Vuk's later deprecatory judgement is probably a case not of false but of undue modesty. His principal biographer, Ljubomir Stojanović, judged that it was by no means bad, considered as a first attempt at a Serbian grammar; the exposition of Serbian forms, Vuk's greatest contribution, was indeed excellent, and if his exposition of grammatical rules was inadequate, this only represented the generally deficient state of knowledge among the Serbs of Vuk's time.

Of more interest to a later generation than the substance of the grammar are Vuk's prefatory writings in connection with it. Vuk had incidentally mentioned the motives for undertaking the grammar in the preface to his first *Song-book*. He set them out much more explicitly in his advertisement for subscribers to the grammar:

For some years the Serbs have been emerging from the darkness of ignorance and have begun to be active in the field of literature. But the beginning of every action is difficult and beset by various obstacles, and in this undertaking of ours two obstacles have appeared, of which the greater is this: Serb writers, from the beginning until today, have never agreed about the language in which they wrote. Some began to write pure Slavonic; others, realizing that those Serbs for whom they were writing do not understand the Slavonic language, began to write a simple Serbian language such as the people themselves speak; others again thought it most unseemly and extraordinary to write books in simple Serbian, so they began to write in a new language, somewhere between Serbian and Slavonic. These three sorts of writer may still be found among our people. The first sort, who write in Slavonic and

---

[1] Mrazović's grammar was itself modelled on Russian grammars of the seventeenth century.

demand that all writing should be in Slavonic, are very few. The second and third sorts are by now more or less mixed up, and want to write in their own mother-tongue, like the other peoples of Europe; but the lack of any written rules of the Serbian language hinders their desire, presents them with difficulties and causes disagreement among them.

In writing this grammar, Vuk concludes, his wish had been to ease the writer's task.

Conscious from the beginning that his individual works were part of a plan for linguistic reform, Vuk gives here a typically simple and trenchant account of the state of the Serbian literary language as he knew it; but if the reader is to understand the full difficulty of the task which he had undertaken in evolving an agreed basis for a popular Serbian style, some account is necessary of the evolution of Serbian literary language in the eighteenth and early nineteenth century (something has already been said about this in Chapter V).

Down to about 1730 the Church Slavonic language was used for liturgical purposes and for such literature as existed (almost exclusively ecclesiastical). In 1727 the Russian teachers sent by the Orthodox Synod in Moscow to help in the education of the Serb community in Hungary, isolated as it was in a Catholic environment, introduced devotional literature written in the Russian language. The original liturgical books, written in Church Slavonic, were becoming increasingly unintelligible to the Serbian people as a whole; but, instead of trying to approximate the language of ritual and church literature to that of the common people, the Serbian Orthodox authorities, under Russian influence, adopted a new sort of old Slavonic, which became known as Slavonic-Serbian but was in fact closer to Russian than to Serb.[1] At the same time it was widely (and erroneously) believed that the old Slavonic language, in one form or another, was the original tongue from which the 'popular' Slavonic languages (including Serbian as spoken in the eighteenth century) derived—as French, Italian, and Spanish from the original Latin. Slavonic thus came to have a special prestige among the educated, while 'popular' Serbian was regarded as a degenerate mixture. Suvorov, the head of the Russian mission in 1727, spoke of 'popular' Serbian as the 'Hungarian-Turkish-German-Serbian language', and this came

[1] For a slightly fuller treatment of this subject see Appendix B.

to represent the view of many educated Serbs as well. In fact, not only did Slavonic-Serbian gain ground as a literary language during the second half of the eighteenth century, but it also began to have some vogue as a spoken language for the Serbian educated classes in the Austrian Empire.

In the meantime there was for many years virtually no literature in anything purporting to be popular Serbian. Zaharija Orphelin, who wrote Slavonic-Serbian, promised at one stage to use the popular tongue as well as Slavonic-Serbian in his *Serbo-Slavonic Magazine*; but it was not until the works of Dositej Obradović began to appear in 1783 that 'popular' Serbian received any firm literary encouragement. At the same time the cause of the 'popular' Serbian language received a severe setback. The language question became most unhappily connected with questions of interdenominational and international politics. The Austrian Government under Joseph II was anxious to secularize the education of its Serb as of its other subjects, partly in order to undermine Russian influence and weaken the link between the Serbian and Russian Orthodox Churches.[1] It thus encouraged the use of 'popular' language, rather than of Slavonic-Serbian, in Serbian elementary schools. Moreover it tried at the same time to substitute the Latin for the Cyrillic script. In 1779 a decree was issued forbidding the use of Cyrillic script except for Church literature, and this was only grudgingly rescinded after much agitation by the Orthodox Church hierarchy. It was particularly unfortunate for the development of Serbian literature that this bitter quarrel between the Austrian Government and the Orthodox Church about linguistic questions broke out at the time when Dositej Obradović was trying without any political afterthought to further the education of the Serb community through publications in 'popular' language. The Orthodox hierarchy began to look on national education, in schools or through books, as an essentially Austrian policy and as a prelude to Catholicization—they had no difficulty in regarding the anticlerical Dositej as in league, consciously or unconsciously, with their Catholic enemies. In particular Stefan Stratimirović, who became Metropolitan of Karlovci in 1790, conducted a fierce

[1] In fact this was already much weakened since the days of Suvorov's mission. The most important link between the Serbs of the Austrian Empire and Russia in the second half of the eighteenth century were the Serb officers who had joined the Russian official service, and often risen high in it.

campaign against 'Dositejism', and disciplined his own clergy sternly on this subject.

Thus Vuk's triple classification—pure Slavonic, simple 'popular' Serbian, and a mixed language—concealed some major political and religious snags. In one respect it was already out of date. There were hardly any proponents left of the 'pure Slavonic' language (whatever it might be). The obvious difference was between those who wanted to use the simple 'popular' language for literary purposes—and Dositej was regarded as their champion —and those, led by the Metropolitan Stratimirović, who favoured at least for profane literature the 'mixed language'—a 'popular' mode, enriched with Slavonic words. Again, Vuk's classification was misleading, in that few, if any, writers at this time dared to say that for literary purposes they favoured a purely 'popular' style. The real debate was between the various proponents of the mixed style. This could clearly mean many things to many people, and not all those who preached it commended themselves to the Church. In any case, this was a subject on which it was much easier to state blameless principles than to work out any satisfactory practice.

Vuk's own views on what constituted truly 'popular' language were not by any means fixed at this time. In a review written for the Vienna *Serbian News* in February 1814, he stated a general principle—the 'popular' language must be 'smoothed out', but never so as to lose its true character. Thus new words should be allowed for new ideas, but they must be Slavonic not foreign (e.g. *zvanično*, for 'official', not *oficialno*). No foreign words should be used if Serbian words existed for the same idea. Slavonic rather than Serbian words might be used, but they should be given as Serbian a form as possible. And so on. But in fact Vuk's own practice was far from consistent in these early years of writing, and his early works were full of what he would later have regarded as Slavonicisms.

Closely connected with the debate on popular style was the debate on the alphabet to be used in popular literature. This is also a subject to which some allusion has been made in Chapter V; it was of great importance for Vuk and his contemporaries. Very briefly, there were some Slavonic letters for which the Serbian language had no sound, and some which represented unnecessary duplication; while the Serbian language contained some other sounds for which there was no Slavonic sign. The Slavonic alphabet, with its 40 letters, was both an over-complicated and an inadequate instrument for the denotation of any form of 'popular' or 'mixed' Serbian language (the present Serbo-Croat alphabet in the form finally given to it by Vuk contains only 26 letters; a rather fuller account of the alphabetical problem is given in Appendix B). Confusion was increased, as Russian literature began to circulate or to be known among the Serb community, by the fact that there were now two Russian alphabets—the old Slavonic for ecclesiastical books, and for others the civil script, introduced in 1708 by Peter the Great.[1]

It was in fact on the alphabetical question that young Serb intellectuals had already made their voices heard most clearly against the Orthodox hierarchy. The book from which Vuk had tried to read a lesson in strategy to Karadjordje's Council had been printed (in 1805) in an alphabet which omitted the Russian 'hard sign'. It was regarded, said Vuk, as something unnatural, like a calf without horns. A drastic and sensible proposal for alphabetical reform, typified by the abolition of the 'hard sign', had been published in 1810 by Savo Mrkalj under the title *The Hardness of the Hard Sign, or the Sifting of the Alphabet*. Mrkalj justified his proposals very reasonably by insisting that in the absence of reform children wasted up to four years in learning[2] to read. It was he who first popularized for Serbia the maxim of the German grammarian Adelung: 'Write as you speak'—a maxim inseparably associated in modern Yugoslavia with Vuk, who appropriated it.

The Metropolitan Stratimirović reacted strongly to Mrkalj's work. He induced the Austrian authorities not only to forbid its further circulation, but also to order that no further books in the new Serbian alphabet should be printed. He was in fact even more opposed to alphabetical than to linguistic reform. So far as language was concerned, he could afford to express himself in

---

[1] See B. H. Sumner, *Peter the Great*, English Universities Press, 1950, p. 206: 'The new type was of considerable importance in emphasising the growing cultural secularization which had indeed begun before his day, but was now so marked in the increase of non-religious and of foreign books and in the developing taste for the Western cult of classicism and for Western romantic tales.'

Between 1750 and 1800, 40 per cent of the 8,000 books published in Russia were secular (James H. Billington, *The Icon and the Axe*, Weidenfeld and Nicolson, 1966, p. 214).

[2] Rather similarly, it was reckoned in 1958 that a simplification of Chinese 'characters' would save schoolchildren two years in attaining minimum literacy.

GRAMMAR AND 'POPULAR SONGS'

favour of a mixed style; the proposals in favour of it were various and vague, no one had come out clearly in favour of a radical interpretation, and partial reforms could be made which did not endanger the essence of the Slavonic-Serb language. Alphabetical reform on the other hand was more obviously and immediately opposed to Church tradition and practice; it seemed to be designed to open the door to Latin script and Catholicism.

Vuk's own views on what kind of alphabet could practically be adopted, quite apart from what was theoretically desirable, wavered at first with the strength of the opposition which he encountered; neither in his *Grammar* nor in his *Song-book* did he go all the way with Mrkalj's projected reform (he did not evolve his own final style of spelling till 1818). But he was aware that his orthography was a challenge to the traditionalists and foresaw the outcry which might be raised against his work, particularly in view of his own lack of obvious qualifications for it. To quote from the Preface to the Grammar:

The first and greatest criticism which will meet my Grammar will be on the score of the method of spelling. In truth I doubted much and pondered about this, but finally it seemed to me that the easiest way to adapt Serb orthography was to the principle: 'Speak as you write; and read as it is written.' Everyone will agree that the sort of orthography which falls under this principle is easiest and best. Whether my own method of spelling leads to it, must be judged by the wiser patrons of Serb literature. Only I would ask: let no one judge any method from superior learning or hearsay until he has read the whole and can judge of it without prejudice.

Vuk continued in a famous passage which proved to be all too prophetic: 'None the less, true tenderness for my race has urged me on and may lead me once and for all through this thorny thicket, even though on the other side I shall come through all torn and bleeding; still the path will be known by which someone else can decide more easily to make his way.'

By the end of June 1814, Vuk's work on his *Grammar* was done, and he made his way back to Vienna for four months to supervise the final stages of printing of the *Song-book* and to give the *Grammar* to the press. He missed Kopitar who had gone to Paris to organize the return to Vienna of books 'liberated' by Napoleon in the course of his residences there, and the two friends thus had further occasion for correspondence. By the end of October 1814, the

Song-book and *Grammar* had both appeared, and Vuk was again on his way to Buda and by gradual stages to Sremski Karlovci.

The winter of 1814–15 was not an encouraging time for him, for his first published works showed every sign of having at best fallen flat. As regards the *Song-book*, there was at first no published criticism in Serbian papers—printed literary criticism was not a regular feature at this time. The songs were not accessible to the Serbs of Serbia who might have relished them, and the Serb community in Hungary preferred a more artificial and literary style of poetry, with perhaps a small admixture of folk-song. Those who looked at the *Song-book* may well have been discouraged by the orthography. It was not until Jakob Grimm published his review in 1815 that it achieved recognition (more will be said of this in the next section); and Vuk achieved some small international reputation before being accepted by his own countrymen.

If the reaction to the *Song-book* was disappointing, Vuk's *Grammar* earned him virtually nothing but notoriety. The list of subscribers was very small and included only five or six of the intelligentsia—for Vuk was a completely unknown writer. Those who did subscribe to it were disappointed, having hoped for a grammar not of the popular but of the current literary tongue. There was virtually no sale, but enough circulation to excite charges of heresy against Vuk from the ecclesiastical authorities for his new orthography. Again it was not until well into 1815 that he received some recognition and comfort in the form of a glowing review from Kopitar.

2

Vuk spent the first half of 1815 in the Srem province, centred first on Sremski Karlovci, where his father was still living, and then on the monastery of Šišatovac. Here his host was the Archimandrite Lukian Mušicki, whom Vuk had suspected of teasing him in his schoolboy days and had come near to attacking in the preface to his first *Song-book*. Whatever the initial suspicions may have been on either side, Vuk and Mušicki at this stage became close friends, and Mušicki was enthusiastic about Vuk's work. This consisted in the early months of 1815 in the collection of more 'popular songs', especially the narrative and heroic kind, and at Karlovci Vuk made a great find, through his cousin Obrad, in

GRAMMAR AND 'POPULAR SONGS' 107

the person of Tešan Podrugović. This was the man of whom he wrote later:[1]

Though there are enough people who know many songs, it is still hard to find anyone who remembers them well and clearly. In this regard Tešan Podrugović (God rest his soul) was the first and best of all whom I have found and heard these ten years past. He came from somewhere between Bosnia and Hercegovina and first of all became a merchant; but afterwards he killed a Turk, went off to be a *hajduk*, and as a *hajduk* crossed into Serbia in 1807. . . .

Vuk continued his story in another passage:

. . . I found him at the beginning of 1815 in the greatest poverty at Karlovci (in the Srem, where he was cutting reeds in the marshland and carrying them on his back to town to sell them for a living). When I realized what songs he knew, and how many, I paid him by the day what he needed to live on and began to listen and take down songs from him. . . . But when afterwards, just before Easter, there was a rising against the Turks in Serbia,[2] it was as if a hundred thorns had got under his skin. I just managed somehow to keep him back over Easter, and wrote down some of the songs which he had recited to me in the wagon on the way from Karlovci; then immediately after Easter I took him by cart to Mitrovica, and from there he crossed into Serbia to fight the Turks again. When the Serbs made peace with the Turks that autumn, he went off to Bosnia; he settled in after his usual manner, collected a few horses and set up somewhere in the district of Srebnička to live as a carrier. But shortly afterwards some Turks beat him up, and he died of his injuries. When I took down songs from him, I don't know that he was much more than forty years old. He was a sensible fellow, and honest for a *hajduk*. He always liked to tell funny stories; in telling them he would never laugh, but put on something of a scowl. He knew at least another hundred heroic songs, all like those which I took down from him, and particularly about *hajduks* and leaders of outlaw bands from the Primorje, Bosnia, and Hercegovina (including fifteen about the Captain Mijat alone). Up to this time I've never come on anyone who knows songs as he knew them. Each of his songs was a good one, for he really understood and felt them (all the more since he didn't sing, but only recited), and thought about what he was saying.

[1] The passages on Tešan Podrugović are taken from Vuk's introductions to Books I and IV of the 'Leipzig' edition of his 'popular songs' (Leipzig, 1824, and Vienna, 1833). A translation of the greater part of the former is given at Appendix E.
[2] This was the 'Takova Buna' (revolt of Takovo) of April 1815, by which Miloš Obrenović established his position.

Tešan Podrugović was the first great artist that Vuk seems to have heard, at least in his adult years, in the singing of traditional narrative songs. In his childhood at Tršić he had listened to the traditional style applied to accounts of contemporary battles, or parodied in the record of village wooings; but Podrugović seems to have been a 'singer' of a completely different class from any known by Vuk hitherto.

Vuk could not have been aware from the first of the full value of his findings—that could only be established by comparison with other and lesser singers. In the meantime he was oppressed by lack of money, and by the onset of doubts which afflicted him often in the next years, whether he ought to commit himself finally to a literary life. He had evidently expressed such doubts to Kopitar, and the latter not only wrote to him words of consolation and encouragement, but proposed to him a literary plan. The nature of it can be seen from Vuk's reply to Kopitar of 8/20 April, the essential passages of which ran as follows:

Karlovci, 8/20 April, 1815

Good and dear friend,

I received your letter of (11 April) with indescribable joy. In truth I do not know if anyone in this world has been so blessed in friendship as I with you. I await impatiently the day when I shall come to you and embrace and kiss you; but it cannot be before August. In the meantime I shall search out popular songs (on this account I must travel through the Banat to Oršava, since a lady[1] from these parts has written to me saying that she has collected more than twenty songs), and I shall collect other material for various purposes and then when I come we can work on it. As for money, I think that I shall have enough to spend a winter there [in Vienna], and that in the meantime I can somehow earn as much again. Only I'm afraid that you may go away from Vienna, for Živkovic tells me that you're leaving it for good! I have collected a good many popular songs (I've already got more than 200 women's songs, and of heroic songs I have more than 20 on Prince Marko[2] alone, and shall get more). But if all the Serbian popular songs were collected and printed without picking and choosing, I assure you that it would be a book almost as big as the whole Bible.

As for *Volkssagen* [*sic*: folk-tales], I don't properly know what they are; if they are the stories told by ordinary people, then they exist

[1] Sara Karapandja, one of a famous East Serbian family.
[2] These were collected from Tešan Podrugović. On Prince Marko ('Marko Kraljević') see Appendix A, no. 6.

among the Serbs, just like the songs. Out of those which I alone have in my head, I could print a little book like the *Song-book*. There are some very fine and admirable ones, but for the most part they are indecent. I shall bring you a few, partly in my head, partly written, by way of example; then if you like them, we can easily get more of them. Proverbs are harder to collect, because one must wait until they come up in talk. As for a translation of the Bible into Serb, that would be a glorious and useful thing; but it should be for someone else, and not for me, since for that you need a number of people who know different languages.

Today I was with Mušicki. . . . As for Mušicki's not writing to you, there will be two reasons for that—his laziness and—various affairs. He really loves you and respects and honours you according to your merits but he seems to be lazy about writing. When I was with him last winter in February, he was saying even then that he would write to you straightaway; so it looks as if he has become lazy and neglectful. Now when I went to see him, he said that he would write to you by the first post, but I was sitting there ten days, and he said that he'd hardly begun. From this I conclude that he must be lazy about writing.

Here I am now at my *Grammar* and the Serbian alphabet. No one has frightened me or convinced me that this is not the proper way. I pay no attention to those who clatter like a chain on a cart, and I can convince any sensible and free-thinking man that this is the way it ought to be. But people don't like getting away from the old lettering. Some stick to it for their own gain; some are afraid, like small children beginning to walk on their own; and some just make a noise according to what others tell them. Well, let them all say what they like. When I come to you in Vienna, we shall print in the way which is most correct according to common sense and the essence of the language. I think that the Serbs should not stick for ever to the mistakes of other people (I mean the letters which they get from the Russians and the Greeks), but should be free for once to do something sensible on their own, even if other peoples have made their mistakes. And now is the time for this action, since it is already beginning—and up to now we haven't got a single book in proper and pure Serbian language.—Where I am now, I have to write with the 'hard sign'[1]—when I come to you, I shall try to publish a complete Serbian grammar, for which I'm steadily collecting odd material. . . .

The day after tomorrow I set out for Šišatovac again and shall be there till May . . . I'd be very pleased if by the 15th May I could get . . . the review of my *Grammar*; but if they praise the *Grammar*, that won't be to Mušicki's liking, for he said to me: 'I shall tell Kopitar, he can

---

[1] Vuk was writing from Karlovci, and felt bound to respect the susceptibilities of the Metropolitan Stratimirović and his entourage.

praise the *Song-book* as much as can be; but as for the *Grammar*, if I were there, I'd be pulling a little at his coat tails!

P.S. Your 'sister-in-law'[1] will now be coming at Easter to Šišatovac with her sister and mother; and I shall convey your greeting to her. It would be very tedious for me to come to Vienna and not find you there, for Stibšić doesn't understand either the language or things in general; and in such songs there must be some playful allusions to breasts and bosom.

This letter has been quoted at length for various reasons. It illustrates the tone of the friendship between Vuk and Kopitar, and the scope of the literary collaboration between them. Vuk carried out in the course of the next few years the programme set for him, though his translation of the Bible was not printed, for reasons which will become apparent, until 1847. His zeal in the collection of 'popular songs' is apparent; so is his continuing worry over alphabetical reform and his readiness to make some tactical concessions to the clergy of the Srem by using the detested and unnecessary 'hard sign' for the time being. (Kopitar was in fact to urge him a little later to pluck up his courage and be more consistent.) Perhaps the most humanly interesting point of the letter is the judgement on Mušicki. Whether or not Mušicki had taken note of Vuk's remarks in the preface to the first *Song-book*, he had clearly now been won over by Kopitar's introduction and Vuk's own personality to at least some of Vuk's causes, and in particular to renewed activity in the collection of 'popular songs'. He allowed Vuk to stay—not without risk to his ecclesiastical reputation—at the monastery of Šišatovac, showed him much personal kindness, contributed a number of songs to Vuk's second collection, and was in constant and intimate correspondence with Vuk over the next three years. Vuk however seems to have been, to say the least, very objective about Mušicki even in the days of their most intimate friendship.

In the spring of 1815 at Šišatovac, Vuk made another contact of great importance to his collection of ballads and particularly of contemporary songs. This was with the blind singer, Philip Višnjić, and again Vuk has himself left a short sketch of him, written some time later:

Philip Višnjić crossed into Serbia in 1804, the summer that the

[1] From 1814, there had been a standing joke between Vuk and Kopitar about marrying Kopitar to the sister of Vuk's cousin, Savka Živković.

Serbian forces retreated over the Drina, and from then until 1813 he lived only in the Serbian camps around the Drina (in 1810 he was at Loznica... when it was being defended against the Turks). In 1813 when the Turks reconquered Serbia, he fled with his family to the Srem, and settled in the village of Grk. I had heard that he knew some good songs, particularly about the times of Karadjordje,[1] and got him to come to Šišatovac in 1815 (after Podrugović had left me). I then took down from him not only the songs here printed but also a further three from Karadjordje's time, which I have left over to make a fifth book with, if God grant me health. By and large I think that Philip himself composed all those new songs of the times of Karadjordje. He told me that he became blind as a young man as the result of the smallpox, and then went around the whole Pashalik [province] of Bosnia and right down to Skadar, begging and singing to the *gusle*. I tried to persuade him to go back to Serbia, in the hope that he might thus compose some new songs, but I never succeeded in doing so, as he was very well-off in the Srem; wherever he went, people made much of him and gave him presents for his singing. He sent his son to school in Grk. He had his own horse and cart and had become a proper gentleman. A few years ago[2] I heard that he had died in Grk. When I took down songs from him, he was about 50 years old.

Towards the end of July 1815, Vuk had collected enough material for his second *Song-book* and set out again for Vienna, where he was to supervise the printing of it. This was a discouraging experience. Davidović had issued an advertisement for subscribers in June. By August only 25 subscribers had appeared, and eventually not more than 200 were mustered of the 600 which Vuk thought necessary. The list of copies to be sent to subscribers (which totalled 369) was probably largely fictitious—representing a new way of paying various old debts, contracted in the years 1811–13—and Vuk remained heavily in debt to Davidović for printing as a result. His disappointment is made clear in the preface to this second collection; he had hoped, he said, to publish a third and a fourth volume of songs, for which all the material was

---

[1] For a full-scale study of Višnjić's life and work, see M. Panić-Surep, *Philip Višnjić, Pesnik Bune*, Prosveta, Belgrade, 1956 and 1967. The connection between blindness and the gift of, or compulsion to, song is at least as old as Homeric legend. On the tradition in Yugoslavia, see Matija Murko, *Tragom Srpsko-Hrvatske narodne epike*, Zagreb, 1951, pp. 207–14. There was traditionally said to be a 'blind man's academy' at Irig in the Fruška Gora, north of Belgrade, where blind men were trained for singing and learned a sort of professional slang.

[2] The passage quoted was written in 1833 (introduction to Book IV of the 'Leipzig' collection of 'popular songs').

present, but he saw now that such plans were nothing but castles in the air.

Vuk dedicated his second collection to Kopitar—this was the first occasion on which he publicly acknowledged the debt to his great friend and literary mentor. In the dedication he records that he had debated with himself whether to address it to Kopitar or Mušicki; if Kopitar was the first to publish the songs, it was Mušicki who had first collected them. This passage he afterwards described as just a formal compliment.[1] It may indeed have contained some conscious exaggeration, but this was a time when Vuk was genuinely indebted to Mušicki for hospitality and perhaps for some stimulus too. Vuk was later apt to let his emotions colour his historical sense, and the near-dedication can be taken fairly literally.

As the first *Song-book* was devoted largely to the lyrical 'women's songs', so the second was devoted mainly to the Serb heroic songs, which thus appeared publicly for the first time in any numbers.[2] The way was now prepared for Vuk's ultimate break-through to the world of European scholarship and literature and the agent of this break-through was at hand. The great German philologist Jakob Grimm had spent some nine months in Vienna from October 1814 to June 1815, initially as a member of the Duke of Hesse-Kassel's delegation to the Vienna Congress. He did not neglect his private work,[3] and at the insistence of Kopitar began to study Slavonic languages, with particular attention to Serbian. On his return to Kassel, he wrote a review of Vuk's first *Song-book*, which was printed, again at Kopitar's instance, in the *Wiener Allgemeine Literarische Zeitung* of 15 September 1815. Grimm's was a thorough review even in those days of leisurely and large-scale literary criticism. He took Serbian lyric poetry seriously, even if his later reviews of the collections of mainly epic songs are more interesting. He remarks on the easy and natural personifications of Serbian poems:

This innocent poetry brings animals and plants into conversation with

---

[1] In his polemic writings of 1842, when he was defending himself against the charge of wholesale plagiarization from Mušicki and others.

[2] A few heroic songs had been published at the end of Vuk's first *Song-book*.

[3] Grimm was in fact active at this time in the political as well as the diplomatic and literary fields. From October 1814 to June 1815, he wrote a number of anonymous articles on German affairs for Görres's *Rheinische Merkur*. See W. Schoof, *Jakob Grimm: aus seinem Leben*, Bonn, 1961.

people, in order to pour out the full riches of its heart in the presence of quiet and trusted nature . . . what a gay and intimate note is sounded, when conversation is struck up with a star, or a meadow, or a river. . . . Nightingales and hawks bring messages, and ravens croak with hollow voice. . . . I know of no people that can display such a consummate wealth of love-songs, except for Solomon's *Song of Songs* in the Scriptures. Our old German *Minnelieder* came from the depth of the singers' hearts, and are more tender than any others, but are not so fresh and lively as these Serbian songs. And our popular love-songs on the other hand, while quite as fresh and perhaps gayer, are hardly as bold in execution. . . . Of all Slavonic races, the Serbs are by virtue of their language (so rich and suitable for poetry) the most blessed with poems, songs, and stories, and it looks as if the good God had by this rich gift of popular poetry wished to make up to them for their lack of books.

This was the highest praise from the best qualified source in Europe.

VIII

DICTIONARY AND MARRIAGE

1

VUK's main preoccupation for the next three years (autumn 1815 to the end of 1818) was the preparation and publication of his *Serbian Dictionary*, the idea of which Kopitar had put into his head early in 1814 as part of a literary programme. It was during Vuk's three-month stay in Vienna from August 1815 that Kopitar began to exert serious pressure on him. The method was described later by Vuk to Sreznevski:

> Kopitar had advised me earlier to busy myself with the collection of Serbian popular words. I'd promised him to do so, but nothing came of it then. Later on, he came to me all of a sudden and brought a whole pile of paper cut up into little slips. 'Now you think of the words which you know are in popular use, and write them down on these slips of paper, each on its own slip. Then little by little you'll collect a whole dictionary full.' The work wasn't hard, and I began to attend to it seriously. To make it easier for me, Kopitar gave me various dictionaries to look at. In fact, I glanced at these dictionaries rather than reading them, and it was much more out of my own head that I wrote down the words on my slips of paper; I never took from dictionaries words which I did not know with absolute assurance to be in popular use. When I came back to Vienna in 1816, I brought with me a fair-size book of slips with Serbian words. . . .

The preliminary work of collecting and noting the Serbian words—which proved to be much the easiest part of the whole affair—was done early in 1816, between Karlovci and Šišatovac, where Vuk was again staying with Mušicki. By March he was already asking Frušić to insert an announcement in the *Serbian News* about the forthcoming appearance of the *Dictionary*, and telling Kopitar to set to work on attracting subscribers. In April he had collected twenty thousand words, and set out for Belgrade via Sremska Mitrovica and Šabac.

The ostensible and perhaps the only reason for his journey was

DICTIONARY AND MARRIAGE

to make a tour in Serbia in order to record new words and dialect variations. Serbia was again comparatively peaceful. By now the effective ruler of the country was a man who will figure largely in later chapters. Miloš Obrenović was born about 1780 into a rich peasant family, and before 1804 had been engaged in cattle-dealing and in the salt trade. During the war he did not play a particularly prominent part in the fighting, but emerged as a shrewd and successful captain. Moreover he survived a major clash with Karadjordje without being virtually exiled, like some of the other generals. In 1813 he elected to stay behind in Serbia after the collapse, instead of going to Austria or Russia, like so many of his colleagues. He settled for a policy of nominal collaboration with the Turks, fostering national resistance in the meantime as best he could. His chosen role was a highly dangerous one, brilliantly performed. In spring 1815 he led a further rising (the 'Takovo revolt') against the Turks—he had little choice but to do so, if he was to retain any credit in Serbia[1]—and then negotiated a settlement with them, as the one man who could ensure a reasonable degree of order for them in their unruly province. This settlement enabled him eventually to run the government of Serbia, nominally as an agent of the Sultan, and in fact with a good deal of independence. As conditions stabilized, many of those Serbs who had fled over the Sava or Danube with Karadjordje in 1813 began to return and settle down again.

Vuk's own journey to Belgrade in the spring of 1816 may conceivably have had some political undertones. From the autumn of 1815 he had been in touch with Jakob Nenadović, one of Karadjordje's chieftains, now in exile. Vuk had begun to collect from him historical data about the uprising of 1804, but he also sent messages to him from Serbia couched in rather naïvely cryptic language. These could have had (there is no proof), or have been thought to have, some reference to the hopes cherished by a number of Serb

[1] The nominal object of the Takovo rising was not to regain independence for Serbia, but to make the Turks apply the full terms of the Treaty of Bucharest. It was a genuinely national movement; Vuk says that even the substantial property-owners backed it, in contrast to that of 1804. Miloš was bound to go along with it, more particularly as he had made no move while the Turks suppressed a revolt of the previous autumn ('Hadzi Prodan's rising'). It was after this occasion that Miloš uttered one of his most famous *mots*. A Turkish official pointed to the severed head of a suspected rebel, and said to Miloš: 'Soon it will be your turn.' Miloš replied: 'My own head I threw into the [executioner's] bag long ago, and it's someone else's that I carry around.'

exiles for a new uprising, led by Karadjordje (who was by 1816 in St. Petersburg and in touch with the Greek Hetaireia),[1] to complete the liberation of Serbia and to coincide with a rising in Greece. It is certain that from the autumn of 1815 onwards Vuk was an object of suspicion to the Vienna police for contact with Serbian exiles and at least one Russian officer of Serb origin. Kopitar had to reassure the police that Vuk was not a Russian agent.

Probably Vuk had no close connection with high international politics and his journey to Serbia certainly had a literary object important to him—the collection of new words for his *Dictionary*. It is, however, likely that during his visit to Belgrade Vuk examined carefully other possibilities for a new career in the Serbia of Miloš Obrenović. His correspondence of 1816–17 contains many allusions to such ideas. He was particularly drawn to Negotin and the Krajina district, where he had served in 1811–13 and probably made some profits in the salt trade. Vuk was in touch with Sara Mihailova Karapandžić, who cherished a faithful and perhaps romantic friendship for him from those days, about the possibility of settling again in this district, if necessary in the employment of a Turkish commander (who was however reported to have 'too many Greeks in his service already'). Shortly after, his old companion Stefan Živković strongly recommended to him the prospects of living as a small farmer in the Šabac or Valjevo district, and making a living by brewing *rakija*. Vuk continued to think, at least till the end of 1817, of moving to Serbia and abandoning the literary life. In June 1816, however, he decided to return to Austria. Among his reasons was no doubt the tender feeling, of which more is to be said in this chapter, between him and his future wife, Anna Kraus.

At all events, he made his way from Belgrade, without journeying further southwards, to stay with Mušicki at Šišatovac and from there at the end of August 1816 to Vienna again. Round about this time the Metropolitan Stratimirović had issued an order against giving hospitality to laymen in monasteries; the order was not the occasion of Vuk's departure, but no doubt Mušicki was glad enough to see his guest leave. In a letter of 1817, he described to Vuk the wigging which Stratimirović gave him for harbouring

---

[1] The Hetaireia (the full title was 'philiké Hetaireia' or 'friendly society') was founded at Odessa in 1814, as a secret society of expatriate Greeks to further the independence of their native land; it had an elaborate hierarchy, somewhat like that of the Freemasons.

Vuk at Šišatovac: 'How could you keep that blasphemer among your priests, take him around the monasteries, and try to secure a place for him?' In another letter he described to Vuk how he had had to hide Vuk's portrait beneath another in his house, to escape the eye of one of the Metropolitan's emissaries—'Had he seen it, I know that he would have denounced me, and an anathema would have arrived, ordering that it too should be "cast out, driven forth and expelled".' Vuk was already a doubtful friend for a cleric.

2

On Vuk's return to Vienna in August 1816, Kopitar and he began serious joint work on the final version of his *Dictionary*. The general proceedings were outlined later to Sreznevski:

Kopitar would come to my house every day late in the afternoon, taking no notice of rain or mud, and we'd sit at our job until dark. I would take the bits of paper one after another and explain to him the meaning of each word. I'd explain until I could see that Kopitar completely understood, and he would then translate the words into German and Latin, consulting in doubtful cases Adelung . . . and other dictionaries. Sometimes, if he thought necessary, he would ask me to write down an example to make it easier to understand the sense of a word, or to give a full description of some objects, customs, etc. Our work grew day by day, and in this way the dictionary was ready for printing and printed in 1818. That period of daily conversations with Kopitar will always be unforgettable for me. It was then that my earlier, general, and instinctive knowledge of the Serbian language was enlivened into full consciousness. Every day I had the opportunity of thinking about the form of words, their grammatical declension, the different pronunciation of them in local dialects, and the syntactical arrangement of words.

The work proceeded fast and the *Dictionary* in Serbian, German, and Latin was finished in April 1817. The real difficulties were still to come and were concerned with the printing. The first obstacle was set in Vuk's path by the Metropolitan Stratimirović. He was at this time not irrevocably hostile to Vuk; he had not liked the orthography of the *Grammar*, but seemed to approve the *Song-books* and other expressions of national culture. He was, however, intent on preserving the domination of the Orthodox Church over the cultural life of the Serb community in the

Austrian Empire. The publication of Vuk's first works in Vienna was in contravention of the monopoly of printing books in Serbian given to the Serbian press at Buda by Leopold II (newspapers were a different matter). It was Stratimirović who stirred the Buda firm to protest, and their complaint was successful; from 1816 there was a temporary ban on the printing of Serbian books in Vienna. Kopitar tried various ways round. Davidović, editor of the *Serbian News*, tried to get a licence for a new Serbian press to print books. Kopitar himself, together with Schnürer, owner of the existing Serb press in Vienna, tried to move the Court Chancellery to give special treatment to Vuk's *Dictionary*, on the ground that it was only one-third a Serbian book (one-third being Latin, and the remaining one-third German). Before any decision could be given on this ingenious plea, Kopitar had solved this particular problem by persuading the Armenian Mehitarists to start on printing the *Dictionary*.[1]

There remained the worst obstacle of all, finance. As usual the amount of subscriptions collected was nowhere near enough to cover the cost of printing, and the costs, when a printer had been found, were constantly underestimated. The details of Vuk's appeals for money and the names of his benefactors are of little interest to the English reader. They involved, however, Vuk's first contact with Miloš Obrenović in Serbia; Miloš had sent a gift of 100 ducats to Davidović for the *Serbian News*; and this encouraged Vuk to appeal to him by letter in October 1816. The letter marked the beginning of a curiously close but always cautious and often hostile relationship between two of the founding fathers of Serbia. Vuk wrote to Miloš that he should subscribe to the printing of the *Dictionary* in return for the honour of having it dedicated to him and specified the following reasons:

1. You will thus confer great benefit and glory on the whole Serb people, and especially in Serbia; and for the benefit and glory of the Serb people you have spared neither your blood nor your life.
2. You will give me the help and succour that is fitting; for I am your only true author from Serbia, and I have made cheerful the countenance of all Serbs and done them honour.

[1] The Mehitarists were Armenian Catholic monks of an order founded in the seventeenth century with the object of converting their fellow countrymen. They migrated from Istanbul via the Morea to Venice, where they founded a press; thence after 1770 to Trieste; and finally in 1810 to Vienna, where they started to print in 1811.

DICTIONARY AND MARRIAGE

3. I shall dedicate this book to your glorious name, and this shall be as a crown for all your glorious manly deeds. The world will see that, apart from all your brave and far-famed deeds, you are concerned for the enlightenment of the Serb people, and for this all Slavonic peoples from Peter's town [St. Petersburg] to Dubrovnik will be thankful to you. The heart of every true Serb from the Adriatic sea to Timok, from Montenegro to Pest . . . will leap for joy, when he sees a Serbian dictionary, written by a Serb, printed at the expense of the first man and head of all the Serbs and dedicated to his glorious name. A grateful posterity will read and tell with joy and gratitude a thousand years afterwards in what manner, and at what time, you paid for the printing of the first Serbian dictionary.

The tone of Vuk's letter is far from humble, and the style is that curious mixture of literary formality and precise common sense which is typical of his earlier writings. He envisaged his dictionary as much more than a labour of lexicography. It was to be, in a Herderian formula suggested by Mušicki, a 'Treasury of Serbian popular thought'—or, in a more detailed and less intelligible phrase, of 'Serbian intellectual nationhood'. It is doubtful whether Miloš Obrenović was at any time very susceptible to such lofty thoughts, and the money that came into his hands was devoted mainly to bribing the Turks and building up his personal position. After prolonged negotiations with Frušić, who followed up Vuk's letter with a visit to Belgrade, Miloš's best offer was 50 ducats on the appearance of the book; negotiations fell through, though the knowledge that they were being conducted may have helped Vuk to obtain money from other Serb benefactors.

At this stage, his thoughts had turned to getting financial support from Russian and Austrian official quarters. In a draft letter addressed but never sent to Mušicki, dated 3 December 1818, he described his further efforts, and gave a bitter account of the pains and misery which he suffered over the *Dictionary*:

The Serbian Dictionary has eaten up my life. I wrote it easily enough, but in having it printed I lost what is man's most precious possession in this world—health. From last summer I have often been pushed so hard that I haven't had a single *kreuzer* (and that in Vienna!). I have sold what I could (in the end the shirts off my back and handkerchiefs out of my pocket—just so as not to die of hunger). I wouldn't ask anything more of Tirka and Maca,[1] who gave me 300 florins last

---

[1] 'Maca', nickname derived from 'Maria', the wife of Todar Tirka, a Serb

year; and for all that other Serb people (or better, hagglers) here cared, I could have died of hunger a hundred times. For example Stevan Konstantinović has a couple of houses here and one in Graz, and is planning to buy a village in the Banat for 1000 silver *forints*—and he wouldn't loan me 50 *forints* for a month, but just said he hadn't the money and that times are such that he can't get that amount in a week of trading. As for Davidović, you know what a big donkey he is from his newspapers and books, and he's just as big a villain. A long time ago I asked him for 200 *forints* to pay for some paper, and he gave it to me without a word, because he thought that I had money; but now when he saw I was in a fix, he worried his brains out asking me for those 200 *forints*, saying that he must have them to pay the police (!). I wanted to go to Razumovski[1] but couldn't get at him, so went off to see his State counsellor Kudriavski, and asked him to get the Prince to put himself down for just 25 books. He said that he'd consult him, and that I should come back in 5 days. When I went to see him after 5 days, he wouldn't admit me but answered by a servant that he had to send off his diplomatic despatches that day, and that I should come at the end of the month, when their accountant would have received money. When I came at the end of the month, he replied by a servant that there was nothing for me. Then I approached Count Jelovkin, the Grand Vizir from Moscow [perhaps Vuk meant Count Golovkin], and he told me curtly that we Serbs are just Germans, that the Muscovites have never cared about us, don't care about us now, and have no cause to do so; that he couldn't give me a single *kreuzer*, much less a hundred florins, of his own or the Tsar's money. He told me to go to the German Government and ask help from them; then he returned to me the second part of the *Song-book* which I had brought him as a gift; saying that he couldn't understand Serb and had no time to read. All this he said to me with a smiling and well-scrubbed Ministerial face. I couldn't say a thing in reply, but began to smile myself, wondering how politics could be so mannerless.

Up to then, it had never occurred to me to go to the German Kaiser, but when Jelovkin mentioned it, despair began to drive me, and I thought to myself: Well, let's try that too, if only to make sure that I've done everything in my power. So that very day I went in the afternoon to the private office to write myself down among those who were going to the Kaiser for an audience. When I arrived at the office, they told me that I couldn't put my name down [*sic*: Vuk clearly meant 'get in']

merchant with whom Vuk had become acquainted in Eastern Serbia in 1813. Maria was by birth one of the Demelić family, from which Vuk later tried to find bridegrooms for Miloš Obrenović's daughters.

[1] Count A. K. Razumovski, the Russian Ambassador and amateur violinist, to whom Beethoven dedicated his three quartets, opus 59.

DICTIONARY AND MARRIAGE

for another 8 days. In the interval I prepared my petition . . . and in this petition I begged the Kaiser to order the Illyrian Chancellery to subscribe for 150 copies, so that I could finish the book and pay for the printing; and I reminded him of how his court in another such case had helped the Franciscan Štuli[1] for some years, etc. After 8 days, I went to see the Kaiser. When I entered the private office at 7 in the morning, there were 100 men and women waiting in one room. I imagined we'd all have our fixed time for talking to the Kaiser, and I thought that we'd go in one by one, as to a priest for confession. Then we went into a big reception room, and stood in order all round, when all of a sudden a whisper began to be heard: 'Is that the Kaiser?' I looked, and there he was going from one to another, taking the petitions from each and asking what it was about. Then I saw what sort of an audience this would be, and began to repent of having given myself so much trouble and climbed so often to the third floor (I'd thought that I'd be received by the Kaiser in his room, and talk to him alone, as man to man); if I'd been near the door, I'd have gone out right away, but seeing that I was on the far side of the hall, I thought to myself: 'Well, things have gone this far, so let them take their course.' When the Kaiser came to me, I gave him my petition, but what could I say to him with such a crowd listening: (I suppose that the whole thing has been arranged so that people can't beg of him personally and reveal all their troubles). When he took my petition, he said that I'd get what I wanted. . . .

Needless to say, Vuk got nothing from the Kaiser's court at this time, and they had already refused him the pension which Kopitar had very hopefully asked for him (1816). Various private contributors came forward, and the Metropolitan Stratimirović himself subscribed 400 *forints*; but by October 1818 printing was again held up for lack of money. Vuk turned once more to the prosperous Serb merchant, Tirka, who had already lent him 3,000 *forints* and refused once to give any further aid. In a desperate letter he begged for the loan of the 2,000 *forints* still necessary to enable printing to be completed: 'I have now no other refuge but you. Now that you have helped me to get so far, and I have swum practically to the end, dont leave me to drown at the last stage. For all the present shortage of money and bad state of trade, you will never feel the absence of these 2,000 *forints*, and they will enable me to finish this work, which is of no small importance.

[1] Joakim Štuli, author of a Serbo-Croat dictionary published 1801–10. This covered the speech of the north-western part of the country only and was printed in Latin letters.

I shall make my own fortune, and will save those 3,000 *forints* which you gave me last year. Without the 2,000 *forints*, I shall be completely overwhelmed, by labour and shame and need and trouble. . . .' Tirka made the further loan, and the printing of the *Dictionary* was completed at the end of 1818.

3

The two previous years were among the most wretched of Vuk's never affluent life. Physical need, and hunger most of all, brought on ill health, at a time when good health and an easy temperament were most needed. Vuk felt acutely the degradation of having virtually to beg from men to whom he felt himself in most ways superior. His natural tone was that which he adopted in the letter to Miloš Obrenović quoted above, and when he could not use it he compensated in private utterance by great bitterness about his fellow Serbs; the remarks about Davidović in the draft letter to Mušicki are paralleled by others in the preface to the *Dictionary*: 'Among our people there are richer men than Tirka, who sit in cafés and at well-set tables and sigh so deeply at any mention of the "people" that you would swear that they'd give their very life's blood for the "people", its good fortune and fame. But let the "people" come into their house and ask not for 5,000 *forints* which Mr. Tirka gave for the *Dictionary*, but for 5,000 pence; they'll start shivering right away as if death itself had come into their presence.' The iron and acid elements in his character were reinforced in this period, and he remained—he had never been anything else—an extremely ill foe.

His bitterness was compounded by his assumption of family responsibilities under difficult circumstances. From the autumn of 1814, when Vuk's landlady in Vienna, Frau Kraus, and her daughter Anna had nursed him through an illness, he had formed an attachment to Anna and from the beginning of 1815 wrote to her as her fiancé (the only love-letters of Vuk which have been preserved are a few dating from this year). The course of true love did not run smooth. Anna's parents, and she herself, were staunch Catholics and were unhappy about her marriage to an Orthodox Serb of free-thinking tendencies. Vuk's own Serb friends were equally doubtful about his choice. A number of letters on the subject between him and Mušicki are preserved. One of these, from Vuk to Mušicki at the end of 1816, illustrates the tone of their correspondence, and Vuk's rather restrained raptures about his fiancée:

> You tell me that there's some Venus blooming for me in Resava [in East Serbia], How am I going to leave your *Messenger*[1] in Vienna in order to go to Resava? Perhaps you'll say, 'Wait a little'? Now, don't tie up the donkey while the grass is growing. Do you realize that by now I'm in my thirtieth year? My Chloe is no great beauty . . . but she's truly most sensible. No Ljubosava[2] in all the world could love and honour me as she has done. . . . And I've found a [Serb] name for her—Milica. If my nationality can be impaired or taken away from me by various clerks and enemies of mine, then be sure that I care nothing for it. I'd become a Turk tomorrow, so long as my friends would say even then that I'd always been a true Serb and would never cease to be. So couldn't you really bless my choice for me?

Vuk himself may have been prepared to give up Anna earlier in 1816 when he was thinking of settling in Serbia again and making plans on the spot to this end. In 1817, however, delays and opposition to the match came from the Kraus family. The marriage contract was signed only in December 1817, and the marriage finally took place in a Catholic Church on 16 January 1818. Only a month later, a son was born to Vuk and Anna, who may have chosen to break her parents' resistance by facing them with a *fait accompli*. Mušicki, on hearing the news of Vuk's marriage, could say no more than that it made him very sad, and that Vuk's marriage with a foreigner would turn many Serbs against him—a prophecy which proved all too accurate.

Vuk's main comfort in the unhappy years 1817–18 lay in his strong sense of the value of his *Dictionary* for the development of the Serb nation; though the same sentiment was a principal cause of unhappiness too, when it seemed that all his work was going to waste. He meant literally enough his remarks (for instance in his letter to Miloš Obrenović) about the glory that would accrue to the Serb people from the *Dictionary*. This was indeed no ordinary dictionary, but a highly original work. Even from the strictly lexicographical point of view, it was virtually all new. Dobrovski

---

[1] Mušicki had wanted Vuk to undertake the editorship of a new Serbian newspaper to be founded in Vienna. The scheme came to nothing.

[2] 'Ljubosava', an imaginary Serb flame of Vuk, with a typically Serbian name, invented by Mušicki.

had thought that there was no need for more than a supplement to previous Slavonic-Serbian dictionaries; but Vuk took from these only what his ears had verified in the common speech of the people. He observed this principle, indeed, so meticulously as to include Serbian words which he had heard but did not fully understand, and Turkish words in common use; though he was anxious ultimately to purify the language, popular usage was the supreme law for him. So far as his experience enabled him to do so, he noted dialect forms for various words, and even went into detail about the exact districts in which such forms were used. In a supplement to his preface, he included a short grammatical essay in which he revised some of the views expressed in his *Grammar* of 1815.

With all this innovation, however, Vuk was much more than a lexicographer and grammarian. He intended the *Dictionary* to make known the life, customs, and to some extent the history of the Serb people. Thus he would illustrate particular words by quoting popular riddles or folk-stories or by describing folk-customs at some length. Some examples of the more narrative entries in the *Dictionary* have already been quoted for their autobiographical interests, and others are translated in Appendix A. It was Kopitar who originally suggested enlarging the scope of the book in this way, but obviously Vuk himself responded with enthusiasm. The result is that the *Dictionary* is one of the best 'lucky dip' books imaginable—it was possible to issue a substantial anthology of the more narrative entries in celebration of the centenary of Vuk's death.[1] In one respect, Vuk's desire to illustrate faithfully popular language and customs, his realism, and, it is fair to say, his own (and Kopitar's) tastes led him too far for his own immediate good. Serbian is a rich and various language and Vuk included in the first edition of the *Dictionary* many words and expressions not common in polite circles, and also a number of stories which would clearly be considered too daring by the dignitaries of the Orthodox Church[2] (in some cases, even where stories were not told in full, there were clear enough allusions to them). Posterity with different ideas about historical accuracy, moral standards,

---

[1] Under the title *Raskovnik* (a magic herb which will open all locks), Prosveta, Belgrade, 1964.

[2] An entry which caused particular and understandable offence to the Orthodox Church authorities was that under *Pričešćalo* or 'Communion'. For a translation of the story told by Vuk under this heading, see Appendix A, no. 12.

DICTIONARY AND MARRIAGE

and humour may be unreservedly grateful to Vuk for his catholic taste and conscientious realism; but the leaders of the Orthodox Church welcomed the chance of being able with some show of reason to accuse Vuk of corrupting the youth and undermining good manners.

4

For the *Dictionary*, when it finally appeared, gave Stratimirović and his followers many other causes for offence. Its publication was an important step in Kopitar's and Vuk's grand design to provide a model for linguistic and orthographic usage, in order to further popular education and the growth of a genuinely popular literature in Serbia. So far as the popular language was concerned, Vuk was attacked mainly for recording vulgar or essentially foreign words. This was a matter for argument. It was, however, indisputable that he had committed himself on the orthographical problem. The process of lexicographical work in itself forced Vuk, even if he had not been willing, to declare where he stood on the crucial question of the alphabet, if only to settle the alphabetical order of the words in the *Dictionary*. While he had wavered on orthographical questions during his first two years of literary work, and debated in detail with Mušicki and other correspondents, for instance about the form of some of the new letters to be put into his revised alphabet, his tone towards the Church authorities and their conservative followers was by 1816–17 quite firm at least in private. He asked Kopitar for example: 'Write to the Bishop of Zagreb [about subscriptions]. I have little hope of our own people, since they think it a blessed thing to fight against the Serbian language. But if God grants that I can get the money from somewhere, I shan't take lessons in Serbian language or spelling from them, but shall write a nice "j"[1] and write my mother-tongue in the way that millions of people talk it. Anyone who wants to show that they speak wrong, and to correct them, is free to try his luck, but he won't drag me into it.' Or he would argue ironically that 'Cyrillic letters are formed only for Holy Scripture. It would be a disgrace for them if we printed in them this simple, degenerate, herdsmen's tongue (as the court of Karlovci call it), particularly with the Serbian accentuation. No, let's leave the Cyrillic letters to priests and monks who anyhow want to have everything different

[1] See Appendix B on the Serb and Slavonic alphabets.

to the rest of the people, and they can shut them up into prayer-books and hymn-books together with the artificial Slavonic language of today.'[1]

The *Dictionary* was ultimately printed in almost the final form of the alphabet adopted by Vuk. He knew that this would cause trouble and wrote in his preface:

> The greatest outcry is going to be against the orthography; but I hope that all our men of letters who know anything about language and spelling will be on my side in this matter, and they will see that the Serbian language cannot be written in any other way than this, the fitting one. Many who know nothing about language, letters, or grammar, think and write that the Serbian language should be written in Slavonic orthography; but the Serbs themselves saw over 500 years ago that this was impossible, and introduced then ... letters which are not to be found in Slavonic books.

On the alphabet Vuk was thus issuing a definite and fairly sharp challenge, but at least he did not do so until the *Dictionary* appeared. On the question of 'popular' language, he had already been the centre of public controversy, ensuring thereby that not only the Orthodox Church authorities but also many 'moderates' in literary affairs should be very ready to criticize his own works. Not even his greatest admirer could deny that he acted in an extremely provocative way. Vuk's behaviour in literary debate is so typical of his character and methods that it must be briefly recorded, however dry the details. In May 1814 he had embodied his views (not yet fully formed) on popular language in a criticism of a novel *The Lonely Lad* by Milovan Vidaković, a noted and senior literary figure of the time,[2] who favoured a 'mixed' form of literary language—based on the popular tongue, but beautified and made smooth by additions from Slavonic forms; Vidaković's theory was not far from Vuk's own at the time. It was his practice which attracted Vuk's criticism; this was not published until September 1815, when it appeared in the *Serbian News*. It was anonymous, but caused a sensation. This was the first occasion on

---

[1] Extract from a letter to Pavle Solarić, who was working at the Serbian press in Venice.

[2] Milovan Vidaković, poet and novelist, 1780–1841. His poems dealt mainly with sacred subjects, his novels were based either on German romantic models, or on moral tales such as Fénélon's *Télémaque*. Jovan Skerlić, the historian of Serb literature, describes his work as a mixture of 'exaggerated fancy and incessant moralizing'.

which any literary criticism had been published in any Serbian newspaper, and it was sharp enough, though purely linguistic. Vuk accused the well-established and popular Vidaković of using too many Slavonic and Magyar provincial forms. Vidaković was furious and hit back in public, asking his anonymous reviewer why he should be expected to write in the language of the kitchen, and why the learned Germans 'don't also write as their swine-herds and goat-herds speak'. He complained of Vuk's lofty and didactic tone and particularly of his implied ban on the use of foreign words—the Germans after all admitted plenty of Latin and French words, but 'we all jump on the wretched Serb who has only just taken a pen into his weak hand, and forbid him even to use his own old Slavonic words . . .'.

Vidaković was not content with a single round of critical battle. In the preface to his next novel, *Ljubomir in Elysium*, published in 1816, he again defended his theory of 'beautified' popular language. Vuk's reply was reserved for some time; Vidaković had complained that Vuk's first criticism had been purely linguistic and had not dwelt on the substance of his edifying tale. Vuk made up for this in his second criticism by printing an enormously long synopsis of *Ljubomir* with special attention to its historical inaccuracies and absurdities (e.g. the drinking of coffee in thirteenth-century Serbia), and a good deal of scorn for its moral tone. Vuk recommended to the author a long list of the best novels for his reading (Kopitar must certainly have inspired this part of his review), including Fielding's *Tomchjonson*, and ended the first half of his criticism by saying that Vidaković clearly knows no 'History, Geography, Logic, Poetry, or Rhetoric; neither does he know what morals or shame or decency are; nor does he know the character of our people, nor anything at all'.

Not unnaturally, Vidaković was infuriated. Another round of public debate took place between the antagonists before Vuk's *Dictionary* reached the hands of readers and reviewers. Vidaković made his case again in the preface of the third part of his *Ljubomir* (1818), and Vuk hit back in an essay (this time under his own name—the first two had been anonymous), which contained two of his most famous controversial passages. Vidaković had expressed the hope that his new volume of *Ljubomir* would not get into the hands of his critic, and proceeded in pathetic tone: 'But even if the candlestick with the candle is put under the bed,[1] it will still shine; the critic cannot put his hand over everyone's eyes to prevent them looking on the midday sun, and seeing the truth.' To which Vuk replied: 'Christ said that the candle would not shine under a bed, and Mr. Vidaković contradicts this. What would a candle be doing under a bed? Wouldn't it be likely to set fire to the bed and burn the house? Mr. Vidaković is welcome to put a candle under the bed in his own house, but we hope that he will first set up house well away from other people.' A passage even more appreciated by Vuk's friends was that in which he defended his own against Vidaković's interpretation of a catch-phrase for anarchy, 'the rule of Baba Smiljana' (which can be roughly translated 'of Granny Smiles'):

It looks to us as if Mr. Candlestick still does not rightly know who Granny Smiles is (though he sticks to her rules so well). Granny Smiles is a great lady, who keeps a school for the Slavonic-Serbian language. Her school prides itself particularly on taking only grown-up and learned people, and on the fact that she is such a good and gracious lady that there are no second and third classes with her, but only top-class people. Though at another school someone might be in the second or third class, with her he may be at the top. Her pupils have no rules but those of 'taste' (each of his own). With her you can't go wrong. Whatever anyone says or writes is correct. With her everyone knows everything. And she is given such a charming name because she smiles on everyone. That is Granny Smiles; all the rest of our grannies talk according to the rules of grammar, and their old men too. . . .

Vuk's intimate friends were delighted by this polemic, but Mušicki and others thought that he had gone too far in attacking the eminent and harmless Vidaković so savagely. The great majority of Serbs were in fact on Vidaković's side. By 1818, however, there was no holding Vuk. His view was that it was better to state clearly his full objectives in the field of linguistic reform, and not to proceed step by step, as Mušicki and others would have wished. He made his clear and full statement in the preface to his *Dictionary*, emphasizing once again the absence of grammatical rules for the Serb language, and the disastrous results of this deficiency for Serbian literature. But this, he says, is a deficiency shared by other Slavonic peoples. It is only the Serbs who suffer from having two languages, Serb and Slavonic (which itself has no proper grammar and rules), and who are trying to

---

[1] 'Bed' stands in the Orthodox text of the Bible for the English 'bushel'.

escape from their troubles by mixing the two to make a third. It is, he says, simply not the case that Slavonic is more truly and originally Serbian than the popular Serbian language then current. There is no need deliberately to beautify this. Why will people not understand that it is useless to make such an attempt according to the dictates of individual taste, and that 'all peoples began to write in the language talked by ploughmen, swineherds, and cattleherds, and then, when their thoughts began to be more refined, the languages became more refined of their own accord?'

Such views were quite enough in themselves to lead Vuk into serious controversy. He seems to have thought, though not explicitly to have claimed at any point, that it was necessary to have a public row at this stage in order to draw attention to the importance of the problem of popular language. He may well have been right about this. It was his own fault, however, that from the first this controversy took on such a bitter and personal tone. One can only guess at Vuk's motives for writing so bitterly; perhaps there was a combination of sheer joy in laying about him with the pen, a deep feeling of inferiority as a 'goatherd' when confronted with so much conventional learning, and much accumulated irritation over the bitter toil of trying to raise money for his publications.

While Vuk tangled in this provocative way with Vidaković, Kopitar ensured that his linguistic views should be taken amiss by the Orthodox hierarchy. Vuk had appealed in March 1818 to the Metropolitan Stratimirović for further help towards publication of the *Dictionary*, and wrote in affecting terms: 'you are my first and only benefactor, whom people must thank for my patriotic feelings'. The effect was spoilt by an article by Kopitar, inserted at the same time as the advertisement for the *Dictionary* in the *Austrian Observer*. The crucial passage ran: 'To the south of Austria there lives a branch of the Slavonic people whose beautiful language is called sometimes Illyrian, sometimes Slavonic and sometimes Serb. This is the language of four to five million people. ... The opponents of this language, certain *viri obscuri*[1] [sic] around the Metropolitan of Karlovci, write in a sort of bogus

---

[1] It seems probable that Kopitar was here alluding to the *Epistolae obscurorum virorum*, a famous polemical work of the early sixteenth century by Ulrich von Hütten, the knightly ally of Martin Luther. It purported to contain letters from Catholic priests and was a bitter satire on the Catholic Church.

literary tongue, meant to be learned, which has no roots among the people.' Kopitar got the better of the ensuing correspondence, but the victory was very far from worth while.

Vuk's literary situation at the end of 1818 may be summed up as follows. His controversial writings and his active correspondence in search of subscribers for the *Dictionary* had ensured that he was well known among the younger generation of Serb men of letters as an energetic and forceful man with 'progressive' views about the need for reforming the alphabet and language. He was indeed, in virtue of his network of correspondents, an obvious centre for any 'popular' movement in Serbian literature. On the other side, he and Kopitar had bitterly offended Stratimirović, who could hardly forgive them for having extracted money from him (and advertised his name among the subscribers) for the *Dictionary*, which proved to be so subversive of proper order in so many respects. Vuk had put off many potential sympathizers, particularly among the older generation, by his savage public controversy with Vidaković. And even his best friends, such as Mušicki, felt that his marriage to a 'foreigner' had been very ill-considered; it could lead to his enemies misrepresenting him as engaged on literary reform in order to undermine Orthodox and Russian influence and to promote Catholic and Austrian interests. Finally his financial situation was desperate, particularly in the light of his marriage and increasing family responsibilities. The balance-sheet was not cheerful.

IX

JOURNEY TO RUSSIA, 1819

I

IN December 1818, Vuk set out for Russia. It was at first sight a desperate undertaking. He had virtually no money, and no certain prospect of earning any at the end of his long journey. He left behind a wife and infant son with no obvious means of subsistence; and another child was on the way. He had further to reckon that, if he gained favour with the Russian authorities, he would lose it with the Austrian Government. In such a case even Kopitar might fail to persuade the Austrian police that Vuk was not a dangerous Russian agent. It is therefore not altogether surprising that he did not inform Kopitar in advance of his new venture.

The reasons for the journey were partly negative. There was no money to be made from Serbian literature, criticism, or philology in Austria or Hungary, Vienna or Buda, and much less in Serbia itself. Vuk had damaged any immediate prospect of writing for profit by his polemics against the Orthodox Church authorities and their literary supporters. His controversies about the alphabet and popular language were moreover beginning to bore alike the editors and the readers of Serbian periodicals. Vuk had little choice but to let things simmer down.

In the meantime there were also some positive reasons in favour of trying his luck in Russia. Vuk was well aware that Russia was a land of rich patrons, who were willing to encourage men of letters. He had admittedly been badly received in 1817 at the Russian Embassy in Vienna, when he had tried to get money from the Ambassador for the publication of his *Dictionary*, but he thought that it might still be possible to have a volume of 'popular songs' published in Russia. He also had some cause for hope in relation to his antiquarian activities. As early as 1815, he had been in correspondence with Atanasije Stojković, a native of the Srem province, who for many years had been a Professor of Physics at

Kharkov University. Stojković had informed him about the desire of the famous Russian connoisseur Count Nikolai Petrovich Rumyantsev to have transcripts of some old Serbian manuscripts. Vuk had refused to help in 1815, on the ground that correspondence with any Russians would cause him political difficulties with the Austrian authorities. From 1816 to 1818, however, he had for his own purposes been transcribing some of the ancient documents transferred to the monasteries of the Fruška Gora in the sixteenth century[1] and still preserved there. Extensive correspondence exists on this subject between him and the Archimandrite Mušicki. Vuk's main object at this time was to assemble as many ancient examples of the Serbian language as possible before writing the introduction to his *Dictionary*. He wanted to prove that the language, in much its present form, had a long continuous history and was not simply a corruption of old Slavonic; as early as 1816 he was thinking of a dictionary of older Serbian words to supplement his *Dictionary* of the spoken and popular tongue. But he may also have had in mind the possibility that Russian patrons might be interested in his work; and in any case by the end of 1818 he had a number of transcripts at his disposal and knew that, once he reached St. Petersburg, these would constitute a recommendation to Count Rumyantsev.

Vuk probably did not know what a distinguished patron he had. A former Minister of Foreign affairs (1807) and Chairman of the State Council (1810), Rumyantsev had been strongly pro-French in his policies, and lost what political influence he had before his retirement in 1814. Since then he had entirely absorbed himself in the collection, study, and publication of source-material on Russia's cultural history, and he made a great contribution to the preservation and rediscovery of the Slavonic cultural heritage.

Vuk had much to gain from Rumyantsev, and he clearly set his hopes on the ambitious target of a pension; but there were other hopes behind his journey to Russia. St. Petersburg was the headquarters of the Russian branch of the Bible Society, founded in 1812. Vuk had for some years been encouraged to prepare a Serbian translation of the New Testament, for use in Serbia and

[1] From the date of the Serbian defeat at Kosovo (1389) onwards, there were frequent waves of Serbian migration to Hungary, particularly after 1459, when the Turks conquered the remnant kingdom of Serbia. In 1483, Matthias Corvinus, King of Hungary, said that in 4 years alone 200,000 Serbs had settled in south Hungary.

the Balkans. The translation had long been a favourite project of Kopitar; the circulation of a version of the New Testament in popular language would, he thought, help to unite the 'Illyrians' of the Austrian Empire, break down the differences between their Churches, weaken the links of the Serbian Orthodox hierarchy with their brothers in Russia, and help to realize his vision of Austria as the centre of the 'enlightened' Slav races. As early as 1815 Kopitar had tried to have Vuk's name brought before the Rev. Robert Pinkerton, the English Bible Society's contact in St. Petersburg with its Russian counterpart (both branches were interested in the distribution of the Scriptures among the Slav populations of South-Eastern Europe).[1]

Nothing came of Kopitar's efforts at this time but the idea of translating the New Testament had been put into Vuk's head. He discussed it with Mušicki during his stays at Šišatovac. Mušicki himself was anxious in 1816 to do the translation, and thought that in any case it must be done by a priest; it would be best if the original Slavonic text were printed with the Serbian translation, and the Serb Metropolitan would be most likely to approve if it were published in St. Petersburg. Vuk at this time discouraged Mušicki, saying (quite possibly with intent to deceive) that the whole project was just one of Kopitar's fantasies; but it is clear from his correspondence that he had studied deeply the text of the New Testament, with a view to translating it himself. He was conscious of his ignorance of Hebrew and Greek as a disqualification for the job, but was ready to work from old Slavonic texts, subject to checking by more expert linguists; and he had no doubt of his own mastery of the popular Serbian language.

In 1818 Kopitar had been in direct contact with the London Bible Society about the possibility of a translation by Vuk, and by the time that Vuk arrived in Russia a preliminary agreement had been reached between the London branch and its Russian counterpart about the division of expenses; the St. Petersburg branch would pay Vuk his author's fee, and the London branch would carry the cost of printing. By the end of 1818, the next step for Vuk was clearly to sign an agreement with the Russian Bible

[1] Kopitar wrote to Silvestre de Sacy, the French orientalist, on the subject in his usual polyglot style: 'J'ai un excellent jeune homme de la Serbie proprement dite, que j'ai employé à écrire la première grammaire Serbienne pour les ὀρθοδοξόυς ... et qui, quant à la pureté de la langue Serbienne, ferait une traduction sans exemple encore parmi les peuples.'

Society, and for this a journey to St. Petersburg was desirable, given the delays and risks in correspondence between the Russian and Austrian capitals.

A further and more personal consideration was certainly important in determining Vuk to make his journey. Since he had entered into polemics in favour of his own alphabetical and linguistic reforms, many conservative Serbs, particularly those closely connected with the Metropolitan Stratimirović, had accused him of being little better than an Austrian and Catholic agent. By 1818 Vuk was suspect not only for his links with the Catholic Kopitar (who was indeed an anti-Russian Austro-Slav) but also for his marriage to an Austrian Catholic. One of the best means of defending himself against these charges would be to go to Russia and forge direct links with Russian literary and cultural personalities; and if it came to a direct choice between Russian and Austrian support, the former, whatever its cost in family troubles, might be more valuable to a man of letters.

So far as immediate monetary difficulties were concerned, Vuk could reckon that the expenses of the journey and of his stay in Russia might be met in part by the generosity of his fellow countrymen abroad. In the eighteenth century, large numbers of Serbs had migrated to Russia from the Austrian Empire in order to better themselves, to escape from the disabilities from which they were there subjected, and to take advantage of the Russian Government's desire for reliable settlers in the Ukraine. When the Banat province was incorporated in Hungary (1751–3), as many as 100,000 Serbs went to settle in south Russia—a sign that, whatever their hardships in the Austrian Empire, they had increased and multiplied since 1690. Many of them made good careers, particularly in the Russian army. The Serbo-Hungarian lawyer and writer, Sava Tekelija, in his account of a journey to Russia in 1812–13, noted the large numbers of Serbs in and near Odessa in particular, and said that the adjoining part of Bessarabia was known as 'Little Serbia'.[1] In 1813 too, after the collapse of Karadjordje's armies, a large number of Serbs had fled to Russia (some of the most prominent had in fact been helped on their way by the Austrian authorities, who did not want to see a further Serbian revolt against the Turks stimulated from their territory). Vuk

---

[1] Sava Tekelija, *Opisanije Života*, part ii, section 6, pp. 204 et seq. (edited by Aleksander Forišković, Belgrade, 1966).

could therefore reasonably count on some contacts and hospitality from his fellow countrymen in Russia. All in all, while the journey to St. Petersburg must have seemed a desperate venture to Kopitar and even more to his own wife, Vuk had some good reasons for trying his luck, and little enough to gain by staying in Vienna. For some time all went reasonably well. A week's journey by coach took Vuk to Cracow. From there he sent his wife in Vienna a sort of will, nominating her sole heir to his property, which consisted mainly of debts owed to him by friends from his days as an official in Karadjordje's administration. The fact that he had to send this document back to Vienna may be taken as another indication that he had left hurriedly, and without thorough discussion of his family affairs (though before leaving he had found time to compile a list of the family land-holdings in his native village, Tršić). In Warsaw, Vuk's next staging-point, he struck lucky, meeting an old Serb friend from 1813, and being introduced by him to the rest of the Serb community—including a patriotic tradesman, who lent him 50 ducats (never to be repaid). Vuk had to wait a month in Warsaw for his passport to Russia, and the onward journey took another twelve days.[1]

2

Vuk arrived at St. Petersburg in February 1819, and was welcomed in Russia, as in Poland, with a warmth that must have exceeded his most optimistic hopes. To the philologists, scholars, and literary men of St. Petersburg, he was the representative of a young Slav nation that had been much in the news, a lexicographer, grammarian, and folklorist with considerable achievements to his credit. His best recommendation, he said, lay in the 30 copies of his *Dictionary* which he brought with him (presumably it was one of these that found its way ultimately to Pushkin's library). The scholars and men of letters of St. Petersburg and Moscow were not deterred by Vuk's quarrels with the Serbian Orthodox Church, if the fame of these had reached their ears through the Serb *émigrés* in Russia. Vuk was a prophet with much notoriety and little honour in his own country; he found himself a much greater man at St. Petersburg than at Vienna or

[1] Vuk spent the time largely in the company of the Polish Sanskrit scholar, Valentin Majevski; they exchanged Serbian and Polish lessons.

Karlovci, and that too in the judgement of a very distinguished company of scholars, Russian and German. Nor was he kept waiting long in St. Petersburg for introductions and for results. His first impressions were given in a letter to Kopitar, dispatched late in March 1819—one of the few documents about Vuk's stay in Russia to survive. It is quoted in full to illustrate not only his literary success but also the domestic cares which pursued him:

Dear Friend,
  On setting out from Warsaw, I left a letter there to be posted to you; I hope that you received it. On Shrove Tuesday I arrived here safe and sound. Adelung, Count Rumyantsev, and everyone else received me as kindly as could be. By this time, I've done two bits of business, with Pinkerton's people and with Count Rumyantsev.
  1. Pinkerton's people have decided to give me 500 ducats for a translation of the New Testament; of this I will be given 150 ducats when I set out from here, and the rest will be given by instalments of 100 ducats [sic] till the work is finished. You will have to look after the paper and printing; not more than 5,000 copies will be printed.
  2. Count Rumyantsev decided to give me 400 ducats to cover a two-year tour of the monasteries of Serbia; of this I will be given 200 ducats when I set out from here to travel via the Bukovina, the Banat, the Srem, and Slavonia; the remaining 200 ducats I shall get in Vienna, when I'm ready to travel further (all this was done for me by Adelung).
  My third and most important job [the matter of the pension] I've hardly yet begun; but I'm hopeful that it too will be settled as it should be,[1] since everywhere I'm well recommended and kindly received (the only trouble is that I have no money, and don't dare to ask it from anyone, so that I may die of hunger in Petersburg). I have made the acquaintance of Karamzin (the other day I lunched at his house with Turgenev, who is director of Golitsin's chancery for religious affairs); of Shishkov (he is now President of the Russian Academy; whenever I go to his house, he reads me his *Slavonic Etymology* in manuscript. To show you what nice things he has—today he told me to come on Good Friday to look at an 'Illyrian dictionary' which he had bought in manuscript from Dobrovski); and of many other learned and well-known Russians. I don't know whether there is anywhere else in the

---

[1] Vuk evidently discussed the subject with Admiral Shishkov, and got what he interpreted as some encouragement—a statement that 'the Imperial Russian Academy may give you a pension'. He alluded to this in a letter of 6 February 1826 to Shishkov, quoted with other documents from Russian archives (principally on the dealings between the Russian Bible Society and Vuk), *Arhivist*, Belgrade, 1963 (Dr. Golub Dobrašinović, 'Nekoliko Dokumenata iz Ruskih Arhiva o Vuku Karadžiću').

world where people take such trouble about books, and such interest in them. There is as much talk and activity about literature here, as there is about trade in the old Fleischmarkt. Every Saturday evening there is a meeting of learned men at Adelung's, and there I had the honour to meet (among others) a well-known German, Count Turn, who is here as Austrian *chargé d'affaires* (today I've got to go to lunch with him, and shall give him this letter to send to you). I'm thinking of staying here for at most two months more, and shall then return to Austria via Moscow and Kiev (so that I shall be at least a proper pilgrim),[1] and in September I hope to reach Vienna. But in the meantime I would ask you to look out for nice lodgings, convenient for me, of three rooms (or two rooms and a bedroom); apart from that they should be (*a*) on the first floor and the staircase should not be too narrow or steep; (*b*) near you, so that you can visit every day, as hitherto. And they shouldn't be right on the Landstrasse—provided that they are not far from you. If however something could be found of this sort at a moderate price, the Landstrasse or Wieden would be all right. Talk about this and look into it with my wife and mother-in-law (and see what can be afforded by way of price; I think that a good apartment would be found on the Landstrasse for 300–500 florins). If Davidović has not received my money from the booksellers of Novi Sad and given it to my wife, by this time she won't have a single penny; so I beg you not to forget to give her a few florins from time to time, until I move from here, when I shall send something to her by coach.

Give my greetings to Maca [Maria Tirka] and to Mr. Tirka. Maca should be godmother to Milutin's sister (or brother), unless my letter comes too late for the christening. If it is a girl be sure to call her Milica, and if it's a boy, you'll also give it a good Serbian name. The New Testament will be printed in Russian this week, and I shall send it to you from the Bukovina by coach together with the other books. When you go on the street for a walk here, you still have to take care that your ears don't fall off for the cold. There is still a constant noise of sledges crossing the Neva on the ice.

The agreement with the Russian Bible Society was signed on 15 April 1819, in much the same terms as forecast by Vuk, who was called in it 'the well-known Serb man of letters'. It was provided that on all questions concerning the printing of the translation the London Bible Society should maintain contact with

[1] The word used by Vuk is 'Hadji', which is still a common part of Moslem surnames in modern Yugoslavia (e.g. Hadjigeorgijev, Hadzivasilijev) indicating that some ancestor had made the pilgrimage to a holy place (most probably Jerusalem).

Kopitar. An interesting minor point in Vuk's letter is his reluctance to talk directly of the Russian Bible Society, and his circumlocution 'Pinkerton's people'. Rather childish it might be thought, when the translation of the New Testament is mentioned in the same sentence; presumably Vuk wished to hide at least something of his activities from the Austrian censors, who might in due course inform the Metropolitan Stratimirović and provoke attempts at preventative action on his part.

On the second main point in Vuk's letter, his dealings with Rumyantsev were not confined to the agreement, with promise of immediate payment, about the collection of ancient documents in Serbia. Vuk left with his patron the transcripts of Serbian royal charters and lists of early Serbian printed books which he had brought with him to Russia. A note of these appeared in the description of Rumyantsev's manuscript collection, which also included the text of questions put by Rumyantsev to Vuk, and of such answers as Vuk, without any books of reference or notes, could give him on the spot.[1] Rumyantsev was favourably impressed and wrote later to his friend the historian and collector of historical documents, A. F. Malinovski, in Moscow:

> I am glad that you have made the acquaintance of this learned and good Serb. I don't know whether he confided to you that he has entered into an arrangement with me, to travel at my expense around all the districts inhabited by the Slav race, and look for documents and manuscripts in every ancient seat of these peoples. Taking into account his great capacity for this work, I think that I can expect important consequences of this undertaking.

It was indeed an undertaking near to Vuk's heart. When he arrived at Moscow from St. Petersburg in June 1819, he devoted himself to study of the old Serbian manuscripts which he found there. He wrote to Kopitar on 26 August:

> In accordance with your recommendation, I spent 17 days there [in Moscow], all the time searching out and studying the oldest manuscripts, and I found a mass of interesting stuff. Dobrovski saw nothing in Moscow, and what he says that he saw he either just noted from a catalogue or looked at it like a Uniat who knows no Slavonic. If God grants that I return to you safe and sound, you'll see what we shall do

[1] For a full account see *Kovčežič*, vi, 1964, 'Prvi Vukovi prepisi starih Slovenskih tekstova', by Djordje Trifunović.

for Slavonic studies. In Moscow all the professors and other learned people received me as kindly as possible, and all took pains to show me everything worth looking at.

In a similar letter to Mušicki he wrote:

> This has been an important journey for a Serb lexicographer. What would you not have given to be with me in Moscow alone, among the archives of the Collegium of Foreign Affairs, or in the Treasure Chamber of the Patriarchate? No Serb up to now has been in Russia with a purpose like mine.
> In Moscow I found a very old Slavonic book of the year 1046! I made a great many notes of all kinds from it. And I found the sword of George [Branković] of Smederevo. . . . All my findings about the Slavonic and Russian language must be printed this winter (not in Davidović's paper[1] but in a special pamphlet). . . .

This is almost all the concrete information which has survived about Vuk's stay in Russia. A few details are however added in a letter written from Vienna eighteen months later, as part of an effort to cheer up the Archimandrite Mušicki and to impress on him the great prospects which were being opened up to the innovators or renovators of Serbian literature. The nature of the exercise may partly account for the rather boastful and naïve tone, as of a bright young boy up from the country and meeting real men of letters for the first time; Vuk was in any case naturally proud of how the mandarins of enlightened St. Petersburg and Moscow received the young cripple from darkest Serbia:

> You ask what the Russians think of my *Dictionary*. The same as the Germans and the Poles. It was my great recommendation in Russia, and brought me into the company of Counts and Princes, Generals and Ministers. In St. Petersburg I read a favourable review in a journal called the *Blagonamerennyi Zhurnal* [the *Well-intentioned Journal*]; and I read another at Kiev in the *Sorevnovatel Prosveshcheniya i blagotvoreniya* [*Promoter of Culture and Charity*]; and I've heard here that a third has appeared in the *Vestnik Evropy* [*Messenger of Europe*]. And have you read that review in the Gottingen academic paper?[2] They showed it to me in St. Petersburg. I hear that there are reviews in

[1] The Vienna *Serbian News*.
[2] Jakob Grimm had written a very favourable review of the *Dictionary* in the *Göttingsche Gelehrte Anzeigen* for 1819, saying that Vuk left his predecessors far behind, and praising him for quoting so much from popular songs, tales, and proverbs; 'We would like to see a complete and elaborated Serbian Mythology from the hand of Mr. Vuk.'

Polish too in some Warsaw newspapers. I took 30 copies of the *Dictionary* with me to St. Petersburg, and if I'd brought 300, they'd have gone like hot cakes. I can tell you that in Moscow I was fairly in the kingdom of my dreams! All the professors received me as you would. From St. Petersburg I had 7 letters of introduction (4 from Turgenev and 3 from others). Malinovski told me that Rumyantsev had written to him on my behalf when sending the dictionary. Dmitrijev [Dmitriev] received me in his ante-room, and by the time that we'd got to the third room to sit down, he had bowed ten times, saying that this was for him a most memorable day (just like any Minister); because, he said, both Turgenev and Karamzin had written on my behalf. Dmitrijev is about 50 years old, or more, but is well and lives better than the Emperor in St. Petersburg; he has been Minister of Justice. Kolajbovic [Kalaidovich] is a young man (about my age), of the lowest officer's rank and poor, but he knows Russian history very well and is acquainted with manuscripts and other antiquities. I was three times with Karamzin; the first time Turgenev took me to lunch, the second time he asked me to lunch at Tsarsko [Tsarskoe] Selo, where he lives in summer; and the third time I took my leave of him when I left St. Petersburg (Tsarsko Selo was on my way, three miles from St. Petersburg). In fact I was with him one more time, with the Copenhagen Professor Raske. Karamzin is a good fellow, fairly old by now, with two daughters to be married. He has made a lot of money with his *Russian History*. I also met Zhukovski, the first poet in Russia today (once we were together at lunch with Karamzin and once with Count Rumyantsev); Turgenev told me that he had sent you some of his (Zhukovski's) poems; I don't know whether you ever got them. And I was a few times with Shishkov, he sent his 4 horse carriage for me, and once he took me to a session of the Russian Academy. He's a very decent man, but old and ill, God knows whether he'll survive this winter.[1]

3

It remains to say something of the Russian scholars, men of letters and patrons whom Vuk mentioned in his correspondence, and of their significance in the Russian context. The most clearly defined group among the names cited by Vuk is formed, naturally enough, by the 'learned men', Adelung, Köppen, Kachenovski (who is mentioned in one of the sentences omitted from a letter here quoted), Malinovski, and Kalaidovich (Vuk's 'Kolajbović'). Most of these were protégés of Rumyantsev, and of foreign

---

[1] Admiral Shishkov did not in fact die till 1841.

JOURNEY TO RUSSIA, 1819

extraction—Friedrich Adelung was born and educated in Germany and settled in Russia in 1794, Köppen's parents were German, and Kachenovski was of Greek descent. These were all men whose names (that of Kalaidovich in particular) were closely associated in Russia with the early period of Slavonic studies, especially with the growth of interest in monuments of Russian antiquity and in the history of Church Slavonic.

Among this group of scholars, it was Adelung, then head of the Institute for Oriental Languages, who was most immediately helpful to Vuk, introducing him personally to Rumyantsev and to the Russian Bible Society. Petr Ivanovich Köppen also did him important service by presenting his work to the educated public of Russia in the literary magazines, and strongly defending Vuk's 'popular' language against those who thought it an offence against the 'Slavonic-Serb' literary tradition. He was also to prove one of Vuk's most faithful and helpful friends in later years. It was incidentally Köppen who induced Vuk to adopt the surname (or clan-name) Karadžić. 'Vuk Stefanović' to a Russian sounded like the normal Russian use of Christian name and patronymic, and implied a surname for more formal use.[1]

It was natural enough that these scholars should be interested in Vuk's work and should take pains to help him during his visit to Russia. Vuk himself was, however, rather more taken up, it seems, with his reception by literary and political figures. Of these, Nikolai Mihailovich Karamzin was the best known. Novelist, author of letters of travel, and historian, he had become by 1819 the Grand Old Man of Russian letters. His novels and letters had not only set the course of Russian literature towards the school of realism that was to dominate the nineteenth century, but had also established a new form of literary language, based on simple popular speech (though not identical with it) and remote from the lofty classical style, which involved adherence to Church Slavonic forms. Karamzin was a 'Westerner' not only in matters of style; it was he who had in 1802 founded the *Vestnik Evropy* (Messenger of Europe), which became very influential. This was edited *de facto* by Kachenovski, who had printed in it a full review of Vuk's *Dictionary*.

[1] In 1829 and 1842–3 Vuk's enemies made his change of style a theme for mockery, suggesting that he was trying to better himself socially by adopting a clan name to which he had no right.

Vasilii Andreevich Zhukovski too, generally regarded as the father of the romantic school in Russian poetry, had been launched on his literary career by Karamzin and was much influenced by Western writing—he had translated Pope, Gray, La Fontaine, Byron, and some of the German Romantics, and contributed much to the formation of a new language and style. It would be pleasant to think that Vuk was able to discuss with Karamzin and Zhukovski the various conceptions of the 'middle style' which he and others were trying with so much controversy to evolve for Serb literature; but there is unfortunately no evidence that he did so.

Both Karamzin and Zhukovski were attracted by court life. The former lived at Tsarskoe Selo from 1816 onwards and regularly met the Emperor Alexander I; even before this time he had submitted to the Tsar memoranda on political conditions in Russia. Zhukovski had become in 1815 tutor to the Tsar's daughter. Both these writers therefore were able to satisfy not only Vuk's literary curiosity but also the taste, which he had not been able to indulge in Vienna, for the company of 'Counts and Princes, Generals and Ministers'. Some of the other contacts which he mentioned in his letters fall into the same double category.

Ivan Ivanovich Dmitriev, who 'bowed ten times' when Vuk came to see him in Moscow, was a poet himself and had been a Member of the State Council and Minister of Justice before he retired in 1814; his principal link with Vuk should have been (there is no direct evidence that it was) the fight which he waged together with Karamzin, and by means of his fables and satires, against the pseudo-classical style in Russian literature.

Aleksandr Ivanovich Turgenev, one of the two Secretaries of the Russian Bible Society, was another who combined high office in the Russian bureaucracy (Head of the Department for Foreign Religions in the Chief Administration for Spiritual Affairs) with literary and historical activity. A brother of Andrei Ivanovich, the poet, and of Nikolai Ivanovich, later well known as a 'Decembrist', he was a close friend of Karamzin and Zhukovski, and well known and liked by the Emperor and Empress. As a young man, he had travelled in other Slav countries and become interested in their history and languages. In 1804 he had actually heard something of the Serb uprising from close quarters, at Karlovci. He was particularly interested in the collecting of original historical

JOURNEY TO RUSSIA, 1819   143

material, and his own *Historiae Russiae Monumenta* . . . was published in 1842 by the Russian Archaeographical Commission. He must therefore have had plenty of common interests with Vuk, apart from the immediate business of the Russian Bible Society. The other principal Russian figure mentioned by Vuk in his letters was Admiral Aleksandr Semyonovich Shishkov, President of the Russian Academy from 1813. 'A very decent man', said Vuk, but he was in outlook far removed from Vuk's other Russian contacts. As a young man on active service, he had learnt to dislike and fear the 'godless French'. His work as a teacher at a naval college then led him to the study of languages and so to translation and original writing—on naval subjects, language and style, and finally on public affairs. He was a patriotic conservative in religious affairs, and was an expert on the history of Church Slavonic; Shishkov was deeply convinced that departure from the linguistic canons of Church Slavonic would undermine morality, and was thus bitterly opposed to Karamzin's 'Gallomania' and new style of writing. He had lofty ideas on the importance of censorship, and by temperament and conviction he was a far more likely friend for the Metropolitan Stratimirović than for Vuk. Shishkov was however interested throughout his life in the smaller Slav Orthodox nations, and presumably in what might be called the conservative side of Vuk's work—the recording of Slav national poems, language, and customs. He was the founder of a patriotic society known as Concourse, which included Russian liberals, as well as conservatives and Old Believers, and from 1813 onwards was in occasional touch with Southern Slav scholars. At all events, there seems to have been no clash of temperament between Shishkov and Vuk; indeed it was to Shishkov that Vuk appealed directly more than once in later years for money to finance his historical publications.

It remains to consider some of the most noteworthy omissions in Vuk's account of his activities in Russia, and to attempt a more general picture of the significance of his visit. In the first place it is sad that Vuk did not meet and mention Pushkin, who though young was very much in the centre of literary life at St. Petersburg. He was in particular a friend of Zhukovski and Aleksandr Turgenev. Moreover, at least by the end of 1820 he was already concerned with some of Vuk's special subjects. In that year he had become acquainted at Kishinev with some of the Serb exiles who had come to Bessarabia after the collapse of the Karadjordje regime, and he showed an interest, which he afterwards developed, in their language and poetry. It is however inconceivable that Vuk should have met Pushkin and not mentioned the fact at some time in his later career, if not in his letters from Russia. Vuk was living at St. Petersburg, as usual, from hand to mouth, and his poverty and pride may well have prevented him from making or pursuing a number of literary contacts. Again there is no sign that Vuk met any of the younger Russian intellectuals later known as 'Decembrists', who had been stimulated by their experiences as officers in France in 1813–14 to think of radical political and social reforms, and formed secret societies which ultimately led to the rising of December 1825.[1]

More interesting and significant is the apparently very limited nature of Vuk's dealings with and knowledge of the Russian Bible Society. This was founded late in 1812, partly as the result of the activities of its English counterpart. The London Society remained closely linked with it, and maintained their resident representative in St. Petersburg. But the Russian Society was very much more than a model of the English, and at the time of Vuk's visit had a quite peculiar place in Russian political and cultural life. The main force behind it was its president, Prince Aleksandr Golitsyn. He found in the text of the scriptures and in the practice of the Protestant Pietists, then established for some time in Russia, an inspiration lacking in the Orthodox Church. In 1810 he became head of the newly established Directorate of Spiritual Affairs. At that time Golitsyn was close to the Tsar, whom he persuaded in turn to read the scriptures and to attend meetings in his interconfessional chapel. The Russian Bible Society was, by circulating the New Testament, to be the main instrument of the 'spiritual mobilization' which Alexander I wanted to achieve in Russia (late in 1812 he delayed his pursuit of Napoleon in order to meet a representative of the English Society). One of the objects of the Russian Society was to 'reveal to the Orthodox Church its errors, revive its faith, and thus begin a reformation in Russia', and among its leading members were a Uniate, a Roman Catholic ecclesiastic, and some of the less dogmatic representatives of the Orthodox Church. In 1816, after the establishment of the 'Holy Alliance', Golitsyn was appointed Minister of Education, and in

---

[1] One of their societies was called the 'Society of the United Slavs'; but these societies had not been formed at the time of Vuk's journey.

1817 head of a new organization, the Ministry of Spiritual Affairs and Public Education (which included the Holy Synod). Prominent German preachers (Catholic as well as Protestant) were invited to Russia to help Golitsyn devise a system under which 'simple unlearned people' could be 'tutored by the Holy Ghost'.[1] Not least important, Golitsyn encouraged the expansion of a more mystical type of Freemasonry in Russia, to correspond on a 'higher' plane with the new provincial 'chapters' of the Bible Society, and the branches of the philanthropic society 'Lovers of Humanity', founded by Alexander himself.

Vuk's work in Russia was connected with the simple and original objectives of the Russian Bible Society—the dissemination of the Scriptures in the authorized Church Slavonic version and the propagation of them in other languages among Christians of other faiths or non-Christians. In 1816, the Society with the Emperor's personal backing, and that of the Holy Synod, took the important step, offensive to most of the Orthodox hierarchy, of sponsoring a translation of the New Testament into Russian—an exact parallel to what Vuk wanted to undertake for Serbia. This appeared in 1818, and by 1819 the Society had published or was preparing the publication of translations of the New Testament in twelve languages, including Polish (in 1824 a Bulgarian translation appeared). But this activity, as well as the mystical flights of Higher Order Masonry, aroused bitter opposition from the Orthodox hierarchy, and Alexander's own enthusiasm began to wane. In 1824 Golitsyn was replaced as Minister of Education by the 'very decent' Admiral Shishkov (one of his first acts was to forbid students to read the Russian translation of the New Testament). In the same year Golitsyn resigned from the presidency of the Russian Bible Society. It decreased rapidly in importance and was dissolved in 1826.

4

There is no echo of Golitsyn's lofty enthusiasms or of the ecclesiastical counter-intrigues either in Vuk's letters from Russia, where he might well have hesitated to mention them, or in any of his subsequent writings. From this and from Vuk's other

[1] See James Billington, op. cit., pp. 281 et seq., and Hugh Seton-Watson, *The Russian Empire, 1801–1917*, Oxford. 1967, pp. 164 et seq.

silences, the simplest conclusion is that his visit to Russia and his dealings there should be taken exactly at their face value. He was of course not a complete innocent in matters of international politics. Already he had acted as intermediary, not necessarily for political purposes, between Serb exiles in Austria and his countrymen remaining in Serbia; this was one of the reasons for which he had been under periodic suspicion from the police in Vienna. There is moreover one passage in Vuk's later writings[1] describing a meeting between himself and Petar Dobrnjac, one of Karadjordje's former generals, in Bessarabia in 1819. But this too would seem to have been in all probability accidental, and without political intent.

The Russian authorities on their side are not likely at this period to have thought seriously of using Vuk for political purposes. In the first place they may well have suspected him of being an Austrian spy. In the second place they do not seem to have been planning at this time to stimulate Serbian national feeling against the Turks. They had certainly given some diplomatic support in 1817 to the Serbs. Their Ambassador at Constantinople, Count Stroganov, was instructed to reassert Russian interest in the execution of the articles of the Treaty of Bucharest (1812) governing the status of the Serbs within the Ottoman Empire. Further negotiations between the Turks and the Serbs were started in 1819 while Vuk was still in Russia. But the Russians were not prepared to apply any strong pressure on Turkey. And if they had wanted agents to foster Serbian national resistance in this context, a number of the exiled followers of Karadjordje were still in Bessarabia, and were better suited than Vuk to such a task.

As a political representative of an oppressed Slav nation, Vuk thus had little to hope for from the Russian authorities. Certainly he was launched with an éclat quite unexpected and very flattering to him among Russian scholars and literary men, many of whom had important political connections. In the person of Admiral Shishkov he met an important conservative political leader. But he was treated by all of them as a man of letters and an archaeologist, 'a learned and good Serb', to quote Rumyantsev's phrase.

[1] The work in which Vuk mentions Dobrnjac is *The Governing Council in the Time of Karadjordje*, published in 1860, when Miloš had died and could no longer be displeased at the thought of Vuk having been in touch with one of his potential rivals.

And he seems even as such not to have been at this stage in sight of getting a pension from the Russian Government. On his side, he seems to have known nothing of any incipient movement within Russia to liberate the Slavs outside it. It would of course not be surprising that he should keep quiet at the time about contact with any such movement; but once again there is no indication in any of his later works, or in records of meetings with him, that such contact took place.

In fact one of the most curious points about Vuk's Russian journey is how little long-term effect it seems to have made on his mind. It was the first of his journeys outside Serbia and Austria, and it brought him into contact with a literary world (all politics apart) which, as he recognized at the time in his letters, was far more stimulating than anything which he had known in Vienna. But he spoke and wrote little or nothing about it in later years. The truth seems to be that, along with his great faculty for concentration, he possessed a great talent for excluding anything from his mind that did not directly affect his career. Russia and the Russians remained for him primarily and almost exclusively a possible source of gifts, pensions, patronage, and even employment. It was not his business to concern himself with their literature and politics. It is perhaps in this sense that Vuk's Russian journey throws most light on his character.

What little else is known of Vuk's travels in Russia can be described again in his own words. He wrote to Kopitar from Kishinev on 26 August 1819:

A holy blessing on you from all the Serb sacred books in Moscow, and from the miracle workers of Kiev, and from the *simple* Russian people, their language and songs! . . .

I didn't want to travel from Moscow by coach, I hired an *izvozchik* [driver] to Kiev, and with him began to learn a bit of Russian. We stopped in the Orlov province for two days, and there I wrote down a few Russian songs from the lips of Russian women and girls (and these may be the first Russian songs—or words, for that matter, taken down as sung or spoken by the people).[1] So I took 17 days on the journey to Kiev. There I settled for a few days and finished my pilgrimage, making my homage to all the holy relics and kissing them. From Kiev to Kishinev it was a 9-days' journey, and here I've been almost a month;

---

[1] Vuk had either forgotten the collections (e.g.) of Novikov and Kirsh Danilov or regarded them as insufficiently authentic.

in five days more at most I intend to set out by Hotin to Černović which is as far from here as Buda from Vienna. From Černović one ought to be able to strike straight through the Banat and Srem, but for the present I can't; I shall take a seat in a coach, and then direct to you. Please look after the print and get it ready, and then we'll start work as soon as I come ...' [on the translation of the New Testament].

Just think of all our troubles! I'd written this letter to send you from Kishinev, but when they asked me 10 *groš* for it at the post, I kept it back. The devil then prevented me from travelling straight from Kishinev to Černović, and turned me back so that I had to strike through Moldavia and Wallachia. When I got to Jaš, there was the plague! All inns were shut, and quarantine stations were set up right down to Bucharest. Then I turned back to the German border in the Bukovina, and now I've had to stay 10 days here in quarantine (well, thank God it isn't 40!)

Another 6 days and I'll get out, and so direct to you via Černović and Lvov.

This is a high-spirited letter, but as Vuk tried to make his way home the troubles of his family in Vienna were weighing heavily upon him. Already he had heard from his wife the tragic news that their son Milutin had died. Vuk wrote pathetically in his imperfect German to his poor wife: 'Alle kleine Kinder die ich hier gesehen habe, alle habe ich mit grösster Freude mit ihm verglichen, und ich habe in sich gedacht; er wird auch so laufen und lachen, bis ich nach Hause kom und jetzt ist das alles ein Traum.' ('All the little children that I've seen here, I've compared with him with the utmost pleasure, and thought to myself: he'll be walking and smiling like this, by the time that I get home. And now that's nothing but a dream.') Vuk sent his wife what money he could from St. Petersburg, and hoped that the advance payments received from Rumyantsev and the Bible Society would enable him to return with something in hand. But the long journey and the delays cost him dear. From Lvov he wrote to Mušicki in September:

Do you realize that I'm going home to my wife without any money?! Of 400 ducats nothing remains but what will cover my expenses to Vienna!! Say that of these 400 ducats I gave 60 for various Russian books; the rest has all gone on carriers, innkeepers, or shopkeepers. Please by your faith as a Serb, find some kind of means of sending if only 200 florins for me to pick up in Vienna. I shall certainly pay you back in the new year, for God will give me the means of earning it then. See to it in God's name, and send me that much money right away, then we'll easily make out for the rest. If you don't send it to me, I shall have to sell to the dealers one way or another all the Russian books which. I've brought with me all this way with unheard-of toil and trouble.

Vuk in fact arrived in Vienna penniless in October 1819. He found his wife in utter penury and a new-born daughter already dead. The immediate balance-sheet of his Russian journey was miserably negative; he had nothing in his pocket and he had mortgaged to Rumyantsev and the Bible Society his work for months to come. Even to him, and much more to his wife, it can have been of small comfort in November 1819 that he had entered the world of international scholarship and had made personal friends—particularly Köppen—who were to do him sterling service in the future. With hindsight however we can see that the long-term gains of Vuk's journey were large and that his stay in St. Petersburg was another of the important turning-points in his life. In the Vojvodina and Vienna he was still nothing but a controversialist, but in the wider world he was beginning to be recognized as a notable scholar and linguistic expert.

X

VUK AND MILOŠ OBRENOVIĆ

I

IT is, one may say as usual, uncertain how Vuk contrived to keep himself and his family alive after his return to Vienna; gifts and loans from friends were probably forthcoming, and he had eventually to sell all the books which he had brought with him from Russia (some, at a good price, to Kopitar and Dobrovski). In the meantime he was working mainly at the translation of the New Testament promised to the Russian Bible Society, for which he had already received some advance payment. Kopitar had to check Vuk's translation from the old Slavonic texts against the Greek and Latin versions, and it was with this joint work in view that Vuk had been anxious to find lodgings conveniently near him. It was clear from the first that the translation was not going to have an easy birth. The Metropolitan Stratimirović was against the project from the start. Kopitar was known to him by reputation as a Catholic and an 'Austrianizer'; Vuk himself was, in Stratimirović's view, undermining by his linguistic reforms the authority of the Church and its influence on education and literature. Moreover Vuk had to some extent outwitted him by securing his financial support and approval for the *Dictionary*, which had then proved to be in more than one respect disagreeable to him. Thus even if Stratimirović had had no objection to the general circulation of the New Testament in popularly intelligible form, he was clearly going to object to Vuk becoming the Martin Luther of Serbia.

Vuk realized what he was up against. Anxious to have his version printed as soon as it was ready, he first tried to get the London Bible Society's permission to circumvent Stratimirović. He proposed to their officials in St. Petersburg that the translation should be printed at Leipzig and that approval for publication should be sought from the Prince Bishop of Montenegro;[1] but

---

[1] Petar I, Prince Bishop (*Vladika*) of Montenegro from 1782 to 1830.

they insisted that Stratimirović must himself authorize printing and circulation for his own province, the Srem, and for Serbia itself. Vuk then tried to work on Stratimirović himself by flattery and the gift of some books and manuscripts from Russia. He wrote to Stratimirović (in the old style of lettering): 'I could collect for Your Excellency such things as no one has been able to find until today, and such as today no one else could find for any price.' If Stratimirović would consent, Vuk's zeal would be redoubled: 'For I would know that the protector of our people takes pleasure in my work and labours; whereas now my pains and toil are for my own pleasure alone.'

Vuk's journey to Russia had indeed had some of its intended effect on the Orthodox Church authorities; he was less suspect than before of being an Austrian agent. Stratimirović accepted his flattery and gifts and for the time being did not encourage further attacks on him. But permission was not given either in the summer of 1820 nor during the lifetime of Stratimirović for the printing of Vuk's version of the New Testament.

2

Vuk's translation had been his principal task in the winter of 1819–20, but he had thrown himself once more into the linguistic and orthographic controversies which he had done so much to stimulate before his journey to Russia. Soon after his return to Vienna he had met the then doyen of Slav studies, the Abbé Dobrovski, and had typically entered into intense argument with him on linguistic questions, rather than bowing to his authority.[1] The main issue between them was whether, as Dobrovski thought, the Serbian language was a later distortion of the Russian; or whether, as Vuk maintained, the Serbian and Russian languages were equally old and both derived from an earlier form of Slavonic. Vuk argued his case with force and a remarkable sophistication; and later linguistic studies have proved him nearer right than the great Dobrovski.

The critical articles or reviews which Vuk published or wrote

[1] In a letter to Frušić of 1819, Vuk gave a lively description of Dobrovski: 'I first saw this Patriarch of Slavonic literature at Davidović's last Saturday . . . great as was my joy at seeing Dobrovski, it was even greater to find in him not some paunchy, dumpy, stooping monk, but a tall, thin old man who really steps out like a young fellow of a third of his years. . . .'

for publication at this time are of only secondary interest today. In main he was hammering home the arguments which he had already advanced (often against the same opponents) in 1816–18. Literary criticism in the normal sense of the words did not interest him. He was concerned only and tirelessly with the need to evolve and stick to precise and definite rules of orthography, grammar, and, so far as possible, linguistic usage. He rejected emphatically the argument that Serbian literature was in its infancy and should not be hobbled by excessive strictness. And, as before, in critical controversy he did not spare his friends and seemed to go out of his way to embitter enemies further.

One of the friends who came under Vuk's fire was the Archimandrite Mušicki and his letters to Mušicki at this period give a good idea of his main critical concerns. They also show him as a staunch and encouraging friend. By the winter of 1819–20 Mušicki was in grave trouble with Stratimirović and the Orthodox Church authorities. They regarded him as a very doubtful supporter of the Church in its linguistic battles with Vuk, and sent a Commission to inquire in no friendly spirit into Mušicki's administration of the monastery of Šišatovac, which had become heavily indebted. By March, Mušicki was suspended from his duties and remained in his monastery as a subordinate, threatened by creditors, perturbed by the scandals being circulated about him, and desperately writing round to friends and un-friends for support. There is something heroic in Vuk's robust attempts to cheer him up and set him to useful work; all this at a time when Vuk himself was in the greatest material difficulties and had no obvious prospects of success open to him. It is also typical of Vuk that he should, though in no evil sense, use the occasion of his friend's difficulties to stimulate more active support of his own literary reforms. The following are relevant extracts from Vuk's letters to Mušicki in February/March 1820:

> Don't be afraid! When there's most thunder, there's least rain. . . . You shouldn't take a penny more of the debt on to your shoulders, except for what you spent on your own particular needs, which the monastery was not bound to give you. It's easier for the monastery to take on debts than for you; let people say what they like, they'll do so anyhow and talk all sorts of nonsense. Now your only way out is to work at literature; that is how to cheer yourself up, and to put your enemies to shame, and to make money. Publish a Slavonic grammar, a

history of Serb literature, publish your poetry, and then all will be well! . . . Now is just the time for you to make your appearance on the stage of Serbian letters, so that we can speak up firmly for our own times and lay a foundation for literature. It's high time, and you can see that on the other side there are nothing but a sort of schoolboys and clerks. Don't you see . . . that a ban should be put on such authors, until they can learn to decline nouns and conjugate verbs and conduct discussions according to the rules of Serb syntax.

Now see you drive that wolf from your door, and I shall send you a review with some real bite and fire in it of your *Patriot's Voice*, so that you'll think of it whenever you take pen in hand. Then too you should fix the sentences of Wieland on a board above your table—and in great big letters too—those that *our* Toma Ljubibratić[1] translated thus: 'How silly have our weathercock wits shown themselves in always wishing to please—people who had the capacity for the most beneficial and useful work, had they only wished to apply themselves seriously! Is it not shameful that people of great gifts should lower themselves and pay homage to the taste and prejudices of the uneducated, to whom in fact they should lay down the law?' You should read that every day, when you begin and when you leave off writing. Your only mistake, but a very big one, is to have in mind only some kind of highly cultured readers, . . . some kind of educated part of our people, some sort of Good Taste (now you see I'm no longer joking, I'm really angry); and you don't see that these are just silly clerks. Among all our people today you'd hardly find three capable of judging properly about these things, but first they ask who has written them, and what so-and-so has said, and then they judge according to the answer. *We* are the Platos and Aristotles of our people today. We must scorn all these clerks and write for a grateful posterity, who will be free of all today's nonsense and cultured ignorance, who won't ask where anyone was born, and how he walked and how he behaved himself, but will look at what he left behind him, and by that standard will judge of our wits and our hearts. A leader shouldn't listen to a blind man telling him which road is nicest, he must go in the direction which he sees himself to be best. That's why he's a leader. . . . When I took up my pen, I thought just to write a few words to you, but now I've babbled on perhaps too long. Well, if you don't like anything, just think that I was drunk when I wrote it. For that I'm waiting in fact for some of your holy plum brandy, to mix with my Russian tea in the evening; that's when I'll

[1] Ljubibratić was a pseudonym for Djordje Magarašević, at the time a Professor of literature in the 'Gymnasium' at Karlovci. He had translated an article by the German Wieland on the uselessness of routine books which involve no more mental activity than spinning (the point was directed against the novelist Vidaković).

take a good look at the *Patriot's Voice*. But while I'm sober I must first make notes of what I shall write about and what I shall write. . . .

A little later, Vuk was giving expert advice on how to deal with creditors, telling Mušicki not to humiliate himself, and jollying him along:

. . . I'm absolutely amazed that you can beg of the Metropolitan [Stratimirović] who hates you and prides himself on your misfortune! You know the Serbian saying: 'It's no use begging, if God doesn't help you.' Even in misfortune, one should despise such people; and it doesn't help to despise just them—you have to despise all their silly works too. Publish your Slavonic grammar, and your *Serb literature*, and then you'll have fame and money and credit! Then I've bought two lottery tickets of the Vienna Theatre at Vidin, for which they give prizes of 300,000 silver florins, so you pray to St. Stefan Stiljanović[1] that he should ask God for mine to be a winner. . . .

The final extract from this series of letters[2] is concerned more directly with Vuk's literary activities, and shows more clearly the limits of Vuk's friendship with Mušicki; Vuk never allowed this to temper his own views on really important subjects, such as the Serb alphabet and grammar:

Here's the review for you! [of Mušicki's *Patriot's Voice*] I wrote it for printing in the *Serbian News*, but as it's to your address I'm sending it first for you to see. If it doesn't seem to you very hostile, and you write that I can give it to Davidović, it can be printed (for this purpose I've kept a copy with me); if you don't like to see it printed, you must: (*a*) write a revised ode and recant in it everything criticized in the review and send the ode to Davidović for printing; (*b*) never again in any future ode put in anything criticized in the review. This second clause was drafted by Kopitar, and now I've signed it. Now choose, do you want peace or war? In such things nothing should be pardoned you, first for your own sake, for your honour, and for the life of your poetry; and secondly for the sake of the progress of our literature. . . .

The review of Mušicki's poems in fact remained unpublished.

---

[1] Stiljanović was one of Mušicki's creditors.

[2] 8 March 1820. A recurrent theme of the correspondence was the portrait of Vuk, painted at Šišatovac in 1816, and now wanted by Vuk's wife in Vienna. Mušicki had been forced to conceal this portrait from the ecclesiastical commissioners, as evidence of 'evil communications', under another picture.

3

Vuk's literary and critical work can at best have brought in very little money at this time. By spring 1820, he was looking for other sources of income, in places less expensive than Vienna. He corresponded with his old friend, Dimitrije Frušić, not for the last time, about the possibility of a schoolmaster's post in Trieste where there were a number of prosperous Serb merchants; but the reply was discouraging.[1] In these circumstances Vuk decided to try his luck again in Serbia. Again it meant leaving his wife and a young child behind in Vienna, where they had to rely on Kopitar and a few other much-tried friends to eke out a living. But on the face of it, the search for employment in Serbia was not such a bold venture as the journey to Russia.

Everything depended on the attitude of Miloš Obrenović. By 1819–20 he had further consolidated his personal position as effective ruler of Serbia, and was trying to negotiate at Constantinople further concessions on the road to Serbian independence; he was at this time supported by Russian diplomacy, and his immediate associates at his court were pro-Russian. In this context, Vuk's success in Russia might have additional uses, and would help (as it had helped with the authorities of the Orthodox Church) to dispel any suspicions that he was little better than an Austrian agent. In fact the literary and critical quarrels in which Vuk had involved himself had aroused at most only faint echoes at Miloš's highly materialistic court. So far as his literary mission was concerned, Vuk could reasonably feel that he had a better chance of success in Serbia than among the Serbs of the Austrian Empire. At least there would be less prejudices of an outdated culture to contend with. As he put it himself: 'Here [i.e. in the Srem] the field is overgrown with weeds, and it will need much toil and time to clear and clean it for proper sowing; while there the ground is clean, and all that is needed is some clever and decent workers to sow clean and healthy seed.'

Vuk had indeed very broad ideas of what he might accomplish in Miloš's Serbia. These went far beyond his constant literary and critical aims, and the best account of them (perhaps rather

[1] Frušić said that Serb reaction to Vuk in Trieste would not be hostile so long as he did not ask either for a job or for a loan!

embellished for the occasion) was given by himself in a letter to Miloš dated April 1822—after the failure of his mission:

You yourself know that I wanted (as I told all your advisers more than a hundred times):

(1) To teach you to read and write; and afterwards to arrange to have written for your special use a number of historical and other useful books of various kinds. Then you could have read some of these yourself in your idle hours, and for the others we could have appointed someone to read to you at a fixed time. Thus, since God has given you a sound mind and a good memory, we could have made up for all that you could not do in childhood to prepare for your present state.

(2) To see how we could teach some of the chiefs to read and write after a fashion; and to establish a school for the chiefs' sons and other young men who have some knowledge of reading and writing, where they might be prepared in European fashion over two or three years for state service.

(3) For the junior schools to publish school books in the best European way, so that the Serbs in other lands might learn something from us (as their mother) and that we should not have eternally to copy from other people.

(4) To persuade you to establish at least a minimum of laws, as much as is possible in the present state of this country, so that it might in some small degree resemble a European state.

(5) For me to collect as many popular songs as could be done; to describe the monasteries at least in your district; and to write a Serbian history of our times (which I have begun long ago). . . .

An ambitious programme indeed; but it should be remembered that Vuk could reasonably hope to occupy a prominent position in Miloš's Serbia, where the lack of educated men was almost as great as under Karadjordje, ten years before. Then the young and totally inexperienced Vuk had been given important practical work to do, not without some success. It was quite possible (perhaps he had the example of Karamzin in mind) that he should become one of Miloš's senior advisers, and undertake the work of a Minister of Education.

It was at any rate with these hopes that Vuk set out from Vienna in June 1820. He passed through Buda, Varadin, and Karlovci, where he was pleased to find himself an object of some public interest.[1] In Zemun, immediately over the river Sava from

---

[1] Vuk was particularly pleased at being recognized by some schoolboys. The superintendent of schools in Zemun, Vasilej Vasiljević, was at this time anxious to introduce Vuk's grammar to his schools.

Belgrade, Vuk wrote to ask permission of Miloš Obrenović to attend the Prince's court, mentioning his hopes that he might be allowed to teach Miloš how to read and write and that he might at last receive some of the money originally promised, as he had thought, towards the printing of the *Dictionary*. While he awaited a reply, Vuk took counsel on how best to approach the ruler of Serbia. The advice was to come into his presence with a suitable gift, and when Vuk was summoned in mid-July 1820 he presented Miloš with a new pair of pistols, which made a good impression. For some months, Vuk seems to have made good progress in the ruler's favour. He was at his best clearly a man of spirit and charm (as can be seen from his letters), and when needs must he commanded a greater power of flattery than could be deduced from his controversial writings. Miloš took Vuk with him to his court at Kragujevac, where Vuk took his place at the ruler's table and played cards with him after meals. By the end of October it seemed that Vuk might be making some progress with his plans to act as royal tutor and Minister of Education. He sent to Kopitar for useful maps and books, including *A comparison of Peter the Great with Charlemagne* and a history of Serbia in German, and wrote shortly afterwards that at Miloš's court he lacked nothing except that he was absent from his wife. At first, Miloš was not averse to the thought of learning to read and write (he started to take lessons), or to Vuk's ideas about the institution of schools.[1] Vuk was able to assure him that everything would redound to his own honour and glory, and he could not reasonably be suspected, as so many could at Miloš's court, of the highest political ambitions, or of trying to enrich himself unduly. By the end of the year moreover Vuk's prestige as a scholar and man of letters had been increased by the award of various distinctions from Slav learned societies. The St. Petersburg Society of Lovers of Russian Literature had made him a correspondent member while he was still in Russia and sent him his diploma in December 1820. In the summer of 1820 the Imperial Russian Academy had resolved, on the proposal of its president, Admiral Shishkov, to send him 300

---

[1] Vuk was an advocate of the Bell–Lancaster system, under which the senior pupils were made to do much of the teaching themselves. The method was originated by Dr. Andrew Bell (1753–1832) at an orphanage in Madras. It was popularized by Joseph Lancaster, a Quaker teacher (1778–1838), and widely used in the Ionian Islands under British rule. Vuk saw the method in Russia, where it had been introduced by the Russian Bible Society.

roubles for services rendered and expected, together with the silver medal of the Academy: and in November the Society of Cracow University elected him a correspondent member. Vuk himself was sensitive about his lack of formal education and academic titles, and much relished such compensations; they may indeed have counted for something even at Miloš's court.

4

In February 1821, the books ordered from Kopitar had arrived in Kragujevac: but by this time Vuk's more ambitious plans had already come to nothing, and he was ready to make an early escape from what was becoming an increasingly oppressive and dangerous environment. Miloš was a complex character, who never lost sight of two main objectives; to free Serbia from Turkish rule, and to increase his own power and wealth. He could persuade himself easily and fairly enough that the second objective was an essential preliminary to the first. For the complicated process which Miloš envisaged of securing diplomatic pressure on the Turkish authorities from outside, and of undermining their authority in Serbia by extensive bribery, a concentration of power and wealth in his own hands could reasonably be thought necessary. To achieve it, Miloš had been quite ruthless since 1815 in removing political opponents or potential opponents by open or secret terrorism, and in breaking up within Serbia the old institutions of regional self-government described by Vuk in the passages quoted in Chapter III; they were replaced in fact if not in name by Miloš's nominees, often his relations, who had little if any connection with the district which they ruled, and were ruthless and greedy in the execution of Miloš's policy. Miloš did not tolerate equals around him, and was quick to suspect ambition. In these circumstances, his court at Kragujevac attracted mainly second-rate adventurers, who were concerned entirely with survival, flattery, and self-enrichment, and looked askance at any newcomer of Vuk's ability who had ideas and threatened to diminish their influence with Miloš or his confidence in them. Moreover despite Vuk's pilgrimage to Russia, the underlings of Miloš's court were soon ready to regard him as a secret or potential agent of Austria—or at the very least to use any opportunity for sowing suspicions of this nature in Miloš's mind. Vuk's post from Vienna was regularly opened, and he lived in an atmosphere of intrigue and suspicion which soon became intolerable to him.

The most vivid evidence of this is contained in Vuk's letter to Miloš of April 1822, already quoted, in which Vuk explained his original objectives, and justified his decision to return to Austria. Vuk explained to Miloš how his work had been frustrated by the established court favourites and officials, in particular one Laza Todorović. There is no reason to think that the substance of Vuk's charges was exaggerated:

Laza feared that as soon as you learned as much as he, you would begin to look for counsellors and secretaries other than him; then too he was sore and ashamed that I should do for you what he could not, and feared that you would pay as much attention to me as to him, or more. So he looked on me as his worst enemy and malefactor, and constantly laboured to blacken me and all that I was hoping to do for you, and tried to kill my hopes and to convince me that I had nothing to look for in Serbia. When you said that you were taking me into your court . . . at first he couldn't do anything, and didn't dare to say anything against it; but when we arrived at Kragujevac and you began constantly to summon me and invite me to discussion and ask me various questions, he began to say every day in my presence how he thought that Serbia would win through happily if only its secrets were well kept, and behind my back he expanded on that until he'd estranged me from you. After that he'd talk to me almost every day but shut me up so that I couldn't have a say in anything whatever. It wasn't only that he slandered me as a tool of intriguers, and made it clear that everything was concealed from me, but he would even keep back from me Serbian and German newspapers for a week, until he had read them first. . . . Whenever he read anything good about me in the newspapers, not only would he refuse to show it to you, but he'd also hide it so that others shouldn't read it; but if there was anything bad, then all the servants and maids about the court would know it right away. . . .'

A particular grievance of Vuk was the trouble stimulated by Laza in respect of his translation of the New Testament. The existence of this had become known at court owing to the censorship of Vuk's mail. The Russian Bible Society had written asking him to send them a copy of his translation, for printing at St. Petersburg.[1] Miloš, on learning of this was persuaded to insist that

---

[1] This was after correspondence in which Vuk had asked for a further advance of money, made it clear to the Russian Bible Society that permission to print in Austria would never be given, and suggested printing in Leipzig or St. Petersburg

he must first approve the text himself with a view to publication at Leipzig, and Vuk sent for his text, encouraged by promises of financial help from Miloš and ecclesiastical approval from the Metropolitan of Belgrade, Agatangelos, afterwards Patriarch at Constantinople. In fact there was endless and ill-informed discussion and revision of Vuk's text, and much criticism of his use of popular and unlearned language.[1] Finally the committee set up at Miloš's court to approve or revise the text managed to get the whole question shelved, although as Vuk wrote indignantly to Miloš, the publication of his translation 'would have done more for your honour and glory than the renovation of ten monasteries in Serbia'.

By March 1821 there were further factors, unconnected with Laza Todorović or any of Miloš's other favourites, which made the court of Kragujevac a very unpleasant place for any Serb with memories of the heroic age of the revolt against the Turks. Miloš was determined to work in his own way for the independence of Serbia, and not to risk any premature rising which might fail for lack of diplomatic support from outside and bring the vengeance of the Turks on himself and the Serb nation. There were good reasons for this caution, and the events of 1832 showed that virtual independence was attainable without paying the price of a war; but equally one reason behind Miloš's policy was the desire to preserve without a rival his own position as leader in Serbia. From 1816 onwards the Serbian exiles, who had finally settled in Bessarabia after the collapse of the Karadjordje regime in 1813, had been linked with the Greek revolutionary society known as the Hetaireia, and had been projecting revolts against the Turks in Serbia and other parts of the Balkans to accompany a rising in Greece. It was with this end in view that Karadjordje himself returned to Serbia in 1817. Miloš proceeded to gain credit with the Turks by having him assassinated and thus removed a dangerous rival to his own position. The deed had appeared to many Serbs, including most of the prominent Serbs in the Srem and in Russia, as one of the blackest treachery, and had aroused

with the approval of the Prince Bishop of Montenegro. See *Arhivist* (Belgrade), 1963, 'Nekoliko dokumenata iz ruskih arhiva o Vuku Karadžiću'.

[1] Vuk recorded later, in an uncompleted history of his New Testament translation, that a 'terrible storm was raised' by his use of the normal Serb word for locusts (*skakavac*) instead of the time-honoured and unintelligible *akrid*; 'and whenever they wanted to raise a laugh against me, they would mention this'.

distrust and suspicion at the Russian court. But three years later Miloš again seemed to be justified by results; by September 1820 his own deputation was negotiating at Istanbul, with Russian diplomatic support and with good hope of success, for a further instalment of Serbian independence.

In January 1821 however the situation once more changed suddenly. The supporters of the 'Hetaireia' revolted prematurely against the Turks in Moldavia and Wallachia. In Constantinople the Turks took savage reprisals against the 'Phanariot' Greek Church leaders; and within a short time the revolt of mainland Greece had broken out. This was in fact the beginning of the end of Turkish rule in the Balkans. European public opinion was before long mobilized against Turkish atrocities committed on the sacred soil of Greece, and the Eastern Question acquired a new diplomatic dimension when France and England, as well as Austria and Russia, became once again concerned with it. Immediately, however, there was no diplomatic pressure for intervention against the Turks. On the contrary, at the Congress of Laibach (Ljubljana) early in 1821 Austria and Russia agreed to recognize the inviolable rights of legitimate governments, including that of Turkey, to deal with their internal affairs as they wanted to. This meant that the rising in Moldavia and Wallachia, which had to do without Russian aid, was soon crushed, and that the Turks for the time being had a free hand to deal with the Greek revolt.

In these circumstances, Miloš was particularly anxious to prove to the Turks that he had no connections with the revolt in Wallachia (all the more so as he was in fact in correspondence with its leaders);[1] he ruthlessly suppressed any elements within Serbia, including *hajduk* bands, which might give, or be thought by the Turks to give, aid to the revolt, and he exploited the chance

---

[1] A fascinating picture of the intrigues and counter-intrigues between Alexander Ypsilanti, 'Lieutenant-General of the Arché' of the Hetaireia from 1818, his agents, and Miloš Obrenović, is given in N. Botzaris, *Visions balkaniques dans les préparations de la révolution grecque*, Paris, 1962. Ypsilanti was anxious not to start the revolt in Wallachia until he had secured his flank against the Turks through the co-operation of Miloš. The latter was in negotiation with the Turks in 1819 for the improvement of conditions in Serbia, and was non-committal towards Ypsilanti. When the revolt broke out in Wallachia in March 1821, Miloš was finally determined in his caution by learning that Karadjordje's former generals, Milenko Stojković and Petar Dobrnjać, were serving with Ypsilanti's armies and that the insurgents were also in touch with the Turkish Pasha of Belgrade, in the hope of securing Miloš's deposition.

of exacting extreme penalties from anyone suspected of disloyalty to himself and his chosen men. His methods of repression were as barbarous as those of the Turks themselves, and Serbia must have seemed an extremely good country to escape from by the early months of 1821.

Vuk was happy to get away with little of his original and ambitious programme accomplished. He had collected some more 'popular songs' and folk-stories; he had visited some of the Serbian monasteries to look for ancient documents in his own interest and in that of Count Rumyantsev. The results of his researches (*A Description of Monasteries in Serbia*) he sent to Rumyantsev early in 1822 with a request (cautiously received) for financial help to enable him to undertake further and similar work. Vuk had also wanted for some time to embark on historical work, and during 1820–1 he had gathered some eye-witness material for a history of contemporary Serbia. But his wider schemes for a new system of schools and education had never got off the ground.

His last act during his stay at Miloš's court was to address a petition to the ruler, asking for financial assistance. During his stay at Kragujevac, he had received odd gifts of money from Miloš, which enabled him to send something to his wife in Vienna. He asked now for a regular pension and special help towards the publication of his books. What he needed, he said, was a loan of 10,000 *groš*, such as had been granted to others, towards the printing of the 'popular songs' which he had collected, of his own projected history of contemporary Serbia, and of other useful works by various writers. Vuk's request was typically detailed and factual. Proceeds of the sale of any of his books in Serbia could be held on account against the sum loaned him; he did not ask for the whole sum immediately, but only for a half, to cover the cost of printing the songs and sending some hundreds of copies for sale in Serbia, etc. He promised to devote his whole life to the object of making Miloš's name praised not only in Serbia but also throughout Europe, 'and that not only for today but for as long as there are people in the world'. And, he added, 'it will only add to your glory if you grant a pension to the first writer among your people as a reward for his labours, and to increase his goodwill for the future'. Even Vuk's flattery was often delivered with a due sense of his own dignity.

He received no answer to his petition, and in April 1821 he left

Kragujevac, under escort, for Belgrade. In one respect at least his journey was lucky. His escort Andjelko Vuković, one of Miloš's bodyguard, proved to be not only a good singer of tales, but also as anxious as Vuk could have wished to have his songs recorded for posterity.

From Belgrade, Vuk proceeded to Budapest, acting on this occasion as a special courier for Miloš. By reason of the revolt in Moldavia and Wallachia, Miloš had lost direct contact with the Russian consul in Bucharest. He wished to get a message through via the Russian Ambassador in Vienna, but would not give it to Vuk in Kragujevac, for fear that it might be discovered by the Austrian authorities at the frontier post of Zemun. Vuk was to receive the letter either in Zemun or Novi Sad, but on arriving at Zemun was told to go on and take delivery in Buda. From there he wrote to Miloš that he was still awaiting it. He occupied his time in taking the waters against a renewed attack of rheumatism, and in procuring a dye to restore the dark colour to his prematurely greying hair. In the meantime, the tortuous Miloš had entrusted his letter to another messenger, Marko Djordjević, who was to prove an assiduous enemy of Vuk.

5

Vuk's return to Vienna was not a happy one. A second son, Sava, had been born to him in his absence (to become in due course the favourite and great hope of the family). He had been able to send occasional advances of money to his wife, whose letters to him were concerned almost entirely with how to keep herself and the family alive. But Vuk left Belgrade with virtually nothing in his pocket, and had to raise some ready money on his friends' credit without even taking time to ask their leave.[1]

He thus assumed new debts and settled down again in Vienna early in June 1821, to look once more for means of earning a living. A good deal of his time was taken up in the familiar and financially unprofitable controversy about the Serbian alphabet. This continued throughout the year in supplements to the *Serbian*

---

[1] Vuk drew a sum from a Zemun merchant on the account of Nikola Nikolajević, without waiting for his permission. 'Brother and friend,' he wrote when confessing what he had done, 'it is only the utmost need which has driven me to this. I would rather confess my shame to you than to strangers.'

News of Vienna. Vuk as usual received some hard blows, and dealt a number harder than any that he received. He did not tire of repeating and enforcing his views. There is no point in rehearsing here the details of the argument, though it is worth recording that Mušicki intervened emphatically, if anonymously, on Vuk's side. It is however important to remember how much of Vuk's energy and time must have been consumed, at this as at later stages of his life, in the continuous battle for an object which was always quite as important as any other for him.

Vuk's first and best hope on his return to Vienna was to secure the publication of his third collection of 'popular songs'. He had taken down many more of these at Kragujevac and on his travels around Serbia, including a number sung to him by refugees from Bosnia—love-songs and lyrics rather than heroic ballads. The new collection was submitted to Kopitar as Imperial Censor for Slavonic books and he gave his approval as a matter of course. At this point however Vuk's life and work became entangled once again with high international policy. As a result of the decisions of the Laibach Conference, the Austrian Government felt bound to be cautious about allowing the publication of any book which could be held to encourage sedition against any of the established governments of Europe. The Court Chancellery found, on examining Vuk's new collection, that the Serbian 'popular songs', with their echoes of battles long and not so long ago against the Moslem oppressor, were 'written exclusively with the aim of increasing hatred against the Turkish Government'.

The same fate was in store for the history of contemporary Serbia on which Vuk had been working at Kragujevac. His draft *Material for a History of Serbia* was submitted in 1821 to the censorship at Vienna in a shortened form covering mainly the life and times of Miloš Obrenović, and thus most likely to secure his patronage. The head of the Vienna police, Sedlnicki, found that Vuk described events objectively, but Metternich himself ruled that 'at the present moment it would not be right to revive memories of the recent history of a people which by its rebellion against its masters set a precedent for the Greek revolt'.

Vuk's translation of the New Testament was also still subject to the ban of the Metropolitan Stratimirović, who remained watchful for any symptom of disobedience and reacted sharply when in December 1821, the *Serbian News* published without previous permission from the Church authorities some specimen passages, provided by Vuk, of the Holy Scriptures in the Bulgarian language. For this and other offences against his authority, Stratimirović lodged complaints against Vuk with the Austrian police in 1822, and Kopitar had to justify his protégé against them. This he did with considerable skill, defending Vuk as a conscious or unconscious agent of the Austrian policy of weaning the Slavs of Austria away from Russian influence. Vuk was protected from police persecution; but his three major literary works of the last year or two were banned and unlikely to see the light of day in Austria.

In partial compensation, Vuk gained one minor victory over the Austrian censorship. In fulfilment of part of the long term literary programme set for him by Kopitar in 1816, and in accordance with the particular wishes of Jakob Grimm, Vuk had collected some folk-stories from Serbia and published them in supplements to the *Serbian News* (1821) without attracting the notice of the censorship. Vuk was then able to renumber the pages and issue them as a small book. It did not bring him much renown at the time and still less financial profit; but it must have given him some satisfaction to see the stories published, particularly as one of them *Ero from the Other World* (translated at Appendix A, no. 13) was the classic tale of how Serbian peasant wit could make an ass of Turkish authority.

6

By the end of 1821, Vuk was thinking of an expedition to Germany where he had good hopes that, under the patronage of Jakob Grimm, at least his new collection of Serb 'popular songs' might be published. He could not, however, afford the journey, and had to turn once again to beg charity of Miloš Obrenović, even though Miloš had already sent him 400 florins earlier in the year as payment in advance for 100 copies of the third collection of 'popular songs'. In a letter of 22 November 1821, Vuk described piteously and no doubt accurately the conditions of life that had resulted from the ban on publication of his work. All his possessions were in pawn—'even the things most essential for my needs, books and linen and shirts and scarves—both my own and my wife's and children's—have all been sold or pawned'.

He asked for money to take him to Germany where he could get the ballads and history published, and found an ingenious *argumentum ad hominen* from the repercussions of the Greek revolt, which had determined Metternich to forbid publication in Austria:

> You see how throughout Europe there is talk of the new kingdom of Greece, and how in London and Paris money is already being collected to help the Greeks; but there is no mention of the Serbs, it is as if they did not exist. The Greeks will get their freedom before the Serbs, because they have their own agents and friends all over Europe, who will make the necessary efforts for them, and in newspapers, books and magazines publish to the whole world what can be of use to them; while the Serbs have no friends anywhere. . . . Thus you can see for youself that it would be necessary and useful for the present condition of Serbia if I went to Leipzig and travelled round a bit in those parts.

Vuk ended this appeal on the note that this was Miloš's last chance to profit by his services; if his request were refused, he would have to give up any idea of working in Serbia 'since one cannot live for ever on unrequited love and tenderness for one's native land'. Miloš was evidently unmoved, and sent no reply. By now, Vuk's financial situation in Vienna was hopeless, and at the beginning of May he moved to the village of Panjevo, near Temesvar (Timoşoara) in the Banat province. Here his previous benefactor, Maria Tirka, whose husband had finally produced the money necessary for publication of the *Dictionary* in 1818, had arranged for him to stay with her brothers, the Demelićes, representatives of a powerful local family. Vuk's wife and children followed him to Panjevo in the course of the summer, and he was able to pursue in comparative comfort and absence of immediate worry his projected studies—further work on the history of Serbia, and 'the lives of famous Serbs, to be a sort of Serb Plutarch'.

The tone of Vuk's letters to Kopitar at this time is comparatively cheerful. Kopitar held out fair prospects of getting the third collection of songs published in Vienna, as the position of Greece became more settled. But Vuk realized that he was doing no more than marking time in Panjevo. It was no use writing more until he could publish what was already written. The best hope of doing so still lay in a journey to Germany, and the best hope of raising money for the journey remained, for all previous disappointments, in securing or regaining the favour of Miloš.

Vuk set about doing so in various indirect ways. He had already persuaded a young Serb lawyer from Budapest, Jovan Hadzić (afterwards one of his bitterest opponents on linguistic matters) to compose an ode in praise of Miloš, and promised not only to get it published in Vienna, but also to circulate it in translation in Russia. From Panjevo he embarked on a proposal for the marriage of Miloš's daughter, Petrija, to one of the Demelićes, who appeared from Vuk's account to be a paragon. Apart from his heroic stature, large property and undoubted patriotism, he could talk French, Italian, Roumanian, Hungarian, Latin, and classical and demotic Greek. 'Had you been at Tsar Lazar's court', Vuk wrote to Miloš, 'you could without shame have introduced him to all and told that he was your son-in-law.' There were however too many other candidates in the field; and it was nominally for a direct discussion of Vuk's main interest—the publication of his third book of 'popular songs'—that Miloš eventually summoned him again to Kragujevac, where 'we could come to friendly agreements on various subjects better than by correspondence'.

Vuk reached Miloš's capital in mid-August 1822. Once again he had set out in an optimistic spirit, and once again he was quickly disillusioned. He wrote in October to Kopitar that his greatest gain from the journey was to have returned with a whole skin.

It proved that Miloš was much more interested in Vuk's historical work than in the publication of his collections of songs. The immediate cause of Miloš's suspicions was a letter from Vuk, discussing his projects for historical work and addressed to the ruler's nephew, Christofor, in Russia; this was probably opened in Christofor's absence by Mihailo German, Miloš's agent in Russia and a devoted enemy of Vuk, and sent straight to Kragujevac. Miloš wished to know more about the projected *History of Serbia*— and perhaps in particular about the use to which Vuk proposed to put a reproduction of Karadjordje's picture for which he had asked Christofor Obrenović. In fact Miloš had some reason to be on his guard. Vuk had previously talked of his history as one devoted entirely to Miloš's life and times, and it was a work covering this ground only that he had submitted to the censorship in Vienna. He had not disclosed to Miloš that he was also collecting material for a history of wider scope, in which it would be impossible to avoid full discussion of Karadjordje's role. His letter to Christofor Obrenović was thus something of a give-away. No doubt it was made clear to Vuk that Miloš would not tolerate any book which seemed in any way to diminish his own historical importance, and that in any case Metternich's arguments against publication were still valid. This was an immediate disappointment for Vuk, and he also found that since his departure from Serbia in 1821 the atmosphere of Miloš's court had not improved so far as he personally was concerned. Laza Todorović, his old enemy, was reinstated in Miloš's favour and his sentiments towards Vuk had not been improved by the letter of accusations sent by Vuk to Miloš earlier in the year. In general, moreover, the arbitrary and tyrannical character of Miloš was even more marked than in 1820. In the spring of 1821 two of the prominent local chieftains of Serbia had revolted,[1] primarily against the economic policy and exactions of Miloš; but he suspected that the rebellion might either be in support of the 'Hetaireia' revolts in Moldavia and Wallachia, or alternatively a part of a plot against him fostered by the Turkish authorities themselves, who had plenty of experience of prominent vassals ambitious to set up their own power—Ali Pasha of Janina and Pazvan Oglu of Vidin were notable precedents. Miloš in fact had little difficulty in crushing the rebellion but his suspicions remained and were directed against his own prominent subjects.

In the prevailing atmosphere of intrigue and flattery, Vuk's enemies at court did not spare him petty annoyances. This is evident from his own account of the episode which represented the most positive item on the balance sheet of his stay at Kragujevac. He describes as follows the collection of some 'really good' songs from a new source, Starac (old man) Milija:

> I heard at Kragujevac in 1820 that Milija knew particularly the ballads about *The wedding of Maksim Crnojević* and *Banović Stranja*. I'd known some versions of both of these songs since childhood, and had afterwards heard them and had copies of them from a number of people, but never in a version that was entirely to my taste. So I more than once requested His Highness Miloš Obrenović to get Milija to come to Kragujevac, or to send me to see him in the district of Požega. But in spite of all His Highness's promises, somehow my request remained unfulfilled. When I returned in the spring of 1821 from Serbia to Vienna, I made written requests both to His Highness and to

---

[1] The so-called *Abdulina buna* (revolt of Abdula) was organized by the chiefs Marko Todorović Abdula and Stevan Todorović Dobrnjac in the district of Požarevac (east central Serbia), in March 1821.

the late Vasa Popović, at that time the main chief of the Požega district, to have these two songs copied from Milija and sent to me; but they weren't able to do this for me either. When I came back to Kragujevac in the autumn of 1822 at His Highness's invitation, His Highness remembered my oral and written requests. Just as I was retiring from an audience and had kissed his robe and begun to make my farewells, he called up the clerk from his Chancery, and said to him with a smile: 'Laza, write to Chief Vasa that Vuk has arrived. He should come here right away, and bring old Milija with him alive, or carry him here dead. And Vasa should arrange for someone to do Milija's work for him at home till he gets back from here.' After a few days Chief Vasa arrived and with him Starac Milija. But when I met Milija, instead of happiness I found nothing but toil and trouble. Like nearly all the other 'singers' (who are nothing but singers), he couldn't recite the ballads in proper order but only sing them. And not only that; without spirits he wouldn't even sing, and as soon as he'd sipped a little spirits, he'd become so confused and decrepit—whether from old age or because of wounds (for he'd had his head all cut about, fighting with some Turks from Kolashin)—that he couldn't even sing always in the proper order. When I saw this I could think of nothing better than to make sure that he sang each song to me several times until I'd got it well enough by heart to know when he was skipping something; then I'd ask him to sing it slowly to me, drawling out the words, and would write after him, as quickly as I could. When I'd copied down a song like this, he'd have to sing it to me again, and I'd look at my manuscript to see if it was all written down properly. In this way I spent about a fortnight on four songs.

Milija knew a lot more songs, but I never had the chance of copying them. He had become rather bored just sitting there with nothing to do and singing to me, and apart from that there were people around (as is apt to happen at courts) who had nothing better to do than to get a laugh out of everything, and they said to him: 'How comes it that an old and sensible fellow like you is doing business with an idiot? Can't you see that Vuk is just a crazy good-for-nothing? He can't think of anything but songs and such-like nonsense. If you listen to him, you'll waste the whole autumn here. Off home with you, and look to your own affairs.' Thus they talked him round, and one morning, after receiving from His Highness a fine present for time lost to date, he left Kragujevac without telling me. When in after years I asked after him, I was told that he had died.

Vuk's own note on the old man's drinking habits is a typically vivid piece of observation:

He would not drink *rakija* from the cup in which it was brought to him, but had the habit of pouring it into a flask which he wore, and then as he sang would drink a little every hour. He'd toast whoever happened to be with him, as he sat drinking, and when he finished would put back the flask into the holder, without offering it to anyone. If anyone asked him what the *rakija* was like, he'd shake himself and frown and answer: 'Bad, my son, terribly bad, couldn't be worse; it's not God's will that you should drink it.'[1]

There is no evidence that Vuk's life or liberty were immediately endangered during his stay at Kragujevac, in spite of his dark hints to Kopitar, and the undoubted ill will which Mihailo German in St. Petersburg bore against him. But he was getting no further forward in his main task of securing money from Miloš, and evidently felt that the longer he stayed in the very unpleasant surroundings of the court the more likely he was to get into serious trouble. He returned from Kragujevac with his mission unaccomplished, but did not weary in importuning Miloš and his principal officers for money. Early in January 1823 he received rather surprisingly a condescending but favourable reply from Miloš in person; the Prince observed that Vuk wanted some money and had remarked in his letter that the printing of the songs would be in Miloš's own interest: 'You know very well that everyone likes best to sow where he will reap a full harvest; in order to fulfil your wish and to give myself at least some hope of benefit, I hereby inform you that I have decided to make available to you 3,000 *groš*.' Miloš's Chancellery recorded the gift, with the comment (which earns some sympathy) 'so that for once he will stop begging'.

Before receiving his answer from Miloš, Vuk had naturally considered alternatives to his projected journey. He was tempted, for example, by the prospect suggested by Kopitar of assuming the editorship of the *Serbian News*. In Vienna he applied through the Russian Embassy[2] to the Russian Foreign Minister, Count

---

[1] This story particularly pleased Kopitar, who remarked on it in a letter to Grimm of 14 January 1834: 'How do you like Vuk's biographies of the rhapsodes from whose mouth he took down the songs? For example the man of Kragujevac who described his *šlivovica* to everyone as terribly bad, in order not to have to offer it. . . .'

[2] The Russian Ambassador, Yuri Golovkin, had strongly taken up Vuk's case against the Russian Bible Society, and supported Vuk's own contention that owing to the delays and financial difficulties caused by them he had had to neglect the collection of material for Rumyantsev.

Nesselrode, for a pension, and even offered to act as an employee for a Russian Mission in Serbia. But no answer came, and in mid-January Vuk received Miloš's gift. By the beginning of February he was in Vienna again, preparing for the journey to Germany, and at the beginning of March he set out for Prague in the first instance. His stay in Germany was to prove of first-rate importance for his literary career.

XI

GERMANY, 1823-1824

I

VUK left Vienna early in March 1823. His first halt was in Prague, where he spent a few happy days discussing linguistic problems with Dobrovski, and meeting the poet Hanka.[1] ('His wife is young and not bad looking, slender and tall. That's a marvel. As a poet, he ought to have married an ugly woman—"Try to choose, they'll refuse".') From Prague, he went on to Dresden and Leipzig, arriving early in April. Until the end of September he lived alternately in Leipzig and Halle; in Halle he lodged with Johann Severin Vater, a distinguished Professor of Theology and Eastern (Slav) languages at Halle University. Kopitar had written to introduce Vuk to him— the first of his many important services to Vuk during the stay in Germany—and Vater received the guest from Vienna most kindly.

In applying to the Vienna authorities for his passport to Germany, Vuk had stated that he wished to study medicine at Halle University, and in fact he seems to have had some serious intention of doing so, and of thus reducing his own dependence on literary work. He began to attend a course of anatomy at Halle, but found the demonstrations hard to endure—'God preserve us from the smell, it's so foul', he wrote to Kopitar. Moreover the lectures were so widely dispersed about the town that with his lame leg he could not easily get from one to another. Vuk continued his lessons in Leipzig for a short time, but soon gave them up and put himself down for a philosophy course during the summer term, attending lectures on ancient philosophy,

---

[1] Vaclav Hanka (1791-1861) the Czech poet and Slavist. It was he who in 1817 discovered the manuscript of Králové Dvůr in Bohemia, containing 'ancient' Czech poems, and in 1818 claimed to decypher a second 'ancient' manuscript, that of Zelená Hora. Dobrovski and Kopitar from the start disputed the authenticity of the second, and both manuscripts were much later proved to have been forged. The principal champion of scholarly standards in this case was eventually Thomas Masaryk. See Paul Selver, *Masaryk*, London, 1940, ch. vii.

'fundamental philosophy', logic and metaphysics, and experimental physics. It does not appear that the courses made much impression on him; he found that it was late for him (now well on in his thirties) to embark on such completely new subjects, and his mind was clearly ill-suited for generalities and abstractions.

Vuk remained of course mainly concerned with his primary object, of which he had naturally not informed the Austrian passport authorities, the printing of his 'popular songs'. His original intention had been to print only the third collection of them, which consisted of 35 songs about heroic exploits of modern times; but at an early stage of his stay in Leipzig he changed his mind and embarked on a much more ambitious task, which involved not only the third collection, but a much enlarged new edition of the first two collections (of lyrics and ancient songs) originally published in Vienna, 1814–15. It is not certain what inspired him to this larger project. He was always ready to be carried away by his own zeal and enthusiasm—how else could he have rebounded so quickly from his many setbacks?—and on this occasion he had probably convinced himself that his financial prospects were at last good.

Vuk's hopes were by this time set once more on Russian patronage. Before he set out for Leipzig, he had been in correspondence with Adelung at St. Petersburg about plans for further work and further payment by Rumyantsev. In answer to a letter asking for a detailed prospectus, Vuk had proposed that Rumyantsev should finance his stay in Leipzig for a year or at least nine months, in order to bring out a large collection of 'popular songs' (he admitted that these had little bearing on Russian history, but thought them worthy of the patronage of the 'Russian Maecenas'). He could also publish the description of Serbian monasteries already sent to Rumyantsev,[1] and go on further journeys throughout the present area of Yugoslavia and even Bulgaria, to collect further manuscripts and books and to make notes about the monasteries, geography, and statistics. After this he could settle in Vienna to prepare the publication of all this material. Vuk received no reply from Adelung until March 1823, and the answer when it came was cautious. Rumyantsev was favourable to the

---

[1] Compiled during his stay in Serbia in 1820, when he visited the monasteries of Ovčar and Kablar, above the valley of the western Morava between Čačak and Užice.

publication of the 'popular songs' (this had also been urged by Kopitar), but wanted immediate details of how big 'the book' would be and of the costs of printing. Vuk's reply to this was that he was already printing the songs and would need 300 ducats partly for the printers and partly for his own keep (no word of what he had received from Miloš Obrenović). Adelung was disturbed by Vuk's high-handed way; he sent 500 rubles (50 ducats) on account of a Slavonic 'Liturgy' received from Vuk, but for the expenses of printing the songs said that he could not suggest to Rumyantsev more than 150 ducats. In the event Rumyantsev sent a further 500 rubles, but the money did not arrive until Vuk had left Leipzig.

His hope of early financial assistance from Russia was thus frustrated, and in the summer of 1823 he had to embark once more from Germany on the familiar round of begging letters. These included one to Dimitrije Frušić at Trieste, who replied with a brisk sincerity worthy of Vuk himself. He had, he said, no money to give, and could offer no security for a loan from others. He had been thinking of sending a small gift, but Vuk's request for a large sum had upset his plans. Certainly money had been raised for Dositej and others, but it was still owing: 'I shall finish this wretched letter—the most wretched and unhappy for me and others that ever my hand penned, and I conclude with words which come right from my heart at this time (may God grant that in the future I may be able to take a different line and think and act differently); I must say that I'd rather some one tore my heart to pieces with his fingers than asked me for money on loan without security or as a present.' In fact the letter ended with a more cheerful postcript. Just as Frušić was going to send it, he saw a common friend through a window and called him in to hear Vuk's letter and his own reply. 'Man,' said the friend, 'you can't murder poor Vuk like that, I'm convinced that he'll yet do something to help our nation, either there in Leipzig, or later on in Serbia. Here, I'll give him 60 florins, and you another 60, and after that it'll be as God grants.' So Frušić was able to send Vuk 150 florins—(33 ducats, instead of the 50 which he had asked)—together with sharp warnings not to get into such straits again, not to beg constantly, and if he must, at least no more from him (Frušić), who would under no circumstances give any more: 'There are plenty of other families; they too get nothing from me, for I have to save something against old age. I ask your pardon for writing so severely; you must reflect that between friends sincerity and not politics is what is needed.' In fact, Frušić was a good deal better than his word, and raised over 300 florins more for Vuk within the next nine months, as advance payment for copies of the volumes of songs printed at Leipzig.

In the meantime Vuk's health was beginning to show signs of strain, and his worries were increased by the letters reaching him from his wife. That long-suffering woman was in fact better looked after than she had usually been during her husband's long absence. She was settled temporarily no longer at Panjevo but with another Serb family (Tirol) near Temesvar, and Kopitar had been able to provide her with occasional sums of money. Throughout the summer however she wrote bitter complaints to Vuk about her situation and about his neglect of her—it was being rumoured, she said, that he intended to leave her (perhaps she had heard of the possibility that Vuk might accept employment in Russian service). He replied sharply, telling her that if he had more money he would need no reminders from her to send it, and warning her never to send him such letters again. Tirol, who himself heard plenty of Anna's complaints about Vuk, wrote to him taking his side, and suggesting that he should by way of punishment sleep apart from her for a week on his return—perhaps not the most appropriate penalty, given the size of their family.

By August 1823, Vuk had gained little but worry, it seemed, from his venture to Leipzig. It was Kopitar who not only looked after his family but also kept Vuk's courage up by a series of stimulating letters, urging the importance of getting the Serbian songs published quickly. A rather transparent code was evolved between the two correspondents, since the official Austrian attitude was still that the publication would offend Turkish sensibilities. The new or third collection of modern songs (the first to be printed) was known as *Jovan Sestrić* (sister's son—an allusion to a name in the ballad of the *Wedding of Maksim Crnojević*), the second, of ancient songs, was called *Strahinja* (after the famous song of Strahinja Banović), and the first, of lyric songs, *The women's*. Vuk's state of mind just before the new third book came off the press is illustrated by his letter to Kopitar of 11 August 1823:

I received your letter of 23 July, and understand it all. Perhaps I have become (or *been*) rather *kindisch und weibisch* [childish and womanly];

that won't change me at all or turn me from my business, but when I am *sick*, life itself is not dear to me; and now I am really sick. Vater and his wife couldn't have received me better. I would have gone to the inn, but the next day they took me into their house, and brought their own doctor to see me, and made every effort to make things easier for me. Indeed I haven't been in bed up till now, and I'm not in bed now. My illness consists of the following: (1) an ache in the stomach below the chest. (2) all over my body a kind of nervousness and unhappy and impatient feeling, so that if there is anything that is the least unpleasant to me, I feel it immediately in my legs (as if the soles of my feet were getting numb); and that is all the result of worry and *verdruss*.

Thank you for saying that you will send another 50–100 florins to my wife, if necessary; for the moment I think that she is not in need, but should she be so, my mother-in-law will tell you; but I hope that she too (my wife) may soon be able to get something from *Jovan Sestrić*. Sestrić is quite ready but they are making clothes for him to wear on his journey. He wasn't able to bring that drawing with him,[1] but has left it for Strahinjić, who will set out in about a month from now; and then, if I'm neither dead nor any better, I too shall leave Saxony and come to you. What I finish here will be out of the way, and I shall find ways of making up for what I don't finish. My health must come before anything else. 'You may fly, as a slave, but you can't from the grave'....

In mid-August the new collection, Book III of the 'popular songs', containing those of modern times, was ready. Vuk sent 300 copies of the new book to Miloš himself, to whom it was dedicated (incidentally it was in the dedication that Vuk first signed himself formally 'Vuk Stefanović Karadžić'). The other two books were due to be ready in October and December respectively. Kopitar, who was tireless in his suggestions to Vuk for raising money immediately, wrote that at least the lyrical songs (Book I) might better be published in Vienna. 'Women travel around more easily than *hajduks* and heroes, and you would not be risking much by bringing the ladies to Vienna, though I can't guarantee that some informer won't appear. You should bear in mind too that the Kaiser is going to Černovci in the Bukovina, where you once stayed, and will perhaps meet with Alex.' This last is an allusion to the wider context of international politics. Kopitar hoped for a renewal of the Russo-Austrian schemes discussed by Catherine the Great and Joseph II for carving up the Ottoman

---

[1] The drawing was of a figure to appear on the title-page.

Empire in Europe or at least for agreement on dividing it into spheres of influence for Russia and Austria.

In any such division, Serbia and Bosnia would fall to the Austrian Government. Kopitar envisaged that in such circumstances there would be no need to take account of Turkish sensibilities. There would be a large market for Vuk's collection of songs in the newly liberated territories, and in addition there would be a strong and growing interest in German-speaking Austria for the Serbian language and literature. This would therefore be the time for Vuk to publish a German translation of his grammar (of which more later in this chapter).

2

In spite of the prospects thus suggested by Kopitar, Vuk stuck to his plans for printing the other two books in Germany. But he took the further advice given to him by Kopitar to travel and introduce himself personally to the learned world in Germany. From Halle Vuk travelled at the end of September to Kassel, where for the first time he met Jakob Grimm, who had already done him much good service by the reviews printed in the *Göttingsche Gelehrte Anzeigen* (and reprinted in Vienna) of Vuk's first collection of songs and of his *Dictionary*.

Grimm wrote to Kopitar enthusiastically about his meeting with Vuk: 'He gave me great pleasure, and has visited me for a few days. This morning however he's planning to leave already, by way of Göttingen. Yesterday he was talking incidentally about Serb hospitality, and I felt distressed that I could neither put him up in my little house nor entertain him as I'd have liked. That's the way with us learned, pedantic Germans; we may have some feeling for the poetry and simple natural virtues of uncultured peoples, but cannot imitate them properly. I couldn't act as his guide, nor make any expedition with him, I'm so plagued with all kinds of business....' Vuk, also writing to Kopitar, said nothing about any failings in Grimm's hospitality, and expressed amazement at his knowledge of the Serb language.

From Kassel Vuk proceeded to Göttingen and thence to Weimar early in October with a letter of introduction from Grimm to Goethe. The meeting is described in another letter from Vuk to Kopitar (23 October 1823):

I hope that you received my own and Grimm's letters from Kassel. In Weimar I spent eight days, and I can tell you that these were the finest of my life (up to now). I had a letter to Goethe from Grimm, in which he enclosed a German translation of the song *How the Jakšić brothers shared* [a translation will be found in Appendix A, no. 2]. I can't describe to you how Grimm praised our songs in his letter: 'Of all that I have known in this line', he says, 'nothing can be compared with the Serbian', and 'the harder one tries to translate them faithfully, the more one recognizes and feels the inadequacy or imperfection of our language for this task!' I gave Grimm's letter to Goethe's servant in the evening, just when Goethe was getting ready to go out somewhere in his carriage. When the servant had handed over the letter, he told me that His Excellency said it would be particularly agreeable to him if I could come at 11 next day. When I arrived next day, Goethe was waiting for me in the middle of his room; we sat down (after many compliments) on the couch (sofa), on which were spread out Grimm's letter, the translation of *The Jakšić brothers* and a bundle of newspapers; then Goethe, pointing to the newspapers, said: 'You see, today is not the first time that you've been in my room; you've been here with me for a long time now!' When I cast my eyes on the newspapers, there were the reviews of my first *Serbian Grammar* [published in 1816]. You can imagine yourself what a triumph this was for me! Then we talked a good deal about our songs, and he read me *The Jakšić brothers*, asked me how certain lines ran in the original and told me that he himself would hand them in for printing: and he asked me to translate a few songs word for word and send them to him. . . .

Goethe himself wrote to Grimm, thanking him for recommending Vuk to him, and saying that he had much welcomed the chance which the interview had given him of improving his knowledge of Vuk's work. Vuk wrote after his departure from Weimar 'Von innigster Freude ehrfurchtsvollem Dankgefühle durchdrungen' (filled with gratitude, reverence, and the deepest joy) at his reception, and sent Goethe translations of more ballads. The latter replied on 20 December 1823 in a courteous letter:

You have given me very great pleasure by sending me the literal translation of the eminently beautiful Serbian songs, and then doubled and trebled it by your gift of the *Grammar* and *Dictionary*.
Your interesting language has thus made its way amongst us too, and imposed on our scholars the duty of diligently studying it. Excuse me if I ask again for a favour—that you should send me a similar literal

translation of the enclosed Serbian songs, particularly of the last of which the main theme is a fine one.
Be assured of my interest, and best wishes.

Your very devoted
J. W. Goethe

At Weimar, Vuk had not confined his attention to Goethe. In the rest of his letter to Kopitar already quoted, he described his audience with the Grand Duchess of Weimar, Maria Pavlovna, sister of Tsar Alexander, to whom Kopitar had been urging that Vuk should pay his respects. The details of the audience are of little interest; the Grand Duchess showed much consideration, sending her carriage for Vuk and meeting him on the ground floor to spare him the ascent of any stairs, and Vuk himself displayed proper reverence ('she told me to sit down, but I did not think it right to do so'). He probably had hopes of securing a substantial sum of money from the Grand Duchess. Kopitar had persuaded him to ask permission to dedicate to her the first (lyrical) volume of Serbian songs in the new Leipzig edition. Vuk went to much trouble to remove from the songs any hint of indelicacy which might offend the taste of female royalty. He wrote to Kopitar in some doubt on the subject of 'Zweydentige Lieder' (songs of ambiguous meaning) and also debated with him the proper form of dedication to the Grand Duchess. He had thought of a brief letter as follows: 'In collecting the songs of a small Slav nation living among the mountains of the South, and rather neglected than small or unimportant, the author could not possibly add more honour and glory to his native tongue than by bringing this first book to the feet of the amiable sister of his blessed Imperial Majesty. . . .' (The dedication as ultimately published was simpler and less flowery.)

The Grand Duchess, while gracious enough to Vuk on the spot, was a great disappointment to him financially. He earned no more from her patronage than the gift of a snuff box. But his memories of Weimar were glorious enough for the time being. And on his return to Halle in mid-October a surprise awaited him perhaps even more gratifying and useful to him than his reception by Goethe. He found that, owing to the intervention of Vater, the University of Jena had granted him a diploma as Doctor of Philosophy. Such distinctions were important to Vuk in that they put him on an academic level with the learned men of the Serbian

Orthodox Church, and perhaps even more so from the psychological point of view, in that they proved him to his own satisfaction to be no longer the 'simple goatherd'. His desire remained set on an honorary doctorate from Göttingen University, such as had been granted to his main enemy, the Metropolitan Stratimirović (known in his familiar correspondence as 'Uncle Steve'). He was partially satisfied on this point in December 1823, when he was elected a corresponding member of the Learned Society of Göttingen.

3

Vuk's travels to Kassel, Göttingen, and Weimar were an academic and literary triumph for him, but brought him no immediate cash; and a severe blow was in store for him when he got back to Leipzig. The debts on the printing of the enlarged Books I and II of the 'popular songs' were beginning to pile up. He still had no news of any more money from Russia and was already disturbed by the absence of any reply to the letter which he had addressed to Miloš Obrenović in August, enclosing copies of the third collection of songs. Vuk wrote with an air of confidence to Vasa Popović at Miloš's court: 'My hope in our Prince's goodness gives me courage and good cheer.... The holy scripture tells us: "He who believes and holds to the faith shall be saved." Firmer than a rock stands my belief and hope that our Prince will rescue me from poverty.... I dreamt at night that the Prince had sent me an overcoat of red cloth and when I unfolded it, it was full of lice. Now you should know how I interpret this dream: the coat will come soon, and the lice will be coins.'

At this stage, early in 1824, he received a very hostile answer from Miloš Obrenović, in a sense far remote from that of his own Biblical visions. Vuk's enemies at court had been at work on Miloš, who remained highly suspicious of any historical writings, either in prose or verse, about his own life and times. In his letter Miloš expressed grave dissatisfaction that Vuk had embarked on the reprinting of the first and second books of songs, previously published in Vienna, and more particularly that in the third and new book, he had published

an untruthful description of the Battle at Čačak[1] under my leadership.

---

[1] This refers to an important victory for the Serbs in summer 1815, during the 'Takovo revolt'.

... All of us who were present at these events and witnessed them, were disgusted at the lies in your songs, which ought to have been founded on truth, seeing that they are about my own times ... I shall not permit you to circulate among our people lies about my exploits. I, who consider myself the promoter of this part of your song-book, had hoped for something different from you so far as touches my exploits and my own times, and of such lies even in a dream I never dreamt. I assure you that this part of your song-book won't prosper as you thought, and won't be sold as you have reckoned.

Miloš had some cause for his annoyance, which revived all the suspicions, temporarily laid by Vuk in autumn 1822, about his historical writings. Vuk had talked out of him the money for printing the third book of songs on the ground that the songs of modern times would present him in a heroic light, and increase his glory in Serbia and Europe. In fact, Miloš was mentioned only in the ballad of the battle of Čačak and there simply as one of the main chiefs concerned. There was much more in the songs to the glory of Karadjordje and of other leaders of the first Serb revolt. It is not surprising that Miloš was annoyed, and more so that Vuk did not pay more attention to the susceptibilities of his patron. This is perhaps a sign that Vuk was suffering in the early days of his visit to Germany from a certain euphoria about his financial and literary prospects; he seems to have thought (so far as he thought about the subject) that he would soon be released from the necessity of having to beg money from Miloš and to flatter him.

Vuk wrote an immediate answer to the Prince, asking for pardon in a fairly humble tone, mainly on the grounds that songs were not real history. He wanted to show the world by printing one song about Miloš that people did sing of his exploits, and had 'left it for the introduction to the first book[1] to say that among the people there are many more and better songs about you, but up till now I have not been able to collect them'. As for the fact that his history of Miloš had not yet appeared, Vuk said that Miloš himself very well knew the reason for this (it had been banned by the

[1] The enlarged 'first' book (of lyrical songs) was published in the Leipzig edition after the new 'third' book. Vuk was as good as his word, writing as follows in his introduction: 'of recent songs from the year 1815 (and especially about the battles at Požarevac and Dublje) there are many more and much better than the fragments given here at the end of Book III, but so far I have not been able to collect them.' For a full text, see Appendix E.

Viennese censorship). He emphasized the enthusiasm with which the Germans, including Goethe, had received the Serbian songs, and said that this was only a beginning. Vuk wrote further letters on the same lines, and with stress on his growing debts, to Miloš and to Vasa Popović before the end of the year. But there was no answer.

Shortly after this he received a discouraging letter from the Russian Bible Society. They wrote to say that they would be unable to pay the rest of the price agreed in 1819 for his translation of the New Testament since the Metropolitan of Kishinev, whom they had consulted, did not approve publication. Vuk's only financial hopes for the immediate future now rested with Frušić and Adelung (acting for Rumyantsev). Such hopes were, as has already been seen, not entirely disappointed, but money from these sources did not arrive in time to prevent Vuk accumulating a large debt to the printers of the three collections of songs (the last of these was printed before the end of 1823). It was Jakob Grimm who came to the rescue. The German publisher, Reimer, at his instance bought 200 copies of each book, advanced 50 talers to Vuk, and assumed 300 talers of the debt to the printers. This was a generous action, for Vuk was not able to pay in full until 1839. He remained in debt to the extent of nearly 300 talers to the printers, and had to leave with them as security 1178 copies of the Song-books (786 of the first, 336 of the second, and 56 of the third). Vuk made his way once more to Weimar in February 1824 in order to keep in touch with his eminent patrons. Goethe received from him copies of the first two collections. The two had been in correspondence since Vuk's first visit about German translations of certain songs, and Goethe was much interested in publishing some of these. Vuk also brought with him in February 1824 a letter from Professor Vater of Halle, who gave an alarming account of Vuk's health ('it is so undermined that the slightest trouble over printing causes him a sleepless night or other inconvenience') and asked Goethe to put in a good word for Vuk with the Grand Duchess, to whom he presented a copy of the first book of songs, dedicated to her. Vater suggested that she might speak to the Russian Foreign Minister, Count Nesselrode, about Vuk, and Nesselrode would see to it that the Russian Embassy at Vienna looked after him 'as they looked after all those who had fought for

Karadjordje and settled in Bessarabia'.[1] So far as is known nothing came of this request.

By this time Vuk realized that his main hope for any lasting prosperity lay in persuading Miloš Obrenović that it was worth paying him for the services which his publications could render in putting Serbia on to the map of Europe, and in linking its ancient glories with the present reign of Miloš himself. Vuk had begun to sense that Miloš, though offended, was afraid of his pen. This gave him a certain bargaining power, but it could not be exerted from Germany. He made his way via Leipzig to Vienna, where he arrived early in March 1824. Within three months, he had brought this chapter of his relations with Miloš Obrenović to a successful conclusion. The final contacts were made from Zemun—he was clearly reluctant to venture himself once again to Miloš's court— and little is known of the details, but by the end of May Miloš had ordered the payment to Vuk of 1,000 florins. Vuk's debt to the Leipzig printers was paid, and the copies of Books I and II of the songs could be put into circulation.

4

It is surprising at first sight that the Austrian censorship authorities made so little difficulty about this. They had after all objected to publication in Vienna on the ground that it would inflame the nationalist spirit of the Serbs against the Turks, and logically they should have objected hardly less to circulation of the same books, admittedly printed elsewhere, in Austria. In fact before the end of 1823, Vuk had heard from his friend Tirol of difficulties in getting copies of Book III through the customs at Temesvar, and wrote to Kopitar expressing the fear that the authorities in Buda would stop distribution. These fears were not justified, but in spring 1824, Vuk's friend Tirka was denounced to the police for selling copies of Book III in Vienna. The highest police authorities recorded the opinion (14 May 1824) that 'these songs are written with provocative expressions, which should only be read by experienced people, not easily to be led astray, and certainly not

---

[1] In 1813 the Austrian Government had been delighted to rid themselves (to Russian territory) of such potentially dangerous exiles as Karadjordje and some of his captains.

by the youth of Serbia, among whom they could arouse the wish for independence'. The songs seemed to be designed to demonstrate the 'bravery and devotion that should be shown to liberate oneself from one's sovereign lord', and would probably provoke the Slavs of Austria as well to work for their own independence. Kopitar as censor was reproved for carelessness in letting such books circulate.

His defence, in a counter-report to the Vienna police, is extremely interesting. Much of it is irrelevant to the charge of stimulating sedition, and harks back to his defence of Vuk against Stratimirović in 1822, stressing the need to undermine the influence of the Orthodox Church and promote the unity of the Slavs in Austria by encouraging a truly popular language.

The undersigned, convinced that this [the publication of 'popular songs'] was a good cause and also the cause of Austria, suggested to Vuk the idea that a collection of the very fine popular songs of the Serbs would be both a much-loved and an invincible representative of the Serbian mother-tongue, for the songs are sung only by the people who have not learned the church language, and must be pure Serbian. . . . Vuk is a foreigner, but no enemy of Austria. While he fights for his own opinions, of which only he is master, he also fights unconsciously for Austria. . . . Austria can tolerate these songs, because they are not printed here. Russia will take care not to work against this directly. . . . The fruits which this book will bear, in providing the Serbs with their own independent and much-loved literature (which will soon outstrip the Russian in favour, since it will rally them around a national centre), would easily outweigh, through the spirit and tendency of the whole collection, any objections against individual and temporarily perhaps harmful details. . . . Given that this collection is part of a three-volume edition with quite different contents and a purely scientific tendency (as shown in the preface to the *Dictionary*), the censor [Kopitar himself], already advised by competent critics of the author (who is recognized as the Illyrian Homer, Ossian, etc.), found no difficulty in approving it, the more easily as the songs of which suspicion has been expressed, being written in Vuk's alphabet and possessing classical value themselves, are entirely suited to give to Serbian literature, hitherto under Russian influence, a popular instrument much more favourable to Austria. It is indeed just because of these qualities in Vuk's works that the censor is not in the least surprised that our Austrian Russomanes (among whom must be numbered, even if they are quite unaware of it, all Greek Orthodox believers, for purely psychological reasons), have produced priest after priest to lessen their influence. . . .

Whether or not Kopitar's defence, tortuous as it was in argument and phraseology, carried conviction, the circulation of Vuk's Serbian songs in Austria was allowed; indeed to men of an age more advanced in the arts of censorship, it seems that both Miloš and Metternich were rather half-hearted in their opposition—perhaps in both cases tyranny was tempered with *Schlamperei*. The sale of the books among the Serbs in Austria and in Serbia itself was of little financial advantage to Vuk. The clergy in particular were very hesitant about buying, in view of Stratimirović's opposition, and even those people who had promised to subscribe were unwilling to pay up the full amount of their subscription at this stage. There had been a gap of nearly three years between the first advertisement in 1821 and the final appearance of Book III, and the general feeling was 'We've had to wait for the book, and Vuk can wait for his money'.

5

Financially, then, Vuk's expedition to Germany had gained him little or nothing. It was nevertheless an important landmark in his literary life, for it served as nothing else could to bring his work to the notice of a small but highly cultivated public. Vuk had been quite correct in claiming to Miloš Obrenović that the learned Germans were enthusiastic about Serbian poetry and the Serbian language. The most generous recognition for Book III of Vuk's collection had come from Jakob Grimm, whose very detailed review was published in the *Göttingsche Gelehrte Anzeigen* of 5 November 1823. A full translation of this is given at Appendix D, and the following extracts are only those most relevant to Vuk's literary biography:

... The reviewer ... wants to report without delay on an undertaking begun without any noise (as is the way with most good and fruitful things), which in time will make the whole of educated Europe take notice and as a start will inevitably have beneficial effects for the editor's native land.

These Serbian songs are not the result of laborious research in old manuscripts, but have all been recorded from the living voice of the people; perhaps they have never been written down before, and in this sense they are not old, but they are likely to have a long life. Some of them ... celebrate deeds which happened not so much as 20 years ago;

and one cannot detect that those concerned with the older and less definitely historical events of popular songs are any different in style and manner. . . .

The Serbian songs . . . are couched in pure and noble language, while the narration is full, clear, and without confusion from beginning to end. In the Serbian territories there are no crude vulgarities of popular expression. . . .

The Serbian songs provide much-needed and substantial material for the study of epic poetry, which has hitherto been all too one-sided. The second part of Vuk's collection is bound to be of outstanding importance, since it will give us the older songs (the subject-matter of which is more mythical) and is likely to surprise us with many stories hitherto unknown; the first part is reserved for 'women's songs', which could be described as mainly lyrical, and are written in various metres. Even those who in general have no feeling for the simplicity of these compositions, and who are inclined not to rate them so high as we do, can hardly withhold their applause, if they know any of the current Slav languages, from the purity and musical quality of the Serbian tongue. The book will reveal to them a wealth of genuine Slav words, forms, and expressions, which have been unknown or forgotten. The Russian can read himself into the language without difficulty, the Ukrainian even more easily, the Czech and Pole will probably find it more difficult. . . .

Germans who wish to study a Slav language can be recommended the Serbian above all others, because of its clarity, beauty, and (this can be added as the result of Herr Vuk's labours) because of the charm of its historic literature. The principal aid to reading continues to be Vuk's dictionary. His grammar is written only in Serbian; a German translation must and we hope soon will be undertaken. . . .

This was an extremely important advertisement for Vuk. He circulated it widely to his friends, and printed it as part of the introduction to Book I of the 'popular songs' in the Leipzig edition. The echoes of Grimm's praise were heard widely in Europe, as will be shown in the next chapter.

The last sentence cited above from Grimm's review refers to Vuk's *Grammar* (of 1816 revised in 1818 for publication as part of the preface to his *Dictionary*) and to the possibility of a German translation of it being undertaken. Here again Grimm was actively helpful. Vuk's friend from Temesvar, Dimitrij Tirol, had translated it into German some years back, and Vuk had brought with him to Leipzig the manuscript of the translation. Kopitar had urged him to get this checked, preferably by Professor Vater, and published—always with the political requirement at the back of his mind for creating or increasing interest in the Serbian language among the German-speaking Austrians. In fact by the end of October, 1823, Grimm had agreed to take on the task himself, after expressing some hesitations to Kopitar lest he should be overwhelmed with other business and unable to finish it; but 'the subject-matter is very close to my heart, so close that I worked on it for a whole year, and then had to lay it aside for revision'. Grimm's fears were not justified. He found a publisher for a German edition, and extensively revised Vuk's work, leaving out the polemics unsuitable for German readers, adding a section on the gender of nouns, revising the chapter on adjectives and the introductory part on verbs and making other minor alterations. Vuk was entirely happy about the changes and wrote to Grimm expressing his regret that they were not more extensive since 'you are an altogether different sort of grammarian from myself'.

Most important for Vuk was the fact that Grimm wrote a long introduction to the translation. Apart from detailed grammatical observations and some general history of the Slav languages, this contained a section written in the spirit of Vuk and Kopitar on the importance of promoting the use of live and popular language, and an eloquent eulogy of Vuk himself: 'The undertaking of successfully rescuing Serbia and the Serbian language from its shameful and moribund state, has been reserved for our times and for one single man (whose merits, it is true, have been more obvious outside than in his own country). He has shown what can be accomplished in a short time by untiring devotion and fortunate industry. But the achievements which in other lands would have gained for him the crown of public recognition for his services, in his own country have earned him something like persecution.' Grimm went on to say that the collection of 'popular songs' had been as important for linguistic as for poetical studies; the readers of Vuk's *Grammar* and *Dictionary* might indeed think that the songs had been collected entirely to serve as supporting material for them.

Vuk was profoundly thankful for all these services, and not least for the fact that the translation of the *Grammar* was dedicated to Miloš Obrenović—much against the will of Grimm, who had taken a poor view of Miloš's letter to Vuk about Book III of the songs. Thus the great scholar's tribute to Vuk could be brought directly to the notice of the prince who remained for the present his most important patron, and no doubt Miloš's decision to pay Vuk the money to discharge his debt to the Leipzig printers was determined in part by Grimm's opinion.

The list of Grimm's services to Vuk at this time is completed by the review which he wrote on the publication of Books I and II of Vuk's collection. In this he rated them both higher than Book III, which he had so unreservedly praised, and drew particular attention to the songs of the battle of Kosovo and the *Building of Skadar* (Appendix A, no. 2). The main theme of Grimm's review was however the comparison of Serbian with Western and Eastern lyric poetry—a theme likely in particular to interest Goethe, who had recently been engaged on his imitations of Hafiz (the *West-Östliche Divan*). The Serbian lyrics seemed to Grimm to combine the good qualities of both West and East. 'The thoughts are more forcible and colourful than those of the folk-songs of other European countries, but without the bombast and superfine expressions of Arab and Persian poetry. Their smell is sweet without being intoxicating. Their scent is of the rose, not of attar of roses.'

Grimm's reviews had great historical importance for Vuk, and are in themselves interesting. But for the present generation they have not the fascination of Vuk's description of his own work and subject-matter contained in the preface to the new Leipzig edition of Book I (which incorporated, as a start, Grimm's review of Book III). I have already drawn on this preface in Chapter II, and more substantial extracts of it are given in translation at Appendix E. The main themes are: the various types of song—the heroic, sung to the accompaniment of the *gusle*, and the women's songs, sung unaccompanied in unison or two parts; the types of song found in various districts; how they are composed, transmitted, and altered; the language and age of the songs; songs found only in fragments; and the most usual metres. This preface, together with another of Vuk's introductions to one of his later collections, remains the most concentrated distillation of his wisdom and experience on the general subject of 'popular poetry', and an important source for comparative students of epic literature. It is linked with the dominant realities of Vuk's life by the final panegyric of Miloš Obrenović:

That these songs can now appear in this enlarged edition may be counted to the praise of the glorious and honourable Prince of Serbia, the Lord Miloš Obrenović. Although there were people who told him in my presence that this collection of songs was nothing but idle folly, in spite of this, he not only provided singers for me and paid them for the time they lost, but also richly paid me to publish them to the world. When the Serbs get to know better their own popular songs, then this service of his will find proper appreciation.

The tribute is typical of Vuk in that it is combined with a sharp dig at Miloš's courtiers, who had for example persuaded Starac Milija to give up singing for him. Vuk is hardly likely, in view of his correspondence with Miloš over the six months immediately past, to have written it from the depths of his heart; but the fact remains that Miloš not for the first time provided the money—however late and ungraciously—for Vuk's publications, and deserves some share of the credit.

XII

'NATIONAL POETRY' AND ROMANTIC EUROPE

I

THIS is a convenient point at which to pause in the narrative of Vuk's life and to consider what was his relation to other collectors of popular poetry, why such eminent men as Grimm and Goethe were interested in his work, and why the Serbian songs had such a prominent place in the romantic and scholarly vogue for popular poetry that prevailed in Europe during the early years of the nineteenth century.

At that time there was in Western Europe virtually no knowledge of contemporary Serbia and little enough of the national poetry of the South Slavs, though from late in the fifteenth century there is evidence both for the existence of South Slav poetry and for some awareness of it on the part of occasional West European travellers.[1]

The eighteenth century was a period of considerable activity by literary collectors, as well as by singers and poets in the South Slav area. A large number of songs were recorded during the seventeenth and eighteenth centuries principally by men of letters at Dubrovnik, and preserved in various manuscript copies. These were however only discovered during the nineteenth century or later, and had no influence either on Vuk's work or on its reception by the European public.

It was only after 1750 that any South Slav popular songs were

---

[1] The earliest reference in non-Slav literature to South Slav heroic songs occurs in the record of an Embassy from the Emperor Ferdinand I to the Turkish Sultan Suleiman the Magnificent, published by a Slovene interpreter Kuripečić in 1531. He mentions songs chanted in Croatia and Bosnia, and referring to a certain hero Kobilić; this was almost certainly Miloš Obilić, the traditional hero who killed the Turkish Sultan Murad at Kosovo in 1389. See Appendix A, no. 5. For further details on this and other points in the notes to this chapter, see Dragutin Subotić, *Yugoslav Popular Ballads, their Origin and Development*, Cambridge, 1932.

printed and at all widely circulated in the present area of Yugoslavia, or began to attract any attention outside it. The first notable figure in this story was a Dalmatian friar, Andrija Kačić Miošić, who travelled widely as a Papal legate in Dalmatia, Bosnia, and Hercegovina and was an enthusiast for Slav history. In 1756 he published at Venice a collection of material, including nearly 140 mainly patriotic poems, to illustrate historical events (with a distinctly pro-Papal bias) under the title of *Razgovor ugodni Naroda Slovinskoga* (*A Pleasant Relation of the Slavonic People*). Most of the poems were written by himself in the spirit of popular poetry, and derived from printed, written, and oral sources; but the collection also included a few songs in their original form. Before he arrived at Vienna in 1813, Vuk had seen and read this book. It was regarded by Kopitar and other men of letters early in the nineteenth century as a collection of genuine Slav popular poetry, and it is uncertain exactly when Vuk himself became quite clear that Kačić's book (to which he referred in the introduction to his first collection) was mainly 'artificial' poetry. What is certain is that both directly, when he read it, and indirectly, when Kopitar talked to him of it, Kačić's book provided an important stimulus to Vuk for the further collection of popular poetry.

The only other literary stimulus which had affected Vuk before his meeting with Kopitar was, according to his own account, the sight of a collection of Russian songs. There was a good deal of coming and going between the Serbs in the Austrian Empire and the large Serb emigration in Russia, and it is not surprising that such a book should have reached Vuk's hands, but its identity is uncertain. The taste for popular poetry had been widely cultivated in Russia during the late eighteenth century. An important date in the process was 1779, when Nicholas Novikov (intellectual reformer, organizer, and mystic) took over the Moscow University Press. Here were published in the 1780s comprehensive collections of Russian folk-tales, songs, and popular legends, edited by Chulkov, and in 1790–1 the *Novikov Song-book*, which was most influential in the development of later Russian literature. This was followed by collections of 'byline' or narrative poems, one of the most famous of which was edited (1804) by Kirsha Danilov. It may well have been this which, before the end of 1813, came into Vuk's hands from one of his numerous Serb contemporaries who had travelled in Russia (or from a Russian officer in Eastern Serbia), and which he mentioned as an inspiration in the preface to his first *Song-book*.

2

Vuk's horizon in 1813 was strictly limited, but Kopitar viewed the collection and publication of 'popular songs' not only with his own Austro-Slav political ideas in mind, but also against the current literary demand in Western Europe. This was determined not least by the romantic vogue for ancient poetry and folk-song which had grown up by the end of the eighteenth century. The beginnings of it may be dated from 1760, when James Macpherson published his *Fragments of Ancient Poetry*, a collection of 16 poems adapted from old Irish songs which had been transmitted to Scotland in the eighth or ninth centuries A.D. The *Fragments* were followed by further adaptations or inventions of Macpherson, *Fingal* in 1762 and *Tenore* in 1763, the two poems being published together as *Ossian* in 1773. Macpherson was at best very free in his treatment of any originals which he possessed, and always refused to produce them; but the poems, however spurious, were exactly suited to the literary taste of the time in England, and, it was soon to appear, far beyond. It was due to their influence, for example, that the name 'Oscar' was dignified by the Royal Houses of Scandinavia; and, for Goethe's young Werther, Homer was 'superseded in my heart by the divine Ossian'.

A much more solid and equally important contribution both to the study of national poetry, and to the European mode for it, was the *Reliques of Ancient Poetry* published in England by the Rev. Thomas Percy of Oxford between 1760 and 1765. About one-third of these were derived from a genuine seventeenth-century manuscript, which included the famous ballads of Chevy Chase, the battle of Otterburn, and Sir Patrick Spens.

Shortly after the publication of Percy's *Reliques*, the West European mode for national poetry began to be extended to Dalmatia. In 1770 the Italian Alberto Fortis, scientist, traveller, poet, and friend of Cesarotti, the Italian translator of Ossian, made a tour of the Dalmatian coast. He was interested in the Slav peasants of the area (*Morlacchi* as they were then called),[1] and was

[1] The word 'Morlak' (or 'Morlaque' or 'Morlacchi') seems to have been derived from 'Moro-Vlach', suggesting a kind of Mediterranean Slav.

accompanied by his friend, John Symonds, Professor of Modern History at Cambridge, who had a particular penchant for folk-lore and poetry. As a result of his journey, Fortis published in 1771 his *Observations on the Islands of Cherso and Ossero* at the end of which he recorded one of Kačić's songs, the *Song of Miloš Kobilić and Vuk Branković* from the Kosovo cycle. Fortis followed up his first volume in 1774 with the more famous *Voyage in Dalmatia*, including a chapter specially written at the request of Symonds and his other prominent English friends[1] on the customs of the 'Morlaks'. At the end of this chapter he printed (from an original, long undiscovered) what was for many years the most internationally famous of all the narrative songs—the *Hasanaginica* or 'Mournful song of the noble wife of Asan Aga'.[2]

The Germans were the first to look with the new interest stimulated by Ossian and Percy on these works of the South Slavs. The author of the German translation of Ossian, a Jesuit Michel Denis, became acquainted with Fortis's *Observations* and wrote to Klopstock about the poems there printed. Klopstock was much interested and wished to include translations, both poetical and literal, in a collection of old German poems which he was hoping to edit. But the project hung fire, and it was left to Herder ten years later to include translations from South Slav poetry in an anthology. Herder, while preserving Rousseau's distinction between 'natural' and 'artificial' poetry, both refined it and gave it substance.[3] In 1778–9 he published his famous and enormously influential collection of national poetry (*Volkslieder* or 'Popular Songs', better known by the title of the second edition *Stimmen der Völker* or 'Voices of the Peoples'). These volumes included German translations of the two South Slav songs already mentioned—the story of Miloš Kobilić and the *Hasanaginica*—the latter in an excellent second-hand version made by the young Goethe from a German translation of the *Voyage in Dalmatia*. Goethe republished his version in the second volume of his own

[1] Lord Bute, to whom Macpherson had dedicated his *Fingal*; John Strange, British resident at Venice; and F. Harvey, Bishop of Londonderry. See Miodrag Ibrovac, *Claude Fauriel et la fortune européenne des poésies populaires grecque et serbe*, Paris, 1966, pp. 257–8. This is a book very rich in information about the reactions in Europe, and particularly in France and Germany, to Serbian popular songs.
[2] For an English translation of this, see Appendix A, no. 1.
[3] Rousseau's most specific words on the subject occur in his *Dictionnaire de musique*, 1765; he was interested as much in the musical as in the verbal elements of popular song.

collected poems, and subsequently the *Hasanaginica* was translated from this German version into other languages—for instance by Sir Walter Scott in one of his least happy verse exercises.[1] When the vogue for Serb ballads was firmly established, the *Hasanaginica* came to serve ingenious littérateurs, anxious to exploit the current fashion, as a model which they could imitate freely, or as a foundation (often the only one) on which they could build imaginative constructions about the habits and poetry of the 'Morlaks'.

Herder's collections deepened and further stimulated the interest of the general literary and artistic public of Western Europe in 'natural', national or 'popular' poetry. They included many of the Scottish ballads which, together with those in Walter Scott's *Minstrelsy of the Scottish Border*, came to enjoy particular fame in the Europe of the romantic era; the great Viennese composers of the time profited from and served to heighten romantic enthusiasm for them. From 1799 almost until his death in 1809, Haydn was in correspondence with the publisher George Thomson of Edinburgh, who sent him Scottish and Welsh songs for harmonization.[2] And in 1813, the year when Vuk first arrived in Vienna, Beethoven's first collection of settings of Irish songs was published.

The general appetite for the natural and the national, particularly in more exotic forms, had been further if less directly stimulated by another major poetic force of the time. Byron published his *Childe Harold* in 1812, and for the next two decades at least there was a considerable vogue for the sort of Near Eastern local colour which he had made familiar. 'Morlaks' and Serbs were acceptable substitutes for Greeks and 'Giaours'.

3

At a very different and higher intellectual level, there existed in Western Europe by 1813 a number of eminent scholars ready to

[1] Scott's first stanza runs as follows:
>What glimmers yonder so white on the mountain,
>Glimmers so white where the sycamores grow,
>Is it wild swans around Vaga's fair fountain?
>Or is it a wreath of the wintry snow?

[2] See H. C. Robbins Landon, *The Collected Correspondence and London Notebooks of Joseph Haydn*, Barrie and Rockliff, 1959, especially pp. xxiv–xxv and 192 et seq. It seems that Haydn organized a team of pupils in Vienna to harmonize Scottish melodies, and thus to exploit the current vogue for them.

welcome the work of Vuk as a comparatively scientific collector of 'popular songs', stories, and language (though neither he nor they would have found it easy or desirable to separate the ethnographic aspect from the romantic spirit of his work). The publication of Percy's *Reliques* had stimulated during the second half of the eighteenth century a revival of scholarly as well as of literary interest in early poetry and in the problems of epic composition. This revival was most marked in Germany. The *Nibelungenlied* was discovered in 1782, and in 1795 F. A. Wolf published his *Prolegomena ad Homerum*, in which he revived the theory that the *Iliad* was a concatenation of heroic lays, the work of various poets, and that the final assembly was only made in the sixth century B.C., much later than the date of the constituent parts. Such discoveries and theories of course had no direct effect on Vuk himself, but Kopitar was well aware of them, and of the academic and antiquarian market, so to speak, for original Serbian poetry resulting from the new interest in comparative epic studies. From a passage in the introduction to Vuk's first *Song-book*, it looks as if Kopitar had discussed Wolf's Homeric theories with him.

By 1814, therefore, when Vuk's first collection was published in Vienna, there was a certain vogue among European scholars as well as amateurs of literature for national or popular poetry, and South Slav contributions to the genre were not entirely unknown, owing to the popularity of Goethe's *Hasanaginica*. The eventual success, however, of Vuk's collections owed a very great deal to the personal interest which Jakob Grimm came to take in all branches of his work. There were in fact strange affinities between the work and character of these two men, almost contemporaries (Grimm was born in 1785 and died in 1863), but educated in such very different circumstances. The following words written in a memorial notice for Grimm, early in 1863, could be applied almost without change to Vuk, even if his work was on a completely different scale: 'His grammar and dictionary exceeded the bounds that might be set for himself by an industrious man who did not want to devote himself exclusively to them. The main characteristic of his work, which informs all its branches, is the inner inclination of the heart towards the poetry of the national mind.'[1]

Grimm was one of the greatest scholars of his own or any other

[1] *Frankfurter Didaskalia*, 24 March 1863. Quoted in W. Schoof, op. cit.

time in the field of comparative literature; he had himself discovered in 1812 one of the classics of German medieval literature, the *Lay of Hildebrand*. It was against the background of his unrivalled general knowledge of early epic literature that he judged the Serbian poetry reproduced by Vuk; and it was with the support of Grimm's great prestige as a scholar and critic that Vuk was presented to the learned and literary Europe of his time.

While Grimm was in attendance on the Duke of Kassel at the Congress of Vienna, there were also present in Vienna many German authors and foreign diplomats, who were glad to act as patrons of literature and the other arts. Grimm profited from this coincidence in order to promote a plan for organizing on an international basis the collection of the traditions of various nations, in which their poetry was to have a prominent place. He himself drew up an appeal to be circulated with this end in view. This reached Vuk via Kopitar, and it was Kopitar who interested Grimm in Vuk's first collection and his *Grammar* (published in 1815). Kopitar also sent him literal German translations of the Serbian songs (some twenty of these were edited and published by Klemens Brentano in 1818),[1] and Grimm sent copies of these to a number of his friends, including Goethe. In 1816 he was contemplating an edition of translations of Serbian and Greek 'popular' poems in a single volume, but this came to nothing, owing to the dilatory habits of his correspondent, Baron Werner von Haxthausen, who was to translate the Greek poems.[2] In the meantime Goethe had been approached directly by Kopitar, who in 1815 had sent him a copy of Vuk's first collection, together with literal translations, notes about Vuk himself and the Serbian alphabet, and Kopitar's own reviews from the Vienna newspapers. The book contained a dedicatory inscription: 'Dem grössten Deutschen sendet, nebst dem original des Klaggesangs von der edlen Frauen des Helden Hassan-Aga, auch die erste Lieferung serbischer Volkslieder ein Slave' ('A Slav sends to the greatest of all Germans this first collection of Serbian national songs, together with the original of the lament of the noble wife of the hero Hassan-Aga'). Goethe's diaries show that he read and reread the translations, and he asked for a translation of Vuk's second collection.

[1] In an anthology compiled by F. Förster under the title *Die Sängerfahrt*.
[2] Baron Werner von Haxthausen had been introduced both to Serb and to Greek popular literature by Kopitar. See Ibrovac, op. cit., p. 71.

He also received two more Serbian songs in 1818, sent to him by Šafařík, along with six Czech poems, and expressed particular interest in one of these ('The marriage of Hajkuna').

Before 1822 'national poetry' remained a very secondary preoccupation for the Great Cham of European literature.[1] At this time, however, his interest in national and popular poetry revived, not least owing to the receipt of some Greek national songs in translation. The outbreak of the Greek revolt against the Turks in 1821 stimulated public taste for the literature of modern Greece and the energies of those, like Haxthausen, who had collected Greek poems (in many ways similar to the Serbian poems of Karadjordje's time) from refugees in Vienna and elsewhere. A famous and influential translation of such Greek poems was published by the Frenchman, Claude Fauriel, shortly after Vuk's three collections had appeared in their original form at Leipzig (1823), and attracted much attention among the philhellene public of Western Europe. Further translations of Fauriel's work into German appeared at much the same time as the German translations of Vuk's Serbian poems, which probably derived some benefit from the fashionable enthusiasm for Greece—much as Vuk himself (who was anti-Greek) would have disliked the thought.

Goethe himself, as well as Grimm, rated the Serbian songs, particularly the heroic ones, higher than the Greek. His taste at this period favoured those poems which were more remote in time and less concerned with war and battle. Apropos of the more contemporary Greek poems, he expressed himself strongly in 1825: 'Schlagt ihn tot! Schlagt ihn tot! Lorbeern her! Blut! Blut!... das ist noch keine Poesie!' ('Strike him dead! Strike him dead! Bring the laurels! Blood! Blood! That's no kind of poetry!') In 1824-6, however, Goethe devoted much time and energy to the Serbian songs. He was helped enthusiastically not only by Grimm, but also by a young lady who wrote under the name of Talvj. This pseudonym was formed from the initial letters of her name, Therese Albertine Luise von Jakob; she was the daughter of a Professor of Philosophy, and had as a young girl spent some years

---

[1] Grimm wrote to Kopitar at the end of 1823: 'Goethe is now too far advanced in years and has too many interests for anything serious to be expected from him . . .; he sniffs at single flowers of popular poetry and gets enjoyment from them; but to look after a whole garden full is no longer for him. . . .'

in Russia. It was Grimm who introduced her to Serbian poetry and to Vuk himself, whom she had met in Halle during the autumn of 1823; to ingratiate herself with the great Goethe she took up the detailed study and translation of the Serbian poems in Vuk's collection, learning the language as she went along from her previous knowledge of Russian.

Goethe's first step after Vuk's second visit to him in February 1824 was to publish in his review *Kunst und Altherthum* ('Art and Antiquity') the translation of the Serbian poem *Dioba Jakšića* ('How the Jakšić brothers shared'), which he had received from Grimm. To accompany this and other translations he prepared a commentary, in which he talked of Vuk, praised Grimm's account of the Serbian poems, recommended urgently the study of the Serbian language, and ended with a 'nice anecdote which has pleased me'. His own translation of the *Hasanaginica* had been used, he was told, as an example to encourage certain Serbs living in Vienna, who feared that they might incur mockery for transcribing such simple national songs. 'So wirkt ein treues aus Herz und Sinn hervortretendes Unternehmen eine Weile fort und bringt in der spätesten Zeit die erwünschtesten Früchte.' ('Thus an enterprise undertaken sincerely from the heart and mind can operate over the long term and bring forth at last the most desirable fruits.') Goethe's commentary remained unpublished, as it was overtaken in his view by other material which Grimm sent to him, including the German translation of Vuk's *Grammar*, with Grimm's own extensive introduction. Grimm also sent a translation of his own favourite heroic poem, *The building of Skadar*,[1] apologizing for its inadequacy in a letter to Goethe of 8 May 1824: 'The beauty of [the poem's] form should not be judged by my faithful but imperfect translation. Satisfactory renderings of Serbian national songs—as of all others—are hard to arrive at. The epic formulae and repetitions which are so natural in the original become forced and halting in the imitation. . . .'

Goethe found the story of the poem shocking—it relates how an innocent mother was walled in as a human sacrifice when the building of the town of Skadar was hindered by a jealous Goddess —but it was in fact printed along with another translation by Miss 'Talvj'[2] in *Kunst und Altherthum* early in 1825. On this occasion

---

[1] An English translation will be found in Appendix A, no. 3.
[2] 'Talvj' (1797–1870) later married an American theologian, Edward Robinson,

Goethe published a revised commentary, which occupied 25 pages of his review. This reflected some highly individual opinions. He was no more enthusiastic about the warrior chiefs of the heroic Serbs than he had been about the crude heroes of the Nibelungenlied, which he regarded as a product of medieval darkness. In general, Goethe was opposed to the considered judgement of Grimm on the merits of the various types of Serbian songs, and preferred the lyrical to the heroic strain. The lyrics he found 'charming', 'admirable', 'infinitely tender', and compared them in conversation with Eckermann to the *Song of Songs*, which, as Eckermann said, meant a great deal from him. But in any case, however selective and idiosyncratic his praise, it was a most precious advertisement to the literary world in Germany of the value of Serbian popular poetry; it also contained a preliminary puff for the translations of Miss 'Talvj', a woman, as Goethe described her, 'of distinguished capacity and talent'.

Two volumes of these translations were published, with a historical introduction, in 1825 and 1826. 'Talvj's' work was not particularly accurate or poetic, but it had a considerable success. It inspired numerous imitators or successors in Germany, chief among them one Wilhelm Gerhard, also patronized by Goethe, who had the advantage of knowing Sima Milutinović[1] (by 1827 engaged on an epic poem about Karadjordje's revolt) and learning something of the Serbian language from him. The German vogue for Serbian poems hardly outlasted Goethe, who at the very end of his life spoke wistfully of his activity in this field to his old friend, Chancellor von Müller: 'That was a happy time, when the translation of the Serbian poems was first on our agenda, and we were transplanted with so much fresh energy into that strange world. But that's all long ago, and I have no taste for it any more.' All that survived of this activity later was a musical echo of Serbian poetry as of Scottish ballads; German translations of individual songs were republished in settings by

and lived in the U.S.A. An occasional correspondent of Vuk, she sent him a copy of *Uncle Tom's Cabin*, when it first appeared. He remarked that the conditions depicted there much resembled those of Serbia in his youth.

[1] Milutinović's poem was called the *Serbianka*. Goethe noticed its existence in an article published in *Kunst und Altherthum*, March 1827, remarking that its sense and tone was much that of earlier Serb epic songs, and expressing the hope that Gerhard would translate it. The gossip of the time, mentioned more than once in Kopitar's correspondence with Grimm, was that Milutinović was hopelessly in love with 'Talvj'.

Carl Loewe ('Talvj's' brother-in-law), Brahms, and many less eminent composers.[1]

4

Fortis's *Voyage in Dalmatia* had evoked a separate echo in France, where a translation had appeared in 1778.[2] Interest in the 'Morlaques' revived when in 1809 the short-lived French province of Illyria was constituted. The sensitive administrators of the Napoleonic era were thus enabled to absorb the exotic atmosphere of Slovenia and Dalmatia. They were indeed officially encouraged to further the scientific investigation of the national cultures of Europe. Napoleon had, for example, founded a Celtic Academy in 1807, which drew up a questionnaire[3] and established methods for collecting national poetry.

In particular, the librarian appointed to the French Governor of Ljubljana in 1812, Charles Nodier, was a man of letters. He was able to introduce some local colour (including songs alleged to originate in Illyria) into the novels of the horrific *Udolpho* genre which he published in 1818 and 1821.[4] He also published in the Ljubljana *Télégraphe officiel* articles (1813) on *Poésies illyriennes*, describing the 'simple and touching' songs of Illyria, which depict 'in marvellous fashion the most tender sentiments known to man'. In Nodier's opinion they are quite as good as Ossian, and he ventures the bold theory that 'the fortunate neighbourhood of Greece' had given additional inspiration to the 'bard of the Julian Alps'. Nodier's articles are typical in that they cite none of the poems on which they comment except the inevitable *Hasanaginica*; but they are valuable as further evidence of the appetite, stimulated by Herder and Rousseau for exotic national poetry and for the artistic productions of natural uncorrupted minds.

[1] See J. Milović, *Goethe, seine Zeitgenossen und serbo-kroatische Volkspoesie*, Leipzig, 1941, pp. 209-15. Brahms set translations from the Serbo-Croat by Siegfried Kapper, who knew Vuk personally. Grimm had expressed the wish in his review of Vuk's first *Song-book* (1815) to hear the original melodies of the songs; some of these were then harmonized by a Polish musician, Franciszek Mirecki, and published as the first examples of specifically Serbian secular music.

[2] This inspired a novel *Les Morlaques* by 'Justine Wynne' (Comtesse des Ursins et de Rosenberg) in 1788, which was in turn the inspiration of Madam de Stael's *Corinne*.

[3] Jakob Grimm had used this questionnaire as the basis of his appeal of 1815 for the collection of popular traditions and literature.

[4] One of these, *Jean Sbogar*, figures among the fashionable romantic works listed in Pushkin, *Eugene Onegin*, III, xii.

The vogue for exotic poetry lasted for some little time in France, and was accompanied by various scholarly studies, particularly those of Fauriel.[1] Lamartine took an interest in Serbian 'popular songs', and introduced motifs from them into his poem *La chute d'un ange*.[2] There was, however, as elsewhere in Western Europe, a good deal more of mode than of scientific curiosity in the literary addiction to Illyria. This was neatly illustrated by one of the most famous and successful hoaxes in literary history: *La Guzla* by Prosper Mérimée was published in 1827. It purported to be a collection of translations of Illyrian or 'Morlaque' poems, collected by the editor from original sources on the Dalmatian coast. Mérimée in his introduction, claimed to have a 'Morlaque' mother, from whom he derived his knowledge of the language and of the Dalmatian coast and interior. The arrangement of the introduction itself may well have been intended as a parody of the scholarly apparatus of Fauriel's translation of modern Greek songs. Mérimée gave a long descriptive biography of his main 'source', the improbably named 'Hyacinthe Maglanovitch'—born in 1757, kidnapped by gypsies, escaped to become a *Hajduk*, etc. 'Hyacinthe' was 'almost the only "*guzla*" player who was also a poet', and one 'had to make him drunk if any profit was to be derived from one's introduction' (this suggests some acquaintance with Vuk's methods of collection!). Mérimée gave a detailed description of the manner of chanting 'Morlaque' songs, which involved 'at the end of each verse, a great wolf-like cry'. It was all a very thorough hoax, and even the title *La Guzla* (prima facie a grammatical howler, since in Serbia at least *gusle* is a feminine plural) was an ingenious mystification; it was an anagram of the word 'Gazul', from the title of another of Mérimée's books *Le Théâtre de Clara Gazul*.

Mérimée gave a public account of his deception in 1840. In 1827, he said, he was a romantic and admired only foreign poetry, especially Scottish ballads: 'Point de salut sans la couleur locale.' He wanted to travel with a friend far from English tourists, down the Adriatic coast, but lacked money. The idea occurred to him at this point 'd'écrire en avance notre voyage, de la vendre

[1] Fauriel's main work in this connection was his *Chants populaires de la Grèce moderne*, Tome Ier, *Chants historiques*, Paris, 1824. See Ibrovac, op. cit., pp. 135 et seq.
[2] See N. Banašević, '*La chute d'un ange et la poésie populaire serbe*', in *Revue des études slaves*, vol. xxxi, Paris, 1954.

avantageusement, et d'employer nos bénéfices à reconnaître si nous nous étions trompés dans nos descriptions'. As preparation, he said, he read Fortis's *Travels* and a 'fairly good statistical description of the former Illyrian provinces, drawn up, I think, by a head of department in the Ministry of Foreign Affairs',[1] and learned five or six words of Slav. The text of *La Guzla* was then written in a fortnight and the idea of the subsequent journey abandoned.

This account is probably no more than a half-way house towards the truth. Mérimée in fact had read a good deal of what descriptive literature was available, and the story of the projected journey is no doubt a sort of excuse for the deception practised on his public. He probably had no intention but to enjoy himself and to exploit the literary market for exotic national poems. He must have been entirely delighted by his own success. John Bowring (of whom more in § 5) wrote from England to ask him for his originals, and in Germany Wilhelm Gerhart included some of the poems from *La Guzla* in his next collection of translations. The translation of Mérimée's poems came easily to him, he said, as beneath the French text he sensed the original metre of the 'Illyrian' ballads. Even Vuk himself, called upon to write a notice of the book in a Serbian journal published in Buda, was cautious. 'The songs are genuinely popular, and not bad. But their true worth could be judged only from the originals. It is worth remarking that the title is printed as "gusla" rather than "gusle". But Dalmatian dictionaries give "gusle" in the singular!'

There was however a still more distinguished victim of Mérimée's hoax. Pushkin had prepared by 1835 a small collection of *Songs of the Western Slavs* in translation; these included a number of Mérimée's poems from *La Guzla* as well as songs from Vuk's first collection of 1814 and from the first Leipzig collection of 1823. Before publishing, he inquired through a friend about Mérimée's sources, and Mérimée confessed his deception in a charming letter of January 1835.[2] He hardly knew whether to be more ashamed or proud that his *jeu d'esprit* had brought him into

---

[1] In a letter of 1832 to Pushkin's friend S. A. Sobolevski, Mérimée admitted having derived some details from the reports of the French Consul at 'Bonialouka' (Banja Luka), whose main object was, according to Mérimée, 'prouver que les Bosniaques sont de fiers cochons—et il en donne d'assez bonnes raisons'.

[2] See the Russian Academy's Centenary edition (1937) of Pushkin, *Stihotvoreniya, skazki, poemy, 1831–6*, pp. 22 et seq., 533 et seq.

touch with the great Russian poet. He added some explanation of the motives which led him to it, rather franker than that which he later published. He was, he said, led on partly by the desire to raise a good laugh at the craze for local colour; and one of the most piquant results of his publication had been an outraged protest by Nodier, who accused Mérimée of plagiarizing his mistranslation of the *Hasanaginica*. Mérimée's letter arrived in time to allow Pushkin to add a brief and amused preface to his collection of *Songs of the Western Slavs*, published later in 1835.[1]

5

Not the least important aspect of 'Talvj's' translations was that they circulated beyond Germany and introduced a comparatively wide selection of Serbian songs to English and French devotees of national poetry, who now had something more than the *Hasanaginica* to study. One of the most interesting of this number, and one of the most colourful figures to make an appearance on the edge of Vuk's life was the Englishman, John Bowring. He was a man of many parts. Born in 1792, he devoted the early years of his adult life to trade. In 1821 he spent some time at St. Petersburg and on his return embarked on the publication of a volume of translations of Russian poetry. This was the first of a series which appeared over the next ten years, and included poems from the Dutch, Spanish, Polish, Hungarian, and Czech, as well as from the Serbian, each volume was prefaced by an informative introduction about the people concerned. Bowring was indeed a remarkable linguist, though not so remarkable as he led his public to believe, and a fluent versifier rather than a poet. In the context of Vuk's life and work, it is interesting that he considered it worth while to exploit and foster the current literary taste for 'popular poetry' so assiduously over this period. He was not the first to introduce the literary public in Britain to Slavonic national poetry. A naturalized Pole, Karol Szyrma, had previously published an article on 'Slavonian Traditional Poetry',[2] in which he advertised Slavonic national material as quite in keeping with the current poetic modes of the time. 'There should be born a Sir Walter Scott, to recall from beneath the mountain tombs ... the bold spirit of old Sclavonian chivalry. There should be born Burnses and Ettrick shepherds to

---

[1] His poems of 1835 also include a separate translation of the opening passage of the *Hasanaginica*.   [2] *Blackwood's Magazine*, September 1821.

give us an ideal of agricultural and pastoral life. . . . Many should be born who would follow Lord Byron, who, by choosing our Mazeppa for his poem, has not in the least disgraced his pen, nor wronged his wild imagination. . . . Its wildness had rather been gratified on the wild places of Ukraine.'

Bowring himself was much more than an amateur man of letters. It is significant (for the literary tastes of the time were often linked with political convictions) that he was from 1821 onwards an active supporter of 'national liberation movements' and an opponent of 'reaction'. He acted as confidential courier between the British and Portuguese Governments in 1822 (to warn the Portuguese of a proposed invasion by the Bourbons), and was caught and arrested in France. From his prison at Boulogne in the winter of 1822–3 he worked at further translations of Russian poetry, and corresponded with Fauriel, the French translator of Greek national poems (he intended to add a Greek volume to his series). In the spring of 1823, released from prison as the result of an outcry in the House of Commons, he became secretary of the newly formed London Committee for Help to the Greeks, and corresponded with Lord Byron about supplies.

Bowring had in 1821 got to know Jeremy Bentham, whose collected works he afterwards edited. The philosopher had a high opinion of him—'A better heart never existed, and will never exist', he wrote to a Portuguese correspondent; 'you have called me a citizen of the world, and so I am—but not more than him', and in 1824, Bowring was appointed editor of the influential magazine founded by Bentham, the *Westminster Review*. It was while he held this post that he entered into correspondence with Kopitar (to whom he was introduced by Šafařík). At the end of 1825, Kopitar sent him Vuk's collections in the original, and at the same time he acquired the 'Talvj' translations. In July 1826, Bowring published in the *Westminster Review* a notice of Vuk's three volumes, and included twelve of his own translations, done in fact almost entirely from the German version. It is pleasant to view Vuk for a moment through Benthamite spectacles:

> We think it is very interesting and a very delightful thing to be enabled to share in the sympathies and to understand the habitual thoughts and feelings of any large portion of our fellow-men; to watch the dawn and progress of civilisation among them; and to welcome the birth and growth of science and literature, by which individuals and nations

become, as it were, admitted into the great community of intelligent men.... When the first step is taken; when knowledge begins to circulate; when books become the receptacle and the standard of a language; when tradition gives place to history, and all the vague and misty fables, which one barbarous age communicates orally to another, are superseded by the record of authentic facts, the seed of improvement is planted, and will probably germinate; the impulse is given which is now acting with such wonderful, such increasing effect, upon the intelligence, the virtue and the happiness of the whole world.

Vuk would himself have made as lofty claims for the circulation of knowledge through books, particularly if, as he himself so ardently desired, these become the 'receptacle and standard of a language'; but he would have found it hard to detect many signs of 'germinating improvement' in Serbia at the time.

In April 1827, Bowring's translations were published under the title of *Servian Popular Poetry*, with an introduction by Bowring and dedicatory verses to Vuk himself, with whom he had been in nominal correspondence since December 1826 (it was in fact Kopitar who composed the answers).[1] The first and last stanzas of the dedication illustrate Bowring's qualities as a poet:

> My friend! it is thou, it is thou
> Who hast ushered these gems into day;
> T'is my pride and my privilege now
> To honour—I fain would repay
> Thy toils, and would bind round thy brow
> The laurels that grow o'er thy lay.
>
> . . . . . .
>
> Thy tenement is but of clay:
> Thou art frailer than most of us be:
> Yet a sunshine has lighted thy way,
> Whose effluence is sunshine to me:—
> And t'is sweet o'er thy Servia to stray
> And to listen, pale minstrel, to thee.

The introduction further illustrates Bowring's extreme remoteness from the Serbian scene and his idealization of Vuk's activities:

---

[1] Vuk first heard of Bowring from Šafařík, late in 1826. Thereafter an active correspondence was opened between them, with Kopitar drafting for Vuk. There was no real meeting of minds; Bowring wanted more Serbian songs, in case the vogue lasted. Vuk and Kopitar were much more concerned with getting Bowring to mediate with the London Bible Society over Vuk's translation of the New Testament (see Chapter XIV, § 2) and to sponsor an English translation of Ranke's *Die serbische Revolution* (see Chapter XIII, § 6).

Of late the influence of those [in Serbia] who have endeavoured to make literature subserve the interests and the happiness of the many rather than the few . . . has led to the prevalence of Serb over Slavonian books. . . . A feeble and crippled frame unfitted him [Vuk] for bodily labour, and all his thoughts and all his ardour attached themselves to intellectual exertions. . . . The Emperor Nicholas in that spirit so honourable to many of the autocrats of Russia has conferred on him a pension of 100 ducats, and he now pursues his interesting enquiries and from time to time exerts that creating and regenerating power which has called the poetry of Servia into existence and established for it a permanent reputation.

The accuracy of Bowring's scholarship may be deduced from the incidental statements in his introduction that Hungarian is a Slav language and that Serbian is a sort of hellenized Russian, modified by the proximity of Greece. He was, moreover, disingenuous in that he failed to acknowledge the extent of his debt to 'Talvj's' translation (as she herself was quick to note). With all this, Bowring's energy, fluency, and versatility are not to be scorned, and his volume was well received by the fairly small public for which it was presumably intended. The *London Review* of April 1827 wrote of the 'Servian' poems: 'In short, nothing can be more remarkable than the purity of these compositions, their amiable simplicity, and their agreeable fancies.'

The translations are said to be 'the most valuable and the most delightful of the anthologies, which the industry and the talent of Mr. Bowring has imported into his native language'. And kind words are said of the author, in connection with the dedicatory verses quoted above:

There is prefixed to the volume a copy of verses addressed to Dr. Vuk Karatschich by the translator, Mr. Bowring. Though we suppose that he never saw the poor crippled *literatus* from Hungary, yet this poem speaks to him in the language of friendship, and almost of affection. Through the whole of Mr. Bowring's writings, this warm and generous sympathy with foreign and distant individuals, whose tie with him is solely that of kindred labours, is highly characteristic. The same facile and generous sympathy, not only with persons, but with their feelings, their habits and their language, renders Mr. Bowring not only one of the most amiable of men, but one of the ablest and readiest transfusers of the spirit of national poetry.

This is a kind of critical epitaph on the literary phase of Bowring's career.[1] It cannot be said that his efforts to introduce the British public to Slavonic national poetry had any very lasting results; the vogue for 'ballads' was soon to be exhausted and in Britain there was no contemporary student of philology and ancient European literature as a whole to compare with Grimm.

Altogether the publication of the 'Talvj' translations of Vuk's collections had produced over a number of years some far-moving ripples on the stream of European literature; but the international fame which it brought to Vuk was both limited and temporary, and did little to help him with his major immediate problems of keeping alive and reforming Serbian literature.

[1] Between 1835 and 1849 Bowring served twice as an M.P. In 1849 he was appointed British Consul in Canton. In 1854 he became Governor of Hong Kong and Commissioner for Trade with China, and was knighted. A strong proponent of a forward policy in China, he bore considerable responsibility for the Anglo-Chinese war of 1856–60. See Douglas Hurd, *The Arrow War*, Collins, London, 1967. He died in 1872.

XIII

HISTORICAL WRITING

I

By the end of the summer of 1824, Vuk had settled again in Vienna with his family. For the next four years his main occupation was with historical writing, and the publication of the historical work which he had already written; and in 1824-5 he suffered what at first appeared to be a disastrous set-back to his plans.

It will be remembered that, when Vuk left Miloš's court at the end of 1821 for Vienna, he brought with him the manuscript of a history of Miloš and his times. He failed to get this published in Vienna, and took the manuscript with him to Leipzig in 1823, hoping to publish in Germany (he had almost certainly discussed this possibility with Miloš during his short stay in Serbia in autumn 1822). However, after reaching Germany, Vuk decided, in a rare fit of caution, to make sure that there was no objection to publication from Russian officials who might conceivably take offence at the account of some of Miloš's international dealings. In spring 1823 therefore he sent his manuscript (written in German, not in Serb) to his friend Adelung at St. Petersburg, asking him to get clearance for it from the Imperial Ministry of Foreign Affairs.

Here Vuk ran into trouble with Miloš's agent in Russia, Mihailo German-Teodorović. This unsavoury character, described usually as German, was a Macedonian adventurer, who had gained Miloš's confidence in 1815 and secured for himself the post of Agent-plenipotentiary with the Russian Consul at Bucharest. His talents seem to have been mainly for secret police work, which no doubt recommended him to Miloš. German feared that Vuk would gain undue influence with Miloš, and therefore did all he could to discredit Vuk, who believed, perhaps with reason, that German was ready to plot against his life.

German had been told about Vuk's activities as a historian at the end of 1821 by his kinsman Marko Djordjević, and decided that everything must be done to prevent publication; the history might reveal his own activities in Russia on Miloš's behalf, and completely upset his position. His immediate reaction had been to embroil Vuk with Miloš in the matter of Vuk's letter to Christofor Obrenović. Vuk had managed, as will be remembered, to talk himself out of trouble before he went to Leipzig, but had aroused Miloš's suspicions again by his publication of the new book of 'popular songs' in Leipzig, which did not present the ruler in a sufficiently flattering light. Now Miloš, having learnt from German that Vuk had submitted an historical work to the Russian Foreign Ministry, issued a further warning when he granted Vuk his 1,000 florins in June 1824:

Moreover, my dear Vuk, I must not omit the recommendation that in writing my history you should strictly observe the most complete silence in surveying even the smallest details of my dealings and relations with any foreign power, and should in the course of your narrative confine yourself to my exploits in Serbia. Indeed my present political position demands of me that no allusion of whatever nature should be made to any European power. I expect and demand of you that you should so conduct yourself in this connection. I also think that it would be best, before your *History* is printed and published, to send it to me here for previous inspection; and if this is impossible, it remains for you to observe most strictly the rules here laid down, otherwise you will turn your good friend into your most bitter enemy. Moreover you must not make any mention in your *History* of the previous type of Government [i.e. Karadjordje].

Vuk recognized the hand of German in this letter. In the meantime he had heard from Adelung that on the Russian side there was no objection to the publication of his history of Miloš Obrenović. German had however managed, unknown to Vuk and Adelung, to get the manuscript from the Russian Foreign Ministry; realizing that it was considered blameless, he determined to forestall Vuk and get the credit for it, rather than to try to prevent publication. He wrote to Miloš on 1 May 1824 that there would soon appear in St. Petersburg a book 'from an unknown author, under the title of *The Life and Exploits of the Supreme Serb Leader, Prince Miloš Obrenović, from 1815 to 1822*'. German promised that the book would be dedicated to Miloš, and asked him for his picture to include in it. The request was granted; Vuk had been writing for the same purpose at about the same time, and had met with a refusal, which rankled very much with him.

Towards the end of 1824 Vuk began to suspect some intrigue by German, and he wrote warning Miloš against 'Marko Djordjević's kinsman', who was, he said, no true patriot, and knew little either of Serbia or other countries.[1] Early in January 1825, he learnt that a book about Serbia had just appeared in Russian, but it was not until the second half of May that he realized what German had done with his manuscript in St. Petersburg. By this time, German had achieved a particularly strong position at Miloš's court. In May he had arrived in Zemun as a Russian courier from St. Petersburg bearing a letter from the Tsar's Foreign Minister, Count Nesselrode, which contained news very welcome at Kragujevac. Miloš had written previously informing the Tsar of the suppression early in 1825 of one of the fairly numerous revolts against his rule in Serbia, the so-called 'students' revolt'; this he represented as resulting from a secret agreement between the Serb emigrants in Bessarabia and the leaders of the Greek rebellion against the Turks. Nesselrode's letter assured him that the Tsar was very happy to hear of the suppression of the revolt, and had given orders for a strict watch to be kept on the activities of the Serb emigrants. Miloš was delighted with this news. Apart from the check on the activities of the Karadjordje party outside Serbia, the news that he had the Tsar's support would help to strengthen his position and prestige within his own country. Moreover the Tsar informed him of the instructions given to his Ambassador in Constantinople, who was to urge on the Sultan the release of the Serb delegation there imprisoned by the Sultan[2] and the fulfilment of Article VIII of the Treaty of Bucharest, 'having in mind the loyalty of the Serb people during the disorders in Greece'. This was justification enough for Miloš of his policy of extreme caution *vis-à-vis* the leaders of the Greek revolt, and he was in high good humour with German as his agent in Russia.

Along with Nesselrode's letter, German had brought with him a copy of the new *Life of Miloš Obrenović* in Russian. It was stated in the preface that the work was based on the manuscript life of

[1] German had kept Miloš posted throughout the second half of 1824 about the progress of the history in its Russian translation.

[2] The delegation has been sent to Istanbul in autumn 1820, and was imprisoned in spring 1821, when the Turkish Government suspected Miloš of complicity in the Greek revolt.

Miloš written in German by 'the well-known Serb man of letters, Vuk Karadžić'. But this acknowledgement did nothing to soothe Vuk's outraged feelings. He expressed these in a letter to Miloš, refusing an invitation to come to Kragujevac and receive an oral answer to all his own letters of recent months:

... as I have always told you the truth, I shall not lie to you now, but shall tell you exactly the reasons for which I cannot come to you. The *first* and most important reason is that I do not dare. So far as concerns my old enemies, of whom you know,[1] I would have decided to come; but I am afraid of German. I know very well that a few years ago German wrote against me to you, and talked against me in various places. Now he has even more reason to do so, particularly because of that biography of yourself. The fact that you like German better than myself and trust him more is confirmed by the matter of your portrait, for which I asked you three times without your deigning even to answer me; whereas for German you sent it even as far as Petersburg, so that he could publish it along with the book which he stole from me. And [you like and trust him more] particularly now, when it is said that he has come to you with such good news, at which I heartily rejoice.

The *second* reason is that my health is very bad, and if any annoyance of this kind happened to me there, I would break down altogether and die or go mad.

The *third* reason is this. You know that I am poor, and live from day to day with food that I earn in misery with my life's blood. While I am alive, I still hope that I can somehow feed my wife and children, and that I can comfort them and they me in our wretchedness. But if death were to come on me now, my wife and children might well have to beg.

These are the true reasons which do not allow me for the present to come to you, and I tell them to you openly, as a son who has suffered wrong and injury to the father who kisses his brow....[2]

And now to say a few words about that book which German brought you. It is true that I would much rather have published it myself in Serb than in German, so that it could be said that the book was translated from Serb into Russian (and then most probably there would not be so many mistakes in it as at present); but I am indeed very happy that it has come out even as it is. If it only brings honour and glory (and if possible profit) to you and the Serb people, I don't mind even if

[1] Laza Todorović, particularly. See Chapter X, § 6.
[2] A long passage is omitted, in which Vuk describes his first coming to Miloš's court in 1821 (Chapter X) 'in order to teach you how to read and write and thus to rescue you from shame, that no one might say you were an "illiterate peasant", as was said of Black George'.

German rather than myself is rewarded for it. It has happened often enough in the world that one has ploughed, sown and reaped, and another has done the eating. But as for how my manuscript got into German's hands, ask him and let him tell you, if you do not know already.

Vuk was genuinely afraid to go to Miloš's court when German was there and high in the ruler's favour; not even the possibility of some reward from Miloš for his admitted share in the Russian publication could induce him to take the risk. He sought some financial redress from the Russian Government, sending a memorandum to the Russian Ambassador at Vienna in August 1825, with a full account of his case against German. The Russians gave him an evasive answer, and indicated that his complaints and claims should be addressed to Miloš himself; Vuk did not hesitate to do so, but could get no written answer from Miloš—nothing but messages to come and talk things over, which he feared to do. And there was no further word from the Russian side, even when Kopitar started to press Vuk's claims through Köppen in St. Petersburg.

2

In the summer of 1825 Vuk had embarked on a new project, the production of a Serbian Calendar,[1] which was to include not only the list of saints' and feast days but together with it an *Entertainer* containing a number of informative articles. The whole was to be the first of an annual series published under the title of *Danica* ('Day-star'). A great attraction for Vuk of this form of publication was that it enabled him to work independently of editors, who tended to become tired of his controversial writings. He could also use for the *Day-star* all sorts of material which he had already prepared, and there was no need for any form of literary continuity. Thus for the first number, which he advertised late in the summer of 1825 and published in October, he strung together a linguistic exposition ('The main differences between the Slavonic and Serbian languages') probably written as far back as 1816; a typical hard-hitting piece of linguistic criticism ('Answer

[1] This sort of Calendar with miscellaneous supplements was part of the Serb literary tradition. Some had been published as far back as 1766, and Zaharija Orphelin had produced others from 1783 onwards, with important historical and scientific articles attached.

HISTORICAL WRITING 213

to a Russian Reviewer'); two songs not previously published in his collections (one of which was so far from the Serb norm that Grimm suspected its authenticity); a 'Description of the monasteries of Serbia', compiled from material collected in 1820, when Vuk was executing his antiquarian commission for Rumyantsev; and the 'Life of Hajduk Veljko', one of his masterpieces, composed as part of, or as a pendant to, the history of contemporary Serbia for which he had long been collecting material, and extensively quoted in Chapter V.

Vuk's main difficulties in this new project were two. He was not the first in the field. His friend, Djordje Magarašević of Novi Sad,[1] had already launched a new calendar with supplements (*Letopis*) in 1824. Vuk would have liked to collaborate with him, but could not do so and continue to pursue his own line on orthography. This was the greater loss to Vuk in that a society, the 'Matica Srpska' ('Serbian Queen Bee'), was founded in 1826 to help the *Letopis* on its way, and became an important force for the development of Serb literature. Vuk's *Day-star* therefore had from the first to compete with the *Letopis*, which commanded more support from those who did not wish to break with the Serb Orthodox Church tradition. Moreover Vuk's anthologies were not everyone's idea of entertainment. The original advertisement for subscribers, issued in August 1825, had been cautious about the contents, saying merely that readers would find in this little book something that would be worth reading even after their time. There was the usual problem in finding subscribers. Only at Zemun throughout the whole Srem province would people subscribe in advance. After publication, Vuk wrote as usual to his friends for details of public reaction and sales. The answers were again disappointing. In many cases, Vuk had to reckon with his inveterate enemies. As Mušicki wrote to him, 'many have been put off by your heretical orthography. That's bound to be so if you won't be more human about it.' More important, friends as well as enemies found that there was nothing very entertaining in Vuk's articles, and one of them dared to suggest that in matters of taste 'Vox populi, vox dei'.

[1] In his original *Letopis*, Magarašević had moved several steps towards Vuk's orthography, and drawn on himself the wrath of the Metropolitan Stratimirović. As a result he had to revert to Slavonic letters, give up any idea of association with Vuk, and leave out the calendar from subsequent numbers of *Letopis*. See *Kovčežić*, ii, pp. 98 et seq., article by Dr. Miraš Kićović on 'Vuk o prvim Srpskim Kalendarima'.

Vuk was unwilling to let this pass and repeated his creed. Sound sense and truth must prevail in the end, contemporary taste is wholly unreliable, and 'in writing I never think of today's uneducated readers, but always of true critics and of posterity'. He did, however, promise rather more obvious popular appeal in the next number.

The reaction to the critical and linguistic numbers of Vuk's *Day-star* was copious and on the whole predictably adverse. More interesting are the letters written to him by friends and strangers about his life of Hajduk Veljko, which represented something completely new both for content and style in the field of Serbian historical writing. One of his friends said that 'Livy did not praise Scaevola better or more appropriately in Latin than you have praised Veljko in Serbian. Here is true and original Serbery, Serbinity, or Serbinismus.' Another wrote that he would buy up, if he had the means, all the copies of the *Day-star* sent to him for sale, simply for the style of the life of Veljko. But even among friends praise was not unanimous. Some thought that the portrait was too personal and intimate, and that more space should have been given to Veljko's exploits before 1813. Others, including Mušicki, were disturbed by the realistic expressions put into Veljko's mouth, or suggested by asterisks. Vuk's friend from Panjevo, Tirol, defended him appropriately by saying that this was a description not of Napoleon, Kant, or Shakespeare, but of Veljko and drawn from life. Vuk's post also included one or two letters from the Serbian equivalent of 'Yours faithfully, Disgusted', who revived old insults against him. 'Many believe that if you'd spent the time which you have devoted to writing in keeping pigs or (according to the old custom) sheep, you would have done better, since (1) you would not have exposed your name to lasting disgrace and (2), more important, you would not have seduced your readers, particularly the young ones, into harmful ways. . . .' As for the biography, it hadn't even occasional strength or charm of expression, but 'you write like any granny, who has never seen or heard of anything noble'.

This was an extreme reaction, but the hard fact remained for Vuk that the first number of *Day-star* was nowhere near a financial success. Even his best friends had great difficulty in selling copies, though they were not asking a high price. Moreover the Metropolitan Stratimirović was still on the watch against Vuk, and found

HISTORICAL WRITING

reason to complain to the authorities in Vienna against the censor (Kopitar) for allowing a calendar to circulate in which the Church holidays were described by their current popular names, rather than by their proper Church titles—for instance Vuk had written, according to universal oral usage, 'George's day', rather than giving the full ecclesiastical title 'Saint George the great martyr'. Stratimirović described such usage as 'profanation of the faith'. Kopitar had little difficulty in defending himself,[1] but it was Stratimirović's objections which carried most weight in his own province. When Vuk circulated for sale, along with *Day-star*, some extracts of his translation of the New Testament which had been printed in 1823 at Leipzig,[2] he found an even less receptive public, and was informed that people did not dare to put them on sale because of opposition from Mušicki.

3

Thus the whole *Day-star* experiment was financially profitless and had once more put the Orthodox Church authorities on the alert against Vuk. Even apart from this, Vuk's personal situation in Vienna by the end of 1825 was again very unhappy. He had his wife and three small children to keep, the last of them recently born, and they had recently moved to more expensive lodgings in the Marxergasse.[3] Vuk's creditors pursued him, especially the Mehitarist (Armenian) brothers of Vienna, who had printed his *Dictionary* in 1818, and to whom he still owed money. Their representative called on him every Saturday, in order to hear an account of his financial state. Another severe blow fell on Vuk and

---

[1] Kopitar was able to point to the use of popular titles for familiar saints in old 'Illyrian' calendars, and even in previous writings of Stratimirović himself.

[2] In summer 1823, Vuk's old friend, Stefan Živković, wrote to him that (as proved to be the case) Atanasije Stojković had taken on the business of translating the New Testament for the Russian Bible Society; the Society had decided to deal with Stojković, in spite of strong opposition from the Russian Ambassador in Vienna. On learning of their decision, Vuk printed his extracts in order to keep his own name before the public as the original translator of the New Testament into Serbian.

[3] In spite of Vuk's poverty, his household at the time included a Serb peasant girl, Maria Milovanović, as general help. She was herself a refugee from Serbia and had joined the Karadžić family at Panjevo in 1824. She was devoted to them, and no doubt their company and her keep were her only reward for staying. Vuk taught her to read.

his family in 1825 with the death of Maria Tirka, wife of the rich Serb merchant who had by her financial help done so much to further the publication of Vuk's works from the *Dictionary* onwards.

His frequent appeals to Miloš for money were increasingly urgent. He wrote in August 1825 that he would soon be reduced to begging. 'Then the hearts of your enemies[1] will rejoice, when they can say: "Look! There is the man who sings Miloš's praise and defends him! Now judge for yourself what sort of a friend to him Miloš is!"' Vuk went on to suggest that Miloš should send him money for another long tour to Germany and Paris to publicize the Serb people and Miloš himself by bringing out his history of Miloš in French.

There was no answer to this suggestion, and Vuk turned in despair to Mušicki, who had suggested rather light-heartedly that Vuk should become his literary agent, for an annual salary. Vuk took him up on this 'offer' with one of his most pathetic letters:

> I don't know whether you are jesting or in earnest [about the annual salary], but I have resolved to write to you about it. I cannot describe to you what misery I am in. Believe me, at Christmas I didn't have the money to buy a pound of meat, much less a proper roast! Thinking what day it was, and looking at my children, I wept myself like a little child. . . . It is winter, there's no wood, no food, no money. I think only that I have deserved something better, and that it will be a disgrace to the Serb people that I am living like this. Come on then, what will you pay me a year? I know that you can't give me as much as I need, but give what you can. Anything is better than nothing. Come on, help me at least not to die of hunger and cold this winter, and in the spring I shall fly from Vienna for ever. . . .

Mušicki evidently sent him a small sum in answer to this appeal, but dropped abruptly the notion of a salary, and merely suggested that Vuk should write again to Miloš 'your benefactor, whom you praise to heaven'.

In the spring of 1826, Vuk wrote again to Frušić at Trieste, in spite of the warning against begging which he had received in 1823:

> I have not forgotten what you wrote to me . . . but in my great misery, I have resolved to write to you again, as a true friend, a sensible patriot, and a member of our most patriotic community [the Serbs in Trieste],

---

[1] This refers to Miloš's political enemies among the Austrians in Vienna. See § 4.

which is able to help me. Then if you do help me, it is good fortune for me, and honour and glory for you. And if you don't, I shan't blame myself for not having written, and you won't be able to say: 'If only we had known that Vuk was in such straits, we'd have helped him!'

Vuk went on to suggest that the Trieste community should pay him an annual pension, as the men of Chios had done for Koraes. Again, however, Frušić wrote a friendly, firm, and immediate refusal, saying that he had not dared even to mention any project for helping Vuk outside the circle of his most intimate friends, and they were agreed that in the present condition of trade it was impossible.

By now, Vuk was reaching a new point of desperation. Early in the summer of 1826, he heard of a post (special proof-corrector to the Serbian language press in Buda) which might provide him with a steady income without cutting him off from his literary activities.[1] With this in mind Vuk went to Buda at the beginning of May 1826. His application seems to have been treated quite seriously, but was turned down flatly before the end of June. Kopitar in the meantime did his best to suggest new lines of thought and activity. He reported Grimm's enthusiasm for further folk-tales and fairy-tales in prose, and mentioned the possibility that a rich resident of Buda, Zelić, would found a chair of Slavonic and Serbian studies at Vienna; Vuk would be the obvious candidate and should get in touch personally with Zelić (Vuk replied that this was merely a castle in the air). At the same time, Kopitar was trying to engineer a conciliation between Vuk and Stratimirović, through Šafařík, who was by now Director of the Serbian 'Gymnasium' at Novi Sad. Such a conciliation might have made a large difference to the circulation of Vuk's works in the Srem. After preliminary talks with Šafařík, the Metropolitan consented to see Vuk more than once, and the latter promised to make some concessions on his calendar —he was indeed as good as his word, giving the Slavonic names only for the main feasts and holidays. There was, however, no real reconciliation; Stratimirović, as he told Šafařík, could not forget that Vuk had associated his name with the *Dictionary* which contained so many shameful words, and Vuk absolutely refused to give up his own spelling—'if they think that I shall abandon my

[1] A new director had just been appointed, who refused to do the correcting himself. The result was a large crop of printing errors, complaints from authors, and the institution of a new post for a proof-corrector.

orthography, there will not be any kind of peace—that is something that I can't and won't do'.

In May 1826 however, while Vuk was waiting in Buda for news of the proof-reading post, he received news which indicated an important turn for the better in his material situation. *Ex oriente lux.* Vuk's original patron in Russia, Count Rumyantsev, had died at the beginning of 1826. Vuk had, however, occasionally been in direct correspondence since his return from Russia in 1819 with another powerful patron, Admiral Shishkov, as well as with Adelung and Köppen. Shishkov was interested in the circulation within Austria of the publications of the Russian Academy, and the main concrete possibility discussed had been that with this end in view Vuk should enter into service with the Russian Embassy at Vienna[1] (Vuk had raised this idea himself, but never pursued it very consistently). By the end of 1825 Kopitar, on Vuk's behalf, had reverted to earlier plans. Together with Grimm, he supported Vuk's case for some compensation in the matter of his stolen history; he now pressed strongly on Köppen and Adelung the profit to be derived for Slavonic studies by commissioning from Vuk further antiquarian journeys in Serbia. He urged that Shishkov should be moved to secure for Vuk, through the Russian Academy, at least a two- or three-year 'research grant' of 100 ducats annually: 'I can say with an easy conscience and with the backing of Grimm, yourself [Köppen] and all competent people that I consider Vuk the best head of all the Serbs that I know. Above all he is a grammatical genius.' (A rather strange estimate of his particular talents, as it now appears.) He ought to be allowed to make a prolonged tour in Serbia primarily for linguistic purposes to research properly into the Bulgarian, Macedonian, Vlach (Rumanian), and Albanian tongues, and 'the gain would lie not only in the field of Slavonic linguistic science, but also in the fields of history, geography, and the discovery of manuscripts. All this for 100 ducats a year.'

In St. Petersburg, Köppen was not idle, and it is noteworthy that now for the first time he drew attention to the political advantages to be gained by Russia from fostering Slav studies in the Balkans. After the death of Tsar Alexander in 1825, and the accession of Nicolas I, Russian diplomatic pressure on Turkey was

---

[1] At the end of 1822, Vuk had approached the Russian Embassy in Vienna for employment.

HISTORICAL WRITING 219

considerably increased and a weakening of the Turkish hold on the Balkans was confidently anticipated.[1] It was a good time at which to use all means for strengthening Russian influence, and Köppen wrote to Admiral Shishkov (April 1826) that 'research into the languages and customs of the Danubian peoples would in many ways contribute to the strengthening of their sympathy towards Russia, and would at the same time serve as an advertisement for the Russian Government's new measures of education'.

Already by mid-February 1826 Köppen had begun to give hopeful answers to Kopitar's repeated requests for help to Vuk. He called for a detailed scheme of studies to submit to Admiral Shishkov. Vuk responded enthusiastically, sketching out journeys to Dalmatia and Montenegro, promising to make studies of antiquities, manuscripts, language, and national customs, and warning that such journeys could not be covered by an annual grant of 100 ducats only—he would need expenses too. He made various other suggestions about the finances of printing and publication. But in fact he had already won this battle. His letter crossed with one from Köppen, announcing that, by direct decision of the Tsar, Vuk had already been awarded a pension of 100 ducats a year for life. The news reached Vuk on 16 June 1826.

4

He was of course overjoyed. 'Your letter', he wrote to Köppen, 'warmed me as the sun warms a beggar frozen by winter.' Immediately, however, he could do no more than go about his business in Buda. First he had to arrange for the printing of the next number of *Day-star* (for 1827). This was compiled along the same lines as the first issue, and when it appeared had no greater public success.[2] *Vis-à-vis* Miloš Obrenović, Vuk continued to display

[1] The Serbian delegation at Istanbul was released in spring 1826.
[2] The second *Day-star* included two items of special interest to the student of Vuk's life and work. The first of these was a geographical and statistical survey of Serbia, which was an abbreviation of the introduction to his projected *History of Contemporary Serbia* and contained some of the passages on typical Serbian institutions quoted in Chapters II and III (e.g. those on Spahis and *Hajduks*). The second item was a sketch for a Serbian *Bukvar* ('letter-book') which Vuk had written on his return from Germany. The introduction to it included the passages on the value of literacy quoted in Chapters IV and (to conclude this book) XXI. Appended to it were versions in popular Serbian of the Lord's Prayer and Creed; it was because of these and out of deference to the

great caution; correspondence about German's theft of his history continued, but Vuk was most reluctant, with German still in high favour, to go to Kragujevac to talk things over, as Miloš through various intermediaries urged him to do; and Miloš would give no firm guarantee of financial or personal support for Vuk. For some time Vuk sought indirect ways of ingratiating himself with Miloš, and proving himself a loyal and helpful patriot of Serbia. His son Sava was brought to school in Zemun, so as to remove him from Viennese influences, and Vuk embarked on a fresh round of match-making activities, this time in aid of Miloš's second daughter. His candidate was again Pera Demelić, who had been rejected as a suitor for the elder daughter Petrija. This time, Vuk's recommendation took the roundabout form of editing a life of a distinguished kinsman of Pera, Djordje Arsenijević Emanuel, who had been a general in Russian service. The unfortunate suitor failed again; he harmed his own cause greatly by being seen at Miloš's court in the act of imbibing some herbal tea—a sure sign in hard-drinking Serbia that his health was weak.

Towards the end of 1826 various new factors decided Vuk to risk a further personal confrontation with Miloš. The grant of a pension from Tsar Nicolas I was proof that Vuk had become *persona grata* to the Russian court and was more important in Russian eyes than German had indicated. This was a consideration which had some effect on Miloš. When Vuk informed him of his new circumstances Miloš gave a favourable reply to the request for money to finance publication in Serbian of the *History of Contemporary Serbia* (in effect a life of Miloš himself). In mid-December 1826 Vuk received a gift of 1,000 *groš* from Miloš's treasury and shortly afterwards an invitation to talk with Miloš at Kragujevac, a sum of 500 *groš* in respect of expenses to be incurred in the journey, and a hint that this journey was urgently necessary ('In inviting you His Highness says that, should you not come now, you would lose much consideration with him').

Vuk was still reluctant but set out for Serbia and reached Kragujevac by gradual stages in March 1827. This time his fears proved to be entirely unjustified. German was still at Miloš's court, but Miloš ordered a confrontation between him and Vuk. German openly admitted the theft of Vuk's manuscript, and Miloš spoke

well-known views of the Metropolitan Stratimirović that the Viennese authorities prevented its separate publication.

sharply of his conduct. Vuk was allotted 1,000 florins (5,000 *groš*), partly as damages, and the money was paid to him immediately. Moreover orders were given for a portrait of Miloš to be handed over to him as a sign of favour when he returned via Belgrade.

Miloš in fact had this time some far-reaching plans for employing Vuk in entirely new business, resulting from the recent strengthening of his own international position. In October 1826, the Russians and Turks had signed the Convention of Akerman, of which Article V, referring back to the Treaty of Bucharest (1812), guaranteed to the Serbs self-government, a ceiling to the tribute to be paid to the Turks, a ban on further settlement in the country by the Turks, and the protection of Russia. Miloš Obrenović himself received the rank of Prince. On hearing the news through his agent German, Miloš had summoned an Assembly to announce the new dispensation, and appointed a delegation to negotiate with the Turkish Government at Constantinople the execution of the relevant clauses. Not for the first or last time the Turks showed themselves masters of delaying tactics in the vital negotiations of detail. Meanwhile, however, Miloš could reasonably think that Serbia was on the point of emerging as an independent European state. He also thought that, with international public opinion in view, the time had come to establish there some modern democratic-looking institutions. In particular he wanted to set up a printing press and a paper factory in Serbia, and it was mainly for this purpose that he wished to talk with Vuk at the beginning of 1827.

When Vuk returned to Vienna in April, he was charged with the task of ordering all the machinery for the new press, and of finding a partner to act with Miloš in financing a paper factory. By the end of April 1827, Vuk had got some way in negotiations and wrote asking approval for a further journey to Leipzig in this connection.[1] For some time he received no answer from Kragujevac. Things were not going well in the negotiations at Constantinople, and by the end of June Miloš had lost interest in his own hopeful projects. Vuk was told to stay in Vienna, get on with his private affairs, and publish the next number of *Day-star*, not forgetting to 'save as much as possible from the sum of money granted to you'. He

[1] Vuk was in touch with a Viennese manufacturer, Anton Strauss, whose terms were 10,000 florins for the press, 2,000 for the paper factory, and no partnership with Miloš.

returned to the charge with plans for a less ambitious type of printing press, but received a further negative answer in October.

5

All in all Vuk's circumstances were brighter than they had been for many years. He was reconciled with Miloš and was also beginning at last to see some fruits of his previous literary work. Bowring's English translation of his Serbian 'popular songs' had reached him and inspired him with plans for further collections, about which he began to correspond with Mušicki and others. His reputation was spreading fast in Slav countries outside Serbia[1] as the result of the publication of his Leipzig collections of poems and the translations of them. The obvious course for him at this stage was to concentrate on the work of collecting and publicizing further specimens of Serbian popular speech and poetry. This would not necessarily involve him in the extended journeys of which he had written to Admiral Shishkov, but it would satisfy his Russian patrons and increase his growing fame throughout the Slavonic lands of Eastern Europe.

Kopitar urged Vuk constantly in this direction and tried to enlist Grimm's sympathy, but came across stubborn resistance from Vuk himself. The basic difficulty was that Vuk's mind at this period was strongly set on historical writing. His motives were no doubt mixed. In the first place he realized clearly (and he was still ambitious) that his best opportunities for future work, as administrator and not only as a man of letters, lay in Serbia. Even if he were not able to get a major post in the administration of Serbia, Miloš remained the patron from whom he had most to hope from the financial point of view—and, with however bad a grace and however much sadistic teasing, Miloš had in fact given a good deal of money to Vuk over the years. Vuk's own interests therefore demanded the conciliation of the Prince. And Miloš would, as he was aware, want of him in future more historical writing and less writing on literary, linguistic, or ethnographic questions.

Vuk must also have been aware from the first that historical work on behalf of Miloš would involve at worst some flattery and at best some suppression of the whole truth. Nevertheless, Miloš's

[1] In 1827, for example, a collection of popular songs was dedicated to him by the Czech František Čolakovski.

desire for historical writing about contemporary Serbia was not entirely selfish. At a time when it seemed that Serbia would soon gain its autonomy and take up a place among the nations of Europe, Miloš was anxious to see that the exploits of the Serb people as well as his own were well publicized. Vuk himself was a patriotic Serb and these ideas accorded with his own inclinations. He had seen how much the cause of the Greek rebellion had gained by the publicity given to it in Europe (and he probably had no clear idea of the special appeal which the descendants of the ancient Greeks could make to the classically educated ruling classes of Western Europe). As a good Serb, Vuk much resented the Greek propaganda appeal to those Europeans who had paid little attention to the pioneer Serb revolt of 1804.[1] From 1825 to 1827, Vuk had occasionally toyed with the idea of travelling to France and England in order to acquaint people there with Serb exploits. From the summer of 1827 onwards he seems to have felt that he would achieve this purpose best by devoting himself in Vienna and Buda to historical writing.

This decision was, however, to involve him in political difficulties and awkwardness in personal relationships, quite apart from the conflicts with his own historical conscience. Any work on contemporary Serbia which was more than fair to Miloš Obrenović was bound in the circumstances of 1827 to cause political controversy in Austria. Miloš's reputation was very bad there at the time. In 1826 he had put down one of the periodic revolts against his autocratic rule (Čarapić's rebellion) with the utmost cruelty.[2] The drafters of the rebels' proclamation had had their hands and tongue cut off, and two of them, who had escaped to Austria, were shown there in their mutilated state as an example of Miloš's barbarity (one even had an audience with the Kaiser). Agitation against Miloš was widespread, and such patriotic Serbs as Sima Milutinović made their feelings clear from abroad. It was, however, largely fostered by the former members of the Greek Hetaireia who fully reciprocated Serb hostility to Greece, and in particular would never forgive Miloš for his passivity at the time when they

[1] For a typical expression of Vuk's views on the Greeks, see Appendix A, no. 11.
[2] Djordje Čarapić and Mihailo (Mija) Belisavljević, a Belgrade teacher, led a rising against Miloš in 1826, proclaiming that 'whoever brought Miloš's head would receive 50,000 ducats a year'. Čarapić was killed; Belisavljević was captured and had both his hands and 'a small part of his tongue' cut off.

had tried to organize a revolt against the Turks throughout the whole Balkan Peninsula (1819). By the end of 1827, moreover, the propaganda against Miloš had a wider significance. It was beginning to be clear that the Serbo-Turkish negotiations about the implementation of the Akerman Convention were held up, and there were plenty of voices in Vienna to say that this was all to the good; Serbia under Miloš was not fit to be an autonomous state, and Russian protection would involve new dangers for Austria. In these circumstances Vuk, as a good Serb patriot with an eye to what he himself might accomplish in an independent Serbia, was more than ever determined to advertise Serbian achievements in the past and to prove that Serbia deserved its freedom.

The first major historical work which he wanted to publish at this stage, for patriotic and personal reasons, was a new and much enlarged version of the life of Miloš Obrenović, of which the pirated Russian edition had given him so much trouble. The new version covered the years 1765–1813. In writing it Vuk as a historian came up immediately against his major dilemma; he could not write an entirely objective work which would please Miloš, nor a selective one which could not be exploited against himself by Miloš's enemies and his own. Trouble on either hand would tend to discredit the Serbian cause with European opinion. His own dearest personal relationships were also involved in the same dilemma. Kopitar wrote to Vuk early in 1828: 'Again I beg of you to think in this business of those nearest to you and on generations to come. In the first class will fall myself and Hadjić and all the other reviewers. We shall call you a "hireling" and "beggar" and shall hate you as long as your hero lasts, and mock you when he falls.'[1] No doubt in making his appeal to Vuk, Kopitar had in mind wider and political considerations as well as friendship and historical reputation. It looked as if Miloš at this stage was staking his political future and that of Serbia as a whole

[1] When Vuk had set out for Serbia in 1829, Kopitar wrote angrily to Grimm (23 May): 'Vuk is off with bag and baggage, wife and children to Zemun. He'll leave the family there and will go to Serbia himself to intrigue and speculate. Strange that revolutions accustom men to trouble and intrigue, and that they come actually to need them! For example, Vuk could live perfectly well even in Vienna from the Russian pension (which he owed to your pressure on Köppen), the yearly publication of his *Day-star* and other odd books. But no! he prefers to intrigue (in hard fact to beg) with Miloš, and in the end has to argue about two, three, or four hundred florins—the cost of his gypsy wanderings!'

on Russian support against the Turks and ultimate Russian protection. If this was the case, and if Vuk declared himself an unqualified supporter of Miloš by publishing an uncritical biography of him at this time, Vuk would thereby become *persona non grata* in Vienna and could not act any longer as the instrument of Kopitar's long-term policy—the establishment within Austria of a Slav counterweight to Imperial Russia.

Vuk evidently decided to risk the longer-term political difficulties which could follow the publication of his selective historical work on Miloš. No doubt he had already decided that he might well want to leave Vienna in any case. It was his own conscience as a historian which caused him most trouble, and in deciding to go ahead with publication, he felt bound to justify himself as best he could in the face of Kopitar's objections. He wrote to his old friend: 'I shall be careful not to lie, and, where the truth cannot be told, I shall just pass over it nice and quietly.' In the preface to the work as finally published, Vuk dwelt on the difficulty of writing history about people still living, and said that nevertheless he had always kept in sight truth and posterity. He had told the story plainly, and left it for others to make judgements; 'and if in spite of my wishes and labour something has been left out, this is due either to ignorance or to human weakness'. By and large, Vuk stuck to his own rules of near-objectivity. His worst crime against the truth was blackening the character of Peter Moler, representing him as plotting with the Turks against Miloš in 1816, whereas in fact he was in touch with the Serb refugees in Austria and Bessarabia, and was suspicious of Miloš's relations with the Turks. Vuk had good reason to know the truth of the case, since he himself had been in political correspondence with Jakob Nenadović and probably other exiled leaders of Karadjordje's administration in 1815–16; it was no doubt precisely for this reason, in order to exculpate himself with Miloš for his own past, that he inserted the passage on Moler, which had not appeared in the manuscript stolen by German. Elsewhere Vuk made his work acceptable to Miloš, where necessary, by *suppressio veri* or *suggestio falsi*. The most notable instance of the former was his brief reference to the murder of Karadjordje in 1817. In the context of a revolt against Miloš which took place after Karadjordje's death, Vuk wrote as follows: 'Here mention may be made of Karadjordje's return to Serbia (in the month of June 1817), and his death.'

Vuk had further and obvious difficulties in presenting the right sort of picture of Miloš himself. A realistic portrait in the style of Vuk's sketch of Hajduk Veljko would have been a great gift to posterity, but this was clearly out of the question. Vuk had to content himself with omitting Miloš's vices (which certainly developed mainly after he had come to power), and giving an accurate catalogue of his virtues—his close links with the common people and skill in dealing with them, his political skill in negotiation with the Turks, and his sympathetic attitude towards heroic conduct as the last resort only of the sensible man.

In spite of these defects Vuk's history of the times of Miloš Obrenović illustrated many of his typical virtues as a historian, and was calculated to present the Serbian nation to a European public in a heroic light. Moreover in spite of the liberties which he had taken with the truth, Vuk was by no means certain of how Miloš would receive the work. The Prince was by this time ready to belittle not only Karadjordje's part in the revolt of 1804, but also the importance of that revolt in the process of achieving Serb independence. Vuk could not do that much violence to his own conscience, and gave a reasonably truthful picture of the events of 1804–13, with some exaggeration of Miloš's own role. He hesitated to go to Miloš's court in order to receive some reward for his not entirely creditable labours until he received a letter from Davidović, Miloš's secretary at that time, to say that the *Life* had satisfied everyone.

6

It cannot have been easy for Vuk to do violence to his own conscience as a historian. In that letter of 1822 to Christofor Obrenović which had caused him so much trouble with Miloš, he had stated clearly and movingly his idea of the historian's task and explained his own historical method:

I am not writing a history of contemporary Serbian politics, but a 'Serbian history of our time', or more exactly from the year 1791 when the Serbian revolt had its beginning. . . . Now you must understand what stirred and drove me on to undertake this work. We see that all our old history is covered in darkness, and we all blame our forefathers for writing and leaving nothing for us; and we see that our descendants will blame us in the same way if we do not write and leave anything for them.

I have talked with some of the Serb leaders about various events at which I was present with them, and they cannot tell me exactly what happened. And when we who were concerned and witnessed such things with our own eyes are covered by the black earth, what can then be truly related about this time which has been so important for our people? The sources for our history will then be all sorts of fairy tales and conjectures by foreign writers, which are already being maintained and passed off for truth. That is why, when I was still in Serbia, I was anxious to write this history and asked various questions and made various notes. I was born and brought up in Serbia and can recall the state of Serbia under the *Dahijas* and before their time. I was there when the first revolt began in 1804 and in 1813 when it finished, and for those ten years I was busy in various public affairs and knew personally nearly all the important leaders, and talked with many of them and ate and drank in their company. Moreover both for these ten years and afterwards down to this day, I have questioned Serbs and Turks alike and taken all possible pains to find out the time, cause, and occasion of this revolt, and after that its course and ending (1813); and then the further beginning (1814 or 1815) and, if we live to see it, some proper ending....

In this history of mine, I'm not trying to set an example to our Serb orators and historians; I have just tried to set everything down as simply—without any art or philosophy—as one Serb would tell it to another. And I have set myself a rule, not to praise or blame anyone nor to find anything laughable or strange, but simply to say what happened, and then the readers can judge for themselves what is for praise and what for blame, what is strange and what laughable.

Soon after publishing the history of Miloš and his times Vuk had the opportunity of embarking on some historical work which conformed far more closely to his taste for objectivity. In the autumn of 1827 he had met in Vienna Leopold Ranke, then thirty-two years of age, a Professor of Berlin University, and already known for his work on Roman history. Ranke had come to Vienna to study Venetian documents, and had become interested from this angle in the political history of south-eastern Europe. Vienna was a centre for refugee Greeks, Serbs, and others, and through Kopitar (whom he naturally met at the Imperial Library) Ranke began to make contact with some of these. Vuk, on his return from arranging the printing of his life of Miloš at Buda, was among the first to be introduced, and by the summer of 1828 Ranke had been persuaded to engage in close collaboration with him on a history in German of the Serbian revolution. The two men were clearly congenial to each other. Fifty years later, Ranke recalled how that summer 'every day I heard my unforgettable friend Vuk coming upstairs—he had a wooden leg—to tell me about the Serbs'. He greatly appreciated Vuk's natural talents: 'Never have I known a man, born in humble circumstances, with such great aptitude for deep and scientific work on linguistic subjects and the history of his country.' And Vuk himself had pasted into his own copy of his *Dictionary* a sheet of paper on which was written another testimonial from Ranke: 'Of all the barbarians whom I have known, Vuk is the only one who has never taken the wrong direction intellectually.'

In the recent history of Serbia Ranke found a subject to fascinate him. 'To the depths of my heart and soul', he wrote in the notes above quoted, 'I was touched by their history with its lively relation about a movement of the broadest historical and political significance.' And again: 'It was particularly interesting and instructive for me to learn the origins of the Serbian revolt from a direct oral account, irrespective of what was generally thought about it in Vienna.' In a letter sent to his brother Heinrich shortly after he had left Vienna in 1828, Ranke wrote: 'Lastly, in Vienna I got to know a people which has been living in subjection, with patriarchal customs and a poetic way of thinking, capable of transforming these into the hard reality of war, when the time came to liberate itself—the Serbs, whose poetry you will certainly have seen.'

Ranke's *The Serbian Revolution* was published in Hamburg in 1829. The exact proportion of Vuk's share in it cannot be determined. Ranke wrote to his brother (in the letter quoted above) that he had tried to put together a new history of the Serbs 'from Vuk's papers'. In the introduction to the original edition, Ranke said that the data used were drawn from the accounts of those who had themselves taken part in the revolt, and that 'other memorials, letters, and documents of that time had been assembled by the trusty collector of Serbian popular poetry, Vuk Stefanović Karadžić'. In the introduction to the second edition (1844), Ranke wrote that in 1829 he had used as a foundation what Vuk had told him, but had checked carefully every fact and word that Vuk had given him, with the informants introduced to him by Vuk himself. Thus the order and arrangement of the book was his own (Ranke's), but the credit for the selection of material belonged to Vuk.

It seems likely that Vuk's part in the collaboration was rather greater than is implied in the last sentence. Vuk was by 1828 not just a good teller of anecdotes but a well-practised historian, of a simple but very effective genre. Moreover his philosophy of historical method, quoted above, is remarkably similar to Ranke's famous principle of relating the facts exactly as they were ('wie es eigentlich gewesen'). In the text of Ranke's original edition there are many passages which might have been taken direct from completed works of Vuk. Such works certainly existed either in published form (the contributions to *Day-star*) or in manuscript (the material which Vuk had been collecting since 1820 for his *History of Contemporary Serbia*, of which the published *Life of Miloš* was only a part).[1] Both Vuk and Ranke spoke in letters of 1829–30 of a 'common work' (not that this proves a great deal), and Vuk used similar phrases ('the book which I wrote together with Professor Ranke') on other and later occasions. Ranke moreover conscientiously continued to send Vuk half his monetary takings for the work.

Whatever Vuk's exact share in Ranke's book, there were excellent reasons, both in 1829 and in 1844 (the date of the second edition) for Vuk's name not to appear on the title page. This was a more objective work than Vuk's *Life of Miloš*, and by letting it appear under Ranke's name only in 1829, he could claim credit for helping to publicize Serbia in German-speaking Europe, and avoid blame for the unprejudiced judgements about Karadjordje which would anger Miloš. In 1844, Karadjordje's son had succeeded to the throne of Serbia, and Vuk did not want to be too openly associated with a work which was equally unprejudiced about Miloš Obrenović.

The individual voice of Ranke is probably to be heard most clearly at the end of his history, where he speculated on the present and future position of Serbia, and, after expressing the view that further progress towards independence could be achieved by Miloš alone, qualified it by saying that Miloš's own position could best be secured by introducing a constitution, guaranteeing personal security and property and freedom of religion, and introducing a new educational system. The flattery of Miloš may have been inspired by Vuk; the qualification may have put some ideas into his mind.

[1] In 1826 Vuk had tried, through Adelung, to have a Russian translation of the full work published. Later in the same year Vuk had given his material to the Czech Abbé Fesl, who would, Vuk hoped, publish it under his own name, and thus enjoy greater freedom vis-à-vis Miloš. Vuk gave up this idea in 1829 when he found that Fesl had begun to incorporate unreliable material as well.

XIV

SERBIA, 1828–1832: VUK AND MILOŠ

I

BY late summer 1828, Vuk's work of collaboration with Ranke had come to an end, and he was anxious to make his way to Serbia, in order to resume direct contact with Miloš and to procure literary and antiquarian material for his Russian academic patrons; but the Viennese police were suspicious of him, thinking that he wanted, after visiting Serbia, to return to Vienna as Miloš's agent. It was not until late September that he received his passport to travel to Zemun on the Austro-Serbian frontier, and then only through the intervention of Kopitar. From Zemun he crossed into Serbia at Miloš's invitation, reaching Miloš's court at Kragujevac in mid-November.

Here he was told that Miloš wanted him to draft a set of laws for Serbia. The plan was that he should first translate the Code Napoléon into Serbian (with the aid of one clerk), and that afterwards a commission, with Davidović (formerly editor of the *Serbian News*) as chairman, should decide how much of the code was applicable to conditions in Serbia. The whole work was to be finished in six months.

In the event, Vuk translated most of the criminal code in about a month, and then returned to Vienna until the spring of 1829. Miloš Obrenović wanted him to look out for a resident court physician, and for a professor to teach his sons French. The Austrian authorities were persuaded to pass Vuk quickly through the quarantine procedure at Zemun by a suitable gift and a typical letter from Miloš, in which (so he himself told Vuk) he argued that Vuk had 'already been plagued by the plague, when his leg became as it is now, so that they needn't fear catching it from him. "This", he told Vuk, "is a joke, so don't be offended."'

Vuk himself had other reasons for a visit to Vienna. He wanted in particular to bring his family back with him to Zemun, and settle them there within easy reach of Serbia. He made strenuous efforts during his stay in Austria to execute Miloš's commissions, but without success, earning some harsh words from his master. In the meantime his principal creditor for the printing of *Day-star* was on his tracks; he was glad to return to Belgrade, and by the end of May he had embarked again on the work of translating laws.

The history of Vuk's next three years in and out of Serbia is a curious tragi-comedy, which can only be understood if both Vuk's and Miloš's long-term interests are borne in mind. Vuk's most lasting concern was to secure a pension from Miloš, and a base from which he could make journeys to collect more material for his powerful Russian patrons. He was certainly ambitious, as a good patriot, to serve his country as well as he could at this crucial stage of its development. Perhaps he also cherished the hope, which he had conceived in 1820, of establishing a proper educational system in Serbia and taking some important part in administering it; but he knew enough by 1828 of Miloš's method and personality to be aware that such plans might very easily be frustrated.

So far as Miloš himself was concerned, Vuk could be a useful instrument. Vuk's was one of the very few Serbian names known outside Serbia. Miloš could expect to gain some credit in Europe by having it known that Vuk was preparing a code of laws or was occupying some high official position. Vuk could also conceivably be useful as a source of intelligence about the ways of the Western nations, and could help Miloš in interpreting them. But Miloš's main motive was almost certainly to have Vuk closely under his eye, and to see that Vuk did not have the chance of publishing anything that might be considered in or outside Serbia as discreditable to Miloš and his regime. The implications of this were that Vuk could make himself a very considerable nuisance to Miloš by his writing, and that he was too well-known a figure outside Serbia to be removed by the drastic methods generally used by Miloš to rid himself of his local opponents. By the end of 1831, Vuk himself was beginning to grasp this situation; at least he began to see that his writings could do Miloš a great deal of harm, though understandably enough he was by no means certain that Miloš would not resort to extreme methods against him. This is the background against which must be viewed the strange duel between Vuk and Miloš over the years 1829–32.

Miloš was at best a rough master, and the manners of his

sycophantic courtiers were rougher still. The work of his legislative commission was a minor bit of showmanship, so far as he was concerned; he did not intend to have his personal rule seriously cramped by a constitution. And he may have thought it salutary to humiliate Vuk and reduce him to the level of other humble obedient servants, while keeping him out of harm's way. At any rate the work of translation was not only 'pure slavery' to Vuk, as he put it himself, but in 1829 was carried out in miserable conditions. The story of Vuk's work on the commission was vividly told by himself in a letter of December 1829 to Kopitar:

> When I left my family in Zemun and came back to Serbia last spring, I found that the others had got no further with the laws, except that my former clerk had got through the translation of the criminal code as best he could. The civil laws and code they had sent to Šabac, to some Greek teacher, and he had translated them quite unintelligibly; at many points one could have burst with laughter on reading his translation, for he knew neither Serb nor German.[1] The criminal code was loaded on to me again, to translate with a new clerk (and here no excuses would get me out of it). Meanwhile the 'Legislative Commission' was set up . . . and I was made responsible for questions of style and language. When I began at the start to discuss and argue on how things should be written, the rest (and particularly the simple chiefs) insisted that in committee we should just read things out, to decide what should be used for our purposes and what not. As for style and language, let us argue about that afterwards, and do what we like. And so in two or three weeks, we got through (that is we read out) all the criminal laws and marked what we should take over. Then the chiefs went off home, and left the clerk with me to put them into proper style and make a fair copy. But this clerk was one of the Prince's men; every now and then he had had to leave the commission and read the newspapers[2] or something like that, and now hardly looked at the laws every third day. So the work on the laws was more or less suspended. Meantime, I was preparing to travel in the districts of Požega and Užice and to Studenica (to look for old songs, church manuscripts, etc.) but instead of giving permission, they fairly pitched into me, saying that I wanted to neglect their business, for which I'd been invited to Serbia, for my own nonsense, etc. . . .

---

[1] Vuk's enemies made fun of his own ignorance of foreign languages in this connection, saying that he confused the French *hypothèque* (pledge) with *apothèque* (an apothecary's place of work).

[2] 'Reading the newspapers' in this context meant 'reading them aloud' to Miloš or one of his high officials.

By the end of September half the civil code, as well as the criminal code, was more or less finished. In the meantime however Vuk, whose health was genuinely frail (he was probably liable also to severe fits of hypochondria), had found the various quarters allotted to him in Kragujevac hopelessly inadequate and the food and mess-life in the Legislative Commission completely distasteful to him. Towards the end of September 1829, he became seriously ill with a sort of malaria, and wrote a desperate letter to his best friend at Court, Vasa Popović, the brother-in-law of Miloš Obrenović:

On your departure [from Kragujevac] I complained to you and to Dr. Stejić[1] that I had caught cold and feared that I was becoming ill. Unfortunately my fears were not in vain, for the afternoon of the very same day when you left a terrible fever took hold of me, which since then has attacked me constantly every day. And so I most humbly beg you to kiss the Prince's robe and hand on my behalf, and to beg him in the name of God and man to be so good as:

(1) to send Dr. Stejić here at once, to rid me of this fever, before I catch some other infection and am quite done for;

(2) if he really wants these laws to be finally written, to appoint another place for the work, where I could have a room such as I need and want; and also to lay down what shall be my monthly pay, so that I can pay a servant to look after me and feed and clothe myself and meet my other needs. . . .

If I'm unhappy about myself and my quarters and way of life, how can I get round to drafting laws? You know what our old women say: 'The merry heart spins the most.' That's God's truth! If to my great sorrow I have to torture myself trying to understand French laws and to choose some of them and apply them properly to the Serbs, I think that it isn't for the good of the Prince that I should also have to worry myself to death with quarters that are too small, with no service, no clothes, and so on. . . .

Vuk recognized that, in asking for the services of Miloš's doctor, he had done something which would be regarded by the men of Miloš's court as unpardonably impudent. He received a further gift of money (300 *groš*), though no word of any regular salary,

[1] Jovan Stejić (1803–53) finished his medical studies in Vienna in 1829 and immediately afterwards came to work at Miloš's court. An author of philosophic as well as medical works, he was among the founders of the Serb Society for Literary Culture (Chapter XVII); he was an opponent of Vuk's orthography, but not among his open enemies.

and was told officially by Vasa Popović that he could join his family in Zemun until his health was restored, and then come back to Serbia again. The detailed answer to Vuk's despairing letter took a form very typical of Miloš's court. The men of his immediate entourage were always on the watch for a chance to ingratiate themselves with Miloš by crude practical jokes or obscenities which appealed to him. A large official envelope, sealed in proper form, was on this occasion sent to a member of the Legislative Commission, Vuk's old enemy, Laza Todorović. It was labelled 'Urgent', and the messenger insisted on a gratuity for delivering it. The addressee thus thought that the envelope contained some particularly good news. The contents proved to be a passport and a covering letter which, by an arrangement concerted in advance with Miloš's secretary, had to be seen by the whole company before they were given to Vuk himself. The passport ran as follows:

I, Amidža [a nickname given by Miloš to one of his main courtiers, Sima Milosavljević Paštrmac], the first and last, who am empowered to issue all sorts of passports to men, women, old and young, healthy and decrepit alike, declare by this passport that the holder, Mr. Vuk Stefanović from Trrršić in Jadar, who has recently entitled himself a man of Drobnjak from Petnica,[1] is travelling from here [Kragujevac] by the Belgrade ferry to Zemun, and further so long as his wooden leg will last.

Personal Description

Name and Christian name: Vuk Stefanović Karadžić from Trrršić.[2] In his youth a goatherd and now a writer of Serb grammar.
Mouth: like the start of a stocking.
Nose: like a blue tomato [aubergine].
Distinguishing marks: None, but if he were to be looked at from behind, it might be thought that he had a broken leg.

The text of the passport was illustrated by a sketch of Vuk on his travels at the monastery of Rakovica, quarrelling with his roommate for the use of a jug as a chamberpot.

The accompanying letter was more viciously rude. Vuk's request for a visit from Miloš's doctor was contemptuously rejected. Miloš himself, it was said, relied on his constitution alone to shake

---

[1] This was a dig at Vuk's claim to be descended from a distinguished Montenegrin clan, the Karadžićes from the village of Petnica in the district of Drobnjak.
[2] The spelling 'Trrršić' was a dig at Vuk's rustic accent.

off fevers, and in any case Dr. Stejić would not come without the prospect of a reasonable fee. Vuk was not the only man who could write laws, and in any case his laws might come out as crippled as himself. As for an apartment, it would be best for him to live in a brothel, where he would not find the winters tedious. He had been accused of stealing a jug for use as a chamberpot; it would be best for him simply to dig a hole underneath the bed for his needs. Vuk's whole letter spoke of nothing but money and debts. He had better join the household of the Pasha of Belgrade and his son; the latter would pay him for services rendered hitherto by his notorious boy-friend Tamindjija; and he would perhaps earn more if he had his other leg shortened and went around on all fours.

The passport and letter were by no means unique instances of rudery among Miloš's inner circle of courtiers. Miloš himself thoroughly enjoyed humiliating his subjects in these ways and was anxious to have news from the Legislative Commission of how Vuk had behaved on seeing the letter. Laza Todorović excused himself for not having kept Miloš currently informed by saying that for long he had not been able to describe the scene for laughing at the memory of it:

When we handed the letter and passport to Vuk, he looked right away at the signature, and seeing his kinsman's name[1] as well as the drawing on the passport, he said: 'Well, no doubt these are some jokes of my cousin's'; then he began to read the passport out aloud, laughing, but his cheeks began to burn. The very same day he ordered a wagon to take him to Zemun. As he sat in it next day, he called me to him and said: 'As I said before, these are some jokes of my cousin, such as he lately played on Tsvetko [Rajović], but it will all pass soon enough. When I get over to Zemun, I shall write to his Royal Highness and thank him for his kindness in the past, and recommend myself to it for the future. Then if His Highness calls me again to work out laws together, I shall come at once!' That's how things worked out here with Vuk.

Whatever Vuk's inner feelings about the behaviour of Miloš and his courtiers, he still calculated that there was a brighter future for him in Serbia than in Vienna. Others beside himself had been temporarily humiliated by Amidža's sort of practical joke. So far

[1] 'Amidža' shared a patron saint (St. George) with Vuk, i.e. they had a common *Slava*, the saint's day on which families celebrated the conversion of their ancestors to Christianity (the custom still holds in Serbia). It was this link that made 'Amidza' claim kinship.

as Miloš had been genuinely angered by his request about Dr. Stejić, the Prince's wrath was likely to pass soon enough, and whatever was said in Amidža's letter about Vuk's dispensability, he knew that there was a lot of work for him to do, and that Miloš was aware of this. Vuk proved to be justified in swallowing his pride. In answer to his congratulations on the occasion of Christmas, Miloš wrote summoning him to Kragujevac, where he was to have a special room in the same house as Dr. Stejić—'and for the rest we shall come to an agreement when you arrive'.

2

When Vuk arrived in Kragujevac, he was appointed as a member of the People's Court there, with a salary of 4,200 *groš* annually, and free house and board; his work was to be the same as before—the drafting of a legal code—and he continued at it for the next eight months. In the spring of 1830, the Legislative Commission was reformed with Vuk as President. He supplied himself through Kopitar with further editions and translations of the Code Napoléon, and worked through them. Probably however he was cynical about the work of the Commission. Apart from the quality of its other members, it seemed very unlikely that Miloš was ready to take any legal code seriously.

The first clear sign of his doing so would be permission to print it; Vuk had hoped that he might be allowed to travel to St. Petersburg in the summer of 1830 for this purpose, but permission was not forthcoming. The laws were copied fair in Vuk's own system of orthography (he had at least that satisfaction), read aloud to the Assembly and approved there, but never published further. Miloš stuck to the sentiment of one of his own *obiter dicta* that it was better to rule without laws, otherwise a ruler 'was bound to a bit of paper, and could do nothing either for good or ill'.

At least the early months of 1830 passed quietly and profitably for Vuk, and he was able to make one extensive journey in Serbia, visiting the famous old monastery of Studenica, for the collection of antiquities and songs. In September he had two months' leave of absence to visit his family in Zemun, and returned to Serbia at the end of October. Here he was soon faced with another of Miloš's jokes, less personally offensive than Amidza's passport and letter, but more damaging to him in the long run. Vuk had brought with him to Serbia at the beginning of 1830 a copy of his revised translation of the New Testament. He hoped to have it approved by Miloš and the Metropolitan of Belgrade, printed in Russian, and circulated in Serbia without hindrance from the Metropolitan Stratimirović at Karlovci. What Vuk did not know for certain was that his translation, submitted in 1823 by the Russian Bible Society to the judgement of the Serb Metropolitan at Kishinev, had also been used as a basis for a new translation made by Atanasije Stojković,[1] and that the Serbian Church authorities in Russia had pronounced this latter to be more correct. There was therefore in fact little hope of getting his own version printed in Russia. In the meantime he had tried in 1827 to interest Miloš once more in his translation, but Miloš had no intention of making difficulties for himself with the Orthodox Church. 'So far as the Church is concerned', he said, 'I want to leave everything behind me exactly as it is today.' In 1828 Miloš gave Vuk more encouragement, it seems as the result of a direct approach from a representative of the London Bible Society.[2] It is doubtful however whether he was sincere and by 1830 Vuk's influence, at least so far as the Bible was concerned, was being steadily undermined. Miloš's main inspiration in this matter had in fact been one of his new court favourites, Panta Hadji Stoilo, a Macedonian who had set up as a merchant in Zemun, and done good services to Miloš in this capacity—'mad rather than vicious' as Vuk afterwards described him. Throughout 1830 he had been playing on Miloš's vanity and stirring up trouble against Vuk as one who was set on eradicating the good old Slavonic ways and breaking the age-old link with Russia. Miloš was in any case not averse, as he himself approached the long-coveted position of hereditary Prince of Serbia, to a reconciliation with that well-established power, the Metropolitan Stratimirović.

This was the background of a new 'joke' by Miloš at Vuk's expense. In the autumn of 1830 preparations were being made for

[1] Vuk had had some warning of this in 1823 from Stefan Živković.
[2] The Revd. H. D. Leeves, the Society's representative in Istanbul, had been approached directly by Vuk in 1827 about the possibility of getting Vuk's version published; he knew of Stojković's version, and was forced to consult the Serbian delegation in Istanbul (which included Vuk's old enemies, Laza Todorović and Marko Djordjević) about the relative merits of the two versions. Not surprisingly, they voted for Stojković's, but Leeves was very cautious about it when reporting to London.

a new solemn declaration from the Sultan, granting Serbia a further measure of independence, and Miloš himself the hereditary Princedom. It was as part of these preparations that the Assembly was gathered to hear and approve the code of laws worked out by Vuk's Commission. At the same time Miloš asked the priests and other competent people gathered there for an opinion on Vuk's translation of the New Testament. All the priests, and many of the others, delivered themselves of an Opinion, which had of course been approved in advance by Miloš himself; this was to the effect that the Serbs needed no other gospel than what was now read out to them in church. The Opinion was embodied in a document characteristic of Miloš's methods. It was said that Vuk had applied to the undersigned, to confirm that his translation was accurate and written in pure Serb language. They excused themselves, as simple and unlearned people, from giving any such confirmation, and expressed their astonishment that such a highly learned man should ask it of them. But though they knew that Vuk was born and brought up with them in Serbia (i.e. that he had no particular educational qualifications), and even given the fact that 'in some of his publications, and particularly in his *Dictionary*, he had brought such reproach on the Serb people, and had even laid hands on the very foundation of their faith, describing the most sacred things with such scorn that it is a grave offence for a Christian to think and much more to speak such words, and still more to publish them, so that foreigners read his inventions as the truth', Vuk should still not regard them as opponents of his intentions. He should turn to the learned Serbs in Austria, and get approval from the Metropolitan Court at Karlovci; then the signatories of the Opinion would accept his work and recognize it as good. To the Opinion was appended a list of stories[1] and expressions from Vuk's *Dictionary*, together with notes by the signatories, a great deal more subversive to good morals than anything written by Vuk himself.

Thus twelve years after the publication of the *Dictionary*, Vuk was faced once more with the accusations originally launched against it by the Metropolitan Stratimirović; and this time they were embodied in a document signed by the best educated men in what was soon to become the near-independent state of Serbia, including his genuine friend and patron, Chief Vasa Popović, and

---

[1] Particularly that about the Communion (Appendix A, no. 12).

his former friend, Davidović, once the editor of the *Serbian News* and now Miloš's secretary. Those who failed to sign the Opinion hastened to back it up with a letter in the same sense, saying that no good literary fruits could be expected from one who had had most of his education from the *hajduks* Čurčija and Veljko, and that such a crooked little man as Vuk could only be expected to produce a crooked style. The main consolation for Vuk must have been that nearly all the signatories of the Opinion were notoriously venal or cowardly. The document had obviously been approved in advance by Miloš himself. Miloš was known to change his mind often enough on matters which interested him as little as Serb orthography and the correct version of the New Testament; and, as and when he did so, his courtiers would come round quickly and obediently enough.

Vuk prudently swallowed his anger once more, and affected to accept the Opinion calmly, as a nine-days' wonder. It was well for his peace of mind that he did not know more at this time about the further dealings of the London Bible Society. In the course of 1830 they had finally decided against Vuk's Serbian version of the New Testament, and had proceeded with the printing of Stojković's version at Leipzig. This was not put on sale until 1834, and Vuk was unaware until 1832 that it had been printed.

3

Shortly after suffering this second 'joke', Vuk witnessed the proclamation of the new Turkish decree (*Hati Sherif*) in Belgrade on 30 November 1830. Its terms could fairly be held to justify Miloš's policy of patiently waiting on the Great Powers to secure the weakening of the Ottoman Empire, of taking no premature risks by armed action, and of strengthening his own personal position within Serbia. The Pashalik of Belgrade was proclaimed to be henceforth the autonomous Princedom of Serbia. The hereditary rank of Prince was given to Miloš Obrenović. A new and fixed rate was set for the tribute to be paid to the Sultan. Trade within Serbia was to be free; the Turks were to have no powers of interference in the internal administration of Serbia, and were forbidden to settle in Serbian towns. The Serbs were empowered to establish schools and printing presses.

Vuk did not participate in the division of Turkish spoil in

Belgrade (he was staying quietly at the court of Miloš's wife, Princess Ljubica, a long-suffering woman who appreciated Vuk's previous efforts to find husbands for her many daughters). He hoped however that in the general rejoicing and in the new deal of administrative posts he would not be forgotten. Miloš's 'jokes' (if the victims survived) were often followed by compensatory gestures. Vuk's hopes were in this case not deceived. Nothing came of his request for a pension, which, when added to his Russian pension, might relieve him of the necessity of accepting administrative work and leave him free to collect more 'popular songs' and antiquarian treasures. In December 1830, however, Vuk was appointed member of the People's Court or Magistracy of Belgrade, with a salary of 4,200 *groš*—twice as much as was given to any other member of the Court. Vuk wrote to Kopitar: 'So far as my pay and company is concerned, you can say that I am the first-ranking state official in Serbia. But I haven't time even to think about literature.' By April 1831 Vuk had even more reason to make these statements, for he was then promoted to be President of the Court. It was the turn of Panta Hadji and Vuk's other particular enemies to be taken down a peg by Miloš, who was clever enough not to let his favourites establish themselves too long in his favour.

The work of the Magistracy was of the most miscellaneous nature, administrative as well as judicial. It involved, for example, the issue of passports and of permits for the opening of shops, the auction of property forfeited for debt, the fixing of prices for provisions, as well as the proving of wills, and the trial of thieves, murderers, and other criminals. The Magistrates' Court was held in a small square wooden building, not far from the present Cathedral Church of Belgrade, consisting of an ante-room to house the guard, the main room with a table for the magistrates in the middle, their private office on the first floor, and prison cells below ground. Vuk spent his time mainly between the court and the 'Serb café'—probably the 'Znak Pitanja' ('Question mark') which still exists in what is now '7 July street'; in Vuk's time it was a frequent resort for European visitors, and provided him with a substitute for the café life of Vienna to which he had become accustomed.

Vuk had plenty of official duties, but other things too were expected of him. He was one of the few Serbs with good connections abroad and one of his functions was to try to attract to Miloš's Serbia foreigners who could be useful in the new administration. It was at Vuk's initiative that Dimitrije Isailović, a Professor from Sombor (on the frontier between Hungary and the present Vojvodina), came to Belgrade in 1830 and founded the High School. A more famous figure in Slavonic studies, the Czech scholar, Pavle Šafařík, who had taught for many years at Novi Sad, could not be tempted to Belgrade. More important to Miloš, however, than such efforts at recruitment were the services which he thought that Vuk could render as an observer and reporter from Belgrade, particularly of what was going on in Austria-Hungary; Vuk regularly reported on foreign affairs in letters to Miloš. His position was thus more important to Miloš than appeared at first sight; it was also more exposed. His many foreign contacts could be misreported and misinterpreted against him by Miloš's other agents in Belgrade. This applied not least to his continued correspondence with Kopitar in Vienna, and to the messages which reached him from Russia via the Russian agent in Belgrade, the son of the dramatist Kotzebue.[1]

Vuk was soon made aware that he was himself subject to close observation, and that Miloš retained the means of humiliating him again at will. As chief of the Belgrade police Miloš appointed a certain Tsvetko Rajović, who had at the end of 1830 returned from a mission to Russia (he had successfully negotiated the purchase of a printing press for Serbia).[2] In a typical manœuvre Miloš contrived both to humiliate Rajović and to embroil him with Vuk. He was jealous of Rajović's success in Russia, and of the Russian order which had been presented to him. Vuk and other officials were instructed not to give Rajović any chance to talk about his Russian mission, and to treat him badly. Rajović was in consequence very ready to take his revenge by reporting wherever possible against Vuk. He had his chance soon after Vuk took over the presidency of the Magistrates' Court,[3] and soon secured all that he wanted from Miloš; he was to attend meetings of the Court,

---

[1] Kotzebue *père* was a Russian secret agent. It was his murder in 1819 by a young student, Karl Sand, that gave Metternich the excuse to pass the very repressive decrees of Carlsbad, providing for the censorship of the German press.
[2] Instead of that for which Vuk had been negotiating in Vienna.
[3] The point at issue was whether Rajović was correct in reporting the arrival of Karadjordje's son-in-law in Serbia direct to Miloš without informing Vuk.

he alone was empowered to sign the minutes personally (the others could only use a seal), and he was given very wide discretion in political affairs. The Director of Police was in future to take measures against 'persons suspicious from a political point of view' without consulting the Magistrates, and to report to Miloš personally. He was to attend carefully to the conversation and movements of suspects; and by means of reliable contacts he was to 'find out people's secret thoughts and see that they did not disturb the public peace'. This was a comprehensive charter for secret police work, and was liable to turn Vuk and his fellow-magistrates into powerless figure-heads, useful only for show to any European powers with an interest in Serbia.

If Miloš himself had had any intention of working towards constitutional rule, there might have been a part for his Magistrates as well as his secret police to play. But for the time being at least he used his new powers and prestige as hereditary Prince in order to get rich or richer quickly, and as before to divide and crush any possible rivals. Moreover he seemed at this period to be suffering from an extreme 'folie de grandeur'. The atmosphere of Serbia in 1831 is best conveyed in Vuk's own political testament, the letter sent to Miloš in August 1832, and fully quoted in the next chapter. At this period Miloš was at worst a very dangerous ruler, and at best a very arbitrary one with a vicious sense of humour, often exercised against his Magistrates. A typical 'joke' was his ruling in the case of a poor country girl who had given birth to an illegitimate child, and asked not to be subjected to any further official questions on the subject, since she had now found a husband; Miloš agreed to the request, but added that since the bridegroom was so fortunate as to have found a fertile rather than a barren heifer, he should present both the Prince and the Chief Magistrate with a pair of shoes and Vuk should have spurs (presumably because he was unable to ride). Nor did the Prince hesitate to humiliate his Magistrates more directly, if the mood took him—as when there was not enough white wine at the reception given at his residence at Topčider, just to the west of Belgrade, on the occasion of a daughter's marriage. And Vuk, as well as the rest, was aware of cases where instead of 'jokes' or outbreaks of ill temper fatal consequences had followed Miloš's displeasure. Aleksa Popovski, former secretary of the Legislative Commission and an admirer of Vuk, had had the temerity to address a love-letter to Miloš's daughter. He had paid for it with his life, cut to pieces by Miloš's guards at the Prince's orders. In his uncomfortably prominent position, Vuk could not be sure of his personal safety, though there is no record of serious threats to his life; he could be sure only that his work as Chief Magistrate was meaningless and that it left him no time or opportunity for pursuing his literary interests.

4

In these circumstances, he had made up his mind by June 1831 (only two months after becoming Chief Magistrate) that the job was not worth the pay. Alleging ill health, he asked more than once, in letters addressed to Miloš through Vasa Popović, to be retired with a pension. He implied clearly enough what he thought of the usefulness of the Magistrates' Court: 'For president of the Court and of the town of Belgrade you could find someone in practically every village to perform all its duties as well as myself in present circumstances, while if I could live as I want I could achieve something which the average man cannot.' Vuk was determined to leave Serbia and Belgrade, this time with no intention of returning. He might well have found it hard to get permission, had it not been for an outbreak of cholera which began to spread from Zemun to Belgrade. There was a panic, and in the general muddle Vuk was given leave of absence for two months— not without the humiliation of another passport from Amidza describing him as of most deformed shape—'one leg is in truth shorter than the other, but that does not hinder quick movements; his hands are straight and active, but one of them he can't always put where he wants'.

Early in 1831, Vuk had been anxious, in spite of his past experiences in Serbia, to get his family over from Zemun to Belgrade. His wife, who was expecting another child, was most unwilling to come to 'Turkey' and tried in vain to enlist Kopitar's help to persuade Vuk that she should stay in Zemun. Reluctantly she crossed the Sava to spend the month of April 1831 in the strange city of Belgrade. But by September Vuk himself was back in Zemun and not willing to return even for the price of a salary that was for him very handsome (though not regularly paid). Indeed he was ready to give up any future claim to it. This in the light of his previous sufferings is a measure of his fear of Miloš and his followers, and of his disgust at the conditions obtaining in Belgrade.

Vuk was however still not anxious for a complete break with Miloš. He still had hopes of obtaining a pension from him, and indeed had at this time few other obvious possibilities of earning a satisfactory livelihood. He thus had a difficult hand to play in correspondence with Vasa Popović and with Miloš himself. At the end of August 1831 he had been given two months' leave of absence (and had not been paid for his work in August); but by the beginning of November he was absent without leave.

Vuk's tactics were to dwell as much as possible on his sickness, and to say that it would not permit him even to come to Belgrade, much less to travel to Kragujevac for further talks with Miloš about the continued payment of his salary, or the grant of a pension, as Vasa Popović urged him to do.

You know very well [he wrote to Vasa] that I am lame in both legs (for some time this right leg of mine, which is meant to be sound, is worse at the foot than the left is at the knee), and I can hardly move. Apart from this I am so weak generally. The slightest cold gets me down, as well as draughts[1] and the noise of conversation, and rowdy talk, and all sorts of things which people in good health can just laugh at.... Anyone can see from this that I'm not asking for cakes instead of bread, but that it's only the greatest ill fortune which drives me to ask for a pension instead of such an honourable post with so much pay.

Vuk's financial terms were steadily reduced. He had started by asking for full pay during his temporary absence, together with payment of arrears. As his date for return to Serbia was put off into the more distant future, he began to demand a pension in substitute for his pay, and as a reward for his past services to Serbia and to Miloš personally. He enumerated these in the letter already quoted (on the subject of his health), and they make a curious list: (1) Vuk had persuaded Jovan Hadjic Svetić [in 1822] to write a fine ode to Miloš Obrenović (and had incurred Svetić's anger by so doing, since Miloš had not given the expected reward); (2) he had persuaded the famous Grimm to dedicate to Miloš his Serbian grammar in a preface, which would have been considered an honour by Tsar Dušan, Napoleon, or Nicolas of Russia; (3) he

[1] Vuk's susceptibility to draughts and desire to close all doors and windows was a standing joke at Miloš's court.

had described Miloš's glorious exploits in the history now printed in Serbian, Russian, and German. And apart from all this there were the benefits and honours done to the Serb people by Vuk's collections of songs and by 'that book which Professor Ranke and I published in German, for the Russian translation of which he was given the Anna Cross, 2nd class'.

Vasa Popović advised Vuk to drop altogether any talk of reward for his work and to come to Serbia once more to give more detailed reasons for his financial demands. In order to avoid the journey Vuk was then reduced to requesting simply charity from Miloš, and for charity, he said, it was unnecessary to argue in detail—he had written all the justification that he could, and there could be nothing to add by word of mouth. The tone of Vuk's letters was by 1832 unlikely to earn him any favour at court, and his prospects became even more dim when in January 1832, Vasa Popović, his most helpful intermediary, suddenly died. He continued the correspondence direct with Miloš himself, who sent him gifts of money totalling 150 florins; but there was no change in the basic position of either party. Miloš would give no assurance of regular payment if Vuk did not return to Serbia, and Vuk by now would not return at any price.

In the meantime he was also being threatened from another quarter. Vuk, as will be remembered, had long been an object of suspicion to the Austrian police, at first for pro-Russian tendencies, especially after his own journey to Russia and receipt of a pension from the Russian authorities. He had now for some time been suspected of acting as an agent for Miloš Obrenović, especially from the time of the publication of his history. When he returned for a short visit to Vienna in spring 1829 the police had no intention of letting him stay long there. The arrangement by which Vuk's family stayed in Zemun from the summer of 1829 on, and he himself came over to visit them occasionally from Serbia, was the subject of much debate by the highest authorities in Vienna, including Sedlnicki, the Chief of Police, and Metternich himself. It was eventually approved on the sensible grounds that, while Vuk was certainly an agent of Miloš, Miloš would have no difficulty in finding others if necessary; and that while Vuk's family was in Zemun, the police would quite easily keep an eye both on them and on him.

This arrangement lasted until the end of 1831, but it then

became clear to the Austrian authorities, who had access to Vuk's talks with Serbs from Belgrade at the 'parlatorium' (or 'talking-place') in the Zemun quarantine-station and no doubt to his correspondence with Serbia as well, that Vuk had no intention of returning there. They concluded that he wanted to settle down in Austria again as Miloš's agent, and their suspicions were strengthened by information given against Vuk by their own agents in Zemun.

In December 1831 Vuk was told by the local police to get permission from Vienna for his further stay in Zemun. He wrote to Kopitar asking for his intervention, and received a reply suggesting that he apply to the Russians for a passport if the Austrian police continued to show him such ill will. Vuk wrote in despair:

I know for myself that in such circumstances it would be best to get a Russian passport; but how will the Russians give me one, when the Metropolitan's party has spread it about St. Petersburg, as well as around the Serb community in this [Austrian] Empire, that the Austrian Court has hired me, through you, to make Uniates out of the Serbs? Thus I say that I am a real martyr, since to the Austrian police the Metropolitan attacks me as having secret relations [with Miloš], and as being a danger to the Empire, while in Russia he attacks me for being hired to convert people to the Uniate faith. And perhaps the Vienna police think that you too are intriguing with me in the Russian interest against this Empire! . . . So help me God, if I only knew where, I would have run away from Austria and from the Serb people, just to get free of such intrigues!

Just as Vasa Popović had urged him to come to Serbia for a personal reckoning with Miloš Obrenović, Kopitar now tried to persuade him to travel to Vienna in order to have things out personally with the Viennese police. Vuk doubted whether he would be allowed to move from Zemun. He replied to Kopitar's suggestion:

Provided they let me come! Miloš Urošević, a ne'er-do-well of this town, has quarrelled over something with the Burgermaster of Zemun, Captain-Auditor Lazarević, and accused him (I think last summer) to the Emperor himself of planning through my agency to hand over the Srem province to the Serbs. . . . And now that I have come here from Serbia, I think that Urošević has accused me to Vienna of being Miloš Obrenović's spy (as is openly said of me in the streets and inns here).

Vuk's suspicions of Urošević were well founded. The latter had suggested to the Viennese police that the reports of Vuk's being in disfavour with Miloš had been deliberately spread and were only a blind; it would be best either to forbid Vuk's further stay in Austria, or at the least to have him removed from the Austro-Serbian frontier districts. So far as Stratimirović was concerned, Vuk was of course right in regarding him as a powerful and unrelenting enemy, but there is no evidence that there were any direct and particular denunciations from Karlovci in 1831-2.

At the end of 1831, Vuk put in a petition to the Vienna police, asking for permission to spend the rest of the winter in Zemun, and then to move in the spring to Novi Sad, where his son Sava was at school. The proceedings that followed well illustrate the ponderous functioning of the Austrian bureaucracy. The petition was forwarded, together with a favourable opinion of Vuk, by the local authorities at Zemun to the commandant of the fortress at Petrovaradin, by him to the War Council at Vienna, and by the Council to Police Headquarters, with a request for a decision to be taken jointly with the Court Chancellery. The Chief of Police, Sedlnicki, forwarded the documents to Metternich, advising against granting the petition. The reasons advanced in 1829 against letting Vuk stay for long in Zemun were still valid (he would act as Miloš's spy); but in Novi Sad he would have better opportunities of gathering information, and it would be harder to keep an eye on him. Metternich agreed, and on 1 April 1832 Vuk was informed by the Austrian Commander at Zemun that his petition was refused; he must move as soon as possible to Serbia with his whole family.

Vuk was utterly downcast by the decision. He immediately addressed an appeal to the commander at Zemun, explaining the medical causes which made it impossible for him and his family to travel at the time, and adding a whole list of other reasons for rescinding the decision; his wife as a good Viennese Catholic with three daughters to bring up in the faith, could not be expected to live in Serbia, and his own life would be endangered by the opponents who intrigued constantly against his person as well as against his literary work. He wanted to return via Buda (where he needed to take the waters) to Vienna with his family, and then to be free to move as he wished within the Austrian Empire. If this request could not be granted, he must ask for a passport via Buda and Vienna (where he would leave his family) to Russia where he would hope to enjoy the continued favour of Tsar Nicolas. Vuk's appeal was forwarded to Vienna on 20 April 1832, and was followed by various reminders. At the same time he wrote to the Russian Ambassador in Vienna, asking as a Russian pensioner for protection and intervention with the Viennese authorities. The Ambassador, Tatishchev, replied promptly that he could not take up the case, which was a purely internal one for the Austrian authorities; the receipt of a pension from the Russian Government did not make Vuk a Russian subject.

Austrian despotism was however once more tempered, in Vuk's case, by *Schlamperei*. While there was no answer to his appeal, no attempt was made to enforce the departure of him and his family from Zemun to Serbia. In mid-September he was even allowed to send his wife and family to Vienna, but his own fate remained uncertain. Kopitar in Vienna was at a loss how to help his friend. In August 1832 he sent a memorandum to Sedlnicki repeating his favourite thesis that Vuk's literary work had the effect of uniting the Orthodox and Catholic Slavs in Austria, and weakening any feelings of allegiance which they had towards Russia; it was thus much more useful than anything which the Russian-inclined Stratimirović could do for the Austrian Government. It is however doubtful if Kopitar's arguments had the slightest effect at this stage on Vuk's fate. A solution for his immediate problems had to wait until October 1832; it came from an unexpected quarter in an unexpected form.

XV

VUK BREAKS WITH MILOŠ OBRENOVIĆ

I

IN his letters to Miloš about the possibility of a pension, early in 1832, Vuk was already beginning to take a lofty ironic tone likely, if not calculated, to annoy his correspondent. It was one of Vuk's weaknesses that he let his pen run away with him in correspondence as well as in public controversy, and said things which, if true, were all the more likely to irritate rather than to persuade. But he had by now determined not to return to Serbia, and had probably begun to appreciate more highly the one asset which remained to him in dealing with Miloš. The Prince was afraid of Vuk's pen, and Vuk was no longer afraid for his life. He must have reckoned that he had forfeited the hope of any substantial favours from Miloš—at least until the nature of the regime in Serbia was fundamentally changed; he therefore had little to lose by writing against the Prince.

Vuk's first direct passage of arms with Miloš occurred in July 1832, and the occasion was an attempt by the Metropolitan Stratimirović to secure a ban on the use of Vuk's alphabet in the productions of Miloš's new printing press, which had just started to operate in Serbia. The first works to be printed, early in 1832, were two small pamphlets, bound together: *A Poem on the Rising of the Serbs against the Dahijas* and *To the Slavonic-Serbian Race and Community*, both of which had previously been printed in Buda and then banned by the Austrian censorship, presumably on the ground that they would stimulate nationalist feeling against the Turks. In March 1832 a start was made on printing the first book to be given to the press, *An Anthology of Truth and Science* by Jovan Stejić, at that time still Miloš's personal doctor. Half-way through printing, which had been expressly approved by Miloš, he decreed that work must stop until the book was rewritten with the hard sign inserted, 'given that the omission of this letter will resemble Vuk's spelling, and many patriotic people, not only in Serbia but also in Russia, think that this will have bad results; therefore it is not allowed that anything should be printed at our press in accordance with Vuk's spelling'. Stejić was told that he could have his book published elsewhere, but that he would not be free to circulate it in Serbia. He had already suffered from Miloš's caprices in his medical capacity, and concluded that his work in Serbia was becoming too difficult. He left Serbia for Zemun at the end of June 1832 and Vuk reported the case gleefully to Kopitar.

He was glad to see that others too—and men who had been prime favourites at court—could not endure Miloš's rule, and Stejić told him that Miloš was showing signs of incipient madness. Vuk however knew that he had little cause for rejoicing at the occasion of Stejić's departure. Miloš did not interest himself in orthographical matters without strong stimulus from outside; and in this case, the stimulus had come from Stratimirović. The Metropolitan had co-ordinated a campaign with Atanasije Stojković in Russia to warn Miloš of the dangers of Vuk's literary reforms. It was this that drove Miloš first to take action against Stejić's book and, much more important, at the end of 1832 to issue a decree, which remained in force for nearly thirty years, formally forbidding the use of Vuk's orthography.

In the summer of 1832, Vuk decided after talking with Stejić to make a direct but still personal and private attack on the Prince's policy. In July he wrote to Miloš about the dangers of a ruler taking too much on himself in literary questions. Parts of this letter read like an exercise in irony, designed for publicity and not to persuade the recipient. Without doubt, however, it was meant as a sincere effort to convince Miloš that it would be wrong to intervene in the literary or linguistic battle between Vuk and Stratimirović, and that at least the way should still be left open for Vuk's reforms. The main line of argument is as follows: Not even in the most advanced literature is there full agreement between experts on spelling. Literary men must fight out their differences on this matter among themselves. It is unprecedented and dangerous for a Government to make rulings on such things. They will only make fools of themselves. 'Tomorrow . . . people will begin to write and talk against the orders which Your Highness has given, to Your Highness's shame. . . . And, as sure as two and two make four, that shame will be enduring.' In any case, Stejić's book is most unsuitable for Serbian conditions of the day, 'even if hard signs were put into every word, at the end, in the middle, and at the beginning'. What was the censorship doing to let it through? 'Books about the natural rights of man are looked at askance today in a number of European states, where people on the whole enjoy such rights; and to write in Serbia . . . about the right of freedom and equality . . . of property and inheritance—would be more dangerous to you than the proclamations of Čarapić and Mija the teacher.' Given the very small number of literate people in Serbia and the difficulties caused by censorship, it would probably be best for the present simply to close down the press except for passports, proclamations, and newspapers.

Vuk's arguments had no immediate effects except to make Miloš turn once more to Stratimirović for confirmation of the advice which he had already given. Some of them however may not have been entirely wasted. For example, Vuk made considerable use of the implication that, while the Prince may do no wrong, he may receive much misleading advice. Knowing Miloš's highly suspicious nature, and having suffered from it greatly himself, Vuk was making a deliberate attempt to discredit his enemies at court by suggestions that their advice would bring Miloš into contempt and might even lead to a renewal of political unrest in Serbia.

The letter of July seems at this distance of time to be a warning shot for a much more serious attack. Vuk realized by this time the unique nature of his experience of Miloš's rule in Serbia. For some time he seems to have envisaged a sort of 'acquit de conscience' for the book on Miloš which he had published in 1828. His first idea was to write frank notes for posterity about Miloš's regime under the title: *Material for a Serbian History* [i.e. history of Serbia] *of Our Time*. The work was never finished, but Vuk prepared a skeleton plan (as for all his major works) which has been preserved, together with extensive notes for the first half of the projected work and a short introduction. He noted that his health would probably not allow him to write anything more systematic, and that he was putting down relevant points in no proper order, just as they occurred to him; they might be of use to some future historian, and, as he had described the glorious exploits of Miloš, posterity had the right to demand of him some account of Miloš's moral character and evil deeds. As he put it himself:

VUK BREAKS WITH MILOŠ OBRENOVIĆ

In the time of Karadjordje, when Miloš was under the rule of his brother and of Karadjordje himself, he was really, as far as I have been able to ascertain, to be classed among the orderly and honest leaders, as is told (perhaps a little poetically) on page 50 of his *Life* [Vuk's work of 1828]. But now, as I left him in Serbia last autumn, he knows not what is sinful or shameful, and has not the slightest conscience in his breast; to put it as shortly as possible, he can be called a real tyrant and completely amoral. It would be great good fortune if his deeds did not give proof of this, and if I were to be caught lying.'

The skeleton headings under which Vuk intended to group his notes were:

I. Rude jokes;
II. Selfishness and suspicion of all other people;
III. Arbitrary rule and government of the country and people;
IV. Undignified behaviour and lying;
V. Domestic life;
VI. Like finds out like [birds of a feather].

The notes under the first three headings were quite full, and constitute the primary sources for a number of passages in Chapter XIV. Those under headings IV–VI took the form only of summary headlines. Vuk's manuscript notes were packed away under a mass of covers, with the inscription 'not to be opened in this century'.[1]

By April 1832 Vuk had abandoned his first plan and decided to make his case against Miloš in a very different form. It was at this time that he drafted the famous *Letter to Miloš Obrenović* which is his political testament. The *Letter* is given in full later in this chapter and needs little more introduction. It was based in part on the notes contained in the *Material for a Serbian History*; but Vuk omitted the most offensive examples of Miloš's misdeeds, instead citing in generalized form 'negative examples' of things which a good ruler should not do. The whole letter was drafted so that it could conceivably be sent direct to Miloš, by way of patriotically intentioned advice. It remains however a very direct and hard-hitting indictment of Miloš's regime, and Vuk's humble advice, as in the letter which he sent to Miloš in July 1832, is often hard to distinguish from the most bitter irony. Indeed it is easy to see why, having drafted the letter in April, he hesitated for nearly four months before sending it. If the letter had been written by a

---

[1] They were first published (partially) in *Književnost*, 1947, nos. 9–10.

more sophisticated politician, it would be easy to conclude that the intention had all along been to publish it at the right moment and that it was only a secondary question whether it was received or read by Miloš himself. Vuk however had some reasons for ensuring that Miloš should take it as serious advice. He wanted to embroil the Prince with his advisers, and in summer 1832 he did not know whether he might not soon be forced to leave Zemun and return to Serbia. It was Miloš himself who was responsible for the publicity which the letter received before the end of 1832.[1] It is thus fair to take seriously, if not completely at their face value, Vuk's professions that the letter was inspired by a genuine sense of duty to his country and a desire to convert Miloš to better ways, rather than by a spirit of revenge and a determination to show Miloš up to the world outside Serbia; but Vuk must always have had in mind the idea of publishing the letter sometime or of exercising pressure on Miloš by the threat to do so.

2

The text of Vuk's *Letter to Miloš Obrenović* runs as follows (the notes on the text, printed here as footnotes, are in some cases Vuk's own, but not all Vuk's notes have been reproduced here):

Zemun—12 April 1832
(not dispatched till 13 August)
Your Highness, Most Gracious Lord!

Everyone wants to know what others judge, think, and say about him. For rulers and governors of the people this is especially needful and they spend untold riches to find out. I remember that Your Highness too, through the Magistracy and local government of Belgrade when I was President of it, enjoined on the Director of the Belgrade Police, Tsvjetko Rajović, as a special duty to give you the names of those who were not content with Your Highness's rule. All this encourages me to inform you of the main heads of discontent with your rule in Serbia, and to explain my own thoughts about this, feeling that there is at present no better way of displaying my gratitude and devotion to you.

It is true that, as our ancestors said, no one can bake cakes to suit all tastes, but with your rule today it could fairly be said that practically

[1] The letter to Miloš was in fact printed first in 1843 in the Belgrade *Serbian Courier*, in a context very unfavourable to Vuk, and as part of Jovan Hadzić-Svetić's campaign to discredit him. See Chapter XVI, § 4.

no one in Serbia is satisfied. If one started to analyse and dissect this further, it would be found that the most discontented are those officials who are closest to Your Highness and most often in your company, and the happiest those who have no kind of acquaintance with Your Highness.

The various causes of this discontent could be roughly divided under two main heads. People are discontented either because they cannot live according to their wishes and capabilities, and their lives or reputation are insecure, and they are not lords of the property which God has given them or which they have justly and laboriously acquired; or again because no such effort and labour is devoted to the common weal as they think is both needful and possible. There is no need for me here to recite by name all those known by me to be discontented, or to relate the causes of their unhappiness; and I do not want to do so, first (apart from other reasons) because I would not wish it to be said or thought that I was attacking anyone out of envy or malice, and secondly, in case this letter should, contrary to my intentions and wishes, do harm instead of good to anyone. But I shall, by way of example, name things which are no secret and could not bring harm to anyone.

Your Highness can probably remember what Stojan Simić said to you at Požarevac in 1830, when you were annoyed at the idea of a *Ferman* from Constantinople laying down that there must be a Senate in Serbia, in agreement with which the Prince should rule the land and people: 'Do not be angry; whatever is in the *Ferman*, while you are alive, things will never be different from what they are today; and after your death those who are still living will make some different arrangement with your successors.' I often heard this same Simić openly say: 'I never like to be in the same place as His Highness—when he's in Požarevac, I prefer to be in Kragujevac, and when he comes to Kragujevac, I go to Požarevac, and hope we don't meet on the way.' When your Highness was at Kragujevac in 1830, preparing for an inquiry at Jagodina against the chief Mileta Radojković, one of your best-known officials came up to me behind your back and said: 'Do you know why this is being done?' When I told him that I didn't know, he went on: 'Simply in order to blacken Mileta's name and lessen his merits; our Prince doesn't want anyone in Serbia but himself to have merit or honour or good name.' Those sentiments for which last year Živan Parazlama was expelled from Belgrade are echoed not only in the hearts of everyone in Belgrade, Šabac, and Smederevo (and of many notables all over the country) but also here in Austria—probably as the result of complaints by the merchants of Belgrade. It is said that under no Turkish governor were there worse exactions than there are today, and that in the last two years twenty-two thousand *groš* of work-tax[1] alone have been paid for the two residences of Your Highness. Thus too the stock dealers of Serbia, and especially the pig-dealers, have complained and go on complaining, at the fact that Your Highness with your partners has gained control of their whole business, and completely ruined them, etc.

Let me say again briefly: in Serbia, no one, precisely no one, is content with Your Highness's Government, except your two sons: and if they were a little older, perhaps they would be as discontented as anyone else. The happier anyone pretends to be, and the more he shouts: 'God grant you long life, my Lord! Your health, my Lord, and our good luck!', the more discontented he is, and he will only be putting on a show to mask his discontent. However you need not think that all who are discontented with your rule are your enemies. Your Highness knows very well that there is no one more discontented with you and your rule than your own wife, but yet you have no better friend in all Serbia than her.[2] As for your brother Jefrem, I don't know whether he is any more content with your rule than any other official, but he would die for you tomorrow, and the same could be said for many other officials. Apart from this, I think that, to judge by the standards of justice and sound common sense, it would be hard to count it against anyone that he is discontented. For to speak directly, Black George's [Karadjordje's] rule was far better for officials and all men of note than your own; yet you yourself rebelled against that, and today if you were in the place of any of your own officials, you would be no less, if no more, discontented than they. And all your officials and companions have as much heart, understanding, desire, will, and all other passions and spiritual qualities as you, for they are exactly the same kind of person as yourself.

I expect that Your Highness, like any clever and sensible ruler, wants to do everything possible to make your compatriots happy; and therefore I venture most humbly to point out here how I think that you could turn their discontent into content.

First of all I would say, as a rule by which everything else can be judged, *that the true profit of every ruler is only that which is of profit to his people too; and that anything which is harmful to the people cannot be of any true profit to the ruler.* Holding fast to this principle, I think:

---

[1] Vuk says in his own note to this passage that the Serb chiefs traditionally had the right to command some days of labour on the spot from people residing on their land. Miloš had started to make his subjects travel long distances to forced work. The work tax (*kuluk*) was called 'slavery' (*robija* = 'robot'), in the Srem province.

[2] *Vuk's note*: 'Not only does Miloš keep mistresses openly, in the sight of his wife (one of them she herself killed with a pistol at Crnvića in 1819), but also to spite her he does everything to shame her family and friends. . . .'

1. You ought to give the people a *code of laws*, or, as they usually say now in Europe, a *constitution*. I don't mean by this a French or English or new Greek kind of constitution; but, roughly speaking, *that the method of government should be determined, and a government constituted* by means of a *Ferman* or *Hati-sherif* (anyone who recommends or approves some other method is deceiving you and leading you astray); *that everyone should have security of life, property, and honour; that everyone should be free to work at whatever job he likes, provided it does no harm to others, and to live as he likes; that everyone should know what he should do so as to stand in no fear of you or anyone else; that no one should be able to compel others forcibly to serve him*[1]*; that it should be clearly known which official is the senior and which the junior; that without proper cause and judgement no official should be expelled from service, or be moved down to a lesser rank; that no one should be forced against his will to take on any service; and that every official should be able to resign when he wants*: Such a principle would be necessary for our officials only in their present condition; as their condition improved, few of them would want to refuse posts and even fewer to resign without special reasons from posts given to them. But until this state of affairs comes about and is confirmed, it will be impossible to do anything sensible about our laws either—just as it is impossible to make a house or any other form of building until a foundation is laid.

A code of laws of this kind should not simply be imposed on the people, but you must announce them to a full assembly, take an oath to abide by them, and confirm that anyone who transgresses and neglects them, be he who he may, is an enemy of his people and country and will be judged as such. Then what is established and confirmed in this way must be cherished and kept as a most holy object. And in order that everyone may more easily become acquainted with their good fortune, and conduct themselves accordingly in gratitude to you, you should print the whole thing, send a copy to every village, and apart from that let it be sold in every district, so that anyone who wants can buy it cheaply.

Perhaps it will be said that Your Highness will lose by establishing a constitutional government and giving a proper set of laws to the people; but I think that, far from losing anything, you will gain by it more than anyone else. When everyone in the land has security of life and property and honour, then only will you yourself have security for your own life, property, and honour, and not only you for your lifetime but your children after you. While as long as you have the power to ruin anyone without any cause, to take from him all that he has or indeed any part

---

[1] Vuk notes at this point that any servant who tried to leave Miloš's court was first beaten and then forced to enter service again.

of his property, and to disgrace him, so long the people has the right, as best it can, to do with you and your children as it likes.

In such affairs, you should put no trust in decrees by the Sultan, or in formal oaths by the people, and still less in your armed bands, your soldiers, and your guard. In our times, as you can see, there are enough examples in Europe of peoples casting down and persecuting kings, whose kingdoms have lasted God knows for how many generations; and how much more easily can this happen in Serbia! There everyone remembers the time when you were as they are today: they can say that it is they themselves who with their toil and riches and blood and service bought for you the lordship and power and right which you think that you have over them, and that they did not choose you of their own free will, but were forced according to your wishes to confirm you in power.[1] (I am only putting this to Your Highness, you know better than I what our countrymen are and how in such matters people can say their mind openly only when they are in power); then too you are not yourself the true Lord of the people and country, but have two great Tsars above you who cannot look on indifferently while the people complain of your rule. As for your bands and soldiers and guard, I think that ruler in a bad way who has to maintain them in order to preserve him from his own people! The greatest security for a ruler in his own country should be the love of his people, their satisfaction with his rule, and their conviction that on his death things can only get worse, and in no way better for them.

Thus the benefits of a constitutional Government are great and important, as are those of a popular code of laws. To look at the matter from three points of view:

(a) In Serbia today there is no constitutional government in the proper sense of the word; you yourself are the whole government. When you are at Kragujevac, then the government too is at Kragujevac; when you are at Požarevac, then it is at Požarevac; when you are at Topčider, then it is there; when you are travelling, the government is travelling too; and if you die tomorrow, which God forbid, the government would be dead too, and then might would be right. . . .

[1] Vuk's note pours scorn on Miloš's popular credentials: 'It is true that he has a few documents confirming that the people elect him as their master and ruler; but when people have to choose what some one else wants, there is no choice in the proper sense of the word. . . . When Miloš heard from the papers that in France and England deputies came to Parliament with full powers, shortly before the Assembly in Kragujevac in 1830 he had full powers made out in his Chancellery and sent round to the chiefs to be distributed to those who came to the Assembly; then to be sure that it was all in French and English style, when the deputies assembled at Kragujevac, he sent his clerks nominally to inspect the documents giving full powers and in fact to take them back from the deputies.'

(b) If a constitutional government were established in Serbia, then it would enjoy the confidence which is proper and necessary, both with foreign powers and with private individuals; for such a government would consider well in advance its decisions and actions, and would stick firmly to whatever was decided or done (according to the popular saying 'An Empire doesn't go back on its word', which applies not only to Emperors but to all rulers and governments). Then it would not be necessary to *establish a special scale* of 600 thalers a year[1] for doctors (for there are very few who are willing to come of their own free will), but according to terms publicly fixed by the government, doctors would come to Serbia in the numbers required for 300 thalers, and they would be much more satisfactory than those who come now for the promised fee of 600 thalers. And similarly, apart from doctors, numbers of decent, notable, and useful people from all ranks of society would come to Serbia without special invitation. Whereas now, as you have at times said yourself, those who come are mostly good-for-nothings, frauds, and cheats,[2] who elsewhere would either not be able to make a living, or not as well as in Serbia; and even such people are not satisfied (probably there are among them men who came to Your Highness without a penny in their pockets, and can now count their ducats in thousands; yet given that they cannot enjoy their wealth as they wish, but have to hide it, as a snake its legs, they would run away to Austria, if only they could make off with what they own, and didn't hope that there would soon be a big change in Serbia, and that they would then be able to grab another thousand or so by investing along with Your Highness.

(c) Even the wisest ruler, who has spent all his youth in learning how to rule, still cannot govern a state properly on his own, if only because a single man can hardly manage one small village properly on his own, much less a whole country and people; secondly because 'four eyes see better than two'; and thirdly, because even the wisest and best educated ruler is still a man, exposed to all human passions and weaknesses, so that he may do wrong to someone out of anger or some other such passion; or in return for some land, he might to the general misfortune and his own misfortune and special shame, give a particular job to someone, for whom it is by no means suitable; for example he might appoint a hedgehog to carry his written and oral messages, or a wolf to guard sheep or a donkey to decide whether the crow sings better than the nightingale, etc.[3]

---

[1] Vuk says in his note that the salary of 600 thalers was only equalled by that paid to Miloš's brothers; but that payment of all salaries was highly irregular.

[2] In a bitter and detailed note about Miloš's staff, Vuk says that he could not trust any true Serb to work with him, so that important places at court were filled almost exclusively by foreigners.

[3] Perhaps a reminiscence of one of the German 'popular songs' in the collection *Des Knaben Wunderhorn*, to which Kopitar had introduced Vuk in 1813–14.

If *officials* were granted a proper code, not only would the present officials be glad to serve, thanking God and you for their good fortune, but also everyone would work to get their children educated and trained to be officials. But now you see that many of the most notable officials would rather put their sons into business or trade than see them training for an official career, and would rather marry their daughters to any kind of dealer than to an official. Your Highness considers himself as no less than the chiefs of Karavlaška [Wallachia] or Karabogdanska [Moldavia], but compared with their officials, Your Highness's men are nothing but beggars and slaves. And, to leave Karavlaška and Karabogdanska aside, and turn to the Turks (who are still thought of as barbarians in Europe), look at the sort of permanent regulations which there are for Turkish officials! I would not compare Your Highness with the Sultan, and your officials with the Vizirs and other officials of the Sultan and the Turkish state; but let us say that you are like some provincial Pasha (probably you are greater) and your officials like those in his Pashalik. Don't let us talk here of the lordly style in which the noblemen live or the Generals, judges, treasurers, honourable counsellors, and many other officials of the Turkish Government or Vizir, but let us turn to Belgrade, where the Turks share power and dominion with the Serbs, and look at Sadik Effendi, who is only a Clerk of the Taxes, riding around Belgrade on his charger, and living better and more finely than any of Your Highness's officials!

The nobles and great men of any country (and in Serbia only the officials are in this class) represent the people, and when things go well with them, they will on their own account take care of their ruler, fearing to lose their own prosperity along with him; but when they have nothing to lose, they will desire any kind of change, in the hope that things will be better for them.

Apart from this, officials are as necessary to every ruler and government as wings to an eagle, or hands to a man. And so all sensible rulers and governments have always tried (and still try) to satisfy the good and worthy officials, who constitute their greatest fortune, with everything possible—riches and honour and praise—so that these could wish for nothing more than to be graciously allowed still to give faithful and honourable service. This is the origin of the various ranks, orders, and pensions (given either to officials during their lifetime or to their families after their death), of gifts of all kinds (in goods or land), and memorials after their death, such as the Russians put up to Suvarov [*sic*], Rumyantsev, etc. It is true enough that people have existed, and still perhaps exist here and there, who have served only for the profit of their native country, and without regard to what they get out of the service themselves; but normally when a decent official notices that his ruler or government does not pay him the proper honour and respect (and much more if they overwhelm him with shame), he will no longer have any true desire to serve, and will either look for ways to leave the service, or if he cannot by any means earn a living without it, will from that point on serve out of sheer poverty and only for the sake of the pay. As for hereditary ranks and lordships, I have in truth never been a great supporter of this custom nor am I today. However I think it right to mention here to Your Highness that I do not know whether anywhere else on earth there is a country in which only the ruler has hereditary rights, and no one else has any security of any possession even for his own lifetime, much less for his heirs. How can such a state have any firm and lasting existence? Can and will people suffer that a single man should have everything, rule and dominion, riches, honour, and glory, and the rest nothing? And anyone who has achieved this by force and pressure, must live ever in fear, for force cannot last for ever and what force has taken and held may properly be regained too by force.

If all that I have mentioned here could be arranged immediately and completely in the proper way, there would be no need to say any more; the code of laws would satisfy the most important of the malcontents and constitutional government the rest. But considering that there is small hope of seeing all this achieved immediately and completely, I shall point out what else I think should be done. Thus:

2. *Forced labour should be abolished and no one should have to pay 'free gifts'.* Just as it is recorded in history that once Serbs used to go from Niš and Smederevo to Jedrena and Constantinople to cut grass for the Sultan, so it will be told that from the Užice and Soko districts people came to mow for Your Highness around Kragujevac and Belgrade; and that the merchants and craftsmen of Kragujevac, Belgrade, and Požarevac had to shut their shops and come out with their helpers and apprentices and house servants to buy hay from Your Highness. Last year in the Magistrates' Court of the town and district of Belgrade, the elders of the villages on the road between Belgrade and Kragujevac complained that Your Highness's guards, if their horses tired or did not please them, would leave them at the inns to be fed at the village's expense, and would take the first horse they found in the village; then when this too broke down, they would take another, and leave it anywhere, so that people would lose a few days in looking for their horses. And it was not only Your Highness's guards that did this, but big-bellied Gaja too when taking the treasure chest from Kragujevac to Belgrade (no doubt for a fee), or bringing things for Your Highness from Belgrade to Kragujevac, would drive the oxen from the villages cursing people's fathers and mothers, and saying: 'This is the Prince's

property; just you dare to refuse us oxen and leave it standing on the road.' And at that time when the elders of these villages complained of this, Captain Golub said that because of such happenings the villagers of Grocka had sold practically all their horses. As far as I was able, I tried to calm down all these plaintiffs, assuring them that this was done without Your Highness's knowledge, and promising them that we would inform Your Highness and that it would not happen in future. Indeed I proposed afterwards that you should be informed, but the rest of the Magistrates, who had long been better acquainted with such goings on, said that this could not be allowed. Last year it was rumoured that Your Highness was thinking of ordering that labour should not be done for any of the officials and only for yourself; but in my opinion this would be even worse, for at present the hatred and discontent of the people at forced labour is shared between you and the officials, but in that case it would all fall on you, and what is more you would add the officials to the number of the discontented.

Therefore I think that it would be best if compulsory labour were completely abolished, except for the needs of local authorities (the building of roads, bridges, etc.), and with it the provision of horses and hospitality on official journeys.[1] When anyone is travelling he should himself look after the expense of his journey and how he is to be fed. If he is travelling on state business, the State should provide him with money for expenses, as is done throughout Europe; e.g. couriers are given what is necessary for expenses at particular points, and then pay their way like everyone else—even the Turks have begun this method with their Tartars. As a substitute for compulsory labour and the provision of horses and hospitality on journeys, Your Highness should be allotted suitable compensation in money. Then when anyone wants to do business with you, your officials can seek them out at your expense, as other people would do, and wherever you travel yourself, your officials can prepare lodgings for ready money. If things were arranged in this way, the people with whom you would lodge, and those who live on the routes by which you travel, would count it their greatest good fortune, instead of their greatest curse, as at present, that they live where they do.

3. *Schools* should be set up. In my opinion, Serbia today has no greater lack or more urgent need than in the matter of capable people for the public service.

I have nothing against Mišić, Vačić, etc. [further names of Miloš's

[1] Vuk related in a note how Miloš in 1831, on arrival at his residence in Topčider, exploded to the Magistrates about the quality of the wine provided. They managed to secure for that evening so much champagne (at 13 *zwanzigers* a bottle) that even the servants at table drank their fill; and afterwards Miloš's servants took care to order all of the best in advance.

own employees of the time]. These are all people who could be usefully employed on business within their capacities, and who deserve honour and respect, like many other comrades, for their services. But in modern conditions it would be impossible to govern a well-established state with such people (any more than with Pavle Radomirović and chief Vasa Popović), much less to bring order into an unsettled country—and simply to govern as the Turks governed, or in some respects rather worse, is of little profit to the people or honour to the rulers.

Our lack cannot be made good by Serbs born and educated outside Serbia (in the Austrian Empire), if only because they cannot enjoy the true confidence of the people, and secondly because they have not learnt what is necessary for the present condition of Serbia. Thus it was that when I came from Vienna to Serbia in 1820, with the particular object of preparing people for official service, I proposed, as is very well known to Your Highness, that we should bring together some young men of 15 to 20 years, chosen throughout the country, with some small knowledge of reading and writing, and that with them we should establish a *High School*, in which three able and sensible teachers would give a three-year course in *general world history, geography, statistics, Serb grammar, with something on higher mathematics, rhetoric, laws, the history of aesthetics, logic, physics, etc*. After three years of this our young men would have been better fitted for official service than any who have done twelve years of schooling in Budapest. And any of them who showed a special gift and inclination to science could, I thought, have been sent to Europe at State expense to have further courses in science and languages.[1] Then for the primary schools I thought that little by little school books should be prepared in the Serbian language, according to the best European models, which could then have been circulated among all the other Serbs, under Austrian as well as under Turkish rule. To make all this easier of accomplishment and to make the fame of Your Highness altogether complete, I intended first of all to teach Your Highness to read and write, and then to compose a few books for Your Highness, some to be read aloud to you at appointed times, and others for you to read by yourself in idle hours. Not to mention here Charlemagne, who learned to read and write after he became King and had married, I might say that if Milenko [Stojković] could learn at Odessa, and Vujića [Vulicević] at Constantinople, both of them older than Your Highness, indeed Your Highness could have learned much more easily and quickly than either. But these patriotic plans of mine, like many others, came to nothing, Your Highness best knows how, and this is no place to talk about that. Then in 1830 I did all that I could

---

[1] By 1842 young Serbs were being in fact sent to Vienna for advanced studies (see Chapter XVI, § 3).

to bring Mr. Isailović into Serbia to start the High School, and it nominally started up at the beginning of 1831 (ten years, that is, after my plans), but up to this day there is no kind of progress there. Those few children who went last year nominally to the first class, are going to the same class this year and learning the same subjects, and if the government continues to be as far behind in this matter as it has been up till now, things will be no different a year hence. Twelve years ago one such High School would have been enough for all your territory; by now four generations of students would have graduated from it, and if in each of these, taking one with another, there had been no more than twenty boys, still each district would have had some competent people, and it would not be necessary now to take in all sorts of rogues and cheats from this side [i.e. Austria] as clerks, teachers, and priests. Now however in the present condition of Serbia three such schools should be set up, one in Šumadija, another to the east beyond the Morava, and a third to the west beyond the Kolubara—and apart from these a proper 'Gymnasium', and then working upwards gradually, a Lyceum and a University.

But who is going to do all this? Isailović certainly is one of the best-educated Serbs in Hungary, and could profess various subjects in any Serbian University. But to establish and manage Serbian schools as they should be, I think that we need some Šafarik or Ranke. And, until a constitutional government is set up and confirmed in Serbia, it will not be easy to attract such people there, or to expect any real profit or progress from them, even if they could be found and brought over. Even Your Highness's children would I think best be educated in the Pages' Corps School at St. Petersburg, or anywhere else in Europe; for everywhere they would receive better education than they could in Serbia under present conditions.[1]

You need have no fear of educated people stirring up trouble against the government or delay setting up schools out of suspicion on that ground. In my opinion educated people (who must inevitably be good as well) are very happy to obey a sensible and just government, for they know that human society cannot exist without rule, and that everyone cannot be an Emperor or King, or Prince, or even an official or a rich man; and if a government is not just, even the most uneducated people will rise against it. One doesn't need to look far for examples of this. It wasn't education that made the Serbs revolt against the *Dahijas*, or you against Suleiman Pasha; and if among those who have risen against Your Highness there was one who could read, there would

[1] Vuk remarks in his note that Miloš's son, Milan (who reigned briefly from 1839, when Miloš was exiled, until his death in 1840), was already completely spoiled, and 'could not even spare a human glance' for the most senior officials. Vuk had urged Miloš in vain to send him to St. Petersburg.

be at least three who couldn't. Even the teacher Miloje, who is taken as proof that educated people are rebellious and that there is no need for schools, had about as much real knowledge in his head (and that is what we are talking about) as Amidja or Milisav Laporac [two of Miloš's officials]. And even if we were to suppose it true that educated people recognize injustice quicker than uneducated, and find it more intolerable, and that people cannot learn to recognize injustice of their own accord, without being shown, or to distinguish evil from good, even so Serbia is not all alone in the world and isolated from the rest of it. There are only the Sava and the Danube which separate it on one side from the Austrian Empire and Karavlaška—and from these countries people are constantly coming and going to and from Serbia; on the other side too there are the Greeks revolting with support from the French, and even the Turks continuously reforming themselves these last few years after the European model (and even before this, as subject to some kind of regular rule, whatever it was like, they have been much better ordered than Serbia).

Thus, if it is Your Highness's pleasure that people in Serbia should not revolt against you, I think that it won't help you much to be frightened of schools and education. It would be better first to give your people a proper code of laws and to order the country so that every sensible and honourable man, judging things according to common sense, could not wish for any improvement; and secondly to do everything possible to let people become prosperous—for at the beginning of the revolt against the *Dahijas*, we saw that the most ardent revolutionaries were those who had no possessions, while those who had even the smallest possessions, even though subject to the greatest oppression, strained every nerve to damp down the revolt; and this is everywhere in the nature of things—the man with nothing to lose can by and large hope to gain something from changes and revolutions, and the man who owns something is unwilling to put it to risk without the strongest compulsion.

4. Just as every man should be free to go about his private business as he likes, so it might be said that Your Highness is free to trade with his own money; but given that Your Highness's dealings may do harm to other people, and particularly to tradesmen, or even simply give cause for others to think and speak evil of you, I would say that Your Highness ought not to do any trade in anything either directly or in partnership with anyone.[1] It is well known to Your Highness that

---

[1] Vuk's note refers to Miloš's partnerships with cattle- and pig-dealers, and his monopoly of the salt-trade from Wallachia (cf. Chapter VIII, § 1 for Vuk's own former interest in this). 'The truth is that in Serbia it's a great honour to be Miloš's partner, but anyone who has once gone into partnership with him will seldom, without compulsion, press to be his partner again; for normally he

nothing told so much against Mladen Milovanović as his trading and partnerships, and much as was said at that time against Mladen, even more is said now against Your Highness; for once the masses start blaspheming, they'll not only say what is true, but add what is false. Thus for example on both sides of the river it is said that Your Highness, for the sake of yourself and your own gain, and to the obvious undoing of all other traders and the detriment of the nation itself, has published and renewed the edict that 'no one shall give credit to any tradesman, and that anyone who does shall have no right of recovery'; for, people say, it is only Your Highness's partners who can always buy for ready money, but other tradesmen have never traded without credit and cannot do so now.

5. People should never do anything of which they should be ashamed, for it is impossible to conceal anything in this world. A mass of things are happening in Serbia which people over there are afraid even to hear about, much more to tell or ask about, but here in Austria they are related openly in the streets and shops and coffee-houses. Even in Serbia however you should not think everything to be concealed which is not openly talked about, or everything to be to people's liking of which there is no open complaint. I have often seen with my own eyes and heard with my own ears how your young men laugh behind your back at things which they approve and praise in your presence. In countries where rather freer speech is allowed, the rulers can find out more easily what the people are thinking and saying; but where no one dares[1] to point to the truth or the real state of public opinion, it is hard to find out what is being thought and said, and moreover people load on to the ruler the blame not only for what he has done, but also for much else which he has not done—as for example in Austria, and perhaps in Serbia too, practically every time that a Serb official dies, it is said that he was murdered, poisoned, etc. Now in such conditions such stories may very well be accepted as true by posterity, and nowadays every European ruler thinks as much of the glory and name that will be his after his death, as of God and his immortal soul.

For other reasons too a sensible man, even at the summit of strength and power should not do anything which could reasonably be held

is a partner for profit alone and does not want to hear anything about losses. For example they say that last year he gave the pig-dealers maize from his tithes, so that he could share the profits of pig-feeding. But when he saw that the fat pigs were being sold cheap and at a loss, he said to his partners that they must pay him such and such a price for the maize, and sell the pigs on their own account, as best they could.'

[1] Vuk describes in his note how Miloš openly threatened all who wanted to be wiser than ('that is to think differently from') himself, and how if corrected by Miloš after giving a perfectly sound opinion, the courtiers said: 'So it is, my Lord, I did not know' or 'I didn't properly understand your question'.

against him at a time of great difficulty and misery for him. In this world even power which seems to have the broadest base may easily be overturned. We have but to think of Mladen (Milovanović), how in 1811 he moved things at his will, not only in Belgrade but also throughout Serbia, and in 1822 at Kragujevac anyone who wanted could make mock of him; or of Napoleon who in 1810 could give orders and set up kings throughout Europe, but in 1815 the people were pulling down memorials to him in Paris and he was a prisoner on St. Helena.

6. It is good to know what people think and say, but unnecessary to punish everyone who says something against you—particularly if they happen, unfortunately, to be right. Many a time people say something in jest or anger, or whatever the occasion may be, simply as words, and with no intention or possibility of doing any kind of harm. In such circumstances, I think that the government or ruler would do much better to try to put things right, if criticism has been just and they can do so, rather than to bully people and drag them to court and punish them. If whoever has been talking is in the wrong and has no intention or chance of doing harm, perhaps the best of all would be simply to rebuke him, so that he himself sees that he was wrong, or to leave him to say whatever he wants, provided that he does his job properly.

7. I cannot refrain here at the end of this letter from recalling to Your Highness one other important thing which in my opinion no true Serb or sensible man can approve, and that is that you have bought villages in Karavlaška. By this action you have clearly shown, to the very great disgrace of yourself and the Serb people, that you think it a better and safer thing to be a landlord in Karavlaška than a Prince in Serbia, and that you live in Serbia only from day to day, in order to accumulate all the money that you can (just as others around you pile up money to invest it); and then as soon as anything goes in the least wrong you will run to Karavlaška. It is bad enough if such an idea has occurred to you casually, and much worse if this is what you have been expecting. Then indeed your enemies could wish for no better revenge. You should know that only in Serbia can you be a ruler and live like a ruler, and as soon as you move from Serbia for good, to whatever country, you must be prepared to hear such reproaches as were publicly made to Mladen [Milovanović] at Kragujevac in 1822, and much worse too. Even if you carried off to Karavlaška as much wealth again as you now possess, still you would be a foreigner who doesn't know the language and a simple peasant among the proud nobles of Karavlaška with their European-style education; you would be nothing but the last of the nobles and Grica Opran[1] would be senior to you there and more influential.

---

[1] A Wallachian merchant and former partner of Miloš, who bought these villages for him.

Besides some new Ratković or Urošević[1] might turn up, who could not be reconciled by all your wealth; and, God knows, there might be found people in Serbia who would burn the houses in the villages that you are building over there, and could give you sleepless nights even in Bucharest.

What useful things could be done for the people in Serbia—and things that would be specially glorious for you—with those ten thousand ducats which you have invested in a foreign land to buy villages there! And if you had merely intended to put the money by for a rainy day, you could have given it to a bank in St. Petersburg, and just with the interest you could have paid all the teachers for a Serbian University, or sent at least twenty children to Europe to learn various sciences and skills, or you could have built and maintained one main hospital at Kragujevac and smaller ones at various other towns.

Here then are the ways in which I think that to Your Highness's own profit and glory you could satisfy all those who are now dissatisfied. Then Serbia would be like a European state of its own size; its sons who live in it would not wish to be the subjects of other powers, and any foreigner who came to it would wish to be subject to its laws. But if Your Highness sticks to the sort of rule which you have exercised hitherto and exercise today, there can be no greater joy for your enemies. Men of honesty and repute from other countries will keep clear of Serbia, and even among its own inhabitants those who have the slightest reputation and power will wish to clear out of it.

If however you are happy to go on ruling in the present way to the end of your days, or have to be forced by someone else to give a proper constitution to your people and country, then perhaps monuments will be put up in Serbia to Djak and Čarapic;[2] and all the others who for faults like theirs have died at your hands, will be counted as martyrs for the laws and freedom of the Serb people, even more than if they had died at Mišar or Deligrad[3] or anywhere else, fighting against their open enemies.

With all my heart I wish that Your Highness may not, to the great and lasting disgrace of yourself, your family, and all your friends and loyal subjects, abandon to another the glory which should be yours! This wish, combined with my genuine love, gratitude, and loyalty towards Your Highness, and my love for our native land, has driven

[1] Two merchants of Zemun, who claimed that the Serbian Government was in debt to them since Karadjordje's time.
[2] 'The student's revolt' (*Djakova Buna*) broke out in January 1825 and spread over most of Central Serbia. It was led by a former priest and clerk at the time of Karadjordje's revolt, Miloje Popović Djak ('the student'), and was directed against many of the abuses mentioned by Vuk in his letter.
[3] Deligrad; a notable battle of Karadjordje against the Turks in 1809.

me to write you this letter. Many and many a time, and particularly at Kragujevac in 1830, I intended and prepared to talk orally to Your Highness on these subjects, but various adverse circumstances never allowed me to do so. And now I have had all sorts of hesitations and mental conflicts about it, fearing that I might offend Your Highness and thus turn from myself the favour shown to me hitherto; but in the end I have scorned my own interest in favour of that of Your Highness and our country, and thought it better that I should tell you all this in writing than that you should have the lesson read to you later by other rebels like Djak.

I do not want to impose myself on Your Highness as a teacher; I simply tell you my opinion, which is the fruit not so much of any great learning or experience, as of long meditation about the profit and good and ill fortune of our people and country.

Your Highness's most humble servant,
Vuk Stefanović Karadžić

3

The consequences of Vuk's letter look at this interval of time like pure comedy. Miloš read it at Kragujevac on 15 August 1832. He was beside himself with rage. It was many years since anyone had dared to write to him in this tone. He had of course no intention of reforming his own ways of rule. Immediately he tore up the letter, forbade the secretary who had read it out to him to reveal its contents, and proceeded to spread about a suitable version of them. Vuk, he said, had written that his officials and even his own family were working against him, and that there was even a plot against his life (no doubt he divined Vuk's intention of making bad blood at his court). In Vuk's words, he then gave orders to his three senior officials, Aleksa Simić, Tsvetko Rajović, and Panta Hadji-Stoilo to go to the meeting-place at Zemun and there publicly 'on behalf of His Highness and (according to his orders) of themselves to (in good Serb) * * * *[1] my father and mother and kin and kindred unto the ninth generation'.

The Kragujevac trio reported to Miloš with relish on their own performance. Simić began: 'Vuk! What have we done to you that you have described us in such black colours to His Highness, us and all his first officials, not sparing even his illustrious family, and presenting us as traitors to His Highness and our country.

[1] Vuk's asterisks.

Why, you wretched, worthless, shameless and malicious creature?' Tsvetko then took up the running: 'Vuk! Who are you to put counsel on paper and send it flying to our Prince... with design to blacken him in his subjects' eyes and them in his, you wretched lame imp of hell? With your long teeth you love to bite all who come your way...!' Panta said his piece third, 'in a loud and angry voice'—'Vuk, we thought you were a Serb writer and moralist, but you are just a scoundrel who loves to spread all sorts of evil and poison many people', etc.

These edifying words were uttered as loud as possible in front of the largest possible audience at the meeting-place. Vuk, according to the official account sent to Miloš, tried in vain to defend himself and professed his sorrow at having sent the letter. He himself wrote to Kopitar that he had taken all the abuse quietly without any kind of angry or abusive expression on his own side. His doom was then pronounced. He was deprived for ever of the Prince's goodwill 'as a thankless and shameless creature, who had trod underfoot the bread and all those other great benefits offered to him; as for that other benefit which remained to him [his pension from Russia], the Prince would do his best to have it withdrawn from him as one who openly did ill to those who had shown him kindness'. Finally the messengers conveyed to Vuk an injunction not to write to anyone in Serbia, and cursed him formally together with his advisers.

Miloš professed himself delighted with the way in which his instructions had been carried out, and asked for a report on local opinion about Vuk (he received an obsequious reply on this subject). At the same time he sent to Panta a complaint against Vuk to be forwarded to the Austrian commander of Petrovaradin (the senior Austrian officer in the district), saying that Vuk was stirring up a revolt in Serbia by his demagogic agitation, and citing Vuk's letter in evidence. As he knew that the Austrian Emperor would not tolerate any subversion of any constitutional government, Miloš hoped that he would not allow the peace of Serbia to be disturbed further by Vuk's continued stay on the frontier, and begged for him to be removed. The commander of Petrovaradin, Radošević, received this letter on 1 September and immediately asked General Voigt, the Austrian commander at Zemun, to send him a German translation of Vuk's letter. This Vuk was of course very happy to provide, together with a covering note explaining the reasons which had induced him to leave Belgrade, and the high patriotic motives which had inspired him to write to Miloš. His letter, he said, was not designed as propaganda, but was of a purely private character, and in sending it he had recommended that it be read out only by the most confidential of Miloš's secretaries.

In the meantime further publicity had been given to the whole business by the interview between Vuk and Miloš's emissaries at the Zemun meeting-place. Vuk sent copies of the letter to Kopitar and simultaneously to his contact at the Russian Embassy at Vienna, the Orthodox priest Meglitski. In both cases he advertised in covering notes (no doubt for the eyes of any intercepting policeman) that the letter had been written out of purely patriotic (and not seditious) motives.

Radošević received his copy of the letter at Petrovaradin and was properly shocked by its tone. He wrote to Voigt at Zemun that it contained insulting attacks on Miloš and his government, and that he was recommending to the War Council in Vienna the removal of Vuk from the frontier district. Vuk was to be warned against any kind of agitation, on pain of imprisonment. At the same time he wrote a conciliatory reply to Miloš telling him of the action in hand.

There the matter rested for over six weeks. Vuk had in the meantime managed to send his family to Vienna, but was increasingly anxious about his own status on Austrian territory, and by mid-October was arguing pathetically and without any undertone of irony that if he was really considered such a dangerous character, Vienna was surely the best place in which to supervise him. Radošević's request for a ruling went the round of high offices in Vienna, with the translation of Vuk's letter to Miloš attached. On 3 October, Sedlnicki, the chief of police, submitted it to Metternich with the recommendation that for the present Vuk should be ordered to stay at Buda (where he wanted to go in any case for the waters). Metternich agreed, adding that he should subsequently be summoned to return to Vienna (which was of course Vuk's greatest wish). The President of the War Council ultimately informed Radošević by a decision dated 9 October that Vuk might be allowed to stay in Austria, but, because of the complaints of Miloš Obrenović, only subject to the strictest supervision. By 24 October, Vuk had been informed that he might leave Zemun for Buda, and at Buda early in November he was told that he might return to Vienna.

Miloš's reaction to the famous letter thus had results entirely favourable to Vuk, although all parties concerned regarded it as a dangerous document. As a result of Miloš's complaints to the Austrian authorities, Vuk was not only able but forced to leave Zemun, and allowed to rejoin his family in Vienna. Owing to the faultless functioning of the Austrian bureaucratic machine, a large number of important Austrian officials had read in full Vuk's charges against Miloš. They may not have been convinced by them, or in all cases particularly concerned; but at least they could hardly doubt Vuk's sincerity. From now on it would be extremely hard for them to regard him as a dangerous agent for Miloš Obrenović. Thus with no reference to his own immediate intentions and against those of his enemies, Vuk had won a considerable victory. His hopes of securing a base for new operations in Serbia had been blasted entirely; but at least he was able, against all the odds, to retreat safely to his old base in Vienna.

XVI

VUK AND THE RULERS OF SERBIA
1832–1845

I

VUK's situation on his return to Vienna in November 1832 was cheerless enough in itself, even though it compared favourably with the prospects facing him a few months earlier. He was cautious enough not to advertise widely the full story of his letter to Miloš and departure from Zemun. Wisely, he wanted to leave the way open for a reconciliation with the ruler of Serbia, and he was sufficiently experienced in Miloš's ways to know that their relations could change very quickly for the better as well as for the worse.

Vuk's friends were glad that he had returned from politics or administration to literature, but he did not always make it easy for them to help him to find the means of making a living. Kopitar at this time was hoping to revive the *Serbian News* which had ceased publication in 1822. He had previously tried to persuade Vuk to take on the editorship.[1] Now in 1832 he tried flattery, in the hope of tying Vuk down in Vienna: 'Erasmus got along well, indeed very well, with Emperors, Kings and Popes who tripped over themselves to give him honours and recognition, but he always just thanked them politely, and stayed until his death with his printer, Frobenius, living freely and in peace at his studies. You should do the same.' But Vuk was still unwilling, in spite of his need. Kopitar declared that he no longer had any faith in the possibility of Vuk settling to a methodical and long-term job; he was probably right and Vuk was no doubt right too in feeling that such work was not for him.

In the meantime Vuk planned the production of further 'national' literature—the fourth volume of his 'popular songs', including the heroic songs of modern times, was published at Leipzig in 1834.

---

[1] The *Serbian News* had been started in Vienna in 1813 (just before Vuk's arrival there) under the editorship of Davidović. Kopitar had tried to revive it with Vuk as editor in 1826.

He engaged on the editing and publication of Luka Milovanov's *Examination of Serb Poetry*—a work of piety to the memory of an old friend, who had recently died in Buda. Another of his calendars, with supplementary material, was published in 1834 and included some further history of the 1804 rising and some 'popular tales'. He corresponded further with Ranke, sending him material about the contemporary Bosnian rebellion against the Turks.[1] And inevitably he embarked on his habitual series of requests for financial help.

As in 1823, his most active and best friend proved to be Dimitrije Frušić at Trieste, who not only sent him a little ready money, but also stimulated the passing of a resolution by the Serbian communal council of Trieste to give Vuk a hundred florins yearly.[2] This decision was communicated to Vuk at the end of May 1833, together with rather over one hundred florins by way of subscriptions for the fourth book of 'popular songs'. The first yearly payment from the Trieste council was made at the beginning of 1834, but it is not clear whether it was regularly renewed thereafter.

This was a start towards financial rehabilitation, but the Trieste gift added to Vuk's Russian pension was far from compensating him for the loss of the salary which he had received, however irregularly, in Miloš's service (840 florins a year). He was not tempted by indirect offers which reached him as early as January 1833 to return to Serbia and receive a handsome pension on condition that he wrote no more. At this period, Vuk's work was planned mainly with an eye on securing Russian patronage and pay on an increased scale. His movements were also determined by a chance encounter at Vienna in June 1833. It was at this time that Petar Petrović Njegoš,[3] afterwards to become the most famous poet in

---

[1] In 1831 and 1833 there were rebellions led by the Bosnian nobles (Moslems themselves); these were caused by Turkish attempts at administrative reform.

[2] This decision concluded a detailed correspondence in which Vuk tried to get through Frušić a guarantee that the Serb community at Trieste would subscribe for 300 copies of each of his works as it appeared, and Frušić tried to get Vuk to collaborate in founding a Serbian language press at Trieste.

[3] Petar II Petrović Njegoš (1813–51) succeeded his uncle, Petar I, as Prince Bishop of Montenegro in 1830. His most famous poetic work, *Gorski Vjenac* ('The Mountain Wreath'), was published in 1847. From 1827 to 1830 he was tutored by Sima Milutinović. He warmly admired the works of Lukian Mušicki, but had little in common with him as a poet. Under Vuk's influence he collected popular poetry in Montenegro, and wrote some poems himself in popular style, published with others in *Srpsko Ogledalo* ('The Serbian Mirror') in 1845. On Njegoš as a reforming ruler, see Appendix F; and in general Milovan Djilas, *Njegoš, Poet, Prince, Bishop*, Harcourt, Brace & World, New York, 1966.

the Serbian language, stayed briefly in Vienna on his way from Cetinje to St. Petersburg, where he was to be consecrated as Bishop of Montenegro. Vuk wrote to Mušicki about their first meeting: 'Petar Petrović is not yet twenty years old, but bigger and more handsome than any grenadier in Vienna! Not only does he know Serbian very well to read and write, but he also composes fine verses. . . . He thinks that there is no finer language in the world than our popular tongue (and he's right to think so, even if it were not true). Uncle Steve [Stratimirović] complained to him of you and me, and he defended us both. . . .'

It seems that from the first encounter Vuk and Njegoš were attracted to each other. Njegoš was shown Vuk's translation of the New Testament, gave it his formal approval,[1] and defended it in conversation with the Metropolitan Stratimirović, who was also in Vienna at the time and naturally had a meeting with the future Prince Bishop of Montenegro. Vuk in turn introduced Njegoš to the Mehitarist monks, in the hope that they would print his early poems *The Voice of the Mountaineer*. This project fell through according to precedent, when the Austrian censorship pronounced the poems likely to inflame Slav opinion against the Turks. The bad news reached Njegoš in 1834 after he had returned to Cetinje. It confirmed him more strongly in the determination which he had already formed to set up a new printing press in Montenegro, where the first Serb books in Cyrillic lettering had been printed in the sixteenth century. Njegoš had brought a press and Slavonic letters with him from Russia, and he now wrote to Vuk, asking him to provide matrices for his own new Serbian letters (*j*, *lj* and *nj*).

Vuk travelled first to Buda for this purpose and then in June 1834 set out himself for Cetinje, via Trieste, Dubrovnik (where he was the guest of the Russian consul and carefully watched by

[1] Njegoš provided Vuk with a certificate to the effect that the translation was pure and correct, and that his wish was to see it published for the spiritual salvation of the Serb people (dated 9 October 1833; see N. Banašević, 'Njegošev odnos prema Vuku . . .', in *Prilozi*, xx, nos. 1–2).

On 14 January 1834, Kopitar wrote to Grimm that Njegoš had given final approval for printing Vuk's translation, and asked Grimm to get Ranke to speed up the mediation which he had undertaken between Vuk and the London Bible Society: 'Wuk hat nun vom Erzbischof von Montenegro, der soeben von Petersburg aus ordiniert worden, also orthodox in hohem Grade ist, ohne suspicione et exceptione major, seine Übersetzung des N. Test. nicht nur gebilligt, sondern mit optamus imprimi ad fidei et literaturae incrementum, erledigt erhalten.' But it became evident before long that nothing would come of the negotiations with the London Bible Society.

Austrian police agents), and Kotor. He reached Cetinje in mid-September. As usual, there were a number of motives behind his journey. On the way and in Montenegro itself he could collect more popular songs, words, and expressions, and make notes of the antiquities—all of which might be useful in securing more money from Russia. He was also directly interested himself in the establishment of a printing press at Cetinje, under the control of the friendly Njegoš. It could print not only the ruler's poems but also works by Vuk himself; a new one (a collection of proverbs) was now ready for the press, and he thought at the time, erroneously, that his translation of the New Testament might also be published in Montenegro.

In fact, Vuk's health did not permit him to stay more than two months in Cetinje in the autumn of 1834, and two weeks in the summer of 1835; but the balance between achievement and hope was on this occasion not too unfavourable for him. On his journey, in Montenegro, and in Dubrovnik where he passed most of the winter 1834–5, he was able to collect a large number of new songs, expressions, and words (more will be said in the next chapter about the linguistic results of his journey). He arranged for the printing at Cetinje of his *Proverbs*, which appeared in 1836. The collection of this work had caused him a lot of trouble, since, as he remarked, people cannot recite proverbs to you; you have continuously to listen to their conversation and wait for the proverbs to turn up. The publication too had been long delayed, and it was thus a relief to Vuk to get it off his shoulders.[1] Much the most important result of Vuk's visit to Cetinje, however, was that he was able to collect on the spot ample material for his descriptive book *Montenegro and the Gulf of Kotor*, of which a brief description is given at Appendix F.

2

In Montenegro Vuk had found a rich store of material, and a hero in the person of the ruler, whose efforts to reform and civilize the Montenegrin clan system he deeply admired. But it had also

[1] Vuk had corresponded as far back as 1824 with a certain Samuilo Ilić, who had also been collecting proverbs, about a joint production and promised to let Ilić include his own material in his book. But there was some delay, and when Ilić raised the matter again in 1832, he had become a monk. As a result of a letter to Ilić from Vuk, suggesting that some of his proverbs might be too earthy, Stratimirović raised further complaints with the Vienna police about Kopitar's fitness to exercise the function of censor.

become clear that in Montenegrin conditions he could not work, even if Njegoš was ready to become his principal patron. At the end of summer 1835, after a leisurely progress along the Dalmatian coast, Vuk returned to Vienna, to work on the poetic, linguistic, and ethnographic material which he had collected on his long journey. This was a pattern often to recur in the next years—journeying in the summer, to be followed in the autumn and winter by digestion of the mental sustenance absorbed. His finances were by now in a rather better state than usual. By the time of his return to Vienna he had received a further 100 florins from Frušić at Trieste, with the promise of more. The Russian Academy too, at the instance of Shishkov, to whom Vuk had appealed directly, sent him 100 ducats as reward for his labours in Montenegro and on the Dalmatian coast. But the best and most surprising news for Vuk, rumoured for some time and received in fairly reliable form after his return, was the grant of a pension by Miloš Obrenović. It took Vuk some time to get final confirmation, but in a letter of February 1836, Miloš assured him that 'as a reward for his labours on Serb literature' he would in future receive two annual payments each of 100 talers. 'It is my wish', Miloš continued, 'that you should in the future also try always and unremittingly to contribute to our literature, that it may be richer and more glorious.' Vuk was not backward in his thanks:

No letter in all my life has given me greater joy than this. Even now I am as it were drunk with joy. Welcome and precious as is the favour of Your Highness as a help to livelihood in my feeble old age [Vuk was not yet 50 at the time], it is even more welcome and precious as a sign of Your Highness's favour and kind inclination towards me.... To the utmost of my powers I shall strive day and night to show myself before the world worthy of this your favour. Up to now too I have worked as I best could for our literature, chiefly out of my love and tenderness for it and for the glory of our people; but now, knowing that I have such an open benefactor and protector, for all the weakness of my health I feel that my patriotic zeal will gain new strength.

To explain this sudden and total change of front by Miloš (and then by Vuk) it is necessary to go back a little way into the internal history of Serbia. In 1830 Miloš had secured from the Turks the decree (*Hati-Sherif*) making him hereditary Prince of Serbia, and granting Serbia all the principal elements of internal autonomy. This decree had been supplemented by another of 1833 (the additional *Hati-Sherif*), enlarging the bounds of Serbia, and settling finally the conditions under which Turks could remain in the country, the Serb right to exercise customs rights in Belgrade, and the amount of the annual Serb tribute to Turkey—all very important questions. Miloš had now won what was virtually a final victory in his political war against the Turks. This was satisfactory in itself, but meant that he could no longer justify his despotic methods of government by the need to present a united front to the common enemy, and to leave himself a completely free hand and ample resources for dealing with the Turks. As a result, a strong movement grew up, not so much among the peasants as among the more important leaders of Serbia, to curb Miloš's personal powers and to introduce some kind of Council which could exercise control over the Prince's government. Such a Council had existed in the last years of Karadjordje's regime, and had been introduced in 1824 by Miloš himself for a very short period, to be transformed in 1827 into a People's Court with judicial functions only. The Turkish Decrees of 1830 and 1833 provided that in governing Serbia Miloš should be assisted by an Assembly of the chief men of the land—in subsequent clauses this was equated with a Council, whose members could not be removed and replaced without very serious reason. Until 1834 neither the Turks nor Miloš bothered about the execution of these provisions, and Miloš governed entirely through his Court Chancellery; but by 1834 the growth of opposition in Serbia led Miloš to take some action, if only for show. He summoned the National Assembly and with its approval set up new Ministries, for foreign affairs, war, finance, justice, and education.

This was by no means enough for his principal opponents, substantial men who were largely concerned with breaking Miloš's monopoly rights and having their share in the booty and economic opportunities resulting from Turkish withdrawal. In January 1835 occurred what was known as 'Mileta's revolt'. Taking advantage of the Prince's absence, Mileta Radojković, one of Miloš's district governors, backed by a number of others and a force of 5,000 men, settled in the capital, Kragujevac, and demanded the setting up of a responsible State Council to form the executive side of Government in conjunction with the Prince. Miloš was taken by surprise and frightened for his life. He gave in immediately and agreed in February 1835 to what became known as the 'Constitution of the

Visitation' (from the Church feast on which it was voted). It had a very short life. The Russian, Austrian, and Turkish Governments all agreed that it was too liberal in tendency, and that certain clauses (e.g. that providing for a national flag) were inconsistent with Serbia's status as a dependency of Turkey.

Miloš was happy enough to see the constitution withdrawn, but he had undergone a severe shock, and it seems that his thoughts turned to the dire prophesies of Vuk in his letter of 1832. Miloš recognized their justice, and perhaps thought this a good moment to conciliate Vuk and do something to prevent that powerful pen from being employed against him. Thus it was that the reconciliation between Vuk and Miloš took place, and on terms favourable to Vuk. Admiral Shishkov, not without some prompting, wrote a letter of thanks to Miloš for his generosity to Vuk; this served as a timely reminder that Vuk had important patrons in Russia who would soon be informed if his pension was not paid.

From 1834 until 1845 Vuk's literary work and financial stability depended to a great extent on the vicissitudes of Serbian politics, which were often in their turn a matter of much concern to the Great Powers. The rest of this chapter will be devoted to the story of Vuk's relations with the rulers and leading politicians of Serbia during this period and of the literary work resulting from them (plenty of Vuk's output fell outside this category).

The receipt of a pension from Miloš from 1836 onwards committed Vuk, as the Prince no doubt foresaw, to his side in the international politics of Serbia. This was the more unfortunate for Vuk in that Miloš had by no means succeeded in reconciling the so-called 'Constitutionalist' opposition, and Vuk found himself being drawn into the anti-constitutional ranks. Miloš had agreed after the suppression of the 'Constitution of the Visitation' to set up a Commission to work out a constitution which would not offend the Great Powers. But he had employed typical delaying tactics, and from 1836 feeling was growing strongly against him. His own brother Jevrem was an important addition to the opposition ranks, which were greatly strengthened also by a change in Russian policy. This was motivated mainly by fear that if Miloš made no concessions he would be replaced by some ruler effectively in the hands of the 'Constitutionalists' and committed to a genuinely liberal policy. The Russians seem to have thought that the best safeguard against such a radical change would be the establishment of a sort of oligarchy under Miloš, on the pattern of the 'General Regulation' promulgated by the Russian General Kiselev for Wallachia in 1831. The Austrians agreed with these ideas, and the Turks did not object. In the meantime however the British Government had decided to work against Russian influence in south-eastern Europe, and to do so in this case by strengthening the hand of Miloš Obrenović. A British consul, D. J. Hodges, was appointed to the Court of Miloš in Belgrade in spring 1837. He was instructed to oppose Russian constitutional ideas but his support of Miloš only served to increase Russian insistence. In October 1837, Prince Dolgoruki came to Belgrade, bringing a special order from Tsar Nicholas I that Miloš should put into effect immediately the clauses of the Turkish Decree of 1830 providing for a Council.

The pressure from in and outside Serbia was growing too strong, and in 1838 Miloš decreed the establishment of a special Commission to elaborate drafts of a constitution and of civil and criminal codes. One member of this Commission was the distinguished Novi Sad lawyer and less distinguished littérateur, Jovan Hadzić-Svetić,[1] and his appointment led Vuk into a lot of trouble. Hadzić had in 1826 been one of the founders of the Matica Srpska Society for the propagation of literature and culture and for the publication of books. The society played an important and useful part in the development of Serb literature, but Vuk quarrelled almost immediately with the Matičari ('Matica men') and their journal, *Letopis*, on the question of orthography. The other side, and Hadzić not least, reciprocated his hostility.[2] For some time they remained in personal relations, but Vuk regarded Hadzić as at best a conceited amateur in matters of literature; and Hadzić on his side never forgave Vuk for printing in the *Day-star* of 1834 a

[1] Jovan Hadzić-Svetić (1799–1869) had been editor of the Matica Srpska's *Letopis* ('Calendar') in 1830–1. In the literary field he was most famous at the time as a poet and translator of Latin and German classics. Vuk's first contact with him in 1822 had been friendly. In 1836 Miloš asked the Austrian Government to allow Hadzić to come to Belgrade in order to help in drafting new civil and criminal codes for Serbia, based on Austrian models rather than on the Code Napoléon, which Vuk had tried to adapt for Serbian use.

[2] The Matica Srpska, following the lead of Djordje Magarašević, tried to remain neutral on the question of orthography. This was bad enough in the eyes of Vuk, who thought that those who were not for him were against him. Vuk's quarrel with Magarašević was precipitated by a favourable review in *Letopis* of one of Hadzić's translations, which seemed to Vuk implicitly to detract from the merits of his own work.

letter minimizing his part in the establishment of the Matica and decrying his literary abilities.

In February 1838, as soon as he had joined the new Constitutional Commission, Hadzić openly sided with the 'constitutionalist' opposition to Miloš. The Prince sought for means of discrediting him, and did not need to look further than Vuk, who was ready enough to attack Hadzić as well as to earn an increase in his pension from Miloš. A fairly suitable reason was also ready to hand for such an attack. In 1837 Hadzić had published at Novi Sad a small brochure called *Linguistic Details*, with very miscellaneous contents. The first half contained advice to Serb grammarians, the second a disquisition on the etymology of the words *Knez* (the Serbian for 'Prince'), *Knjaz* (the corresponding word in Russian), and *Zakon* (the Serbian for 'law'): Hadzić was clearly adapting his linguistic studies to his new position as drafter of laws for the Principality of Serbia. Vuk's *Reply to the Details* was published in February 1839. This was the first round of a prolonged and furious literary duel, with political implications which proved very awkward for Vuk.

He had much the better of the linguistic argument, the details of which are of little interest to present-day readers; he enjoyed himself a good deal at Hadzić's expense, pointing the ludicrous contrast between the author's own usage and his pretensions to lay down the law for all grammarians of his own and previous times—'not to mention those visits paid to him, he tells us, by the Muses'. There was however one weak point in Vuk's *Reply*, and that was the date of its appearance. Hadzić was quick to ask why this skilled controversialist had taken nearly two years to comment on his own slight pamphlet; and he was quick to answer his own question correctly. Vuk had waited for orders before writing.

This was the most telling argument in Hadzić's *Reply to the Reply* or *Crushing Blow* (*Utuk*). It also contained in undeveloped form many of the charges of plagiarism made more fully against Vuk later in his life.[1] Miloš typically hedged his bets in the controversy which he had inspired. He expressed his sympathy to Hadzić about Vuk's attack, and offered to have any counter-attack

---

[1] For example, that his grammar of 1814 had been the work of Luka Milovanov; that the introduction to his first *Song-book* had been written by Sima Milutinović; that the new letters in his orthography were not his own invention, etc.

by Hadzić printed at the Serbian national press in Belgrade; but he also rubbed salt in Hadzić's wounds in his own letter of condolence by giving a résumé of Vuk's charges.

3

Vuk was soon threatened with graver troubles. He travelled to Belgrade in May 1839 to put forward personally a request for an increase in his pension. This was passed on by Miloš to his new Council, who decided that 'not only should Vuk's pension not be increased, but that in future it should not be paid at all'. The decision was no doubt intended as a punishment against Vuk for attacking the 'constitutionalist' Hadzić. It was in fact reversed at the next meeting of the Council, but the second decision was not signed 'since at this session all those members were not present who had attended when it was concluded not to give any pension to Vuk'. And immediately after this, Vuk lost his royal patron in Serbia.

Hard pressed by his 'constitutionalist' opponents, Miloš had in 1838 invited the Turkish Government to send a deputation to Belgrade, in order to discuss all open political questions with himself and the 'constitutionalists'. He hoped thus to by-pass the Russian and Austrian representatives in Belgrade and perhaps to get some support from the British Government, who might bring influence to bear on the Porte. The Turks appeared to agree to this sort of procedure, and put forward a counter-suggestion that Miloš should send a deputation to Constantinople. This he did, though well aware that the Serb delegation might let him down.[1] The work in Constantinople lasted for several months, and was finally embodied in a decree published in Belgrade in February 1839. The contents were worse than Miloš's worst fears. Legislative power was in effect to be shared between him and a Council headed by his brother, and at this time bitter enemy, Jevrem. Executive power remained to some extent with the Prince, but he was bound to exercise it in conjunction with the Council and not exclusively through a Governmental civil service. At the end of April 1839, Miloš tried to organize a revolt against the new Council, but it was promptly and severely repressed. He had little choice but to abdicate in favour of his son, Milan, who was

[1] Miloš told the members of the delegation to study carefully Matthew 6: 24: 'No man can serve two masters.' He, if anyone, ought to have known better.

already mortally ill; and on 3 June he left Serbia for those properties in Rumania the purchase of which Vuk had criticized so bitterly in his letter of 1832.

This was a moment of great difficulty and some danger for Vuk. He was not left long in uncertainty about his fate, for on 23 June the Council finally gave its decision, confirmed by the Regency ten days later, to continue paying him the pension which he had received hitherto, but not to increase it. To attain this limited success, Vuk had had to rely very much, in dealing with the victorious 'constitutionalists', on his letter of 1832 to Miloš; he arranged for copies to be given to the office of the Regency and to the Council, and tried to inspire publicity in Vienna in order to ingratiate himself with the new rulers of Serbia. Vuk's courting of the new regime was far from dignified, and laid him open to charges afterwards made against him, by Hadžić in particular, of time-serving and opportunism. He could and did argue that he had done the best possible service to Miloš by his letter of 1832, that in 1835 Miloš had seen the justice of his arguments, and that he abandoned the Prince's cause only in 1839 when Miloš seemed to have reverted to his former ways. But not surprisingly some of the mud thrown at Vuk stuck.

By November 1839 he was back in Vienna, and looking for further literary employment. Ranke, with whom he remained in correspondence, was thinking at this time of issuing a new and revised edition of his *Serbian Revolution*, and Vuk was anxious to travel to Berlin, where he could help in the preparation of the book; but he could not find money for the journey. By the spring of 1840, however, it seemed that political conditions in Serbia were becoming stabilized under the Regency Council, and that there was again a chance of fruitful work there, both literary and political. In 1838, Miloš had held out prospects to Vuk of making him a member of the Council, and now Vuk raised again the subjects both of employment on the Council and of an increase of his pension in various letters addressed to Jevrem Obrenović and Prince Mihail (who had succeeded to the throne late in 1839) among others. He evidently had had some encouragement from within Serbia for doing so. Writing to Jovan Gavrilović, a member of the Regency Council, Vuk said:

As for what you write, that there is talk in Belgrade (and that too in high quarters) that it would be worth my while to come and play a real part

VUK AND THE RULERS OF SERBIA, 1832-1845

in working for the progress of the country, I am inexpressibly pleased. For the common good of our people I'd go as far as America. More than once I've come to Serbia with my head and my pack full of patriotic plans, simply to be able to do something of use to our people; but when I'd seen that it couldn't be done, then with sorrow I've turned back to this side [to Vienna], in order to serve our people from here as best I could. And now too I'm not living in Vienna just because life is more agreeable to me here than there, but simply in order to be of more use to Serbia and the Serbian people. . . .

In fact, Vuk was more interested in securing an increased pension and going on with his literary work than in any further administrative job. He put his point more frankly in a letter of about the same time (February 1840) to Dr. Jovan Stejić, formerly physician to Miloš, who had now returned to Serbia after nearly eight years of absence: 'As regards a post, I would accept one if elected to the Council, but I'm not going to beg anyone for this; for, partly because of the state of my health, partly for love of peace and quiet, and partly too because of my literary work (which is dearer to me than all the honours and riches of this world) I'd rather have 600 talers of pension [Vuk was then receiving 200 from the Serbian Government] than be made a Councillor with a salary of 2,000. And so I say, that if I accepted any post, I'd accept it *only for the public good*. . . .'

Vuk's correspondence on this subject came to nothing. His conditions were too stiff, and he refused to consider any humbler post. It was in the meantime Miloš Obrenović, from the estates which he cultivated so shrewdly in Wallachia, who provided Vuk with literary and financial encouragement. Miloš had by no means abandoned political ambitions; he watched for a favourable chance of returning to the Serbian throne at his son's expense, and cultivated Vuk as a possible and eminent supporter. In June 1840 Miloš sent 300 florins to help in the publication at Vienna of the first book of the enlarged and revised collection of 'popular songs' which Vuk planned to issue as the result of his most recent journeys. The accompanying letter was full of noble sentiment: 'Never falter in your zeal, dear Mr. Karadžić! Your fatherland will take pride in this work of yours, as the work of its son; while other peoples, turning their attention to our people's qualities, will wish, to our great benefit, to become better acquainted with them.'

In the meantime, the Serbian regime had found some new work

for him to do, supervising the studies of a number of young officials who had been sent to Vienna at the end of 1839 to learn French and German. Vuk's duties, which he took seriously, were evidently rather delicate, since the students, in the words of his report to the Ministry in Belgrade 'do not regard it as a favour that the Government sent them here, but think and say that they are sacrificing themselves for the people, and that the Government deceived them by removing them from their posts and promising more than it performs for them; apart from this, they think that they are no longer students or children, to be given orders on how to behave themselves, but are ex-officials and grown men, who know this without telling . . .'.[1]

This curious interlude in Vuk's career shows that he had by the end of 1841 achieved reasonably good relations with the new Obrenović Government. He felt that he stood well enough with the Serbian regime to renew his requests for an increase in his pension, and in May 1842 Prince Mihail confirmed the Council's decision to raise the pension from 200 to 400 talers a year. But Prince Mihail was very far from secure on the throne of Serbia, even if he had been formally invested at Constantinople with his princely dignity. His supporters of the 'constitutionalist' party were divided, and its powerful leader, Vučić, had come to the conclusion that he could not realize his aims while the Obrenović family reigned. He turned against Mihail, and exploited the unpopularity of the young Prince's administrative reforms, which involved increased taxation. The Turkish Government too began to intrigue through the Pasha of Belgrade in Serbian internal affairs. Above all, Miloš himself with all the resources of his experience, of money derived from his Wallachian estates and of a network of agents in Serbia, began to scheme very actively against his own son. From 1840 he was supported by his influential wife, Ljubica, who had remained in Serbia and had come to the conclusion that Miloš's political skill was necessary to cope with the difficulties of government there. It was Miloš who did most to prepare the ground for his own son's abdication, while Princess Ljubica encouraged two unsuccessful revolts in Serbia itself. But it was not

[1] The reaction of the Ministry of Education in Belgrade to the expression of the students' view was that they must sign a declaration in the presence of the Vienna police, to the effect that they had come to Austria of their own free will. They were outraged by this demand, but Vuk managed to settle things tactfully.

Miloš who profited from the weakening of his son's regime. In August 1842, the king-making leader of the 'constitutionalist' party, Vučić, organized a successful coup against Prince Mihail. The latter crossed the Sava into exile at Zemun, and the Serbian Assembly proclaimed Karadjordje's son, Alexander Karadjordjević, as Prince, the Turkish Government publishing its confirmatory decree in October. In the summer of 1841 the Turks, who had a good idea of the subversive part which Miloš was playing against them throughout Eastern Europe, succeeded in having him banished from Wallachia to Vienna, from which he could not make his influence felt so strongly in Serbia.

4

This political peripeteia was a matter of great personal concern to Vuk. Whatever he may have said about Miloš Obrenović in 1832, the new regime regarded him as irrevocably devoted to the Obrenović family, and lost little time in depriving him of the pension which he had fought so hard to have increased. As a result, Vuk now began openly to act as a political agent for Miloš. During the reign of Mihail, he had kept his hands clean and Mihail's own agents in Vienna regarded him as harmless and an admirer of the reigning Prince, even if he kept up his contacts with Miloš for the sake of his own livelihood. His own views were probably best expressed in a letter of 1840: 'You ask what I think about Serbia, and on what side I am. It's difficult to answer *in writing*. You know that I recognised as clearly as anyone the mistakes of Miloš's rule; but given that after him things immediately *became worse in Serbia and remain so till now*, I'd say it would be best if he came back to Serbia again and lived and died there with his son. From this you can see that I'm on the side of the young Prince [Mihail] and *of the people*.' In the autumn of 1842 Vuk evidently calculated that in the light of his past record it would be at best a long-term process to reconcile himself with the new Karadjordje regime, while Miloš was so to speak a patron in the hand. Miloš himself was not convinced that the new regime had come to stay; the Russian Government had immediately protested about the Assembly's election of Alexander Karadjordjević and about Turkish confirmation of the election, and Miloš thought that he or Mihail or both might still fish with success in the troubled waters. Vuk went as his messenger in October 1842 to Mihail at Zemun, with a letter instructing him how to behave towards the Pasha, the foreign consuls, and the political leaders in Serbia. A lively correspondence developed, Vuk informing Miloš currently of conditions in Serbia, and receiving in turn new directives for Mihail. It proved however that the Russians were not hostile to Alexander Karadjordjević personally. All they wanted was to protest for the record against the principle of popular election. At their insistence a new election was held for the office of Prince of Serbia in spring 1843. Vuk reported on developments from Zemun and professed optimism, but the result of the new election was in fact a foregone conclusion.[1] The Obrenović dynasty had to wait its turn for some years.

With the return of the Karadjordjević dynasty, Hadzić resumed his attack on Vuk in spring 1843, and attempted completely to discredit him as a historian and as a political opportunist. The instrument he used for this purpose was a newspaper founded by the Karadjordje Government in March 1843, known as the *Serb Courier*, and designed particularly to increase the prestige of the new regime abroad. In a whole series of articles, Hadzić dissected Vuk's career and tried to prove that from the first he was nothing but a paid tool of the Obrenović family. It was due to Vuk's propaganda that the fame of Karadjordje was hardly known abroad; Vuk had consistently under-estimated the part played by Karadjordje in the uprising of 1804, had even blackened his reputation, and had induced Ranke to commit the same faults. Until 1830, Vuk was led on by promises of receiving an estate in his native Tršić. When, instead of this, he had to content himself with the presidency of the Belgrade Magistrates' Court, he turned against Miloš and wrote the famous letter of 1832 (which Hadzić published in the *Serb Courier* for the first time). Vuk, Hadzić said, was induced not to publish this only by substantial bribes, and when Miloš was exiled in 1839 did not hesitate to advertise it.

[1] A minor and curious embarrassment for Vuk lay at this time in the political speculations of Kopitar, who was suggesting to mutual friends that Vuk himself should be the new 'Grand Vizier' or even Prince of Serbia. Kopitar wrote to Ranke a few months later (in 1844) asking him to recommend Vuk for the post of Prince in the introduction to his new edition of *The Serbian Revolution*. Vuk himself wrote to Ranke in July 1844: 'I most sincerely hope that you will do nothing of the sort. People would laugh at us both, and it would be particularly harmful to me . . .' (no doubt Vuk was thinking of the suspicions which would be raised in the minds both of Aleksander Karadjordje and of Miloš).

Recently he had again engaged in political intrigues for the Obrenović interest, which was consistently contrary to that of the Serb people. Apart from his ignoble political conduct, he had pursued only private ends in his literary work. In particular Vuk had not been the first to collect 'popular songs'; he relied on the work of many others in this field, and was careful to appropriate all the credit himself.[1] These and other incidental accusations were renewed or initiated by Hadzić and many of them are of considerable interest. They must have made disagreeable reading for Vuk, but were developed with too much obvious personal animus to persuade many of those who were not already against him. Much the most substantial of Hadzić's accusations related to the inconsistency between Vuk's life of Miloš Obrenović, published in 1828, and the picture of his rule given in the letter of 1832. If Hadzić had confined himself to this point, he would probably have made a more fully convincing case.

Vuk's reply was issued almost a year later in April 1844. It was published as a special pamphlet, of which Vuk sent a number of copies to the Serbian Minister of Finance, Pavel Stanišić, for distribution to influential men in Serbia, with a covering letter emphasizing the loyalty with which he had in his time served the Karadjordje regime.[2]

Vuk's reply was written in a much more sober tone than that of Hadzić's attacks, and he scored some good points of detail. As a client of Miloš, who still hoped to get a pension from Alexander Karadjordjević, he had to tread carefully and avoid the total political commitment of Hadzić. This was to some extent an advantage. His conclusion on Serbia's alternate ruling houses was excellently judicious: 'I don't say, and I have never said, that Prince Miloš was more deserving than Karadjordje; but I still think any sensible person must admit that, apart from Karadjordje, no Serb did more for the freedom of our people than Miloš Obrenović. . . . Those who think that one can't praise Karadjordje

[1] The charge about 'popular songs' had already been given currency in Serb newspapers during 1841-2. Vuk's final answer to them was printed in the Budapest newspaper *Skoroteći* under the title 'The true cause and beginning of my collecting our popular songs'; see Chapter VI, § 2, for extensive quotations from a parallel account given at about the same time to the Russian scholar Sreznevski.

[2] 'In the ten years of the Karadjordje regime, I had ten houses burnt; my father would put them up in the autumn, and the Turks would burn them in the spring.'

without abusing Miloš Obrenović, are bad friends to Karadjordje; and those are bad friends of Miloš who think that one cannot praise him without abusing Karadjordje.' On the letter of 1832, Vuk of course had a more difficult task. He acquitted himself with dignity, but not entirely convincingly. If all that Hadzić said about the letter was true,

still no one could rightly and sensibly say that this in itself proved that there was no truth in what I wrote before about Serbia and Prince Miloš. If there could be found in the letter anything directly contrary to what I wrote and published before, it would still be worth examining just how and why that came about. Sensible and unprejudiced people might then justify me by reflecting for example that things could in truth have been as I described in the first place and then have changed; or that I only afterwards discovered the full truth; or that what I first wrote was for publication, and about a living Head of State, while the letter was for his own eyes, etc.

All reasonable arguments, but very defensive. It was to this point particularly that Hadzić returned in his second *Crushing Blow* published in 1845. Vuk may have thought back regretfully to Kopitar's warnings in 1828 about the possible dangers to his reputation as an objective historian involved in publishing the life of Miloš. Hadzić however did not make the most of his opportunity. In 1845 again he obscured his principal point by a lot of skilful and amusing lawyerly argument about inessentials; by the time this pamphlet appeared, Vuk's position was much more secure, and he wisely left it unanswered.

5

The revival in Vuk's fortunes between 1841 and 1845 was partly due to the work on linguistic questions (discussed in the next chapter) which he was enabled and indeed encouraged to do in Serbia under the new Karadjordje regime. Principally however Vuk owed the favourable and final turn in his luck to the Obrenović family. Miloš had contributed handsomely from his exile in Wallachia to the cost of publication in 1841 of the first book of Vuk's revised (Vienna) edition of 'popular songs' (devoted, as in the previous editions, to the 'women's' or lyrical songs). But the sales were meagre, and left Vuk so heavily indebted to the printers that there could be no question of publishing further volumes in the revised series. This was all the more disappointing to him as he had envisaged a grandiose programme of work, for which he had solicited the financial help of the Russian Academy—the publication of an edition of the 'popular songs' enlarged by at least one-third since the Leipzig edition, a new edition of his *Dictionary*, with thirteen thousand new words, a new and enlarged edition of his *Proverbs*, a book of popular tales and riddles, and descriptions of popular customs, mythology, and superstitions, and finally a Serbian grammar. The Russian reply was discouraging; they were interested only in the *Dictionary*; and then only if the words were translated into Russian rather than German. Vuk was too busy with the 'popular songs' to think more of this proposition in 1839 and he concentrated all the more attention in the following years on the patronage of Miloš Obrenović.

He suggested first that Miloš should finance the full programme that he had outlined for the Russian Academy (with the addition of 'a history of our people in modern times'). Very hopefully, he suggested that Miloš should imitate Count Rumyantsev:

... I have decided to put an idea to Your Highness about which I have thought a great deal since the year before last. The Chancellor of the Russian Empire, Count Nikolai Petrovich Rumyantsev, leaving an official post which was the highest in the land after the Tsar, devoted the whole of the rest of his life and all the income of his estate to the benefit of the literature of his people, and thus left a far fairer and more lasting memorial to himself than by any of his previous services. Would not Your Highness wish to be our Rumyantsev? It would not be necessary [and here a slight touch of Vuk's usual realism is apparent] for you to spend all the income of your estates for this purpose, but only a part of it, with which you could for example buy a house in Vienna, then give me the rent of it to dispose of on our literary needs, and the house would always be at your disposition.

Needless to say, Miloš was not inclined to come to any such arrangement in Vuk's favour, and Vuk renewed his efforts to find a second Rumyantsev in Russia, offering his services to the Russian Ministry of Foreign Affairs in a letter designed to dispel the 'constant doubts about his loyalty and inclination towards the Russian Government'.

It was however from Mihail Obrenović that Vuk ultimately

gained some financial security. During the second half of 1842 Vuk had hoped to earn a financial reward from Miloš by his activity as a political agent. Once Alexander Karadjordje had been re-elected, however, he advised Miloš to keep clear of any further intrigue and found another means of service to the Obrenović family. In exile the family had become comparatively, if not very closely, united, mainly because Miloš was able and willing to meet the financial needs of the others. In particular, Miloš was reconciled with his son Mihail. Vuk had met Mihail for the first time in 1841 as a young man of 17, when he was nominally ruler of Serbia, and each had taken to the other. In the autumn of 1843, Mihail was sent by his father on a tour of Europe and Vuk accompanied him as a sort of tutor. They travelled together from Vienna to Prague, Dresden, and Berlin, where Vuk found a French teacher for Mihail, and renewed his own friendship with Ranke, providing him with material for the second edition of his *Serbian Revolution*.

The friendship between Vuk and Mihail was confirmed, and it seems to have been in the course of their travels in 1843-4 that Vuk secured from the young Prince a promise which was of enormous importance to him and was faithfully kept by the Prince. Mihail pledged himself to give Vuk an annual sum of 600 talers to finance the publication of his books. The arrangement had to be kept secret from Miloš, who would have wished to have the sole credit for any patronage of this sort and would have resented the fact that the young Mihail was spending his allowance so wastefully. There is thus no clear contemporary record of the agreement between Vuk and Mihail, and only in 1862, after Miloš's death, did Vuk feel able to refer publicly to the immense debt which he owed to Mihail (then again reigning Prince of Serbia).

The achievement of Vuk's greatest financial ambition early in 1844 did not prevent him from trying to persuade the Government of Russia to increase their pension to him, and the Government of Serbia both to restore theirs and (this was a point on which he always insisted) to pay him the instalments due to him since 1842. He addressed himself to this matter from the moment that he realized that Alexander Karadjordjević was firmly established as Prince. In letters to Vučić, the power behind the throne, Prince Alexander himself, and the Russian envoy, Baron Lieven, Vuk continually protested his loyalty, tried to explain away his connection with Miloš Obrenović in 1842, and attributed his bad standing with the Karadjordjević regime to the slanders of his enemies—no doubt thinking mainly of Hadzič. At the beginning of 1844, Vuk was able to enlist the support of the Prince Bishop of Montenegro, Njegoš, who wrote to Prince Alexander on his behalf that 'as regards Vuk, although his condition may have forced him to ally himself to some extent with the opposite side, you can be firmly and truly convinced that from now on he will be heart and soul devoted to you. What sort of a Serb would he be, who didn't love you!' For some months there was no reply from Belgrade (Vuk ascribed the delay to Hadzić's attacks on him), but in September 1844, Vuk was told that his prospects were good and that he should come personally to Belgrade. He was well received by Prince Alexander and Vučić, and it looked as if he had at last won his case, when a last-minute obstacle appeared. In late September 1844 some Serbs from Austria crossed the Sava, took Šabac and Loznica (the nearest town to Vuk's own native Tršić), and incited a rebellion in the surrounding district of the Mačva.[1] The rebellion was suppressed harshly, and without difficulty but evidence was discovered pointing strongly to the complicity, if not to the full responsibility, of Miloš Obrenović, who had certainly not given up his ambition to return to the Serbian throne. Vuk was still suspected of being Miloš's man, and possibly his political agent. He was told to leave Belgrade for Zemun and returned to Vienna in October 1844 with the question of his pension still unsettled. Fortunately for Vuk, the Serbian Government's agent in Vienna, Wilhelm Hoppe, reported very favourably on his attitude; by December the matter was cleared up, Vučić was satisfied, and on 22 December 1844 the Council of Belgrade finally decided that Vuk should be given a pension of 400 talers. In writing a letter of thanks to Vučić, Vuk continued to insist on his rights: 'It is true that there is no mention of what I have failed to receive for the last two years and some months; but I am grateful for what I have received, and God, who has given it, may yet in time give the rest.' Vučić announced cryptically: 'God may direct the man who needs something along the path of good deeds, and may attract to his good deeds the attention of those in whose power it is to reward such a man. And thus a just wish and intention, executed by good deeds, may always be fulfilled.' Be

[1] This was the rebellion known as the *Katanska Buna* ('hussars' revolt').

this as it may, Vuk received no back payments of his pension until the Obrenović family returned to power in 1859, and continued to regard the Serbian Government as in debt to him.

The long, tortuous and perhaps squalid tale of Vuk's battle for financial independence is now told. Aged by now nearly 60, he had achieved a position from which he could devote his remaining energies, considerably impaired by age and ill health, to the completion of the literary programme which he had set himself. It is however fitting to end this chapter with a brief account of Vuk's relations at this crucial time in his life with Miloš Obrenović, who had so often and with so ill a grace done so much for Vuk in the past, and with whose fate Vuk's was so closely and curiously linked.

The relationship between these two forceful characters remained strangely ambiguous. Miloš, though he knew nothing of Mihail's benefactions to Vuk, was not best pleased by the friendship between them. He was even less pleased by Vuk's success in recovering his pension from the Karadjordjević Government. But, although there were frequent coolnesses and open quarrels, the two returned regularly to a cautious and no doubt cynical friendship. Before Vuk was established in comparative prosperity in 1845, Miloš would help him in Vienna with periodic gifts—as of money to pay his rent—even if he liked to humiliate Vuk by making him ask for the money. Moreover he acquired the habit of using Vuk as a 'man of confidence' in what appear to be the most inappropriate cases. Miloš was for example a devoted wencher until late in life. He liked to set up house with his current favourite, who often bore him children, and, when his fancy changed, to establish his previous 'housekeeper' in an appropriate station of life (in Kragujevac usually by marrying her to one of his courtiers). He kept up this habit in Vienna during the 1840s, and Vuk was among those who had to occupy themselves with the mediation involved, for instance, in marrying off and fixing an appropriate portion for a Circassian girl whom Miloš had brought with him from Constantinople as far back as 1835 (she embarrassed him by raising her price when the wedding guests were already assembled).

The story of the link between Vuk and Miloš may appropriately be concluded with a short verbal sketch from about 1842 by Anastas Jovanović, a student of painting and afterwards the first well-known Serbian photographer:

Vuk would often visit the Prince, and I would listen to them with the greatest pleasure as they told various stories to each other. What a pity that I did not take notes of it all! Once, as they talked, Prince Miloš said to Vuk: 'Vuk, off home with you, I want to have a walk in the Prater, and you, Dauber, come along with me!'

Prince Miloš had the habit of giving nicknames all round. Vuk was called 'Limpy', but never to his face; Zivanović, his secretary, 'The Prior'; Daruba, a Greek tradesman in Vienna, 'The Judge'; and I, 'Dauber'—Prince Mihail too never called me anything else. I waited, then, while the Prince changed his clothes, and, as we set off, we ran into Vuk still on the staircase, descending very carefully with his crutch. As we went down at his own slow pace behind him, step by step, the Prince began to improvise a song:

> 'Forward, Vuk, to drive the Turks before us,
> You the foremost, and then I behind you,
> Steady, though, that I may overtake you,
> That the Turks may not escape our coming.'

From this little portrait, as from other details, one derives the impression that, whatever the ups and downs of their relationship, Vuk and Miloš had in more than twenty years become used and even somehow suited to each other. Money apart, Vuk was by now Miloš's man.

XVII

LINGUISTIC DEBATES AND THE 'ILLYRIAN' MOVEMENT

I

WHILE Vuk was establishing his own financial security, he played a prominent part in the debate on questions of orthography and language which was being initiated or resumed during the 1840s both in Serbia and in the Slav territories of the Austrian Empire. From 1834 onwards Vuk travelled much more widely than before within these territories, and his new experiences were reflected in the development of his linguistic views. At the same time his house was becoming more and more a centre for Slav visitors to Vienna, particularly for Russians interested in Slav languages and customs outside their native country. Thus Vuk naturally became caught up in the development of the 'Illyrian' movement within the Austrian Empire, and had a close view of the ferment among the Austrian Slavs during the years 1848–9.

Vuk's journey to Montenegro in 1834–5 was crucial in turning his attention to the language and customs of the Slavs outside Serbia, the Srem, and Hungary and within the present area of western and south-western Yugoslavia. Vuk and Njegoš met frequently in Vienna in 1836–7, when Vuk was working on his book *Montenegro und die Montenegriner*, published in German in 1837. This was an extremely frank account of a primitive society, and is the most complete of Vuk's ethnographical and sociological publications. A brief account of it is given at Appendix F. Njegoš was rumoured to be annoyed by some of the franker passages in Vuk's work, but he certainly took no serious offence, and continued to see and help Vuk as opportunity offered.

The journey to Montenegro and Dalmatia in 1834–5 also provided Vuk with plenty of further material for his collections of songs and notes on the manners and customs of the country. He added to these in the course of subsequent journeys to the Dalmatian coast and the rugged country of the Velebit mountains behind it. The new edition (1841) of the lyric (or 'women's') book of 'popular songs' bore witness to Vuk's zeal in collecting during this and other journeys. The discovery which seems most to have delighted him personally was that of some professional mourners between Split and Trogir, 'women who will weep and lament for pay over the dead. . . . People say here that this custom has survived from Roman days.'[1] It is plain however from Vuk's correspondence that he was quite as much interested in linguistic questions as in matters of folk-lore during these journeys, and that he was pondering deeply about them at this time.

In 1841 he made another long journey to the coast and the mountains of the hinterland, this time going as far south as Korčula, Kotor, and the edge of Lake Skadar. He was accompanied by Nikolai Ivanovich Nadezhdin, a Russian publicist, archaeologist, and ethnographer, and Dimitri Knjazhevich, a Russian civil servant of South Slav origin, anxious to find traces of his father's family in the Austro-Turkish border country from which they had come.[2] The journey of 1841 marks an interesting stage in Vuk's relations with Russia, which for long after his return from St. Petersburg and Moscow in 1819 had been confined to begging letters addressed to the Russian Academy or the Russian Embassy at Vienna.

For some time he had been in touch with the Russian Slavist, Mihail Petrovich Pogodin, who on visiting Vuk in Vienna in 1837 was shocked to find him in the same clothes which he had worn in 1835 and to see the poverty in which he lived—this 'Slavonic

[1] Vuk described his discovery at length in a letter of the time: 'When in Montenegro, I doubted whether such a thing existed among our people. I looked for them yesterday and succeeded in seeing and hearing them. I had a good deal of trouble in persuading them to begin mourning; once they started, they made an old woman lie down in the middle of the room, to act as the corpse.' In Montenegro, Vuk later heard spontaneous and unpaid mourning songs, which attained a very high artistic level. See J. Šaulić, 'The Oral Women Poets of the Serbs', *Slavonic and East European Review*, vol. xlii, no. 98, December 1963.

[2] N. I. Nadezhdin (1804–56) became a close friend and correspondent of Vuk, and intended to travel with him through Bosnia and Serbia in 1848. The journey had to be put off because of the revolutions of that year. Nadezhdin's diary of his journey with Vuk in 1841 is published (in Serb translation) in *Susreti s Vukom*, Matica Srpska, Belgrade, 1964.

notable of our time, the author who by his researches, publications, and journeys has done most of all for the Slavonic world'. Pogodin was very different in outlook from the Russians whom Vuk had met on his tour in 1819, and with whom he had since corresponded. This young professor of history had strong ideas about Russia's mission among the Western Slavs and in 1838 had formulated the first Russian 'Panslav' programme, which combined the ideas of Russian nationalism and Slav messianism, to culminate in a 'universal monarchy' under Russian leadership.[1] Vuk clearly made a deep impression on Pogodin, who afterwards secured his election to membership of the Moscow Society of Friends of Russian Literature, and collected subscriptions in Russia for the third edition of Vuk's 'popular songs'.

Nadezhdin, who accompanied Vuk on his travels in 1841 and left a detailed diary of the journey, was also a distinguished figure in Russian cultural history, though far removed from Pogodin's Panslavism and social conservatism. He was deeply influenced by the philosophy of Schelling, and was closely associated with the magazine *The European*, founded in 1832. His aim was to link Russia more closely with Western Europe; it was, he thought, the mission of Russia to work for the propagation of a purely spiritual Christianity throughout the world, and to achieve a cultural synthesis which would transcend the old classical and romantic categories.

It is typical of Vuk's concentration on his own affairs that he was on good terms with both Pogodin and Nadezhdin (as he had been with, for example, Admiral Shishkov and Turgenev during his visit to Russia) and that no trace of their wider and contradictory interests appears in the records of their dealings with him. Their converse with Vuk was on an entirely antiquarian or 'folkloristic' basis; Nadezhdin's diary contains a passage which shows what a reputation Vuk had in this field. He describes a stroll in the little town of Gospić (not far from the lakes of Plitvice):

On my way back, I heard clearly the sound of singing from a house next door to the post office. Gaj[2] and Mažuranić had come to meet me. They went into the house to hear the singing, and I followed them. We

---
[1] P. I. Köppen had first drawn Pogodin's attention to Vuk by giving him in 1827 a copy of Vuk's '*Day-star*' for 1826. For further details of Pogodin's descriptions of and correspondence with Vuk, see *Susreti s Vukom*, p. 301.

[2] Both Gaj and Mažuranić were eminent Croatian men of letters. See § 2.

found ourselves in a large room, where ten to fifteen women and girls were at work, sewing and making clothes. . . . They received us cheerfully without any shyness, getting on with their singing and their work together. I was burning with impatience to hear for the first time those Serb popular songs, which have become so famous in Europe thanks to the devotion and labours of Vuk. But, alas, they sang only songs from books, the work of contemporary town writers. So we see education on the march everywhere to the detriment of true popular customs. Apart from that, the singing was very well in time, lively and from the heart, just as with us (in Russia) at village evenings. . .!

Other and less eminent Russians began to appear in Vienna from 1841 onwards to pay their respects to Vuk. In particular the Russian Ministry of Culture sent three young academics on, as it were, travelling scholarships to visit the countries of the Western and Southern Slavs and to learn as much as possible of their history, language, and customs. One of these students[1] was Ismail Ivanovich Sreznevski, candidate at this time for the chair of Slav studies about to be established at Kharkov University. After travelling widely throughout much of the present area of Yugoslavia in the summer (he was not able to accompany Vuk and Nadezhdin), Sreznevski settled down that autumn in Vienna, in a house next door to Vuk's, visited him daily, studied the Serbian language with him, and took notes of his conversation for the biography which he published in 1846; this, the most valuable source about Vuk's early years, has been extensively quoted in Chapters I–V.

The new generation of Russian Slavists were not enthusiastic about Vuk's old mentor, Jernej Kopitar. The two remained close friends, but Vuk was by now completely independent mentally, and the most fruitful period of his association with Kopitar was long past. While Vuk's links with the young generation of Russian Slavists were being formed, Kopitar was ever more pre-occupied with the idea of building up Austria as a rival and specifically Catholic centre of Slav studies. In his last years in fact he did something to justify the hostile propaganda which had for so long

---

[1] The other two Russian travelling scholars were Osip Maksimovich Bodzhansky, who had just defended a thesis at Moscow University on the popular poetry of the Slav peoples (there is no record of his meeting with Vuk); and Piotr Ivanovich Prajs, later to found the chair of Slavonic studies at St. Petersburg, who was most enthusiastic about Vuk as a scholar, a teacher (Prajs took Serbian lessons from him), and a man. See *Susreti s Vukom*, p. 101.

been disseminated about him from Serbia. He even travelled to Rome in 1842 to discuss with the Vatican the foundation of a chair of Church Slavonic language in Vienna, and the establishment of a Cyrillic printing press to help in the dissemination of Catholic propaganda.

In his career and his private life, Kopitar was a disappointed man. His promotion to the rank of Court Councillor (*Hofrat*) was very long delayed, and when it finally came in 1843, it was accompanied by the loss of all his painfully accumulated savings. An interesting sketch of him in the last years of his life was provided by the young Croat publicist, Imbro Tkalac,[1] who was told in 1843 to get through Kopitar an introduction to Vuk. He found Kopitar gloomy and in a bad temper. After a few minutes' conversation,

> Kopitar asked: 'Do you know Vuk?' I answered that I had read his books but did not know him personally, and Kopitar observed: 'You must get to know this extraordinary man. I'm seeing him tomorrow and will take you with me. There's no one else like Vuk. Remember that.'
>
> The next day I went along with Kopitar to Vuk's house. . . . We went into his room. 'Herr von Vuk, here's a young Croat who reads your books.' With these words Kopitar introduced me to Vuk, who rose from his legendary couch to greet us. 'A rare bird, wouldn't you say, this Croat who reads Serbian books?' said Kopitar, with a smile, and I remarked that other Croats too read Vuk's works.—'But they don't learn a thing from them, otherwise they'd write better', said Kopitar and relapsed into his former gloom.

Shortly afterwards Tkalac paid a farewell visit to Kopitar, in order to get a letter of introduction to Ranke in Berlin:

> As we parted, Kopitar said: 'Vuk likes you. Off with you in God's name to Berlin, and give the letter to Ranke. It'll help you, for he knows that I'm not a great writer of letters of recommendation. And tell him that I've reached the last chapter of St. Matthew'—(I didn't understand this phrase at the time, but found afterwards that it meant death was at

---

[1] Imbro Ignjatević Tkalac (1824–1912) did much to publicize Vuk's work among German-speaking Austrians, and in 1854 wrote an article on Vuk for the current edition of Brockhaus's *Lexicon*. He defended Vuk in 1860 against attacks in Russian journals. The passages quoted here and in Chapter XX were probably intended for Tkalac's memoirs, which were completed in manuscript, but burnt at his death. See *Susreti's Vukom*, pp. 109 et seq., 307–8. For a fuller appreciation of Tkalac, see Viktor Novak, *Vuk in Hrvati*, Belgrade, 1967, Chapter IX.

hand)—'and if he wants to see me again, he'd better come to Vienna soon.' Nor did Kopitar deceive himself. In fact he died in the autumn of 1844.

2

Thus Vuk's main link with the world of Austrian officialdom was broken, at a time when his contacts with the Russian Slavophils were becoming close, and when he had started to travel widely in the South Slav lands. He now frequently spent the winter months at Vukovar on the borders of Slavonia (Eastern Croatia) and the Srem, and it was by 1843 natural enough for a young Croat literary journalist like Tkalac to visit him in Vienna. For Vuk was by chance as much as by design becoming associated with the 'Illyrian' movement in Croatia. This was in essence a literary movement, though it was linked with Croat political agitation against Magyar domination (within the Austrian Empire Croatia was subordinated to Hungary), and on a wider basis with the movement for greater unity of the Slavs within and beyond the Austrian Empire. The personal force within the 'Illyrian' movement was provided mainly by the dynamic Ljudevit Gaj. Born in 1809, he had come as a student at Vienna under the influence of the Slovak scholar and publicist, Jan Kollár, who in the 1830s was preaching the idea of the 'mutuality' of the Slavs, and the forging of cultural links between the four main language groups which he distinguished—Russian, Polish, 'Bohemian-Slovak', and 'Illyrian'. The area of the Napoleonic Kingdom of Illyria would in this context have to be enlarged to include most of the present area of Yugoslavia. Kollár's ideas were of course quite unrealistic; no amount of linguistic links could, for example, nullify the hard realities of Russo-Polish tension. Gaj himself was slightly more modest, supporting at one time the idea that Russia should set about mastering the Balkans (rather than Eastern Europe as a whole) with 'Illyrian' (i.e. Croatian) support.[1]

This was a time at which nationalist and literary movements

[1] In 1838, Gaj sent a memorandum to the Tsar on the subject. Even within a strictly South-Eastern European context, any such programme was quite unrealistic, since the Serbs, who of all the South Slavs had the closest links with the Russians, were far more interested in achieving or preserving their independence than in helping the Croats against the Magyars.

could hardly be separated, and Gaj's most effective political work was done by literary means. In 1833 he sought permission to publish in Zagreb a newspaper in the Croat language, which would give the Croats their own organ of publicity against the dominant Magyars. In 1835, his newspaper, the *Illyrian News*, was founded, with the strong support of the Croat politicians, especially Janko Graf Drašković, who at this time founded the Croat National Party. The Hungarians counter-attacked strongly, and secured the support of the Government in Vienna. They were able to point a warning finger at the 'Pan-slav' implications of the 'Illyrian' movement; as a result in January 1843 the very use of the word 'Illyrian' was forbidden from Vienna by governmental decree, and in 1844 the Hungarian diet declared that within six years Magyar was to become the official language of Croatia (even the Croat politicians were fighting for Latin rather than Croat).

The 'Illyrian' movement in fact continued to make progress. The demand for a chair of the Croatian language at Zagreb Academy, the establishment of 'reading halls' in Zagreb and the holding of literary meetings there in the early 1840s, all helped to foster the Croat national spirit against the Hungarians. But the immediate political effect of the 'Illyrian' movement was small; it did no more than prepare the way for common action by the South Slavs in more favourable circumstances. Gaj's most important work lay in establishing a linguistic basis for Croat *rapprochement* with the Serbs and other Slavs, and in adapting the Croat language so as to be more easily intelligible to other South Slavs. It was in this context that Vuk's relations with him and the other 'Illyrians' were to have considerable importance.[1]

Gaj had become acquainted with Vuk's 'popular songs' as a student in 1826 and regarded them as a priceless treasure. The two men met in Vienna in 1833, and in 1835 Gaj, along with his *Illyrian News*, started the publication of a literary periodical, *Day-star*—the same name as that of the annual almanac which Vuk had been publishing in Vienna. Gaj's *Day-star* soon began to appear in the principal Serbian rather than in the normal Croatian dialect (see Appendix C). This was a gesture to promote Serbo-Croat literary

---

[1] As early as 1825, Vuk had been in correspondence with a Croat Catholic, Ignjat Brlić, who in his *Grammar of the Illyrian language*, published in 1833, recommended the complete abandonment of the Latin script and the adoption of Vuk's Cyrillic alphabet.

rapprochement. In the same spirit, Gaj reprinted many of the famous songs from Vuk's collections. As the result of his collaboration with Gaj's *Day-star*, Vuk gained the friendship of many of the younger men of letters in Croatia and had great influence upon them. In 1842 Sreznevski wrote that the 'new School of "Illyrians" holds that it is time for them to learn the language and style of Vuk, and to follow in his footsteps', while in the same year Nadezhdin described Zagreb as the centre of 'Serbo-Catholic literature'.

Vuk approved of the main direction of Gaj's attempts to adapt the literary language of Croatia, but had plenty of detailed criticisms to make. Unlike Kopitar, who disapproved of any attempt to suppress one dialect and impose another as the approved literary language, Vuk was delighted with Gaj's adoption of the main Serbian dialect; his criticisms were reserved for some of the detailed forms which Gaj used; these seemed to Vuk to result from his ignorance of the Serbian language. On this point however it was Kopitar who made the critical running, and Vuk did not enter the lists till after Kopitar's death in 1844. He was more critical from the first of Gaj's attempts to adapt the Latin alphabet to the Serbian linguistic forms.[1] Above all, Vuk was reluctant to see any common South Slav language called 'Illyrian', and to drop the name of 'Serbian'. As early as 1836, he wrote to Justin Mihailović: 'The name too is one of the big difficulties. It is hard to induce them to acknowledge that they are Serbs, and we would be crazy if we agreed to abandon our famous name and to adopt another one which is dead and today has no meaning in itself.'

3

In Belgrade also Vuk was engaged in debates, all too familiar to him, about orthography and language. In 1842-3 these had once more become very live issues in Serbia and, though Vuk's general standing with the new Karadjordjević regime was not good, there was no attempt to prevent a scholar of his eminence in this field from airing his views. Indeed they were solicited. By the early 1840s a comparatively large number of literary journals had begun to appear, or had been resuscitated, in the Serb language,

[1] Gaj's adaptation involved the use of numerous diacritical signs, as in Czech, to modify certain consonants. Kopitar referred to these signs as *Fliegendreck* ('fly-shit').

particularly the *Serbian National Newspaper* (a purely literary one) in Belgrade. In 1841 the Matica Srpska Society decided to examine again the question of Serbian orthography, in order to help the newspapers and particularly their own journal to achieve some kind of uniformity. A special commission was set up under the presidency of Platon Atanacković, an old friend of Vuk. He asked both Vuk and Sava Tekelija, the distinguished conservative patron of the Matica Srpska, to send in papers expressing their views. Their contributions were received early in 1842 and were quite irreconcilable. Sava Tekelija insisted that the right course was to set the clock back for 50 years, and adopt the written form of Slavonic-Serbian as it had existed before Vuk had started his reforming career. Vuk repeated the familiar view which he had first stated in the introduction to his *Dictionary*; he pointed out the difficulties of writing the popular language of Serbia in the old Slavonic letters, and the orthographic inconsistencies of those who tried to do so. The commission formed by Matica Srpska wisely decided to drop the inquiry, since no progress would be possible while Tekelija was alive, and the society depended very much on his patronage (he died in autumn 1842).

In the meantime preparations were being made for the foundation of a new 'Serbian Society for Literary Culture', which held its inaugural meeting in June 1842. The aim of the Society was the 'propagation of scientific knowledge of the Serb language, and principally the formation and perfection of a popular Serb language'. The members (Vuk was elected a 'corresponding member') decided to discuss regularly 'the qualities of our language, both grammatical and lexicographical' and to come to some decision on a suitable orthography at a plenary meeting after three months; until then the Society would stick to the 'usual orthography' but left it to members to make small deviations from its rules. This was a very conservative directive, and was supplemented by a communication suggesting that any inadequacies of the 'popular language' should be made good only from the Slavonic vocabulary, tailored so far as possible to a popular Serbian model. Vuk of course opposed these ideas, but the plenary meeting of the Society, which was due to discuss them, never took place. The political climate of Serbia had become too unsettled (this was just the time of the replacement of Mihail Obrenović by Alexander Karadjordjević), and the Society suspended its work for some two years.

In the interval Vuk was engaged in some less important debates on linguistic questions. In 1843 he published his reply to Hadzić's first *Crushing Blow* (which had appeared in 1839). This was mainly devoted to defence of his own historical and political integrity but contained some devastating counter-attacks on Hadzić's own linguistic theories and qualifications as a writer on linguistic subjects.[1] In 1843-4 Hadzić wisely moved back to historical ground for his attacks on Vuk, and it was not until 1844-5 that battle was rejoined over linguistic questions. The 'Serbian Society for Literary Culture' resumed its work in August 1844, and now devoted its attention principally to the question of coining new terminology for modern sciences, and to the need for some directive about new formations. A number of members applied themselves to particular fields—physics, 'fundamental philosophy', etc.—and, to arouse interest, some of their contributions were circulated to the Belgrade public. Meanwhile, in preparation for the Society's plenary meeting in May 1845, a comprehensive list of new words was collected with the initial letters A, B, and C (and some under D).

Vuk was among those who spoke at the meeting, reading out a letter which he had addressed to the Minister of Culture, Paun Janković, on the subject at issue. His views were that it was premature to work out rules for the formation of new terminology; the field was too wide, and the task too difficult 'particularly for our men of letters, who neither know their own language nor want to learn it...'. The Society should not commit its prestige to work which was bound to be so imperfect. It would do better to ensure that its members really knew their own popular language. The members could justify, if they would only first admit, their ignorance by the plea that they spent their youth learning the sciences in various foreign tongues. Certainly Slavonic and other new coinages should be allowed, but only reluctantly and in case of real need. The danger of total corruption of the true popular

---

[1] The following is a typical passage: 'A botcher is the description of a man who does not properly understand his own business (as for example it is said of a bad painter that he daubs); and a charlatan is the description of someone who not only is a botcher but also sings his own praises and is anxious to convince people that he knows what in fact he does not know. Now I have never said that Mr. Hadzić is a botcher and a charlatan; I have only said that, so far as the learned world is concerned, he could be one if he knew nothing better than he knows the Serb language and etymology.'

language was increasing. Up till now it was only the literary men brought up in Austrian towns who could not distinguish what was truly Serbian. Now, as the result of their books circulating, the opening of offices, the general spread of education, and the establishment of newspapers, printing presses, and learned societies, all run by the Austrian-bred literary class, the process of corruption would be rapid indeed. The primary task of the Society should be to halt this process, and in doing so they could take comfort from the thought that they were following the example of the Russians, who had steadily approximated their literary to their popular language—'for which reason it is easier for us to understand Lomonosov and Derzhavin than Krylov and Pushkin'.[1]

In a second speech a few days later Vuk rubbed salt in the wounds which had had inflicted. He had not meant to propose, he said, as seemed to have been thought, that the Society should undertake the production of an authoritative Grammar. All he had suggested was that members should individually improve their knowledge of their own language. He proceeded to some practical advice—that members should start by reading a few chosen books that were agreed to be good linguistically (he cited Šafařík's *Selected Serbian Reader*); they would then have a linguistic standard by which to judge, and gradually a consensus would be reached of what was and what was not good Serbian. By working along these lines, the Society could do untold good; if they continued to assume that they had no need to learn, things would go from bad to worse, and 'then would be fulfilled what has been said by some learned Russian travellers, that the time will come when Serbs from the Srem, the Bačka, and from Serbia itself will go to Zagreb to learn Serbian. . . . Perhaps many of you think that this could never be. But I say here and now before you all, that if we work at this subject no better than we have done up till now, and the "Illyrians" progress no worse than they have done up to date, then it not only may, but must, come to this.'

The newspaper reports of the debate which followed varied very considerably, according to whether they were inspired by Hadzić, who got in the last word, or Vuk. Vuk's own account of the proceedings after his second speech is the least ambiguous and the most probable. Hadzić, he said, had put forward the thesis that

---

[1] The point being that the Russian of Krylov and Pushkin, being more 'popular', was more idiomatic and less accessible to the non-Russian Slavs.

all were agreed on the need to speak and write the popular Serbian language; the dispute, according to him, was simply between those who wished to add the new words necessary to supplement it according to the rules of etymology, and those who paid no attention to this standard. Vuk replied that first the debate could not properly be limited to the question of supplementary words—the subject was the popular language as a whole; and secondly that those who wished to apply etymological rules had no proper standards or consistency, but just 'wrote as the words came from the pen'. Hadzić repeated the need for new coinages, and denied the need for any self-education by the members of the Society: 'Let each write as he can and wants, and leave the details to posterity for correction.' To which Vuk replied: 'However well and sensibly we work, posterity will have something to do; but why leave for it what we can and ought to do ourselves?' In the end, no vote was taken on Vuk's proposals, and the only agreement was to assemble material for a 'Serbian phraseology'.

On his return to Vienna, Vuk assembled and published before the end of 1845 a number of his recent writings on linguistic subjects. By far the most important of these was the *Conclusion*, a new article, in which Vuk tried to summarize the main objections advanced against his linguistic theories, and to counter them. People said that he was artificially separating the Serbian from the Slavonic language, when there should be no boundary between the two. His reply was that there was a very definite boundary. Slavonic was the language of Church books, Serbian of the living people. If a word occurred in popular speech and in Church books, this did not prove that there were not two languages—only that there were words common to both. The same principles apply to the alphabetical question. There is a Serbian alphabet and a Slavonic alphabet. Those who want to apply the Slavonic alphabet to the Serbian language only make themselves more ridiculous by saying that they must be right 'because the Russians have kept the old Slavonic alphabet'. It was in fact the Russians who first dropped some of the Slavonic letters, and made new ones of their own. 'And so there is at least ten times more difference between the present Russian and the old Slavonic alphabet than between mine and the present Church Slavonic.'

On the question of establishing a literary language Vuk repeated the arguments which he had used nearly thirty years before in the preface to his *Dictionary*, and those which he had recently advanced to the Society for Slavonic Studies. He disapproved of trying to combine various dialects into an artificial literary language. His own standard for good language was the language of Hercegovina and Bosnia, and the most corrupt language of all was that spoken in the Austrianized towns of the Srem.

Those who wished to revive Slavonic for general literary purposes could be neglected, after the death of Sava Tekelija. Those who want to establish a new sort of literary language fall into various errors, in their attempt to find parallels. In Germany, they say, the written language is different from that normally spoken; but in fact it is a development of that spoken in central Germany. In Russia, there has been a 'mixed language', but this is being increasingly abandoned by writers in favour of a purer popular style. The main hindrance in Serbia to using the popular language for literature is that writers in their ignorance are corrupting it. And their main reasons for wishing to create a new literary language are that they haven't thought deep enough on linguistic questions, and that they do not know and will not lower themselves to learn the popular language.

Vuk concluded his exposition with words of the utmost self-confidence:

Any review or printed reply to these my thoughts will give me great pleasure. I do not think that I know everything as well as it can be known, or that I can make no mistakes. I only think that on the main point I am right, but mistakes of detail may well be found in my work even on this. . . . With those who agree with me on the main point, I would be very glad to have discussions about many details, and in writing this pamphlet I have thought in many places how useful this would be. With those of our writers who differ from me in this business, I am angry not for personal reasons but for the sake of our language and of the common benefit. . . .

Vuk distributed his pamphlet free to friends and acquaintances, including the Serbian Minister of Culture, together with a request that the ban of 1832 on his orthography in Serbia should now be lifted. No notice was taken of this request, but the pamphlet had a considerable success. There was of course criticism as well, and Hadzić produced in 1846 another *Crushing Blow*. The argument was again mainly *ad hominem*, and Vuk was accused particularly (and not without some apparent reason) of steadily and deliberately denigrating the Austrian Serbs. On substance, Hadzić repeated his old points that everyone was agreed on the need for popular language and that the main matter at issue was spelling according to etymological principles. He struck new notes of regional rivalry in claiming that it was the best-educated Serbs (i.e. from the Austrian Empire) who should be the arbiters of taste in the formation of a new literary language, and in attacking Vuk for paying too much attention to the 'Illyrian' Catholics. 'Our Illyrian brothers', he wrote, 'must recognize that the Eastern Serbs long anticipated them and thought and did more for the preservation of their language and nationality than did the Illyrians. They must convince themselves once and for all that the Eastern Church is no obstacle to enlightenment and science, and that Cyrillic letters can be written in a good, intelligible and learned style.' These arguments had little effect. Hadzić had by this time been banished from Serbia by the all-powerful Minister, Vučić; he was no longer a formidable foe, although his defence of the Austrian Serbs naturally found a ready audience in Novi Sad, to which he had retired.

The importance of this last round in the long duel between Vuk and his main literary enemy was not intrinsic so much as incidental. A new generation of writers was beginning to appear, and one of them, a young philologist and grammarian Djura Daničić, was inspired by Vuk's *Conclusions* to write his *War for the Serbian language*, a work far more scientific and thorough than Vuk could have produced himself. He was a master of the linguistic science of the day, and documented the main arguments of Vuk, which he adopted, by examples from other Slavonic languages. The work of Daničić finally disposed, as far as serious argument was concerned, of the dilettante approach of Hadzić and his followers.

The *War for the Serbian language* was produced in 1847. The same year saw the publication of two other works which were indirectly important for the success of Vuk's linguistic theories. Njegoš's *Mountain Wreath* marked a departure from the stilted classical style affected by the majority of previous writers of Serbian poetry (including Mušički). A more direct proof that the popular language could be used for literature as well as for controversy was provided by the young poet, Branko Radičević, who in 1847 published his first volume of lyrics written in pure popular style and in Vuk's orthography. Nor could there be any doubt that Branko was directly influenced by Vuk, since he had become a member of Vuk's most intimate domestic circle in Vienna. At the end of 1847 it could therefore be said that after thirty years Vuk's theories were at last making some headway.

4

By this time too Vuk's doctrines about language had come to carry political implications which they had not had in 1817. His opponents, who wanted to keep as close as possible to the Church Slavonic alphabet and vocabulary, were in effect, if not entirely in intention, putting the maximum of obstacles in the way of linguistic and cultural links between the Serbs and the other Southern Slavs. And they were thus opposing, not any Austrian-inspired plot to catholicize the Slavs of the Srem and Serbia, but a Slav-inspired 'Illyrian' movement. Thus Vuk's linguistic work at this stage contributed quite notably to clearing the way towards a united South Slav state. He was of course not unconscious of what he was doing to promote cultural unity. From 1844 onwards, Slavonic 'conversations' (social evenings) and dances were organized in Vienna and attended by representatives of all the Slav groups in the town. Miloš Obrenović and Vuk were prominent figures at some of these gatherings, which had political or nationalist undertones.[1] In Belgrade too there was new interest in the 'Illyrian' movement. When the word 'Illyrian' was banned by the Austrians in Croatia in 1843, Gaj's movement found friendly supporters in Serbia, who gave them monetary help and allowed them to publish (1844) a newspaper *Branislav* ('Defender of the Slavs') to conduct what amounted to an anti-Magyar campaign.

The 'Illyrian' movement thus seemed to be gaining in reality in the years immediately preceding 1848. There is no sign that Vuk was profoundly concerned in the political struggles of the Slavs within the Austrian Empire; but in 1848 it was hardly possible to stay completely aloof. The Paris Revolution in February stimulated revolts throughout Europe. These included a fiercely nationalist movement in Hungary, which claimed the incorporation of Croatia in a unitary Hungarian state, and in Croatia

[1] A list of subscribers to these gatherings has been preserved, in which Croatians, Dalmations, Slovenes, and Serbs are mentioned as 'Illyrians' and 'men of South Slav race'. See *Kovčežić*, iii, pp. 147 et seq., article by Dr. Ljubomir Durković-Jakšić.

THE 'ILLYRIAN' MOVEMENT

counter-demands for more autonomy, not least equal rights for the Croat language in the Croat Church Assembly and the Austrian Reichstag. In May, the Serbs of the Srem province held an anti-Magyar Assembly at Karlovci, demanding ecclesiastical and political autonomy for themselves, electing a *Vojvoda* (Marshal) and nominating their Metropolitan Rajačić as Patriarch to prove their own national autonomy. The Croats and the Serbs of the Srem moreover began to make common cause against the Hungarians. In March the *Serbian Popular News* of Buda changed its name to the *General South Slav and Serbian News*. Gaj met the new Serb Patriarch, Rajačić, in Vienna to promote joint political action, and the 'Vukist' poet, Branko Radičević, called on Croats and Serbs to unite in their struggle against the common enemy. Early in April 1848 Croats and Czechs issued a common proclamation in Vienna to the Southern Slav subjects of Austria. In May the Serbian Assembly at Karlovci resolved that their lands in Hungary, newly christened the 'Vojvodina' (Marshal's province) should be joined to Croatia, Slavonia, and Dalmatia, and that there should be a joint Serbo-Croat Ministry at Zagreb. At Zagreb itself, the Committee of the Parliament demanded similar links between the Croat and Slovene lands. Temporarily there was a common front of the Austrian South Slavs for union within the Austrian Empire.

In the meantime, the Austrian Government, self-exiled to Innsbruck, powerless, and faced with similar important demands from the Czechs, played for time and were inclined at first to back the Hungarians against their Slav populations.[1] In Serbia too, while there was much individual support for the Serbs in the Vojvodina, the Government of Alexander Karadjordjević was cautious. They did not want to provoke Austrian or Russian intervention by too overt support of what might turn into an anti-Austrian movement in the Vojvodina; they did not want to encourage revolutionary social changes there (in fact there was little danger of this); and they feared rightly that Miloš Obrenović would be very ready to claim leadership of the Vojvodina Serbs, and then of a united greater Serbia. This latter fear was shared by the Russian and Turkish Governments, who thought that a greater Serbia led

---

[1] At the same time the appointment of the Croatian nationalist and strong man, Baron Jelačić, to be Governor (*Ban*) of Croatia showed that the Austrians were hedging their bets.

by Miloš might be simply an Austrian protectorate. It is uncertain whether Miloš was in fact plotting to secure either an invitation to Karlovci or his own return to Serbia; but he certainly had plenty of agents in the Vojvodina, and the Karadjordje Government kept a close watch on his movements.[1]

Such was the international context as it immediately affected the South Slavs in June 1848, when the famous Slav Congress met at Prague, intended originally by the Austrian Slavs as a counter-ploy to the German democratic congress at Frankfurt. Here the question of South Slav unity within or outside the Austrian Empire was never specifically discussed. The main debate, joined before the Congress as well as during it, was between Palacky speaking for the Czechs and the Western Slavs, and the Slovak Štur, speaking for the Eastern Slavs and particularly the Poles. The former wished to block both German, Magyar, and Russian expansionism by maintaining a strong Austria, reorganized into a federation of equal nationalities. The latter considered it quite unrealistic to think that any Austrian Government would carry out a pro-Slav policy. The Austro-Slavs agreed with the others on excluding German participation, but otherwise they were defeated all along the line. The agenda of the conference was widened. A *Manifesto to the Nations of Europe* was produced, protesting mainly against the partition of Poland. A Pole, Lubomirski, put forward a draft scheme for 'Slav Unity', and Bakunin his own ideas of 'revolutionary Panslavism', a Slav federation led by Russia. The appeal to the Hapsburgs on behalf of the Czechs and South Slavs was side-tracked. So far as the Serbs and Croats were concerned, the Congress never got down to earth before it was dissolved on 12 June by the artillery of the Austrian General Windischgraetz.

Vuk was one of the Serb delegates to the Congress[2] and was accorded particular honours. But there is no indication that he was particularly active, nor of what his views were on the main themes which were or should have been discussed at the Congress. The

[1] When Miloš arrived at Zagreb from Vienna in May 1848, he was put under house arrest for a few days and deprived of his money by Ljudevit Gaj himself, who was almost certainly acting in concert with the Belgrade authorities and to the embarrassment of Governor Jelačić.

[2] Another was the veteran of the 1804 rising, Prota Matija Nenadović. For an account of Vuk at the Slav Congress by the Czech publicist, Joseph Václav Fritsch, see *Susreti s Vukom*, pp. 129 et seq.

THE 'ILLYRIAN' MOVEMENT

events of the next six months, however, induced Vuk to take a strong 'Austro-Slav' stand; the idea of Austria as the best guarantee of Southern Slav as opposed to Serbian freedom was one with which Kopitar had familiarized him, and he was confirmed in it by the Hungarian behaviour in 1848. He was indeed no admirer of the new Serbian regime in the Vojvodina. The Serb Patriarch, Rajačić, in particular had become an enemy, or unfriend,[1] and in 1849 suppressed a new journal *Napredak* ('Progress') produced at Karlovci and Zemun in Vuk's alphabet. The foreign policy of the Vojvodina Government at first pleased Vuk little more than their attitude on literary questions. He would have preferred to see them making common cause with the Karadjordjević regime against the Turks. But by the end of summer 1848 this was obviously a dream. The Vojvodina Serbs were engaged in war against the Hungarians, and the Austrian Government, no longer needing Hungarian help to put down a rising in Italy, had decided to use their Slav subjects to bring the Hungarian regime under Kossuth to heel. In order to secure the support of the Vojvodina Serbs (many of whom fought in the Austrian army) the Austrians granted them a considerable measure of autonomy under the Patent of Olmütz in December 1848. Vuk was confirmed by these events in his Austro-Slav convictions. He was enthusiastic for Jelačić's early successes against the Hungarians in September, and his enthusiasm was by no means lessened when the Croatian general suppressed the radical October revolution in Vienna, which would effectively have divided Austria into German and Hungarian halves.

By the spring of 1849 however it was plain that the Southern Slavs were gaining very little politically for their support of the Austrian against the Hungarian Governments. On the military front the Hungarians were holding out successfully. On the political front there was little progress in sight. At the Constituent Assembly meeting after the October revolution at Kroměříž, in Moravia, there was no general support for the reconstitution of the Austrian Empire along national and federal lines. The Kroměříž Assembly did not dare to envisage any effective partition of Hungary. The 'Stadion constitution' of March 1849 provided for

---

[1] Stratimirović had died in 1836. He was succeeded in 1837 by Stefan Stanković, who died in 1841. The new Patriarch, Rajačić, had originally befriended Vuk, but was surrounded at Karlovci by conservative advisers, including Jovan Hadzić-Svetić.

the establishment of provinces on national lines throughout the Austrian Empire, including Hungary, but these were to be no more than administrative areas for the convenience of the central Government. There was to be little local autonomy for national minorities within the provinces.

In May 1849, the Hungarian Army capitulated to the troops of the Russian Tsar, who anticipated trouble for Russia from the example of successful Hungarian resistance. The Austrians had nothing more to gain from Serbian support, and there was no effective obstacle to total centralization under the Vienna Government. Croatia and Slovenia were proclaimed a joint Crown Land of Austria (separate from Dalmatia); they were deprived of the provincial Diets which had existed before 1848, and of their linguistic rights. The Serbs of the Vojvodina fared no better. In the summer of 1849, the Vojvodina too was reduced to the pattern of another administrative unit, and the Serbs there were deprived of any special rights. All they gained from the wars of 1848-9 was the right to retain their new name, with the Austrian Kaiser assuming the additional title of Grand Serbian Vojvoda.

In these circumstances, the Southern Slavs of Austria had for the time being no more to hope from political action, and the literary and cultural *rapprochement* among them for which Vuk had been working before 1848 did not seem to be so far below the level of the times. An important stage in this *rapprochement* was marked in March 1850 by the 'Literary Agreement' signed in Vienna by Vuk and Daničić among others on the Serb side, by a number of prominent Croat authors, including Kukuljević and Mažuranić, and by Miklošić for the Slovenians[1] (though he did not carry his countrymen with him). 'Conscious that a single people must have a single literature' and that South Slav literature was not uniform in alphabet, language, or orthography, they agreed that it was not right to mix dialects, but to choose one, and that it was most correct and best to accept the Southern Serbian dialect as the literary one. The agreement was the result of long and continued discussion of Gaj's proposed changes in the Latin alphabet for Croatian use, and of his desire to make the West

---

[1] Franjo Miklošić, Slovene man of letters, succeeded Kopitar both as censor on Illyrian affairs and as librarian of the Vienna Court Library. He helped Vuk after Kopitar's death to complete his translation of the New Testament, and after Vuk's death was one of those who signed an appeal for the publication of his collected works.

Serbian dialect the literary standard. On the first point, Vuk mediated between Gaj and some Dalmatian authors, who were most obstinately opposed to any changes. On the second point, he fully supported Gaj in opposing the creation of an artificial mixed dialect for literary use (which, he thought, could only be justified if the adoption of any single existing one would cause irremediable offence among those who spoke and wrote in the others). And, with much deeper knowledge of the subject than Gaj, he had continued to press the claims of the West Serbian dialect—it was the language of the 'popular songs', and of the Renaissance authors of the Dubrovnik school, and it was 'nearest to the Slavonic way of speaking, from which, as is so often dinned into us, we should not depart'.

The agreement was more important symbolically than practically, at least for a long time. The two alphabets, Cyrillic for the Serbs and Orthodox Southern Slavs and Latin for the Croats, remained; while this was so, it was (and is) difficult to achieve a really common literature for the whole Yugoslav area. Probably the most important immediate result of Vuk's involvement with the 'Illyrians' culminating in the 'Literary Agreement' was that they got to know him personally and to appreciate the Serbian contribution to South Slav literature. The school books for Serb children in Austria, for example, in future included specimens of Serb authors. In the longer term, the Vienna Agreement—one literature, one literary language, and (by implication) two alphabets with equal rights—has served as one of the foundations of the multi-racial Yugoslavia of present times. It was supplemented and its main points were made more explicit in the Novi Sad Agreement of 1954. The basic importance and political implications of this understanding are best appreciated when it is called in question—for example in 1967, when it was suggested that a Croatian translation was needed of the Serbian language as used for official proceedings in Serbia, and vice versa. This proposal would have involved making Croats foreigners in Serbia and Serbs in Croatia, and there was strong Governmental reaction to such a shaking of the foundations of 'brotherhood and unity'. Dusty as many of the details seem of Vuk's linguistic controversies and of his co-operation with the 'Illyrian' movement, it should be recognized that he was working steadily in a direction which made 'brotherhood and unity' possible.

XVIII

VUK AS EDITOR AND ARTIST: SONGS, TALES, AND TRANSLATION OF NEW TESTAMENT

I

FROM 1843 to 1850, Vuk's most obvious activities had been his linguistic controversies and his work with the 'Illyrian' movement. But the secret financial agreement which he had reached with Mihail Obrenović in 1844-5 enabled him to pursue the more comprehensive literary programme which he had long had in mind. In 1845 and 1846 appeared the first-fruits of the agreement—the second and third volumes of Vuk's new and revised edition of the Serb 'popular songs', covering the most ancient heroic songs and those of later times, down to the nineteenth century (the first volume of this edition, covering the 'women's' or lyric songs, had appeared in 1841; a fourth volume, of modern heroic songs, was published in 1862; and a fifth volume, including more modern heroic songs of Montenegro, appeared after Vuk's death).

This is a convenient point at which to give some account of Vuk's work as a collector and editor of 'popular songs' and stories. It would perhaps have surprised Vuk to learn that 'popular songs' were still being collected in Yugoslavia until the time of the Second World War, and can no doubt be found in some districts even today.[1] This fact might seem at first sight hard to reconcile with Vuk's own often expressed conviction that he accomplished

[1] See particularly the account of the journeys undertaken by Dr. Matija Murko in 1930-2 to collect popular poetry in *Tragom srpsko-hrvatske narodne epike*, Zagreb, 1951; and *Serbo-Croatian Heroic Songs*, collected by Milman Parry, edited and translated by Albert B. Lord, Harvard and the Serbian Academy of Sciences, 2 vols., 1954. A recording was recently in circulation of a 'popular song' in traditional style on the death of President Kennedy; and I have heard the exploits of Marshal Tito and the Partisans celebrated by a 'guslar' on a formal occasion. Probably such songs represent an artificial revival, but more natural flowers of 'popular song' may no doubt still be found in remote parts of Yugoslavia.

his work of collection at the last possible moment. Vuk was nevertheless right in thinking that his own work was done at a crucial period. In the first place literacy and oral tradition go ill together. As the former begins to flourish, the latter decays. Serbia at the end of the eighteenth century was almost illiterate; with the establishment of an independent state and the circulation of books and newspapers, the narrative and satirical songs began to lose some of their news value. Moreover as Vuk's and other printed collections of songs were circulated,[1] they became known to a number of the remaining singers, even if these had few other sources of written instruction; and they would thus learn as much of their repertoire from books as from oral transmission. But above all a heroic climate is most favourable for the heroic bard and heroic song. Such a climate was created at the end of the eighteenth and beginning of the nineteenth centuries by the behaviour of the Turkish oppressors and by the wars against them. Where the Turks stayed on, and the Slavs fought against them, as in Bosnia and in Montenegro above all, the heroic song continued to flourish; but in Serbia the tradition of heroic poetry declined when it was no longer possible to find poets with direct experience of war, like Vuk's favourite singer, Tešan Podrugović.[2]

Vuk therefore was able to collect at the right period, and recorded much that would probably have been distorted or forgotten without his work. He had further advantages which more than counter-balanced the absence of a tape-recorder. He came from a notable family of singers, and something has been said in Chapter II of his childhood experience of songs sung by his father and uncle, and by visitors to their house. Given his retentive memory, this meant that Vuk started his work of collection with a good idea of what to look for and where to look for it. He knew

[1] Even during Vuk's lifetime, his was not the only printed collection of 'popular songs' in circulation. See Murko, op. cit., pp. 284–92.
[2] These conditions obtained to a limited extent in 1914, if not in 1941. Murko, op. cit., p. 309, for example quotes a song about the London Conference of 1913, featuring:

'Ministar engleski
Što se Kraljem od Engleske ruča,
Prva glava u Engleskoj slavnoj,
Prva glava, Eduarde Greje.'

('The Minister of England, / He who takes meat with the King of England, / First among the men of famous England, / First among them all, Sir Edward Grey.')

moreover how to handle recalcitrant and thirsty sources, as is shown by his account of how he dealt with Starac Milija; and he was sufficiently a part of the local scene on occasion to be able to note one or two of those satiric songs which must have formed a good part of local literary output and were extremely difficult for a stranger to hear and record.[1]

How important Vuk's village background was for his work of collection is shown by his description of the difficulties involved in getting good versions of the 'women's' or lyrical songs:

Young women and girls are usually ashamed to recite or sing in front of strangers. The more they are asked, the more they resist, and besides all of them seemed to think that I was only looking for songs and writing them down for a joke.... So often enough the best singers would make the excuse that they didn't know or even in some cases answer me: 'We're not blind women to sing and recite to you.'[2] In such cases I could often do no better than give presents to small girls who hadn't acquired this sense of shame; they would then begin to sing, and their elders would correct them, often with scolding ('That's not right, you little devil!') until the elders too became gradually easier and less on their best behaviour.

Vuk himself understood well the suspicion that 'popular songs' were being taken down in a spirit of condescension and mockery. He himself had reacted in this way when Mušicki had first asked the young students at Karlovci to note what they knew.

A different obstacle which Vuk had to surmount at Miloš Obrenović's court was the idea put about by Miloš's favourites that there was something ridiculous in solemnly collecting and publishing the 'women's songs' in particular. Not the least of his merits as a collector was that he had the sense of purpose and strength of mind not to be discouraged by this sort of teasing, to which he was subjected both at Kragujevac and from the more cultured Austro-Serbs, who supported the views of the Metropolitan Stratimirović on the literary value of the lyrical 'popular songs'.

In one respect Vuk as a collector suffered from the inhibitions

[1] Murko, op. cit., p. 71, notes that favourite subjects of satiric songs were still unsuccessful wooings or abductions, that such songs were not easy for a stranger to collect, and that the authors preferred to remain anonymous; cf. Chapter II, § 3.
[2] Cf. p. 111 n. 1, for the correlation between blindness and skill in song.

of his age. Particularly after the outcry raised by the Orthodox Church authorities about the coarse words included in his *Dictionary*, he had to be careful about publishing what he called 'ambiguous' songs (*Zweydeutige Lieder*), which might offend conventionally refined taste. It will be uncertain until Vuk's archives are fully published how much material of this sort was collected and remained unprinted. Much may survive, as for example the fifty songs omitted, according to one of Vuk's letters to Kopitar (of 1823) from the Leipzig edition of the 'women's songs' (Book I of his collection). The songs were put on one side for fear of offending the susceptibilities of the Grand Duchess Maria Pavlovna, to whom they were dedicated. In the same letter Vuk quotes a number of songs which might be considered indelicate or undesirable for other reasons (for instance, as tending to subvert religion), and should perhaps be omitted—one of these he says that he is certainly going to print, but better not at that time.[1] At the other end of the spectrum, it seems unlikely that Vuk or his collaborators noted the words of those 'songs for dancing' which he said were so obscene that they could only be sung in the heart of the dance 'when it was thought that they would not be noticed'. In general however Vuk was far from squeamish, and so far as concerns the text of the heroic and historical songs he would not have to make any concessions to the over-refinement of his readers.

All in all the merits of Vuk as a collector are hardly to be questioned. He was also a very capable organizer of other people's work, and by the 1840s had a large network of contributors (one of his principal cares was that they should remain 'exclusive correspondents' and not record songs for the other collectors who were beginning to appear on the Serb literary scene).

The value of Vuk's editorial work on the material which he

[1] In a letter to Kopitar (of 8 December 1823) Vuk lists first a *double entendre* in the injunctions to a bridegroom ('a rose to whom has been given a sprig of rosemary') to water well his sprig of rosemary. The other instances quoted are of blasphemy (a girl who preferred long nights with her lover to paradise), immorality (a girl who poisoned her brother to gain her lover), and indecency of subject-matter rather than expression (a bet between a girl and her lover on which will be the first to make a wanton move when they spend the night together). Cf. Percy, preface to *Reliques of Ancient Poetry*, 1765: 'In a polished age like the present, I am sensible that many of these reliques of antiquity will require great allowances to be made for them. . . . Great care has been taken to admit nothing immoral or indecent.'

collected has been rather more widely disputed, from his own days onwards. During his lifetime he was criticized mainly for appropriating other people's work and reproducing it without change and without acknowledgement, though in fact he did his best to list his sources as soon as he realized the importance of doing so.[1] In more recent times the tendency has been rather to think that he may unduly have distorted the material which he collected, in the interests of literary standards set by himself.

Vuk was of course no dispassionate and scientifically accurate recorder of folk-lore, and his standards were different from those of the ethnographer of today. In the first place, he had a profound sense of the political value of what he was collecting, and of the importance which it possessed as an embodiment of the Serb national spirit (though this did not prevent him from publishing songs which could well have been considered barbarous and detrimental to Serbian prestige). Secondly—and this is a connected point which it is easy to forget—Vuk was an anthologist, not an indiscriminate collector, of 'popular' material; and thirdly, his work as a selector and editor was determined, no less than his work as a collector, by the way in which he knew his material, so to speak, from the inside.

Vuk selected partly because he soon came to realize, once embarked on his life's work in 1814, what an enormous mass of material was available to the collector. He wrote about this to Kopitar in the letter quoted in Chapter VII, in which he outlined his literary programme. A very large quantity of songs, collected only in the parts of the present area of Yugoslavia to which he had access, was left unedited among Vuk's remains. Four collections were published in his lifetime, and five more volumes after his death from the material found among his papers. Large collections, too, of which something has already been said, were published by other editors after his death; and no doubt there is plenty of traditional material, not least among the Moslem population of Yugoslavia, still to be recorded and published.

Another factor very important in the determination of Vuk's method of work was his own knowledge of the nature of oral transmission, and of the great difference in quality between various singers. Yugoslav heroic and other narrative songs are

[1] For an important list of Vuk's sources see preface to Book IV of the 'Leipzig' edition of 'popular songs', published in 1833.

composed in a very simple metre, natural to the rhythm of the language (the ten-syllable line with stresses on the odd rather than the even syllables, or more technically a trochaic pentameter), and they contain a large number of stock phrases or passages. They were therefore easy to memorize—Vuk himself clearly knew a good number by heart, though no singer himself, as the result of listening in his childhood. They were also easy to compose. As Vuk said, once a man knew some fifty by heart, he would have little difficulty in composing others. Thus new episodes could be added without difficulty to the traditional and historical narratives, or current events recorded in the same style. Moreover it was quite possible that even without the addition of new episodes or any deliberate intent to vary, no song would be sung twice in exactly the same way even by the same singer. A bad singer would spoil his songs progressively, a good one would steadily improve his. It was therefore impossible in Vuk's view to attempt any comprehensive record of all the material available, and of all current versions of each song; moreover to do so would mean perpetuating a lot of bad poetry and this would be contrary to his patriotic duty.

Selection and editing were therefore necessary. Vuk did a good deal of both. It is interesting that some of his best 'collecting agents' expected him to do so, and were ready to admit that the result would be an improvement on the raw material which they had provided.[1] It should be remembered in this connection that, before the days of mechanical aids, taking down songs was a chancy and difficult business, particularly from those artists who sang rather than recited. There were few sources like the admirable Tešan Podrugović, who 'had no idea how to sing, or didn't want to, but just recited songs as from a book'. More often songs had to be collected from singers who performed without thinking of the sense of the words, and Vuk's own account of his troubles with Starac Milija indicates the difficulty of taking down songs in these circumstances.

Both in selecting and editing, Vuk relied in the first place on memory of what he had heard in his youth at Tršić; this often provided him with a standard of comparison and stimulated him to search for fuller or more satisfactory versions of traditional

[1] See a very interesting article by Zhivomir Mladenović in *Kovčežić*, i, pp. 64 et seq., 'Vuk as editor of popular songs', especially p. 72.

themes. In the course of his work he evolved certain editorial standards, which he described in the preface to the fourth collection of his 'Leipzig' edition (1833). A coherent and probable story was a principal requirement. In a 'popular song' one should not necessarily look for historical truth, but the narrative as told by a good singer will never be altogether contrary to 'the sound sense of the people and to what is customary in song'. Vuk proceeds to quote some examples of bad versions. The faults which he notes are inconsistency with the majority of good songs (for instance when Prince Marko is made to carry a gun, this is not only historically wrong, but at variance with a famous passage in another song where he laments the invention of firearms as destructive of the true knightly virtues); internal inconsistency within a single song (as when a mother laments her poverty while her baby lies in a golden cradle); and the introduction of obviously inappropriate stock formulas from other songs.

In accordance with these criteria on subject-matter and with his own sense of verbal style, Vuk certainly made a good many small textual changes both in the songs which he copied himself, and even more in those collected for him by his less experienced and skilful correspondents.

The greatest difficulty in the way of assessing Vuk's own contribution to the texts which he published has lain in his habit of destroying the original versions from which he made copies for printing. There are however a number of cases where the original text from one of Vuk's contributors has been preserved along with his own amended version and the final printed text. It is clear that he made his emendations mainly to satisfy his sense of what was linguistically appropriate, or to preserve the ten-syllable metre strictly. He also did not hesitate to delete odd lines that confused the narrative, to insert others in order to clarify it, and occasionally to add stock similes from other and similar songs in order to enhance the poetic effect. The net result however is artistic editing rather than reconstruction of the original.[1] The work still

[1] See Percy, op. cit.: '. . . the old copies, whether manuscript or printed, were often so defective or corrupted, that a scrupulous adherence to their wretched readings would only have exhibited unintelligible nonsense, or such poor meagre stuff, as neither came from the Bard, nor was worthy the press; when, by a few slight corrections or additions, a most beautiful or interesting sense hath started forth and this so naturally and easily, that the Editor could seldom prevail on himself to indulge the vanity of making a formal claim to the improvement. . . .'

proceeding on Vuk's archives at the Serbian Academy of Science and Art may throw more light on the subject. Here it need only be said that, if Vuk fell short of the textual accuracy which would now be demanded in the reproduction of 'popular' material, he did so for his own good reasons; and that his editorial work was carried out with an artistic sense which it would be hard to equal.

2

In his final collection of fifty 'popular tales', published in 1853,[1] and appropriately dedicated to Jakob Grimm, Vuk's editorial role approximated much more nearly to artistic creation. He himself admittedly said in the Preface to his final collection that all that was necessary for reproducing 'popular tales', as for 'popular songs', was 'to collect them faithfully, and without spoiling or corrupting them'; he went on however immediately to say that 'in the writing of tales, one must use one's head and change the words (not according to one's own taste, but according to the genius of the language), so that the whole is in no respect exaggerated, but the learned can read it and the plain man listen to it'.

The material on which he was working was much less uniform in style and phraseology than the 'popular songs' as transmitted by the best of his singers; apart from a number of customary verbal formulas, the rules and customs of prose narrative were far less definite than those of the epic songs. Moreover most of Vuk's originals had circulated and been collected among the Serbs of urban communities in the Austrian Empire, and had lost in the process something of their original rural flavour. Of the fifty tales published in 1853 only ten represented anything that Vuk himself had heard in their original setting, either in his childhood at Tršić or from his favourite singer of tales, Tešan Podrugović. The others were adaptations partly from printed sources, partly from oral versions already much corrupted (one of the best-known tales was given to him by Prince Mihail Obrenović). Vuk's main aims were to put the stories back into their original rural and heroic setting, and to restore something of pace and logic to

[1] Throughout this section I have relied on Miodrag Popović, *Vuk Stefanović Karadžić*, 1964, pp. 425 et seq.; his comparisons of Vuk's final form with the form of the tales as originally heard are based on Vuk's manuscript remains, preserved at the Serbian Academy of Science and Art.

narrative that had often become overgrown with superfluous detail.

Two of Vuk's most typical versions are given in translation at Appendix A, and his artistry may fairly be judged from these. One or two further examples of his method of work may be given, in the form of pairs of quotations, the first in each case from Vuk's source, the second from Vuk's own version. He was always intent on clarifying the narrative and shortening the rambling sentences. Thus:

(i) (Source) 'There was once a man who had a shepherd or herdsman who served him faithfully.'
(ii) (Vuk) 'A certain man had a servant who had served him faithfully and honestly for many years.'

He cut to the minimum love-interest and evidence of fashionable 'sensibility' (though he also removed the coarser passages on which he had remarked when replying to Kopitar's original inquiry about folk-tales). Thus:

(i) (Source) 'He couldn't cast the girl out of his mind, but was so much in love with her that he was ready to die for her.'
(ii) (Vuk) 'In the end he decided to go out into the world to look for her, and not to come back till he had found her.'

Vuk liked to add touches of true popular idiom to simple phrases. Thus:

(i) (Source) 'Go and tell your father.'
(ii) (Vuk) 'Run quick as quick to your father and tell him what has happened.'

Finally he would add phrases to transport the reader into an epic and archaic world. Thus:

(i) (Source) 'Tell me, when my father was Tsar, where were his weapons and where was his horse?'
(ii) (Vuk) 'Tell me, when my father was Tsar, where were the weapons that he girt on him, and where the horse on which he rode?'

It should not be forgotten that Vuk's object in collecting examples of 'popular' poems and stories was not to facilitate the production of theses on comparative literature. He wanted to exhibit the spirit of Serbia to the world in as pure a form as possible; and for him it was best exemplified by the rural heroic Serbia of medieval times. It was with this in mind that he adapted the 'popular tales' and in so doing accomplished some of his most original literary work.

3

If Vuk was most completely the creative artist in his retelling of 'popular tales', his version of the New Testament was also far from being exclusively a work of scholarship. The publication of Vuk's translation in 1847, and its ultimate circulation in Serbia in 1859, was in the opinion of many Yugoslav critics not only a decisive victory in Vuk's battle with the authorities of the Orthodox Church, but also an important landmark in the development of Serbo-Croat literary prose. Vuk's own preface makes it clear that his first object was to meet the real need for an unambiguous and intelligible translation: 'Judging only by the Slavonic translation, no one can say where it is faithful and where it is not. There are places where no sense can be got out of the words, even if you were to study the Slavonic tongue for a hundred years; and there are others where we are bound to be in considerable doubt whether we have understood or not. So I think that even our greatest experts on the word of God, if up to this time they have had to rely on the Slavonic text alone, will only now and with the help of my translation be able properly to understand many passages of the New Testament.' But accuracy had not been his only aim. He had done all he could to see that his translation was in the purest popular language. The judgement of Daničić, who was academically much better qualified than Vuk, was that his master had triumphantly succeeded in this and had 'raised a memorial to the Serbian tongue such as few peoples can pride themselves on, a memorial which will always clearly illustrate to the learned world the living tongue of the people for whom it was written'.

Vuk did more in his translation than simply reproduce a particular version of popular speech. The view of his most recent Yugoslav biographer is that by fusing some elements of the normal spoken language with some of Church Slavonic he was able to achieve a new popular literary style. His first acquaintance with letters had been in the form of the Church Slavonic psalter and Book of Hours, and he had a deep feeling for the rhythm of the old language. The sureness of his instinct is shown by the fact that some of the occasional Slavonic-type words which he coined for his translation (to cover abstract qualities) were subsequently found in Slavonic texts not available to him. His main effort was to avoid the 'Russifications' of the later Slavonic-Serbian language, which had gained ground in the eighteenth century. And of course he had acquired in the course of his travels a wide knowledge of the varieties of popular speech in much of the present area of Yugoslavia. In his translation of the New Testament he did not confine himself to the dialect of Hercegovina but drew on his full linguistic experience in the choice or formation of words.

It would be out of place in a general work of this nature to try to illustrate in detail the problems which he faced or the skill with which he solved them; but two points may be mentioned where both the problems and the solutions of the original English translators seem to have been parallel. In the Church Slavonic language there were a large number of participles. Vuk in his translation very often got round these by relative clauses or other means, e.g. 'the voice of him that crieth in the wilderness' rather than 'the voice of one crying in the wilderness', or 'out of pity' rather than 'pitying'. Again Church Slavonic, like ancient Greek, was rich in small emphatic particles. These had no equivalent in popular Serb, but in order to preserve something like the rhythm of the original Vuk often replaced them by conjunctions 'and', 'for', etc. The point is a little harder to illustrate in double translation. Where the Old Slavonic text says roughly 'evening thus being come', Vuk's version ran 'and when it was evening'; or for the Old Slavonic 'From thee now shall spring forth', Vuk said 'For from thee shall spring forth'.

Vuk's translation of the New Testament was all in all a considerable artistic achievement, and had a long-term and wide literary effect. It deeply influenced the spoken and written language of the Serb people. Its effect may indeed have been more than literary. Knowledge of the New Testament in their own tongue probably affected the Serbian style of thought, and the resulting links with the traditions of Protestant Christianity perhaps helped to foster that independence of mind and speech for which the Serbs have remained notable.

XIX

PUBLICATION OF NEW TESTAMENT AND REVISED DICTIONARY

I

VUK's translation of the New Testament was substantially the same in 1847 as that which he had made in 1820 after his negotiations with the Russian Bible Society. The story of its final publication and circulation, in which the London Bible Society played an important part, deserves to be briefly told or recapitulated. For some time Vuk's translation had been superseded, so far as the Bible Societies in England and Russia were concerned, by the translation (based on Vuk's) of Atanasije Stojković; this had been printed in Leipzig in 1830, at the expense of the London Bible Society (the Russian was dissolved in 1826). It had not received, any more than Vuk's version, the blessing of the Metropolitan of Karlovci, and was not allowed to circulate either in the Austrian provinces or in Serbia. Nevertheless, it seems that two quite large editions were printed at Leipzig, and that it was a third edition which appeared in 1834. In informing Vuk of this (it was the first that he heard of the publication of the Stojković translation), Šafařík found it impossible to explain how the copies had been disposed of.[1] The mystery is not entirely cleared up by the correspondence of the London Bible Society,[2] though it

---

[1] Šafařík wrote: 'Where have all the copies of the first two editions been distributed? Among the Serbs in Hungary and Slavonia? I haven't seen a single copy; and you assure me that this is the case too in the rest of Serbia. It occurs to me that the Bible Society may have sent the whole edition to Petrograd, where instead of to Serbia it's gone into the fire or the toilet for want of a better destination. . . . It looks as if just this happened to the Bulgarian New Testament, printed at London in 1828 or 1829.'

[2] The relevant extracts were located by Professor Elizabeth Hill in the archives of the Bible Society in London, and copies were presented by her to the Serb Academy of Science and Art for the Vuk Centenary celebrations in 1964. Professor Hill kindly drew my attention to this, and the Academy and the Vuk Museum in Belgrade kindly gave me access to her gift.

emerges from this that 1,000 copies of the 1830 edition went to their depository in London, and that in 1838 900 copies of Serbian New Testaments (presumably the third edition of 1834) were on their hands at Leipzig.

In 1836 Vuk's old and main enemy, the Metropolitan Stratimirović, died, but Vuk did not immediately try to secure the approval of the new Metropolitan for the publication of the New Testament in his own translation. No doubt the thought of the expenses involved was a sufficient deterrent, apart from all his other occupations. It was not until 1845, when he had secured financial help from Prince Mihail, that Vuk reverted to the subject with the Orthodox Church authorities.

The Metropolitan by this time was Josip Rajačić, who as Bishop of Šibenik in Dalmatia had been enthusiastic for Vuk's work, and had collected subscribers for his book of *Proverbs* and description of Montenegro. Rajačić had in 1844 told Vuk that he would give his approval to the translation of the New Testament, and in 1846 promised that it would be allowed to appear with a specific note to that effect. But his assurance of 1846 was accompanied by a request that Vuk should send him the translation for inspection. Vuk had learned bitter lessons about the dangers of sending his manuscripts to the proper authorities. In this case he gave the manuscript instead for printing to the Mehitarist press in Vienna. Only in spring 1847 did he send any text to the Metropolitan Rajačić, and then it was in the form of printed proofs. At the same time he tried to insure against a change of heart on the part of Rajačić by getting an episcopal blessing from Njegoš;[1] but the Prince Bishop of Montenegro was by now unwilling to let himself in for trouble on this issue with the Serbian Orthodox Church: 'If you'd asked my blessing for the liberation of the Serbs from intolerable oppression,' he told Vuk, 'for that I am your only true Bishop, but you're not demanding this, and I'm not the man for what you are asking.'

Vuk's caution with regard to Rajačić was entirely justified. The Metropolitan had agreed with Vuk that a critical comparison of the new version with the Church Slavonic text should be conducted by a committee consisting of Vuk himself, Rajačić, and two of the latter's ecclesiastical staff. This examination was duly begun, but

---

[1] This was the second time of asking; see p. 274 n. 1.

it soon became clear that Rajačić was under strong pressure to oppose Vuk's version. When he realized this, Vuk had his translation published in Vienna without the prior approval of any authority of the Serbian Orthodox Church—but also, as he was able later to point out, without any objection from the Vienna censorship. He included in his preface an implicit challenge to the Church: 'Had the censors at Karlovci specified with regard to my translation whether they had found in it anything against the doctrines of the Church, I would have corrected anything proved to have been a mistake and had the pages on which such things appeared reprinted.'

The reaction of the Church authorities to Vuk's action was predictably violent. In September 1847 the *Serbian News* of Belgrade carried a notice saying that the translation had been published in an underhand way, without the approval of the Church, and that neither the Metropolitan nor the Ministry of Culture would permit its circulation in Serbia. This ban was proclaimed without any consultation of the Council in Belgrade; Vuk, on the advice of friends, protested to the Council against it and took the chance of sending copies of his translation for their inspection. In his covering letter he insisted rather too much to be convincing that he 'loved and honoured our Orthodox Church as much as any Serb'; but his main effort was directed to meet what was now the principal charge against him, that in issuing his translation he was acting as the agent of the Roman Catholic Church, and was helping to facilitate the conversion of the Orthodox population into Uniates. His principal argument was logical enough: 'Why should the propaganda of Rome at its own expense provide our people with what is forbidden to those of its own faith? What would it gain, as an enemy of our faith, by allowing our people to have access to God's word in their own pure tongue; and what harm would that do to us and our faith? Would not this prove that the propaganda of Rome is a much greater friend and benefactor of our people and faith and language than many of our so-called patriots?' With his logical arguments, Vuk typically mixed some hard-hitting debating points against the Austro-Serbs. He was, he said, being persecuted by men who had gone over to Serbia at the sound of money clinking, 'like locusts who go about the world after grass and leaves. And why do they persecute me? Because I am a Serb born, and they think it shame that the learned world should judge from my works that I, who was born and brought up in Serbia and did not spend so long in schools as they, should know something—particularly in what concerns our people—better than the lot of them.' The Belgrade authorities however were not to be moved by logic or emotion.

Public opinion in Serbia, so far as it concerned itself with these things, was behind them or at least did not dare to express itself against them. The newspapers were bitter and frequent in their attacks and even Vuk's firmest supporters on linguistic questions found it hard to defend him against some of the more detailed accusations of the pious and conservative. Thus it was widely felt that Vuk had stuck too closely to the Vulgate text, that he had too often left out familiar verses from the Church Slavonic version; and—an echo of the old criticism of his *Dictionary*—that he had a weakness for coarse and shocking language. Apropos, for instance, of the phrase 'The kings of this world went a-whoring after her', one of his friends wrote that 'these are words which no one would dare to pronounce today in polite society' and 'if Christ himself were to return to earth, I think that today he would pay rather more attention to etiquette and be careful not to offend our weaknesses, just because they are weaknesses. With other peoples this is easier, just as it will become easier with us, when people have gradually become accustomed to seeing such words printed—but with us this has never been the case until the appearance of your *Dictionary*. . . .' To which Vuk briskly replied: 'I am not responsible for the fact that the Holy Scriptures are in certain places not to some people's taste and I think that such people are wrong; anyone who thinks that Holy Writ is holy, should not stretch its words and correct them according to his understanding, but should adapt his understanding to them.'

Vuk's eminent friends were reluctant to get themselves into conflict with the Serbian Orthodox Church by any intervention on his behalf.[1] Vuk's young admirer, Daničić, wrote a full and very favourable review, comparing Vuk's with many previous versions, much to its advantage; but no editor in Serbia or Hungary dared to print this review, and it was not published until 1862. A few favourable criticisms were however published, and one of them caused a good deal of controversy. It was a short notice in the

---

[1] Šafařík was asked to review the translation, but cried off saying that he did little reviewing and that his health was deteriorating.

Russian journal *Northern Bee*, and unfortunately mentioned incidentally that Vuk was under the protection of Prince Miloš Obrenović. Miloš was unwilling that his chances of return to the Serbian throne should be compromised by any quarrel on behalf of Vuk with the Serbian Orthodox Church, and publicly disclaimed any connection with Vuk's translation.[1] The net result of all this was that the translation made no headway in Serbia. The Metropolitan Rajačić had more trouble in stopping its circulation in the Austrian Empire. He rather reluctantly requested the Hungarian Chancellery in Buda to decree the confiscation of the copies already sent to booksellers and the Orthodox Bishop of Temesvar anticipated their decision by forbidding the local bookseller to sell it. Vuk again argued that this action was illegal on the grounds that the translation had been printed without any objection from the censorship in Vienna, and that this in itself implied that circulation should be free. He also argued that in any case it was already circulating 'more or less all around Europe'.[2] No doubt Vuk would have come off worse in this debate too, had not the issue been anticipated by the revolutions of March 1848 and the abolition of the Hungarian Chancellery at Buda.

This opened the way for the free circulation of Vuk's translation among the Serbs of the Vojvodina, Vienna, Trieste, etc. At the same time Vuk's dealings with the English Bible Society, so often frustrated since 1819, at last began to bear fruit. As far back as January 1840, the Society had received a letter from a Vienna correspondent, casting doubt on the value of the Stojković version and reminding them that Vuk's existed and might now obtain ecclesiastical approval for circulation, particularly in Serbia.[3] Nothing seems to have come of this for some time. In the summer of 1848, however, when it was clear that Rajačić's attempt to prevent the circulation of Vuk's translation in Austria-Hungary had failed, Vuk wrote to Bowring in London, sending a presentation copy of his translation for the Bible Society, and suggesting

[1] Miloš went further and attacked the Matica Srpska for not having raised their voice effectively against Vuk's translation.

[2] The basis for this statement was presumably that some copies had been sent by Vuk to friends in Germany.

[3] Kopitar, who was still alive, expressed doubt about the attitudes of the Metropolitan (Stratimirović's immediate successor) and of the Vienna police. In any case it appears from the Bible Society's records that they were unimpressed by their correspondent's suggestion, and authorized only a few weeks later a new edition of the Stojković version.

that they should buy 1,000 copies of his version for £500. Complicated negotiations ensued, involving Vuk and the Society's representatives in Frankfurt and Vienna. An agreement between Vuk and the Bible Society was finally signed in January 1851, on terms rather less favourable than those which he had proposed in 1848.[1] The new edition did not appear until 1857, but shortly afterwards it was allowed to circulate in Serbia, when in 1859 the ban was finally lifted on books printed in Vuk's orthography and imported from abroad into Serbia. The usual criticism was voiced from the usual quarters, and Vuk was defending himself as late as 1862 against published charges that he was exposing the mysteries of Holy Scripture to the common people, whose mind was not fitted to understand it, and that at the prompting of the Vatican his translation exaggerated the role of St. Peter. But by then it was sufficient for Vuk to put his own case to the ruling Prince Mihail Obrenović. The circulation of his translation of the New Testament continued; by this time too the London Bible Society was interested in a Serb translation of the Old Testament, which was entrusted to Daničić, and appeared finally together with a third edition of Vuk's New Testament in 1871.

2

By 1850 the principal item outstanding in the literary programme which Vuk had long before set himself was a revised edition of his *Dictionary*. This finally appeared in 1852. It was much larger than the first edition, including 47,000 instead of 26,000 entries, and covering geographically words from much of Serbia, Croatia, Dalmatia and Montenegro, as well as from Vuk's native district of Jadar and the Srem province, which were the main sources of the words in the first edition. In other respects the *Dictionary* remained, in its second as in its first edition, much more than a linguistic work; it continued to provide as much material for the ethnographer as for the etymologist. Many of the new entries were illustrated by fragments of popular poetry, to show the words in their proper context, and, if Vuk was unwilling to go into etymological history, he again provided his readers with much

---

[1] The original offer (1848) was 2,000 florins (£200) for 1,000 copies, and the right to print a further edition of 5,000 copies.

historical background about the customs and social life of the South Slav peoples.

In preparing the revision of his *Dictionary*, Vuk worked closely with his young and distinguished disciple, Daničić. Their collaboration was not without its difficulties. Daničić had done a great deal of the hard work of collecting the Serb material, as well as translating it into German and Latin. He had hoped to produce, with the prestige of Vuk to back him, a complete and scientific Dictionary, including obsolete as well as current words, and covering written as well as oral sources. Vuk stuck to his own conception of the *Dictionary* as providing a guide exclusively to the living and spoken tongue; he included only words which he himself had heard, or which his main sources guaranteed to be part of current speech in their various districts. It was Vuk who had his way, and Daničić felt a certain bitterness about this, as well as some resentment that Vuk had not been or could not be lavish in paying him for his work, and had acknowledged his massive contribution with nothing more than a reference in the preface.

Any estrangement between the colleagues was however temporary, and the *Dictionary* involved Vuk in much greater difficulties of a familiar kind. There were indeed many advance subscribers to the new edition—more than 300 in Serbia alone. Many eminent Croatians also subscribed, amongst them Jurij Strossmayer, then Bishop of Djakovo, who did much in later years for the cause of 'Illyrian' or Yugoslav unity.[1] But Vuk's enemies in Belgrade, still infuriated by the publication of his New Testament translation, were active against him. The old charge of obscenity was countered by Vuk's advance announcement that doubtful words were omitted in the second edition, and his enemies changed to other though also familiar ground. The nature of their charges emerges from a long letter which Vuk sent in 1851 to an illiterate but influential member of the Council in Belgrade, Stefan Khičanin: 'Last year you told me as I left your house [Vuk had been on a visit to Belgrade in 1850] that there are people who say that the harm done to our country by the collapse of the Kingdom at Kosovo is nothing to that which I want to do with my alphabet; and that I have

---

[1] Jurij Strossmayer (1815–1905) was appointed Bishop of Djakovo in 1849; he spent a large part of the revenue of his see on financing secondary schools and seminaries, where Serbo-Croat rather than Magyar was the language of instruction, and he founded the University of Zagreb.

been bought by the Austrian Government ... in order to make Uniates and Catholics of our people.' Vuk was at pains to show how little money he had received for his translation of the New Testament,[1] and how absurd it was to suspect Kopitar of any catholicizing tendencies. He represented Kopitar as a sceptic about organized religion and argued that he would have become a Court Councillor at Vienna many instead of a few years before his death, had he been such an active Catholic propagandist as he was represented to be in Serbia. A new argument which Vuk introduced was the impropriety or inexpediency of forbidding the circulation of books already printed elsewhere. He cited an interesting contemporary instance of which he may have heard from Ranke. When Strauss's *Life of Christ*—that very important prototype of the new Biblical criticism—was published (in 1835), the King of Prussia was said to have asked an eminent authority whether to forbid its circulation in Prussia, and to have received the answer: 'If the people accepted the thought of the book, then the days of our present Christian faith are over; but in any case, the book is such a work of scholarship that I dare not tell you to ban it.' The most striking proof of how seriously Vuk had taken his opponents' charges, and of his increased self-confidence, was the suggestion that a special commission should be appointed to decide whether these were well-founded; if they were, he said (rather rashly), it was surely a scandal that the Serbian Government should continue to pay him a pension.

Once again however Vuk argued in vain with those in authority. He was allowed to appear personally before the Council in Belgrade in February 1852 and to read out to them his letters. But the crucial session of the Council went against him. The ban on publication in Serbia of books printed in Vuk's alphabet was now extended to cover books imported to Serbia from abroad. Vuk's appeals to the Council and personally to Prince Alexander Karadjordjević went unanswered. The circulation of the second edition of Vuk's *Dictionary* was thus forbidden, and the 300 copies sent from Vienna to subscribers in Serbia were held at the customs house in Belgrade. Eventually Vuk managed to have them transferred to Zemun through the Austrian Consul, and in 1855 the 'Society for Literary Culture' in Belgrade obtained permission to import a few copies for scientific purposes. In the meantime

[1] Vuk failed to mention his contract of 1851 with the Bible Society.

however Vuk had had to refund money to the subscribers from Serbia. Thus the ban on his *Dictionary* was a financial blow to him as well as a severe discouragement. The circulation in Serbia of Vuk's revised *Dictionary*, as of his translation of the New Testament, had to await the restoration of the Obrenović dynasty at the end of the decade.

XX

FAMILY LIFE AND LAST YEARS

I

VUK's financial position was secured by 1845, and by the end of the 1840s he had attained the position of the Grand Old Man of Slavonic Studies in Vienna. His house was a place of resort and pilgrimage for young scholars from the South Slav lands and from Russia in particular. It is largely from their letters, diaries, and reminiscences that we can form some picture of his private life, habits, and conversation in his old age. By 1842 he was settled in new lodgings off the Landstrasse. His wife was still with him, a shadowy figure who survived until well after his own death. Of their numerous children, only two survived by the end of the 1840s, Dimitrije, born in 1836, and Wilhelmina (Mina) born in 1828. Dimitrije grew up to be trained as an officer in the Serbian Army, and survived his parents. He had early become acquainted with a hard-drinking and hard-gambling set of officers, and caused much concern to his ageing parents.[1] Dimitrije was no substitute for Vuk's favourite and most talented son, Sava, who had been sent to St. Petersburg in 1834 as a scholar of the College for young mining engineers, and had died there as a boy of 17 in 1837. Mina was the only surviving child to inherit anything of Vuk's tastes and gifts, and emerges from contemporary accounts as a lively and accomplished person, who must have added much to the attractions of Vuk's house, besides acting as his secretary for correspondence in German and herself translating his *Serbian Popular Tales* into German.

A young Austrian historian and travel-writer, Siegfried Kapper, who made a tour of Bosnia, Serbia, and Bulgaria in 1850–1, left an attractive sketch of life in Vuk's household about 1850:

[1] Dimitrije Karadžić, after nine years of professional training in Austria, Berlin, and Belgium, served in Serbia from 1858 until after Vuk's death. In 1866 he had to resign from the Serb Army and entered Russian service, taking part in the Serbo-Turkish war of 1876. The place and date of his death are uncertain.

Let it be said that no visitor to Vuk Stefanović Karadžić should expect such palaces as France provides for example for her Lamartine. You would not find a servant there either. . . . But all the heartier is the welcome which will be given by the honoured lady of the house or her accomplished daughter. From the hall, you enter straight into the chamber where Vuk works, a large and quite sparsely furnished room, where you may look in vain for the most ordinary conveniences of the average scholar—big bookcases, tables with maps, globes, and rare books. All you'll find is a single and simple old table, a few chairs, and, I think, one bookcase. On the chairs a few books are scattered, but far more loose papers, some proofs, some in manuscript—some corrected, some just begun, some left aside, and some finished. At the table, with his back to the window, sits Vuk, a figure bent with age, with features of the South Slav type and long grey moustaches, a common red fez on his head,[1] and in his hand an old-fashioned plaything from the east, approved at some time by the Church as an aid to piety—a rosary.

From Vuk's room, the visitor entered 'the shrine of Wilhelmina', where she kept her small library 'of the best German, French, Italian, and English authors, together with a selection of the latest literature. In this room she conducted some of her father's correspondence with the learned world of Germany, France, and England; here she would work at the translation of Serbian popular proverbs and tales, which was afterwards to be published in Berlin with a preface by Jakob Grimm; here too she would paint and sketch, in these arts too going well beyond a normal amateur's skill.'

It was in the dining-room, furnished with a piano ('the only luxury article in the house') and with portraits of contemporary Serb heroes, that the Serbs of Vienna would assemble for social gatherings on Sunday afternoons, together with Czechs, Moravians, and Slovenians and occasionally some tradesman or priest from Serbia, Bosnia, Hercegovina, etc. The entertainment was very gay. Immediately after lunch people would come and stay till all hours of the night. The talk would be in German, Serb, Russian, French, Italian, or whatever was convenient for the guests present. A good deal of time would be spent on serious affairs, and only afterwards would merriment prevail. If no one else was there to do so, Vuk's daughter would act as mistress of ceremonies with innocent and occasionally provocative skill. Vuk would generally sit in a corner on his sofa, not

---

[1] The fez was worn by Vuk and others as a sign of patriotic Serbian opposition to the Austrian way of life.

very talkative, fingering his rosary bead by bead, looking on with pleasure and now and again taking part in one or other game. If anyone asked him a question, he would answer briefly but always to the point, or would just smile and shrug his shoulders. By his side sat the lady of the house, an amiable and respectable Viennese; she too would take full delight in the fun, again more as a spectator than as a participant. When we'd had music and touched lightly on serious subjects and grumbled seriously about unimportant ones, it would be time for party games. No one then would despise 'Black Peter' or be afraid of the 'Journey to Hell'. Vuk would agree to play and everyone would smile happily when the old man was the first to get the black mark with a piece of coal, and when in due course the translator of the Holy Scriptures was the first to go down to 'hell'. 'Goodness me' said, a young Serb professor on one occasion, 'isn't it a disgrace, our great Vuk is now where Dante once was!' Then to refresh ourselves after such goings on, they would bring us a snack to eat, and everyone would take particular pleasure in a kind of maize tea; this was a wonderful drink of which the secret was held in Vuk's kitchen alone.

Mina Karadžić was clearly an attractive girl, if no classical beauty, and did not lack suitors at an early age. A serious claimant was the young Russian physician, Flor Ognev, who came to Vienna in 1846 on finishing his studies and fell deeply in love with Mina.[1] He sought and obtained his parents' permission, asked for Mina's hand, and after a long delay the two were formally betrothed in 1847. Thereafter it seems that Vuk made very searching inquiries from Flor's parents about what they could do materially for their son, and pitched his own and Mina's demands very high. She would have to live in Moscow in decent style, by which he understood good lodgings in a fashionable quarter, a carriage, a coachman, cook, at least one housemaid, and two teachers; not at all, in fact, the way of life to which Mina had been brought up. It is hardly surprising that Flor's parents were unwilling to make any such guarantees, and early in June 1848 Mina wrote to Flor in Russia breaking off the engagement.

The whole episode is strange. Admittedly Flor was rather hump-backed, but this seemed to have nothing to do with the case. Vuk must have had plenty of opportunity of discussing

---

[1] For details about the Russian doctor of medicine, Flor Sergievich Ognev, see article by N. Ranošević, *Kovčević*, iii, pp. 142 et seq. Ognev later said that one of Mina's most attractive qualities was 'her presence of mind and daring; when bathing she would jump into the water from a steep and high rock'.

MINA KARADŽIĆ-VUKOMANOVIC
(Vuk's daughter)

Flor's prospects—which in fact proved to be excellent—directly with him in Vienna, and checking on them through some of his Russian friends. Perhaps his wife, still a devout and narrow-minded Catholic, prevailed on her husband and daughter to break off the engagement with an Orthodox Russian; perhaps a new and more favoured suitor had appeared in the Karadžić household.

The most intimate members of Vuk's family circle in the late 1840s and early 1850s were the poet Branko Radičević[1] and the young philologist Djuro Daničić. Mina Karadžić towards the end of her life reminisced about them to a friend:

Do I remember Branko? Are such happy memories so easily forgotten? I think of him often, sometimes with sorrow, sometimes with joy. I would say that I can still see him before my eyes. He was every day in our house, as a son or brother. And that's not surprising. You know how Vuk liked to collect around him our young men of talent, and his sharp eye could not miss Branko's rare wit and warm heart. So Vuk loved Branko as his own, and was a tender father, a true friend, and a conscientious teacher to him. I can only now realize entirely the full worth of this for Branko's mind, and what it meant to him. At that time I was busy, and still had much to learn, and couldn't judge as I can now. Today I know very well what was the reason for this gay young man haunting all day long the serious Vuk's study, and why Branko was so happy to take the old invalid by the hand and escort him to the 'Waterglass' café. . . .

It was widely rumoured at the time by Vuk's enemies that Branko and Daničić were both in love with Mina, and that this was the reason for their frequenting Vuk's house, and supporting his literary theories. Love clearly had little to do with their views on language, but it is at least possible that Vuk had hoped for Branko (who died early in 1853) as a son-in-law. There is an interesting passage in the reminiscences of Imbro Tkalac which bears this out, though the dates are somewhat confused:

After I married in Germany in 1848, and returned in 1849 to Croatia, it was obvious that I should visit Vuk in Vienna myself and introduce

---

[1] Branko Radičević (1824–53) was the most famous Serb lyric poet of the nineteenth century. His first volume of poems was published in 1847, and two others appeared in 1851 and (posthumously) in 1863. In them he broke completely with the 'classical' style affected in the eighteenth century. He was a great admirer of the 'popular poetry' published by Vuk, and himself helped Vuk to collect songs and words. He was also an active and unsparing opponent of Vuk's enemies on linguistic matters.

my wife to him. The ladies were talking separately when Vuk said to me: 'It's odd. I'd always thought that you'd ask for Mina's hand.' These words struck me like a bolt from the blue. I answered that I'd always looked on Mina and loved her as a sister, but had never thought of her as a woman or as a possible wife for me. And I'd never suspected that such a thought had been in Vuk's head. And, finally, would Mina have married me herself? I had the feeling that Vuk wasn't pleased with this reply, so I added: 'Vuk, it seems that we Panslavists are fated to marry Germans. Look at you, Šafařík, Kolár, Palacki, all with German wives! Is it any wonder that I followed your example?' Vuk smiled and said: 'You're absolutely right! Yes, *mein Gott*, when you fall in love, you don't ask what is the girl's nationality. We're all like that in our youth.' Had I been able to guess that Vuk had destined Mina for me after the premature death of Branko Radičević, my life would have taken a completely different direction. . . .

Mina eventually married in 1858 outside the circle of Vuk's Slavist acquaintance. Her choice was a Professor at the Belgrade Lyceum, Aleksa Vukomanović, whose material circumstances were far worse than those of the rejected Flor Ognev. Again there was a long engagement (from 1856) at first kept secret from Vuk and his wife. It was an ill-starred marriage. Within little more than a year, Vukomanović had died, leaving Mina with an infant son, Janko, to devote herself again to the care of her father's last years. Poor Janko, Vuk's only grandchild, suffered much the same fate as his favourite son, Sava. Mina brought up her son in Vienna after Vuk's death; when he had finished his course there at the 'Academic Gymnasium,' she was persuaded against her inclination to send him on a scholarship from the Russian Government to the 'Pages' School' in St. Petersburg. There he died of dysentery in his first year of studies (about 1875). Mina was broken-hearted, cut herself off from the world for several years and died in 1894.

In the early 1850s, however, Vuk's life in Vienna was as settled and fortunate as any that he ever enjoyed. His international fame as a scholar was at its height, and many new distinctions were conferred upon him. In 1848 he had been elected a member of the Viennese Academy, and in 1850 was awarded the Franz Josef Cross by the Kaiser. In the same year he was elected a corresponding member of the Berlin Academy of Sciences at the instance of the brothers Grimm, and of the Russian Geographical Society in St. Petersburg, and was given a diamond ring by Tsar Nicolas I. In 1851 he was also elected corresponding member of the literary

FAMILY LIFE AND LAST YEARS 339

department of the Russian Academy of Sciences. Perhaps his most curious distinction was to become (in 1848) an honorary member of the African Institute of Paris.

Small wonder that Vuk was not easily tempted away from Vienna at this time; efforts were made to attract him to Serbia, but these were unlikely to be successful while the ban on the printing or import of books in his orthography was still in force. He had a good case against the charge of lacking patriotism and put it strongly in a letter of March 1852 to Stanišić, one of the members of the Council in Belgrade:

I live in Vienna, not because life here is more pleasant to me than in Serbia, but simply because I can do more good for our people here than there. The various plots that have been inspired against me in Serbia show that I couldn't have done any of my literary work there; indeed . . . even here my enemies from Serbia worry me and hinder my work.

Thus it's not true that I am at fault for not being in Belgrade among the members of the Council. It would be my fault only if our Government had elected me to the Council and sent me a diploma to that effect, and then I hadn't accepted it. . . .

Please do not think that I intend this letter as a complaint for not being a member of the Council, or that I worry about this; God forbid, I am simply answering your reproach. I would only worry at not being a member of the Council, if I knew that in that position I could do more good for our people than by my literary work, and otherwise not at all.

As for the fact that, if I were a member of the Council in Belgrade, I would have a house, and perhaps some business and some land near Belgrade, that concerns me very little I prefer to have written and published just those two books which my enemies—helped by you, my friends—have banned in Serbia, i.e. the New Testament and *Serbian Dictionary* than to have as much property as all you Councillors and Ministers put together.

2

In fact, though Vuk was unwilling to accept any official position in Serbia under the Karadjordje regime, he travelled regularly between Serbia and Vienna from 1850 to the end of his life; 1853 was the only year in which he did not leave Austria (for fear of the effects in Serbia of the Russo-Turkish war which developed into the Crimean war). In particular Vuk frequently visited the scenes of his childhood at Loznica and Tršić.[1]

---
[1] One of these journeys (1850) was made in the company of Mina and an

Vuk's interest in his native district was not entirely sentimental. He had long cherished the idea of becoming a man of property, and as far back as 1820 there had been talk, not entirely in jest, between him and Miloš Obrenović about the possibility of him becoming a landowner in Tršić.[1] From 1849 on he concerned himself earnestly with the farming of what remained of the Karadžić land in Tršić; from 1851 he began to round this off with fresh purchases; in 1857 he purchased a large property near Loznica for a very considerable sum (over 1,000 ducats) and in doing so incurred debts which were settled for him by Miloš Obrenović in a final act of grace just before Miloš's death in 1860. The business of managing his large new property involved Vuk in a good deal of further expense, and even litigation; his efforts to collect personal debts owed to him at this time reveal a marked streak of peasant meanness.

As has already appeared from the story of Mina's engagement with Flor Ognev, Vuk's ideas of a suitable standard of living had grown with the years, and rather faster than his means. Before 1845 he found it hard to keep alive at all, and afterwards hard to live up to the new standard which he set for himself. His income from the sale of his books was small and irregular. He was generous in giving copies away, not least to students, reading-rooms,[2] etc.; and literary piracy, particularly of the songs about Prince Marko, began to diminish his sales. In fact he needed to build up his assets and credit, and sought to do so as persistently as he had previously begged the means of bare livelihood. His requests covered a hereditary title of nobility and an increase in his pension from the Russian Government, and (a hardy annual) payment of the pension withheld from him by the Karadjordje Government in Serbia in 1842–3.[3]

Irish lady, Mrs. Louise Kerr, who had translated Ranke's *Serbian Revolution* into English, and had been introduced by Ranke to the Karadžić family. Mina left a lively account of the journey in a travel-diary, and there are records of conversations with Mrs. Kerr about it. (See *Susreti s Vukom*, pp. 148 et seq., and *Kovčežić*, vi, pp. 208–11, article by Jeremija D. Mitrović.) It is clear from Vuk's correspondence that he found Mrs. Kerr a nervous and exhausting companion.

[1] One of the charges made against Vuk by Hadzić in 1843 was that he had been bribed to act for Miloš by the promise of the 'Spahiluk' of Tršić. Vuk said in defence that this was just a joke between Miloš and himself, but there are passages in his letters to Vasa Popović at Miloš's court which show Vuk to have thought quite seriously on the subject.

[2] 'Reading-rooms' or study centres were an important means of national self-affirmation for Slavs in the Austrian Empire.

[3] Vuk secured payment of the arrears which he reckoned as his due after the return of Miloš Obrenović to Serbia in 1859.

PLATE 3

VUK'S HOUSE AT TRŠIĆ, AS RESTORED

PLATE 4

VIEW OF BELGRADE, 1849

FAMILY LIFE AND LAST YEARS

In the meantime Vuk's main source of income was the collection and sale of old books and manuscripts. From his earliest years in Vienna he had collected on behalf of Kopitar, who would buy material from him for the Vienna Court Library. By 1840 he had organized a network among his friends for the purchase of specimens which he sold at considerable profit in Berlin as well as Vienna; and from 1845 onwards, he found his main client in Pogodin, the Russian historian. Vuk received large sums from Russia on this account—about 5,000 rubles in 1846-7 alone.

His principal source of books and manuscripts in these years was Dalmatia and Montenegro, and one of his most trusted agents was his old friend from his journey of 1835, Vuk Vrčević, secretary of Prince Danilo of Montenegro (Njegoš's successor) and Austrian Consul at Trebinje. In 1853 they became involved in a sharp exchange of letters about Vuk's prices and profits. Vuk laid down the law in his driest style:

As for those four books which you say were brought to you by a novice from the Monastery of Zhupa, I simply cannot fix a price for them from here, and you, who have been in trade, ought to know that this is impossible; how can a man say openly what he will give for something that he's never seen, and make a bargain on hearing alone? You as my friend and agent should buy as cheaply as you can (like everyone who is buying); and I will give you for all manuscripts, even if you've bought for a few pence, the price which I agreed with you before for the Gospels. For the book, as soon as I've seen what size it is and in what condition, I'll try to give you the best price possible, so that you'll be completely satisfied as you assured me that you've been until now. The price here indicated should be our standard for the future, so never let me hear you ask 'what you should give for something, or what I will pay for it'.

What emerges further from the letter is that Vuk was by this time not the only buyer in the field, and Vrčević thought that he might get a better price from a rival. It is not clear whether he found Vuk's brisk directive satisfactory, but they remained in good relations.

3

Vuk kept back for his own use a number of the old books and manuscripts which reached him. They provided him with further evidence for the thesis which he had defended for over forty years, that Slavonic-Serbian was not merely a debased form of Church Slavonic (or Russian Slavonic), but a separate language and another proof of the independent development of the Serbian people. In 1857 Vuk published in Vienna his last philological work, *Specimens of the Slavonic-Serbian Language*. In the meantime, Djuro Daničić had become the secretary of the 'Serbian Society for Literary Culture', and was steadily preparing the way for the acknowledgement in Serbia of Vuk's alphabet and of his ideas on the Serbian popular language. The struggle was prolonged, and Daničić and Vuk were strongly opposed by the educational authorities in Belgrade.[1] The older generation, particularly in the Vojvodina, remained loyal to the Orthodox Church, and continued to resent Vuk's attacks on the Austrian Serbs.

The conservatives were perhaps at their most aggressive during the brief rebellion of the Serbs against the Hungarians in 1848-9; Branko Radičević recorded at this time some angry passages between them and the 'Vukists' in the inns of Zemun about Vuk's translation of the New Testament. And the feeling persisted for many years after. In 1947, an elderly man, Veljko Petrović, recorded the impressions passed on to him by his father, who as a young student had greeted Vuk at Novi Sad in 1863:

All Novi Sad was agog, Sremski Karlovci too, and all the environs. The news came that Vuk Karadžić was arriving. For one part of the Serbian population he was a father of the people, crowned with glory, like the blessed patriarch of the Bible who pointed the way for his scattered and backward race towards the promised land, awakened in them unsuspected strength, and fought to open up for them an honoured place among the cultured nations; for others, he was the 'lame goatherd', the 'limping devil', agent of Vienna and the Vatican, who was dividing us Serbs from Orthodox Slavdom, from the East, where alone the Slavs had succeeded in creating their independent states and national cultures.

With these two extreme views, people met in public places, in cafés and inns, on the streets, and quarrelled and fought like bitter enemies. Vukists and anti-Vukists were actually compelled by Government decree to avoid each other; one party would use the right side of the street, the other the left, even in church they were divided, and, so to speak, drew demarcation lines for themselves.[2]

The younger generation however was increasingly drawn

[1] The Minister, Dimitrije Crnobarac, went so far as to issue an order prescribing the use in newspapers and official documents of Slavonic forms for certain words.   [2] See *Susreti s Vukom*, pp. 248-51.

towards Vuk's literary doctrines, not least those groups of Serb students who had been sent for higher education to Paris and Berlin. In Belgrade, the young liberal politician, Jevrem Grujić, who was secretary of the Council, was a strong supporter, and the influence of the liberals was strengthened, in this if not in all directions, by the *coup d'état* of December 1858. The Karadjordje regime and the once-powerful Minister, Vučić, had become very unpopular mainly on account of their foreign policy. In 1854 the Turks had secured Serbian neutrality during the Crimean war. Under the Treaty of Paris in 1856, Russia renounced its influence over Serbia's neighbouring protectorates, Moldavia and Wallachia, and renounced any right of protecting the Government of Montenegro. This caused much concern in Serbia; even if under the Treaty of Paris the Turkish rights of garrisoning Serbia were reduced, it was widely felt that Alexander Karadjordjević had become little more than a puppet of Austria, and above all that he had missed opportunities which the crafty Miloš Obrenović would never have let slip for improving Serbia's position *vis-à-vis* the Turks. In 1858 there was a plot against Alexander Karadjordjević, who succeeded in putting it down, but had to accept at Turkish insistence a new Ministry. This lasted less than a year. A National Assembly was summoned[1] and it was this—the 'Assembly of St. Andrew'—that banished Alexander Karadjordjević and his principal Minister Vučić. Miloš Obrenović at last seized the long-awaited chance to return to power, and enjoyed it for a year and a half until his death in September 1860. He was succeeded by Vuk's particular patron and friend, Prince Mihail, and for the last years of his own life Vuk could at length live and work more or less freely. The ban on books printed in his orthography was gradually lifted; first in respect of books imported from outside Serbia, or printed at private presses within Serbia (December 1859), then in respect of books printed at Government expense (December 1860 —this derestriction was very important, since it covered all except primary-school books).[2] Finally, in 1868, after Vuk's death, all governmental regulations on orthography were abolished.

[1] At the insistence of the British Government, after their consul in Belgrade, Fonblanque, had been improperly treated by the Turks.
[2] The first stages of this process did not go smoothly for Vuk, since the Minister of Education maintained his opposition to Vuk's ideas. Vuk published a bitter personal attack on him, and was only saved from prosecution by the intervention of Miloš Obrenović.

From 1859 onwards Vuk spent almost as much time in Serbia as in Vienna (he even persuaded his wife to join him there in the autumn of that year), and travelled to an extent quite remarkable for an ailing man over seventy years of age. His literary work was by now nearly completed. In 1860 he published the last of his historical works, *The Governing Council of Serbia in Karadjordje's Time*, the main theme of which was the way in which Karadjordje weakened the Council in order to break all political opposition to himself, and thereby hastened the collapse of Serbian resistance to the Turkish invasion in 1813. The book was in Vuk's usual realistic vein, and provoked public criticism on this account, which Vuk himself answered. The most interesting points about it are incidental. Firstly, the book sold very well in Serbia, owing to the insistence of Miloš Obrenović's new government that all officials should subscribe for it. Secondly, in defending himself against criticism, Vuk felt bound to allude to Russian slanders against himself and Kopitar. The reference is to A. Hilferding's work *The Western Slavs*, which in 1858 was published simultaneously in Paris and Russia. Hilferding represented a new current of nationalist and Panslav feeling in Russia; he repeated the old charges that Vuk and Kopitar had done their best to break the cultural links between Russia and Serbia, and his accusations were echoed in Russia for some time after this.[1]

4

During the last years of his life, Vuk was something more than a literary figure in Serbia. The liberal leader and author, Jevrem Grujić, described how Vuk played a considerable part in political consultations and coalition-making after the death of Miloš Obrenović in September 1860; he was known as an intimate of Prince Mihail, and apart from that 'Vuk at that time was a man much visited by people of all parties. . . . There was no one more skilful than Vuk at stimulating talk and getting acquainted with other people's views without revealing more of his own than he

---

[1] Even Platon Kulakovski, in his favourable study, *Vuk Karadžić: yevo deyatel'nost' i znatchenie v Serbskoi literature*, Moscow, 1882, says that Hilferding's accusations had some justification in respect of Kopitar. The *Bol'shaya Sovetskaya Entsiklopediya* (2nd edn.) echoes Hilferding's charges against Vuk as well.

FAMILY LIFE AND LAST YEARS

wished, and yet without detracting from the good faith and openness in which talk had begun.' Grujić was ready at this point to put forward Vuk's name for the Ministry of Education, and no doubt Prince Mihail would have been glad to see him there. Vuk would not hear of it—no doubt at 74 he felt himself too old—but he would have liked to enjoy a position on the Prince's Council as a sort of Minister without Portfolio, but with a Ministerial salary. He did not get what he asked for in this respect, but was free with advice on matters of general policy.

The new ruler of Serbia decided in 1860 to use Vuk as a special envoy abroad. There was a strong feeling among the younger generation in Serbia that the time was ripe for a new settlement of accounts with the Turks, if necessary or even preferably by means of war. In Bosnia, Hercegovina, and above all in Montenegro it seemed likely that armed action could be concerted against the Turkish troops; Russia was unlikely to object to a defeat of the Turks and an increase of Serbian influence in the Balkans at this stage, and Austria, after recent defeats by the French in Italy, would not be able to do so effectively. The Montenegrins had fought the Turks successfully in 1853 and had won an important victory at Grahovo in 1858. Their Prince, Danilo, had himself been murdered in 1860, and Mihail Obrenović wished to sound the new ruler, Prince Nicolas. It appears from the report sent to Paris by the French Consul at Skadar that Vuk was empowered to promise him arms, munitions, and 8,000 troops. Mihail and his envoy had however left out of account the French Government, which now exercised an important influence in the Balkans. Prince Mihail's chief Minister, Garašanin,[1] disapproved of what he considered to be Vuk's liberal tendencies in political affairs, and was glad to do Vuk a disservice. At his instance Mihail had sent another envoy to Paris, who in March 1861 strongly advised him not to launch any attack against the Turks. Mihail renounced his agreement with the Montenegrins, and the Serbs did not move when later in the year Turkish armies crushed a fresh revolt in Hercegovina and moved on to defeat the Montenegrins and seal their victory by the Convention of Scutari.

Within Serbia too, Mihail, on Garašanin's advice, pursued the traditional Obrenović policy of waiting on events, not fighting

[1] Garašanin had supported Vuk on linguistic questions during the reign of Prince Alexander Karadjordjević.

the Turks directly, and relying on pressure by the Great Powers on the Porte. In June 1862, while Mihail was on tour in Western Serbia with Vuk, the Turks tried to terrorize the new Government by bombarding the Serbian town of Belgrade from their own fortress. Mihail himself wanted at this stage to adopt a decisive stand and risk war; a proclamation to the Serbian people, announcing a new revolt, was already drafted, but again Garašanin prevailed with counsels of caution. His policy was by no means heroic, and the Bosnians and Montenegrins suffered severely in the meantime at Turkish hands. Vuk travelled to Cetinje in the summer of 1862 nominally for the collection of further songs. He may well have had some political message to carry as well; he was certainly employed by Prince Mihail in Vienna that winter in order to explain Serbian policy to the Montenegrin envoy, Vojvoda Mirko,[1] and to agree with him on monetary help from Serbia. It must be recorded that Vuk's late excursion into diplomacy was a failure, and must have been embarrassing to him. So far as Serbia was concerned, however, Garašanin was justified by subsequent events. Under international pressure, the Turks finally left Belgrade and Serbia without bloodshed in 1867.

5

By the contrast between the armed Serbian revolt of 1804 and the political manœuvring of 1862, we can measure the extent of the change of scene which Vuk had witnessed in the course of his full, various, and combative life. His work and journeyings were nearly at an end. In 1862 the fourth volume of the final collected ('Vienna') edition of his 'popular songs' was published. It was dedicated to Mihail Obrenović and contained the epic songs of the first Serb uprising and of the Montenegrin battles against the Turks in the nineteenth century—an ironic accompaniment to Vuk's diplomatic activity.

Vuk's friendship with Prince Mihail secured for him during the last years of his life a position of prestige in his native Serbia. But he was by this time a figure of symbolic importance in many of the South Slav lands, and as a literary figure was probably best

[1] The 'Vojvodas' were originally the leaders of the armed forces in a clan. In 1804 they were district commanders, and later the most senior generals or 'Marshals' in the Serb Army. Vojvoda Mirko was the father of Prince Nikola of Montenegro.

FAMILY LIFE AND LAST YEARS 347

appreciated outside Serbia. The last picture of all, already quoted in part,[1] shows him at Novi Sad in 1863—the last year of his life:

My father told me that the whole picture and setting was wonderful. They sat the old man in a deep armchair, between two windows. . . . It could clearly be seen that he was weak and invalid, yellow and dry as parchment, but in his clothes and whole appearance completely clean. . . . He was hunched up and his head rather bowed. To prevent his wooden leg from slipping, a 'pouf' was put under it. . . . Someone stood on either side of him ready to jump to his aid and serve him, if he needed anything. . . . Vuk received the [student] delegation with a truly fatherly expression, encouraging them with smiles, and, when the speaker had said his greetings and all three had come up near him, he stroked their hair and kissed their brow and cheeks. In the speech of greeting there must have been some terribly youthful exposition of Vuk's principles, and vows to observe them. . . . Vuk thought it right and necessary to reply immediately to this young generation of his admirers, and that very seriously, warmly and quietly, which was more than could have been expected of him. He thanked them for their love and devotion, and for their loyalty to the principles of popular language and literature (a word which was at the time interpreted very broadly, to cover all varieties of the written and spoken word, and virtually every verbal expression of culture), and of phonetic spelling. He confirmed them in their determination never and under no circumstances to depart from his teaching. They should fight against obsolete customs and principles, against the unfair methods of debate used by the other side, the so-called anti-Vukists, against their lies and slanders. But never should they let their young hearts harbour hatred . . . for his enemies, or regard them as . . . eternal and mortal enemies of the people. It was obvious that trust would prevail, that our side would multiply and grow inexorably, for youth was with us. Most of our enemies of today would be on our side tomorrow. Eventually, willy-nilly, even the most stubborn remnants would have to use the people's language and way of writing. . . .

'We are a small people', he said, 'and under attack from mighty non-Slavonic countries. When once we can shake off the power with which they subdue us, with which they bind us to the chariot of their interests and culture and denationalize us, and can strengthen our resistance and combine for some noble end, we must stop spoiling each other's work. . . . Do not hate each other like mortal enemies, but love each other like brothers.'

Vuk had himself fought hard and bitterly, but there is no

[1] See p. 342 and *Susreti s Vukom*, pp. 248-51.

reason to doubt that he did not want his battles to be pursued by the next generation. He was confident that his ideas had taken root, and he was not deceived.

In the autumn of 1863 he journeyed for the last time to the coast of Montenegro with his daughter Mina, and returned to Vienna in October. His invalid frame was exhausted by continued work and travel. There was however no obvious struggle with death. The last of Vuk's letters to be preserved is dated 16 January 1864; in it he asked an old friend at Zemun for recipes to make some of his favourite Serb dishes. On 26 January, after dictating to his secretary in the morning, he rested on his doctor's orders and died quietly and suddenly in his sleep. A solemn choral service was sung for him by a Serb choir in the chapel of the Russian Embassy at Vienna, and attended by a crowd of young Serb students. Thirty-three years later in 1897 Vuk's bones were brought back to his native Serbia and reburied with much solemnity in Belgrade.

XXI

CONCLUSION

1

THERE are few men who could claim as convincingly as Vuk might have done in his last years that they have set themselves large tasks in their youth and have fully accomplished them in the course of their lives. Vuk had successfully realized all the points in the ambitious programme set for him by Kopitar in 1815. He had compiled a *Grammar* and *Dictionary* of the popular Serbian language, which involved the introduction of a new alphabet and a more logical system of orthography; and he had gone far towards making the popular language into the standard language of literature as well. By collecting 'popular songs' and tales, and by translating the New Testament, he had brought into being a widely accessible and acceptable literature in the popular tongue.

Vuk had moreover undertaken successfully tasks to which neither Kopitar nor himself had looked forward in 1814. His histories, as well as the 'popular songs', had introduced his native Serbia to Europe, and his linguistic reforms had prepared the way for cultural *rapprochement* between the Serbs of Serbia and the South Slav inhabitants of the Austrian Empire. In addition, Vuk had from time to time taken an active if not very glorious part in the administration of the newly emergent state of Serbia.

This is a sufficiently extraordinary record in itself, and the wonder of it is enhanced by consideration of the background against which it was achieved. Even for modern Yugoslavs, for example, the final completeness of Vuk's victory in the linguistic field makes it hard fully to realize how difficult his struggle must have been. Vuk's alphabet and form of language hold the field completely, and it is hard to imagine a different state of things. The English reader of Vuk's life will naturally find it even harder to grasp the full difficulties and importance of his linguistic campaign, or to realize how much and how continuously his energies were absorbed by linguistic controversies. Certainly the intellectual calibre of Vuk's opponents was not always high, and they were not able to point either to a uniform practice or to an established literature on their side. Perhaps something like Vuk's system was bound to be worked out and to prevail in the end. But authority and power were on the side of Vuk's opponents in this controversy. It needed extraordinary energy and application on his part to get the argument on to a rational basis and to win a public for his own views.

The same qualities were necessary for Vuk's work in other fields, such as the collection of popular literature. Here there may have been no rational opposition; the worst that he had to contend with was the spasmodic nature of the interest taken by his chief patron, Miloš Obrenović, the silly practical jokes of Miloš's court, the reluctance of potential sources to take his interest seriously,[1] the unwillingness of subscribers and publishers to venture their money, and the extreme caution of the Austrian censorship.

There was indeed a great variety of external obstacles in Vuk's path, and it is hard to bear in mind, when looking at his life's work as a whole, that he had also to battle for most of his life against miserable poverty and consequent family troubles—of his thirteen children only four survived early childhood, only two lived to be adult, and only one, Mina, was able to give Vuk aid and comfort. Moreover, even allowing that he had a hypochondriac strain in his character, his health was never strong and was often very bad. It was an achievement for Vuk simply to survive and to earn a minimum living in the face of such obstacles. To accomplish his full literary programme in such conditions required extraordinary courage and persistence.

Sheer intellectual energy and determination were thus Vuk's outstanding characteristics. This was perhaps part of his village and ancestral heritage, and it is not surprising that he displayed at times the obverse of the better peasant qualities—a sharpness in controversy which led to unnecessary bitter feelings (his attitude

---

[1] Miss Jelena Šaulić, of the Vuk and Dositej Museum, Belgrade, to whom I am grateful for many most pertinent comments, writes as follows: 'My father told me (and I was able to confirm it as I travelled with him) that nothing had changed even after a hundred years. When he was collecting mourning songs as a student, his uncle was seriously worried and told him reproachfully that it brought disgrace on the whole family for him to waste time at graveyards recording women's nonsense, instead of sitting with men, smoking and listening to their conversation.'

CONCLUSION 351

to Dositej Obradović is perhaps the most painful instance); an insistence on his uttermost rights (no Government servant of any age can deny admiration to Vuk's successful battle over 15 years for the arrears of his pension); and an urge to better his family's social position, most vividly illustrated by the conditions which he set for Mina's Russian suitor.

2

Vuk is often contrasted, as the agent of a dark romantic nationalism, with Dositej Obradović, the rational apostle of the Enlightenment. Dositej was indeed an endearing and attractive figure, who played a very important part in introducing European culture to Serbia. The contrast however can be misleading. Vuk may have set himself to serve national ends, and may have been an overzealous patriot (his rancour against the Greeks is an example). He was certainly passionate in his desire to make Western Europe acquainted with the heroic past of Serbia, its heroic efforts in the later wars against the Turks, and the good old ways of Serbian culture which provided the background for heroism. But any implication that Vuk had cloudy ideas or could have made himself at home with the heroes, real and fictional, of the German Romantic movement is wildly out of place. Vuk had a vigorous, severely practical mind. As he himself said, it was a combination of chances which turned him into a man of books and a writer. Had he not been lame, had he not met Kopitar, had he not married a Viennese, his occupation could obviously have been very different. As it was, while Vuk had developed some interest in popular language and culture before he arrived in Vienna, he was not a literary man in the normal sense. Writing was to him always a means to an end, not the joyful practice of a natural talent. Kopitar convinced him—perhaps he did not need much persuasion—that there was work to be done. Much of it could only be done by writing, and Vuk started to write. He was in fact essentially a propagandist, and one who believed unshakeably in the importance of his message. It was this belief which stimulated him to apply his mental energy in the direction which it finally took, and gave him the determination to carry on in spite of all difficulties.

If determination and force of intellect were the first of Vuk's distinguishing characteristics, his passion for knowledge was equally remarkable. Much of the force behind Vuk's detailed argument for certain forms of language and spelling derived from his firm belief in the intrinsic value of accumulating knowledge about the world. He had that intense faith in the benefits to be gained from book-learning which flourishes most easily where men have had to fight in order to get some little education themselves. He regarded the popular language of Serbia as the best vehicle for the spread of popular education, and the existing chaos of literary forms of language as a serious obstacle; for it could add a year or two to the time needed by a child to reach the point at which he could usefully read for himself and increase his knowledge.

Moreover Vuk was as much convinced as Dositej Obradović or any eighteenth-century philosopher of the ultimate invincibility of right reason, and in consequence of the value of rational argument. The propagandist who is utterly devoted to his aim is not always discriminating in the arguments that he uses or in the quality of his logic. Vuk was certainly ready, when he thought that occasion demanded, to employ personal arguments against his opponents; but he was not given to blackening their characters in order to disprove their reasoning, though he himself constantly had to meet the 'arguments' that he could not be right because he had had no formal education, or that only crooked reasoning could issue from such a crooked frame. Arrogant as Vuk's manners often were in controversy, there is no reason to doubt his own contention that he was always ready to learn if anyone had anything to teach him in his own field, nor his assertion that he measured his own achievements modestly, according to the intellectual standards set for him by Kopitar and Jakob Grimm.

Vuk liked to have his way intellectually, not out of vanity, but because he was assured that he was right, and that it was important for others to learn by reasoning what he had to teach them. He was in fact often pathetically unaware of how little it served his own cause to be right at the wrong time and in the wrong place. A more skilful tactician could have saved himself a lot of trouble by not arguing, or by arguing less abrasively, with for instance the novelist Vidaković in 1816–17. It is however doubtful whether anyone could have combined suppleness in tactics with Vuk's extraordinary persistence in pursuit of his aims; and he could fairly claim at the end of his life that his tactics had been good enough to win him his battles, even if the cost had been heavy.

PLATE 5

VUK AND HIS WIFE IN OLD AGE

3

The third remarkable characteristic of Vuk's intellect was his passion for accuracy of detail and for truth of general impression. This may originally have derived from his professed belief in the importance of his 'conservative' task. He had absorbed Herder's doctrine that the soul of a nation was expressed most clearly in its 'popular' art and literature, and it seemed to him for patriotic motives very important to record such literature accurately and to publicize it as far as possible in Europe. The same sort of feeling led him to record in detail all that he could, not only of the Serbian uprising against the Turks in 1804, but also of Serbian village and rural customs. The Serbs themselves and the nations of Europe (so ready, it seemed to Vuk, to admire the Greek insurgents who had acted so much later) should be put in possession of the full heroic story and of the full background to it. Vuk's passion for truth cannot however be explained entirely by patriotic motives, for he recorded accurately a good deal that the average patriotic historian could have omitted without doing violence to his conscience. He valued the truth, and the fullest truth which he could attain, for the sake of increasing the sum of human knowledge and wisdom, or simply for its own sake.

Vuk had an excellent eye and ear for detail, and any number of illustrations of his stereoscopic vision could be cited from his sociological writings. But he realized that the faithful recording of detail could be misleading and convey much less than the whole truth. A slightly frivolous passage may be cited as a first instance of his meticulous passion for truth, both of detail and of general impression. In the introduction to a late edition of one of his books of 'popular songs' Vuk cites verbatim a long formula of prayer in Montenegro, to be used as the bride leaves her parents' house. It includes the wish that the daughters born of the marriage should be 'good and honest like your mother', and Vuk appends a note: 'This is the form of words, whatever the mother is like. Thus it may happen that people smile to themselves on hearing this prayer.'[1]

---

[1] In the spirit of Vuk himself, I quote another observation of Miss Šaulić, that a smile might be permissible in the case of some minor fault, but that any serious aspersion on a woman's honour in Montenegro was very far from a laughing matter.

It is however in his historical work that Vuk's peculiar combination of short and long sight, so to speak, is most notable and most valuable. As a political and social historian, he thought it his duty to posterity to record exactly the trimmings of a typical *hajduk's* dress, or to make a plausible guess at what a good spahi landlord would say to a peasant whose harvest had been bad. Such realistic reproduction of popular speech as appears in his life of Hajduk Veljko was something very foreign to the polite literary tradition of his time, and in this respect Vuk was a genuine innovator. Probably his peasant upbringing and lack of formal education helped him to look at things straight and call them by their simplest names; he did not see life around him through a filter of current intellectual conceptions, and did not have to rid his mind of the fashionable formulas of the day. When Vuk on occasion tried to use these for his own ends (as in the dedication of his first *Song-book*), common sense kept on breaking through. Indeed he could infuse something of his personality into the most ephemeral of his writings, such as an advertisement for subscribers. Thus:

'The price for subscribers will be 4 *forints*. After printing, if any copies are left over from subscribers, the price will be 6 *forints*. Then too, buyers will have to look for the book and order it themselves, but subscribers will have it dropped right at their doorstep.'

If Vuk's lack of formal education and the preconceptions likely to result from it helped him to see and describe clearly the detail of everyday life, it was perhaps the heroic tone of the great Serbian 'popular songs' which stimulated him to take a wider view of history as he had experienced it. At any rate Vuk's historical and sociological writings are remarkable not only for his meticulous accuracy of detail, but also for his attempt to envisage and convey to his reader the general trend of the events which he describes. He aims at truth of general impression, as well as of particular fact, and can fairly be described as a philosophic historian, even if he had no explicit philosophy of history. By careful selection of concrete and detailed instances, Vuk conveys to the attentive reader a general view of what war and heroic action are about, and this general view is not only more convincing but also more deeply tragic than any amount of laureate biography. Vuk's point, which he makes only implicitly, is that human beings have to be

CONCLUSION

considered in their total historical setting, that they do not rise above their circumstances, but that circumstances can stimulate them to truly heroic action. Thus, when the Turkish rule was reasonably moderate, people did not go to the hills to be *hajduks*; when the Turks were outrageous, they did, but even then they were not inspired only by noble sentiments about patriotism and national liberty. Indeed they would rob anyone to make a living, and could be as much nuisance to Serbian trade as to the Turkish military supply system. All this is plain from Vuk's account; but he also shows that the *hajduk*, whatever his motives, normally rose at least to a certain heroic swagger in his daily life, and was ultimately ready to face his Turkish executioners with defiance and to make a good end. The heroic elements stand out the more clearly and movingly against the background, which Vuk first drew in, of the *hajduk's* normal human failings.

Vuk applies the same philosophy of life to the Serbian uprising of 1804 against the Turks. The Serbs did not plan their 'liberation struggle' far ahead, or embark on it in the name of any resounding slogan. They were, Vuk makes clear, forced into armed resistance by desperation. Even after the fight had begun, those who possessed property of any kind were slow to come forward, and had to be committed to war by their more desperate fellows. Again, when it comes to choosing a leader for the uprising, there are no conventional heroics. Karadjordje does not gain his position by sheer force of character or obvious heroism. He is a well-known *hajduk*, whose qualities will be valuable; but he can also be sacrificed in the event of failure, which many of the Serb notables envisage. Or perhaps no sacrifice will be necessary; the whole uprising can be labelled as a typical *hajduk* movement, and Karadjordje can be allowed to return under guarantee to more peaceable occupations. All this is related by Vuk in matter-of-fact style. Even where his personal sympathies are deeply engaged, as in the portrait of Hajduk Veljko, he records faithfully enough the failings of his hero, in particular his inability to take a broad strategic view. By giving his readers such a vivid idea of the human weaknesses of the leaders of the Serbian uprising, Vuk renders their subsequent exploits both more credible and more moving to the reader. In Vuk's historical writing there are no abstractions and very little generalization; but it is not hard to generalize sensibly and even to construct a philosophy of history from Vuk's simple record of the remarkably wide range of facts that he sees. And in this respect Vuk is not only a very sympathetic but also a very original historian for his time.

4

It may not seem easy to square the idea of Vuk's passionate commitment to the truth, and wherever possible to the whole truth, with the sometimes ignoble circumstances of his life. He was forced not only to beg but also to flatter unworthy patrons. In particular he found it necessary to go against his own historical conscience by publishing in 1827 his history of Miloš Obrenović's life and times, in which he suppressed some well-known facts and hushed up others that were unfavourable to Miloš. His enemies were quick to point the contrast between this work and the revelations contained in the famous letter to Miloš which he wrote in 1832, only five years later. Vuk's defence was skilful but not entirely adequate. It cannot be denied that he was ready on this occasion to sacrifice his own idea of the truth; the incident cannot be called typical, but it throws much light on Vuk's character, and is therefore worth analysing in order to make a final estimate of his personality.

There are two possible defences of this and other minor lapses by Vuk from his intellectual integrity. First, over a long period he often had little choice about how to earn a living for himself and his growing family, to which he had some duty. This defence will not fully cover his major lapse; in 1827 he could in fact have exploited the growing fame of his collections of songs by devoting himself more whole-heartedly to the 'folkloristic' branch of his work, and could perhaps have collected more linguistic and antiquarian material for his Russian patrons. Instead Vuk chose to concentrate on historical writing; this was bound to depend for its success on Miloš's patronage and this in turn could only be earned by flattery. What then is his second defence? It seems doubtful whether Vuk's choice was dictated mainly by the desire to advertise Serbia to Europe, though this certainly played its part. It can, I think, only be justified or explained by reference to his longer-term ambitions. Vuk wanted financial security and a new base in Serbia from which he could pursue his object of linguistic reforms, without incurring hindrances from the Serbian

CONCLUSION 357

Orthodox authorities in the Austrian Empire and in consequence from the Vienna police and censorship. He may well also have had in mind the possibility of taking a senior administrative post under Miloš and introducing a new system of popular education in Serbia. It was probably with such ideas in view that Vuk felt bound to make a really determined attempt to earn Miloš's favour, in spite of some previous experience of his fickleness—and it should be remarked that Vuk did not suffer to the full from Miloš's ways until the period 1828–32.

Such a decision seems to be very much in line with a well-attested trait of Vuk's character. He had set himself certain objectives which he pursued with the utmost determination for fifty years. In concentrating on these he seemed to be able to exclude himself from other forms of intellectual life around him. There is for example nothing in Vuk's letters to indicate that he lived in the Vienna of Beethoven, Schubert, and Grillparzer. Perhaps this is hardly surprising; it is more remarkable that he seems to have isolated himself equally in 1819 from any broader interest in Russian intellectual life, and that at a time when he was in personal contact with a number of its most interesting representatives. Such was the measure of Vuk's concentration on his objectives. This devotion also took more active forms. He mobilized his friends, in a manner somewhat reminiscent of Richard Wagner, to help him financially and otherwise towards the achievement of his life's major aims. Nor did he spare himself and his unfortunate family. In order to preserve his energies for his long-term work, Vuk refused occasional possibilities of more comfortable routine employment (for instance as editor of the Vienna *Serbian News*). His wife could have reproached him with thus sacrificing the lives of those many of their children who died in childhood or infancy. In the same cause Vuk certainly did not spare his own dignity, as witness the constant flow of his begging letters. And it was probably in this cause that in 1827 he made what may have been for him the most painful sacrifice, of his pride as an objective historian and of his undoubted devotion to truth. No doubt he felt some shame at his own action (though he was able to satisfy his historical conscience immediately afterwards by his collaboration with Ranke on *The Serbian Revolution*); and he was certainly reluctant to earn the bad opinion of Kopitar on this occasion. Probably however he comforted himself by thinking that such a sacrifice was necessary in order to gain a position from which he could work more effectively towards his long-term aims.

If this idea is right, then Vuk could have argued to Kopitar and his friends that he was indeed maintaining his essential integrity by continuing to work for his essential objects (though he would never have used such high-flown terms). He would probably have put the matter more quantitatively and said that it was worth circulating something less than the truth in this case, in order to have the opportunity of spreading knowledge more widely later.

Vuk was never one for quixotic heroism, though, like the heroes of his history, he could endure and dare when necessary. For him in fact the end could justify the means, and by the close of his life he could say that the end had indeed been attained. There is some similarity here with the career, if not with the character, of Miloš Obrenović. Miloš too subordinated a great deal to his long-term aim of liberating Serbia by gradual diplomacy and by exploiting the pressure of the Russians and other Great Powers on the Turks. He had no hesitation in sacrificing considerations of personal or even national honour to this end. By 1830 he had attained his goal, without effusion of blood on a national scale; this was a powerful answer, at least, to his critics. Vuk was working in an intellectual element, his choice of means was nicer, and his hands were incomparably cleaner. He neither had so many critics by the end of his life, nor any crimes for which to excuse himself. But he could strongly have defended his occasional less creditable acts, as Miloš his crimes, by the results which he finally achieved.

Such a defence may be repugnant to the moralist even when applied to intellectual rather than political misdeeds. It may indeed fairly be thought that there was something terrible and inhuman about Vuk's concentration on his intellectual tasks and about his occasional subordination of intellectual integrity as well as of family interest to his long-term objectives. I am only concerned here to suggest that Vuk made his sacrifices out of strength rather than weakness of character; and that they were as much heroic as ignoble.

5

For the rest, I must hope that Vuk has spoken sufficiently to the reader for himself through the translations of his work included in

CONCLUSION

the main body of this book and in its appendices. There may have been a terrible element in his energy and concentration; but his writings, apart from their historical and sociological value, are also full of the high spirits and shrewd simplicity which charmed Grimm, Ranke, Prince Mihail of Serbia, and so many young Slavists who saw him in the Vienna home of his evening years.

To close on a personal note, I have had the good fortune to live for six years at one time or another in Vuk's country, and for over three of them I have been much engaged with his works. The freshness of his vision, as well as the keenness of his sight and hearing, have never failed to delight me. I hope sincerely that I have conveyed some of my pleasure to readers in my own country and that I may have encouraged some of them to make Vuk's closer acquaintance. The last words—in praise of writing, and in justification, as it afterwards appears, of his whole life's mission—are Vuk's own, taken from the introduction to a little Serbian spelling-book, published in 1827:

Whatever men may have invented in this world, nothing can be compared with writing. To send your thoughts on a piece of paper over the wide world to friends living far off, to read what others wrote two thousand years ago, and to write what others may read thousands of years from now, this is a skill which almost passes human understanding. It may well be said that he who discovered it was more a God than a human being.

APPENDIX A

I HAVE assembled here a number of translations to illustrate the main text. Section I (nos. 1-4) contains translations of 'popular songs', three heroic, and one comic. Section II (nos. 5-9) contains some descriptions by Vuk of popular beliefs, superstitions, and customs, and Section III (nos. 10-14) some of his 'popular tales', taken from the *Dictionary* as well as from the collection of 1853. I have added, where necessary, brief introductions to the main sections, and introductions and notes to the separate items.

I. 'POPULAR SONGS'

There is no comprehensive collection of English translations, but modern versions of certain groups or cycles of heroic songs are contained in Helen Rootham, *Kossovo; a Translation of the Heroic Songs of the Serbs*, Blackwell, 1920, and D. H. Lowe, *The Ballads of Marko Kraljević*, Cambridge, 1922.

My own translations follow roughly the metre of the originals (on which see Vuk's own comments at the end of Appendix E). I have found however that an exact trochaic pentameter in English is too reminiscent of the *Hiawatha*-type tetrameter, and have therefore deliberately roughened the metre of my own lines, in an attempt to convey something of the stark tone of the original.

1. *Hasanaginica* (The wife of Hasan Aga)

This was the song translated into Italian by the Abbé Fortis, and into German by Goethe (see Chapter XII, § 2), which became the best-known single 'popular song' in early nineteenth-century Europe.

> What shines white there on the green mountain?
> Is it snow, or swans that shine there?
> Were it snow, it would long have melted.
> Were it swans, they would long have flown.
> Neither snow is it nor swans shining,
> But the tents of the Lord Hasan Aga.
> He lies sick there of cruel wounds,
> And his mother and his sister tend him,
> But for shame his dear wife would not come.[1]

[1] The heart of the poem lies in this obscure line. Hasan Aga's wife did not come to tend him, because according to the strictest Mohammedan law she was bound to wait until he sent for her. He evidently thought that she did not care,

When his wounds had begun to heal,
To his true wife thus he sent word:
'Wait for me no more in my white castle,
Nor in my home, nor with my family.'
As the lady understood these words,
Still in sorrow she was thinking of them,
When the horses drew up at her door.
Then did Hasan Aga's lady haste to the
Tower window, there to break her neck.
But her two young daughters ran after her:
'Turn again to us, our dear mother.
This is not our father, Hasan Aga,
But our uncle, Pintorović Bey.'
Then she threw herself upon his neck:
'Ah! my brother, great is my shame,
As he sends me from our five children.'

To her grief, the Bey says not a word,
Puts his hand into his silken pocket,
And gives her the letter of divorcement,
That she take up her marriage-wreath
And return with it back to her mother.
When the lady had read this letter,
Her two sons she kissed on the brow,
Her two daughters on their rosy cheeks;
But from her tender baby in his cradle
No way could she bring herself to part,
Till her brother took her by the hands
And parted her hardly from her baby,
Put her then upon the horse behind him,
And rode with her to his white castle.
There she stayed but for a little time,
But a little time, hardly a week.
A good lady of good parentage,
Many sought the good lady in marriage,
Above all the Cadi of Imoski.
The noble lady begged of her brother:
'Ah! brother, this I would not have,
Give me not in marriage to any man,
Lest my heart break for very sorrow
When I see my poor orphaned children.'

and similarly misinterpreted (at the end of the poem) her effort first to avoid seeing and then to part cheerfully from her children. The whole story well illustrates the difficulty of doing justice in translation to poems which are at crucial points concise and allusive.

But the Bey cared little for her words,
Gave her to the Cadi of Imoski.
Then the lady begged again her brother
That he send a paper, a white letter,
Send it to the Cadi of Imoski:
'Your bride greets you kindly in this letter,
In this letter she thus kindly prays you,
When you have assembled the bridesmen,
And all set out to her white castle,
Bring a long veil with you for the bride,
That may hide her from her orphaned children
When she passes the house of Hasan Aga.'
When the Cadi read the white letter,
He assembled then the noble bridesmen,
And they went together for the bride.
Fairly they came to the bride's house
And returned with her in good cheer.
But when they reached the house of Hasan Aga,
Her two daughters looked down from the window
And her two sons came out in her presence,
Came and spoke thus to their dear mother:
'Come again to us, our dear mother,
Come that we may give you food for supper.'
Then when Hasan Aga's lady heard this,
She spoke thus to the bridesmen's leader
'In God's name, brother and first bridesman,
Halt the horses here beside the court,
That I may give gifts to my poor children.'
So he halted the horses beside the court,
And she gave fine gifts to her children.
To each son, a dagger gilt-handled,
To each daughter, a dress down to the ground,
And she gave a tunic finely sewn
To her little baby in his cradle.
All the while the hero Hasan Aga
Watched, and then he called his sons to him.
'Come to me, my poor unhappy children,
Since you will receive no more kindness
From your mother of the stony heart.'
But when Hasan Aga's lady heard it,
Turning all pale, she fell to the ground,
And straightway she parted with her soul
Out of pity, seeing her poor children.

APPENDIX A

2. *Dioba Jakšića* (How the Jakšić brothers shared)

This is the song of which Goethe was studying a German translation (sent to him by Grimm) when Vuk called on him in October 1823 (Chapter XI, § 2).

The moon speaks hard words to the Day-star:
'Where have you passed your time, star, o Day-star?
Where have you passed, where have you lost your time,
Lost your time for three livelong days?'
The Day-star to the moon makes answer:
'Where have I passed, where have I lost my time?
All over the white town, over Belgrade,
Where I looked and saw a mighty wonder,
How two brothers shared their father's goods,
Dmitar and his brother Bogdan Jakšić.
And the brothers two were well agreed,
And divided well their father's goods.
Dmitar took the land in Karavlaška,
Karavlaška and Karabogdanska,[1] and
All the Banat down to the Danube waters.
Bogdan took the Srem, land of the plain,
The Srem and the plain-land of the Sava
And Serbia, south to Užice town.
Dmitar took the lower part of the town[2]
And Nebojša, the tower on the Danube,
Bogdan took the upper part of the town,
And the Rose church in the midst of it.
On a little point alone they quarrelled,
It was something, it was rather nothing,
A black horse it was and a grey falcon.
Dmitar claimed the horse, as the elder brother,
The black horse he claimed and the grey falcon,
Bogdan would not yield one or the other.
Then at morning when the dawn lightened,
Dmitar mounted on the great black horse
And he took to himself the grey falcon,
Then set out for hunting in the hills,
But he called his love, Andjelija, to him:
"Listen well, Andjelija, my true love,
You must poison Bogdan, my brother,

---

[1] Wallachia and Moldavia.
[2] The town is Belgrade, and the scene is set in the fifteenth century, when it became the centre of the Serb kingdom under Despot Stefan, son of Tsar Lazar.

And if you refuse to poison him,
You must leave me and my white castle!"
When his love, Andjelija, heard his words,
She sat down full of care and sorrow,
Thinking thus, and speaking to herself:
"What does that grey cuckoo[1] want of me?
If I should poison his own good brother,
God would think this a mighty sin,
And men a reproach to me and shame.
Young and old would then say of me.
'Look on her, her the accursed woman,
How she poisoned her own husband's brother!'
But yet if I will not poison him,
I must leave my warrior husband's house."
Thus she thought, and then she had a thought.
She went down to the lower chamber
And took up the great prayer chalice,
Made of pure gold, of beaten gold,
Which she had brought from her father's house.
She filled it full of the red wine,
Then she took it to her husband's brother.
Kissed his garment and kissed his hand,
And before him bowed down to the ground:
"In honour of you, my man's dear brother,
In honour of you I bring the cup and wine,
And do you give me the horse and falcon."
Then at that did Bogdan repent him,
And gave unto her the horse and falcon.
Meanwhile Dmitar all day long on the hill
Hunted, and all day he caught nothing.
Then chance led him, as evening drew on,
To a green lake high among the hills.
On the lake was a duck with golden wings.
Dmitar loosed then the grey falcon,
All to catch the duck with golden wings.
But the duck was no way to be caught
And it seized itself the grey falcon
And it broke the falcon's right wing.
When Dimitrije Jakšić saw this wonder,
Straight he took off his lordly apparel
And swam far into the still lake,

---

[1] i.e. her husband Dmitar: the cuckoo was a bird of ill omen, and according to Serbian legend incorporated the spirit of a woman mourning her lost brother.

All to rescue his grey falcon.
Then he asked of his grey falcon:
"How is it with you, my grey falcon,
How is it without your right wing?"
And the falcon hissed in pain to him:
"Without my right wing I feel now
As a brother feels without his brother."
Dmitar then bethought and called to mind
How his love would poison his own brother.
So he mounted on his mighty horse
And rode at speed to Belgrade city,
That he might yet find his brother living.
When he came there to the Chekmek bridge,
He spurred on his black horse to cross it,
But the horse fell down upon the bridge,
Fell, and falling broke its two forelegs.
When Dmitar saw his own ill hap,
He took the saddle off the mighty horse,
Put it with his cudgel on his shoulder,
And in haste he came to Belgrade town.
When he came, he called straight to his love:
"Andjelija, my own faithful love,
You have not poisoned my own brother?"
And Andjelija to him made answer:
"No, I have not poisoned your own brother,
Rather I have made peace between you."'

3. *Zidanje Skadra* (The building of Skadar)

This was one of Jakob Grimm's favourites among the Serbian 'popular songs'; he sent his own translation of it in May 1824 to Goethe, who found the subject too primitive and barbarous (see Chapter XII, § 3).

Three born brothers were building a town
Three brothers, the three Mrljavčevićes.
One of them was Vukašin, the king;
Uglješa, the captain, was the second;
And the third was Gojko Mrljavčević.
They built Skadar town, on the Bojana,
And they builded it for three long years,
For three years, with three hundred workmen,
Yet they could not raise up the foundation,
And much less build up the town itself.
All that the masons built up by day
Was cast down at night by a spirit.

When the fourth year of work began,
Then the spirit cried from the mountain:
'Spare your trouble, King Vukašin, spare
Your trouble and waste not your wealth!
You will never raise up the foundation,
And much less build up the town itself,
Till you find two creatures of like name,
Till you find a Stoja and a Stojan,[1]
And build boy and girl, brother and sister,
Into the foundations of the tower.
Thus only will the foundations hold,
And thus only will you build your town.'
When the King Vukašin heard these words,
He called to him Desimir his servant:
'Desimir, my dear child Desimir,
Till now you have been my true servant,
And from now on are my dear child;
Take, my son, horses and chariot,
Carry with you six chests of treasure,
And go, my son, throughout the wide world
All to seek two creatures of like name.
Seek, my son, a Stoja and a Stojan,
Boy and girl, brother and sister;
Either seize them or buy them for gold,
And bring them to Skadar on the Bojana,
That we build them into the foundations;
Then may our foundations hold well,
Then may we build up well our town.'
Desimir the servant heard these words,
And he took then horses and chariot,
In them carried six chests of treasure,
And the servant went through the wide world,
Went to seek two creatures of like name.
Thus he sought a Stoja and a Stojan,
Thus he sought them for three long years.
But he found no creatures of like name,
Found neither a Stoja nor a Stojan.
Back he came to Skadar on the Bojana,
Gave back to the King horses and chariot,
Gave back to him the six chests of treasure:
'Here, king, are your horses and chariot,
And here too are your six chests of treasure.

---

[1] The names were presumably chosen for their connection with the Serbian verb 'to stand', 'to stand fast'.

I found not two creatures of like name,
I found not a Stoja and a Stojan.'
When the King Vukašin heard these words,
He called straight to Rade the mason,
Rade called to the three hundred workmen,
And the King began to build up Skadar.
The King built, and the spirit cast down,
Would not let them raise up the foundation,
And much less build up Skadar town.
Then the spirit cried out from the mountain:
'Listen, good Sir, listen, King Vukašin,
Spare your trouble and spend not your wealth!
You will never raise up the foundation,
And much less build up Skadar town!
Here you are, you three born brothers,
And each brother has a faithful love.
One of them will come to the Bojana,
And will bring the workmen's meal tomorrow;
Build her into the high tower's foundation,
Thus will the foundation hold well
Thus will you build up well your town!'
When the King Vukašin heard these words,
He called his two born brothers to him:
'Did you hear those words, my dear brothers,
That the spirit cried out from the mountain?
To no end do we consume our wealth,
She will not let us raise the foundation,
And much less build up Skadar town.
This too said the spirit from the mountain,
That we stand here, we three born brothers,
And each brother has a faithful love.
One of these will come to the Bojana,
And will bring the workmen's meal tomorrow.
We must build her into the foundation,
Thus will the foundation hold well,
Thus shall we build up well our town.
Now swear we on our firm faith in God,
None of us shall tell this to his love,
And thus shall we leave it to fortune,
Which shall come tomorrow to the Bojana.'
Then they swore by their faith in God
That not one should tell it to his love.
And the twilight came thus upon them,
And they went unto the white castle

Where they supped as fitted such great lords,
And each with his love went to lay down.
Listen now, friends, to a great wonder!
King Vukašin broke his solemn promise,
He the first spoke to his true love:
'See that you beware, my true love!
Come not to the Bojana tomorrow,
And bring not their meal to the workmen;
You shall lose your life, if you do so,
They will build you into the foundation.'
Uglješa too broke his solemn promise,
And he too spoke to his true love:
'Do not be deceived, my true love,
Come not to the Bojana tomorrow,
Bring not you their meal to the workmen,
For so you shall die, young as you are,
They will build you into the foundation.'
But young Gojko, he kept his promise,
He said nothing to his own true love.
When at morning the dawn showed its light,
They rose early, the three Mrljačevićes,
And went to the town, to the Bojana.
The time came for taking down the meal,
And it was the Lady Queen's turn.
She turned then to her sister-in-law,
Uglješa, her husband's brother's love;
'Hear my word, dear sister-in-law!
My head is aching—good health be yours—
And I cannot overcome my pain,
Do you take their meal to the workmen.'
Then Uglješa's true wife gave answer:
'Lady Queen, my own sister-in-law,
My hand is aching—good health be yours—
I too cannot overcome my pain,
Go you to our young sister-in-law.'
The Queen went to her young sister-in-law:
'Sister-in-law, sweet young wife of Gojko,
My head is aching—good health be yours—
And I cannot overcome my sickness.
Do you take their meal to the workmen.'
Then the wife of Gojko spake to her:
'Hear, good sister and my lady Queen,
I would gladly obey your command,

But I have a little child to bathe
And some white linen to be washed.'
And the lady Queen replied to her:
'Go', she said, 'my own sister-in-law,
Go and bring their meal to the workmen.
I myself will wash clean your linen,
And your other sister will bathe the child.'
Gojko's young wife then had no choice
But to bring their meal to the workmen.
When she came to the stream of Bojana,
Gojko Mrljavčević saw her there,
And the hero's heart was full of sorrow,
Sorrow for his wife, his own true love,
Sorrow for their baby in its cradle,
For their month-old child that lay there.
From his eyes the tears then poured down.
Then his slender wife set eyes on him;
A few steps and she was by his side,
A few steps, and she spoke softly to him:
'What ails you then, my good lord and master,
That the tears are pouring down your cheeks?'
Then spake to her Gojko Mrljavčević:
'Woe is me, my wife, my own true love,
For I had an apple wrought of gold,
And it fell now into the Bojana,
My sore grief I cannot overcome.'
And his slender bride understood not,
Still she talked to her lord and husband:
'Pray to God that he give you good health,
And they shall make you another apple.'
Then sorrow still sharper came on Gojko,
He was fain to turn his head aside
That he look no more on his true love.
Then his two brothers came upon them,
The two brothers-in-law of Gojko's wife,
And they took her by the white hands,
Led her to the town, to be walled in.
First they cried out to Rade the mason,
And Rade cried to the three hundred workmen.
Still the slender bride stood smiling there,
Still hoping that all was done in jest.
But the three hundred workmen gathered,
Gathered wood and stone all about her,

TRANSLATIONS

Builded them up to the waist about her.
Then she saw the fate that had lighted on her,
In despair she hissed like a wild snake,
And thus she besought her husband's brothers:
'By your faith in God, oh, do not let them
Wall me in that am so young and tender!'
Thus she pleaded, but to no avail,
Her brothers-in-law would not look on her.
Then she cast aside shame and scruple,
Thus beseeching her true lord and husband:
'Good my lord, do not, oh, do not let them
Wall me into the town that am so young!
Go you rather to my old mother,
For my mother has riches enough,
And there buy a slave, man or woman,
That they may build into the foundations.'
Thus she pleaded, but to no avail.
When it was clear to the tender bride,
That no prayers could avail her more,
Then she pleaded to Rade the mason:
'In God's name, brother, Rade the mason,
Leave me here a window for my breasts,
Leave my white breasts without the wall,
So when my infant Jovo shall come,
When he comes, then he may suck my breasts.'
This prayer as a brother Rade answered,
He left there a window for her breasts,
And he left her breasts without the wall.
So whenever her infant Jovo came,
When he came, then he could suck her breasts.
Then in grief she called again to Rade:
'In God's name, brother, Rade the mason,
Leave me here a window for my eyes,
That I may look towards our white castle
When they bring my baby Jovo to me,
And when they shall take him home again.'
This prayer too as a brother Rade answered,
He left there a window for her eyes,
That she might look towards the white castle,
When they brought her baby Jovo to her,
And when they should take him home again.
Thus they built her into the town wall
And they brought the baby in its cradle,

And she suckled it for seven days.
After seven days her voice was silent,
But the milk still flowed for the baby,
And she suckled it for a whole year.
Thus it was, and thus it remains,
Even today the milk will flow there
For a wonder and for the healing
Of any woman that has no milk.

4. *The Wooing of Bazerdjan Sterija*

This is a translation of the lines which Vuk remembered from the parody of a heroic song, composed by his servant, Arsenija Stanojević, at Kladovo or Brza Palanka in 1812 (Chapter V, § 2). Vuk tells the rest of the story in a prose appendix to his record of the verses. I have summarized this at the end of the translation.

Bazerdjan Sterija was drinking wine
In the fortress at Brza Palanka,
In Košara, in his white palace
By the Danube and its waters cold.
Trivun the young servant served the wine,
And when he had drunk his fill of wine,
Then the hero thus began to discourse:
'Ha! Trivun, faithful servant mine,
No wife have I, and I would be married.
I have seen this land and all its towns,
And the Turks' land down to Istanbul,
And the Germans' land to fair Vienna,
Karavlaška and Karabogdanska,
But I found not for myself a maiden,
Till I saw one now in Kladovo,
In the house of Kosta Jermenlija,
And the maiden's name is Helena.
Now you, faithful servant, give me counsel,
Who shall go for us to Kladovo
Who shall ask for me the lovely maiden
(My wife must she be, and your good lady)?'

Then up spake the faithful servant Trivun:
'My good lord, Lord Bazerdjan Sterija,
Send them first the old man Slatinash,
Slatinash, the head man of the Vlachs,
Far and wide men listen to his counsel.
Send as second envoy Jovan Radić,

TRANSLATIONS 373

> For this Radić comes of noble race,
> From the lovely town of Sarajevo;
> Well he knows the land and all its cities
> And his converse is as of a Lord.
> Send as third man Nikola the Greek. . . .'

The three envoys then make their way to the tower of Čotrić (a reference to Vuk's patron, Jefto Savić, from Čotrić), deceive Arso the clerk into giving them a pass to Kladovo for trade (Arso is himself in love with the girl, so they cannot tell him the truth), do their business, and are finally outwitted by Arso.

II. TRADITIONS, SUPERSTITIONS AND CUSTOMS

Items nos. 5 and 6, taken respectively from Vuk's *Dictionary* (1818 edition) and *Life and Customs of the Serb People* (published in 1867, after his death) deal with two famous subjects of Serb heroic song. Nos. 7–9 are included for their folkloristic interest, Nos. 7 and 8 (the *Vampire* and the *Rain-makers*) coming from the *Dictionary* (1818) and No. 9 (*Abduction*) from the *Life and Customs*.

5. *The origin of the name Obilić*

[The hero was probably known originally as Miloš *Kobilić* (son of a mare). One of the genuine 'popular songs' recorded by Kačić in his *Pleasant Relation* (1756) was about Miloš Kobilić and Vuk Branković, traditional hero and villain of the battle of Kosovo. This was reproduced by Alberto Fortis in his *Observations on the Islands of Cherso and Ossero*, 1771 (Chapter XII, § 1). The story here translated is a rationalized account of the origin of the more heroic name *Obilić*.]

The Serbs tell that when Stefan the Mighty was hunting around Cer, he caught sight of a place where the branches of a tree were being bent first down and then up. He went there and found a child with a few sheep, who had struck his axe into a billet and then gone to sleep on his back. When the child breathed out, the branches were carried upwards, and when he took in his breath, they came down to the ground. The Tsar was amazed to see this, and stretched out his hand from the saddle to take the axe, but, lo and behold, he couldn't move it from the billet. Quick as quick the lords and servants got off their horses and all in turn tried with both hands to take the axe out of the billet, but none of them could shift it an inch. So they woke up the child and the Tsar asked him: 'What's your name?' 'Miloš', he answered. 'Have you got a father and mother?' 'Yes, a mother; my father's dead.' 'And where's your mother?' 'Down there in the village, at home.' 'Well, take us home with you.' 'I can't leave the sheep.' Then somehow they persuaded him to drive the sheep and lead them to his home. They were curious to see what he'd do with the axe, and how he'd take it out of the billet, or whether he'd leave it there. As he started to drive the sheep, Miloš just took out the axe with one hand, and put it over his shoulder. When they got to the house, Miloš left the sheep and his unknown guests and disappeared between the buildings to look for his mother. The Tsar dismounted and went after him to make sure that Miloš didn't hide himself somewhere. The Tsar looked through a chink in the wood into a room, and there was Miloš's mother kneading flour. She had thrown her right breast over her left shoulder and her left breast over her right, and Miloš was sucking from behind. The Tsar said: 'Truly, that's an abundant mother who's borne an abundant hero.' He took Miloš away from his mother to the court, and from that time on Miloš was called 'Obilić'.[1]

6. *Marko Kraljević* (Prince Marko)

There is no Serb who doesn't know the name of Marko Kraljević (Prince Marko). Here I shall mention only what is told of him but does not appear much in the ballads.[2] It is said that Marko was much stronger than the men of today and no doubt than those of his own time. ... I myself remember as a boy in the Srem, at the tavern of Krušedol Monastery, where there was a picture of Marko holding an old ox by the tail over his shoulder, and carrying it on his back as he walked on. ... Of his horse Šarac, some say that a fairy gave it to him and some that he bought it from some carriers. Before Šarac, he is said to have changed horses often, and none could carry him; then he saw a mangy piebald colt with these carriers, and thought that it would make a good horse; he took it by the tail to whirl it around (that was his way of trying horses), but it couldn't be moved from the spot; so Marko bought it from the carriers, cured it of the mange and taught it to drink wine.

There are various stories of how Marko Kraljević died. Some tell that somewhere in the large village of Rovina, Mirčeta, a leader of the Karavlachs, shot him with a golden arrow in the mouth and killed him, when the Turks (Marko fighting on the Turkish side) and the Karavlachs were fighting each other; others say that in one of these battles Šarac was caught with him in a bog near the Danube and that both of them were

[1] The adjective 'Obil' means abundant, fertile, and it is under this word that Vuk quotes the story in his *Dictionary*.
[2] Many of Vuk's best songs about Marko Kraljević were collected from Tešan Podrugović, his favourite singer (Chapter VII, § 2).

lost there. In Negotinska Krajina[1] they say that this was in a marsh near Negotin, under the spring of Tsaricina. There is a marsh there to this day, and the foundations of an old church, which is said to have been built over Marko's grave. A third story is that in one of these battles so many people were killed that horses and men were swimming in blood; Marko lifted up his hands to heaven and said, 'My God, what am I to do now?' At that, God took pity on him and by some miraculous means transported him and Šarac to a cave, where they are still alive today. Marko stuck his sword under a beam, or drove it into the stone, laid down and went to sleep, and still sleeps on. In front of Šarac stands some moss, which he eats bit by bit, while the sword is moving gradually from under the beam or out of the stone. When Šarac has eaten up the moss, and the sword emerges from under the beam or out of the stone, Marko then will awaken and go out into the world again. Some say that he fled to the cave the first time that he saw a gun. He made to examine it (to see whether it was in fact like what had been told him) and shot himself in the palm with it, then said: 'Now courage is of no more use, for the worst coward can kill the greatest warrior.'

7. The Wolfcoat or Vampire

'Vampire' is the name given to a man into whom (according to folk stories) some devilish spirit enters forty days after his death and revives him (he becomes a vampire). The vampire then comes out of his grave at night, attacks people in their houses and sucks their blood. A good man cannot become a vampire unless some particular bird flies over his corpse, or some other kind of animal approaches it; so the corpse is always guarded to prevent anything approaching. Vampires appear mainly in the winter (from Christmas to Ascension Day). When there are a lot of deaths in a village, people begin to say that there is a vampire in the churchyard (some will tell how they've seen it at night with a shroud on its shoulder), and to guess who has turned into a vampire. Sometimes they will take a pure black stallion and lead it to the churchyard and round the grave where they fear the vampire may be; it is said that such a stallion can't and won't go past a vampire. If they are convinced in any case and agree to dig up the vampire, all the peasants assemble with a stake of hawthorn (for that is the only wood which a vampire fears) . . . dig up the grave and, if they find in it a corpse which has not decayed, they transfix it with the stake, throw it into the fire and burn it. It is said that they have found such vampires in graves and that they are all blown up fat and red with human blood ('red as a vampire'). The vampire sometimes comes to his wife (especially if she

[1] Negotin, and Negotinska Krajina are in the extreme east of Serbia, near the Rumanian border.

is young and pretty) and sleeps with her. It is said that children born of a vampire have no bones. In times of hunger, vampires are often seen around mills, and granaries or stores of maize. It is said that they all walk with their shrouds over their shoulder. They can squeeze themselves through the smallest hole, so it is no use to shut doors against them any more than against witches.

8. 'Dodole' (The rain-makers)

[I have included this item, partly as a good example of Vuk's folkloristic interests, and partly as an occasion for noting that some of the customs recorded by Vuk are taking a long time to die. J. M. Halpern, in *A Serbian Village* (Columbia, 1958) has published a study of the people and customs of the village of Orašac (where the revolt of 1804 began). This includes (pp. 242 et seq.) an account of rain-making ceremonies very similar to those described by Vuk. A young gypsy girl ('Dodole') is dressed in a skirt and cape of thick leaves and led from house to house. She dances for rain, and chants a song with the refrain 'Oi, Dodo, Dodole' and with verbal reminiscences of the lines recorded by Vuk.]

Some summers when there is a drought, a number of girls go round the village from house to house, and sing and conjure, that rain may fall. One of them strips altogether,[1] and thus bare she binds and covers herself with all sorts of grass and flowers so that her skin cannot be seen at all, and she is called the 'rain-maker' (so it is said of a girl or woman who is wearing an elaborate head-dress 'She's made herself up like a rain-maker'); and thus they go from house to house. When they arrive in front of a house, the rain-maker first dances alone, and the other girls stand in order and sing various songs; then the woman of the house, or someone else, takes a pot or bucket full of water, pours it over the rain-maker, and she must go on dancing and moving all the time. In the rain-makers' songs at the end of each line of whatever kind they sing: 'Oi, dodo, oi dodole', for example:

> Our rain-maker prays to God,
> Oi dodo, oi dodole,
> That the dewy rain may fall,
> Oi dodo, oi dodole.

In present times, the rain-makers dance almost throughout Serbia,[2]

[1] I have translated here the entry under 'Dodole' in the first edition of Vuk's *Dictionary*. In the 1852 edition, no doubt with his eye on the Orthodox clergy, he has the rain-maker stripped only to the shift.

[2] In the later edition, Vuk says that for long all village girls would go 'rain-making', but now (in 1852) it is done mainly by gipsies, who use the opportunity for begging.

TRANSLATIONS 377

but particularly from Valjevo over to Timok. In the Srem, Bačka, and Banat, they danced till recently, but the new priests have forbidden and rooted it out.

9. *Abduction* (Otmica)

[This item is included partly as a prose account of what was clearly one of the favourite subjects for comic songs (Chapter II, § 3), and partly because the custom of abduction, like that of rain-making, persisted in Serbia, at least in a modified form, long after Vuk's death. See Vera Erlich, *Family in Transition, a Study of 300 Yugoslav Villages (1937–1940)*, Princeton University Press, 1966, pp. 199–206.]

In Serbia girls were abducted down to our own times. At a very early age the young men would start on abduction. One would propose to another: 'Come on, friend, let's go after this or that girl.' They go off to abductions armed as if to battle. Sometimes the young men ambush the girls as they watch the stock or go for water, then lay hold on them and take them off. Sometimes they storm into the house at night, like *hajduks*, break it up and bind the girl's father or brother until they can find the girl and take her off. Sometimes the brothers or parents fight the abductors, and then blood flows in plenty; for example in the Jadar district at the village of Klupci in 1805, one of the girl's brothers and one of the abductors were killed, and still they didn't succeed in taking the girl off. Thus abductors do not lightly determine to attack any house where they know that the girl has plenty of relations, and particularly if the village is a compact one; for when the guns begin to fire and a fight starts up, the villagers will all snatch up their guns and run to help. It is a disgrace to any village if girls are taken off from it, and even more so to the abductors, if they return 'barren'. When the abductors catch a girl, they will not let her go, even if they must all die for it; and if the girl starts to struggle and will not go with them, they drag her by the hair and drive her with sticks like a cow among the cabbage. The abductors do not dare to go with the girl to one of their own houses, since the villagers with the girl's family sometimes set out to hunt for them. They take her instead into the woods, and there marry her in some vineyard-worker's or shepherd's hut, or elsewhere in the wood. The priest must marry them, whether he likes it or not, for they will be ready to kill him. When the pursuers come to their village, then the men of the place from which the abductors came will go out to meet them civilly and make peace between the parties. If they are successful, well and good. But if the girl's family goes to complain before the magistrate, then the abductors must appear too with the girl. When the mother sees the girl in the court, she will begin to beat her breasts with her hands and to wail: 'Woe is me! Behold, I am a slave!' When the judgement begins, the magistrate first asks the girl: 'Were you forced, or was it of your own free will?' If she says that she was forced, and does not want to live with the young man either today or tomorrow, not even if they cut her all to bits, then things go badly for the abductors; they will be imprisoned and pay a fine. But if the girl says (as is most often the case): 'There was no force, it was my own free will. I would go with him over hill and stream'; then the abductors give something to the magistrate, make their peace with the girl's family, and take her off home to celebrate the wedding. Sometimes, if the pursuers could not find the abductor with the girl in his village, they have set fire to the houses of the young man who took her off and of all his kin, and burned everything of theirs that would burn, and only after all this have made their peace.

Usually abductions take place only when the young man has asked for the girl and been refused. But sometimes (if they know that permission will not be given) they don't even ask, but start right away with an abduction, even if the young man has never set eyes on the girl. Abduction is practised mainly by young men with no parents, or by those who have parents but pay no attention to them, and go loitering about; few decent young men of decent family will abduct a girl, or go out on an abduction. Black George put a ban on the abduction of girls. He issued a decree saying that every young man by whom an abduction was carried out should be executed, that priests who married any abducted girl should be shaved (un-priested), that the godfather, brother-in-law, and senior bridesman should be flogged, and that each of the rest of those concerned should receive 50 strokes. When the Turks conquered Serbia in 1813, abduction came back again, but afterwards Prince Miloš Obrenović sentenced a number of people according to Karadjordje's rules and completely abolished it in his area of Serbia; under Turkish rule it is presumably practised to this day.

III. POPULAR TALES

Partly as a matter of personal taste, and partly because they illustrate more directly the main text, I have given preference to tales or minor instances of Serb popular humour over the fantastic tales of fairies and wonders, which are in fact more frequent in Vuk's collection of 1853. Something of the flavour of these may however be deduced from no. 14 ('Animal language'). A large selection of the Serb popular tales has been translated into English by Mrs. N. Čurčija-Prodanović, *Yugoslav Folk Tales*, Oxford University Press, 1957 and 1960.

10. *The Ill-speaker*

There was a Bosnian spahi, who had in his village such an ill-tongued man. He was making ready to go to a holy place, and before setting out called the man of ill tongue to him and said: 'You man of ill tongue, I am setting out on a pilgrimage in God's name; be sure to say nothing ill of me, until I come home, and I shall give you a bushel of millet.' 'Very well, my lord', said the man of ill tongue, 'but who will give me the millet if you don't come back?'

11. *'Putting the water on'*

'Put some water on, and I'll be shaved.' 'Put some on, I'm not exactly from Sarajevo (but from near by).' A Turk came into a barber's shop to be shaved, and said when asked that he came from Sarajevo. Out of devilment the barber began to sing the praises of the men of Sarajevo, saying that they were all heroes, and never allowed him to put water on their faces, but were shaved dry. The Turk was well pleased with this, and to show that he too was a hero consented to have a dry shave. But, when it began to hurt him badly and he could stand it no longer, he said: 'Put a little water on, I'm not exactly from Sarajevo, but from near by.'

[Vuk added some comment to his own story as follows:]
I saw with my own eyes something exactly like this in Serbia in 1822. I was travelling from Ram to Kragujevac, and lunching at Svilajnica, in the house of the chief Milosav Zdravković of Resava, and there was a Greek of about 22 years, who had escaped from Greece that summer. He kept on boasting to the lads what heroes they are in Greece and how they admit none to their company who would not be shaved dry. Seeing that the carriage did not come for me immediately after lunch and the next day was a Saint's day (our Lady's), when I heard talk of shaving, I sent for a barber to shave me. When I had been shaved, the lads talked the Greek, whose beard was very thick, into being shaved; and having in mind all the recent boasting about their heroes (among whom he numbered himself) being shaved dry, they told the barber not to wash his face, but just to go ahead with shaving. The barber began his work, and saw that it wasn't going well. The Greek was clenching his teeth and shutting his eyes, so the barber offered in Turkish to put a little water on. The Greek, afraid of being shamed, told him (again in Turkish) just to go on shaving; but when shortly afterwards the barber made the same offer again, the Greek allowed him to put a little water on.[1]

[1] For Vuk's anti-Greek sentiments, see Chapter XIII, § 5. He recorded elsewhere how certain Greeks deliberately put themselves into detachable chains in order to resemble prisoners released in fixed chains according to Turkish custom, and thus to make a better business of begging.

12. Ero's Communion

[Nos. 12 and 13 are typical stories of Ero, the sometimes shrewd simpleton from Hercegovina ('Ero' is short for 'Ercegovinac'). The story of *Ero's Communion* appeared under the heading *Pričeščalo* in Vuk's *Dictionary* (1818), and caused particular scandal in the Orthodox Church (see Chapter VIII, § 3). No. 13, *Ero from the other world*, is mentioned in Chapter X, § 5; it was the subject of a popular Yugoslav opera of the 1930s.]

Some men of Hercegovina with loaded horses (normally they travel with horses and carry all sorts of loads as the men of Bačka do in carts) were passing by a monastery, when one of them said to his friends: 'Here, one of you drive the horses, while I go in for a moment to take the "combunion" and the "chaplice"' (for 'communion' and 'chalice').[1] When he came into the church, he began to shout: 'Come quick, whoever gives the combunion and the chaplice here! I can't wait long, my horses are on the road.' Now when the monks' boys saw him and heard what he said, they realized right away that this was a simple fellow, who perhaps had never in his life seen a church or taken communion before. So they took him off into a corner, and began to ask him whether he had eaten anything before coming to take communion. He told them outright that he had dined (he had eaten a full dish of porridge and I know not what else). Then the boys told him to wait a little, and one of them ran off and brought a cup full of the hottest peppers and vinegar. They told Ero to open his mouth wide and poured it right in. When it began to choke Ero, he put his hands to his mouth and began to run out of the church, but one of the lads was waiting for him at the women's end with a stick: 'Stop, Ero, and I'll give you the "chaplice"!', and thus the boy ran along with him to the doors. When Ero found his way out of the monastery, he met a man leading some children, and asked him where he was taking them. The man said, 'Into the monastery to take communion.' Then Ero said: 'God and God's faith! Maybe someone bigger could stand it, but not one of these little ones could! And then anyone who could stand the combunion will never abide the chaplice.'

13. Ero from the other world

A Turk was digging maize with his wife. At noon he went off to tie up his horses somewhere else and water them, while his wife stayed behind to rest in the shade. Along came Ero.

[1] Ero is made to mispronounce the correct words *pričešće* and *navora* as *pričeščalo* and *navornjak*. I have tried to convey something of the effect in translation. *Češčalo* means a comb, hence 'combunion'.

'God be with you, good lady!'

'God be with you, good peasant! Where do you come from, good peasant?'

'Lady, I come from the other world.'

'In God's name, is that so? And have you seen my Muja there, who died a few months ago?'

'Of course I've seen him, he's my best friend!'

'Well, in God's name, how is he, how is he getting on?'

'Thanks be to God, he's well, but, so help me God, he's in a pretty bad way without money. He hasn't anything to buy tobacco with, or to pay for coffee in company.'

'Well now, are you going back? If I were to send him a little money, could you take it with you?'

'I could, of course I could, I'm just on my way back now.'

So the Turkish woman ran off to the place at which her husband had stripped off his jacket for the heat, took out his purse and gave whatever money was in it to Ero, to take to Muja. Ero grabbed the money, put it into his pocket, and ran off along the brook. Hardly had he disappeared beside the brook, when, lo and behold, there was the Turk, watering his horse, and his wife came to greet him:

'Fancy, husband! Just now there passed this way a peasant from the other world, and said that our Muja was in trouble for lack of money—nothing to buy tobacco with or to pay for coffee in company—so I gave him what money there was in your purse to take along with him.'

And the Turk said: 'Which way has he gone?'

When his wife told him that Ero had gone along the brook, quick as quick he jumped on to his horse bare-back and galloped off along the brook! Now when Ero noticed the Turk galloping after him, he took to his heels. He arrived at a water-mill just under the hill, and ran inside shouting to the miller:

'Run for your life! Here comes a Turk to cut you down, so give me your cap, and you take mine, then run off that way round the mill and up the hill!'

The miller saw the Turk galloping up, took fright and had no time to ask why and wherefore he was to be cut down; so he gave Ero his cap and took Ero's, and ran off above the mill and up the hill. Ero put the miller's cap on his head, took some flour and rubbed it in, and made himself into a proper miller. Then up galloped the Turk to the mill, dismounted and rushed inside:

'Now, good fellow, which way did he take, that man who's just come into your mill?'

Ero replied: 'There you are, look, he's running up the hill, there.'

The Turk said: 'Hold the horse, good fellow.'

So Ero took the horse, and off went the Turk up the hill after the miller, this way and that among the beeches. He caught up with him and laid hold of him, and said: 'You whoreson, where's that money of which you cheated my wife, and were for taking it to Muja in the other world?'

The miller began to cross himself and be amazed: 'God be with you, my lord! I've never seen your wife or Muja or the money.'

And so they passed a full half-hour, until they cleared things up and saw what it was about. Off ran the Turk helter-skelter to the mill, but when he got there, what do you think? Ero had ridden off with the horse and there was no sign of him, and the Turk went back on foot to his wife, with his tail between his legs. When the woman saw him without the horse, she cried out: 'What are you up to, man?'

And he said, with a good oath: 'You sent Muja money to buy coffee and tobacco, and I sent him the horse, so that he won't have to walk.'

14. *Animal Language*

There was once a shepherd who had served his master faithfully and honestly for many years. One day when he was going after his sheep, he heard a sort of screeching in the wood and couldn't think what it was He went off into the wood, following the sound, to see what was up. When he arrived, there was a big blaze and in the blaze a snake screeching. When the shepherd saw it, he stopped to see what the snake would do, for the fire was around it on all sides, and the flames had almost reached up to it. Then the snake called out of the blaze: 'For God's sake, shepherd, help me out of this fire!' So the shepherd stretched out his stick, and the snake got out along the stick, then on to his hand, then from his hand up to his neck, and wound itself around his neck. When the shepherd saw this, he began to wonder and said to the snake: 'What's this? It was an ill hour for me when I helped you out of the fire and did myself in!' The snake answered: 'Don't be afraid, just take me home to my father. He's King of the Snakes.' So the shepherd began to beg the snake and say in excuse that he couldn't leave his sheep, but the snake said: 'Don't worry about the sheep. Nothing will happen to them. Just come along as quick as you can.' Then the shepherd set out with the snake through the wood, and at last came to a gate made of nothing but snakes. When they got there, the snake on the shepherd's neck whistled, and the other snakes unwound themselves right away. Then the snake said to the shepherd: 'When we come to my father's court, he'll give you anything you ask for—silver, gold, or precious stones: but don't you take any of that, just ask for the animal language. He'll hold back for a long time, but will give it to you in the end.'

So they came to the court, and the father, all frightened, asked the snake: 'For God's sake, son, where have you been?' And the snake told all in order, how he'd been surrounded by the fire, and how the shepherd had got him out. Then the Snake-King said to the shepherd: 'What shall I give you in return for saving my son?' The shepherd said: 'I don't want anything, except the animal language.' The King said: 'That's not for you. If I gave it to you, and you told anyone, you'd die at once. So ask for something else, and whatever you want, I'll give you.' At that the shepherd answered: 'If you want to give me anything, give me the animal language. If you won't give me that, well, God be with you! I don't need anything else.' And he made as if to go. Then the King made him turn back and said: 'Stop! Come here, if it's really nothing but that that you want. Open your mouth!' So the shepherd opened his mouth, and the Snake-King spat into it and said: 'Now you spit into my mouth.' The shepherd spat into the King's mouth, and the King again into the shepherd's. So each spat into the other's mouth three times, and then the Snake-King said: 'Now you know the animal language. Go with God's blessing, but if you value your head, tell no one; for if you tell anyone, you'll die on the spot.'

The shepherd went off through the wood, and as he went he heard and understood all that was being said by the birds, and the grasses and everything under the sun. When he got back to his sheep, he found the full number and nothing wrong, and lay down to rest for a bit. Just as he lay down, up flew two crows and alighted on a tree, and began to talk to each other in their own language, saying: 'If that shepherd only knew it, just where that black post is laying, there's a cellar full of silver and gold under the ground.'

When the shepherd heard that, he went off to his master and told him, and the master brought up a cart and forced open the door of the cellar and took the treasure home. This master was an honest man and gave all the treasure to the shepherd saying: 'There, my son, here's all the treasure for you, that's what God gave you. You build a house for yourself and get married and live off the treasure.' The shepherd took the treasure, built a house, got married and little by little became a very rich man—not only in the village but in the whole district there was no one to touch him. He had his own men to look after sheep and cattle, horses and swine; he owned much property and great wealth.

One time at Christmas he said to his wife: 'Get ready wine and spirits and all that we need, and we'll go off tomorrow to the pig farm and bring something to give the shepherds a good time.' His wife obeyed him and did everything as he had ordered. Next day when he'd come back from the pig farm, he said to his shepherds in the evening: 'Now you get together, eat, drink, and be merry, and I'll look after the animals the whole night through.' And so he went and stayed with the animals. When it was about midnight, there were the wolves howling and the dogs barking. The wolves asked in their own tongue: 'What about us coming and doing some damage? Then you could have some meat too.' And the dogs replied in their tongue: 'Come on, and we can all have a good meal.' But among their number there was an old mastiff with only two good teeth in his head. He began to say to the wolves: 'You know what you can do with yourselves. While my two teeth are still in my head, you shan't do any harm to my master!' All the while the master heard and understood all that they said. When the next day dawned, he gave order that all the dogs should be killed off, and only the mastiff left. The servants said to him: 'Surely to God, master, that's a shame!' But he answered: 'You do just what I say!'

Then he set off home with his wife on horseback; he was on a horse and she on a mare. As they rode along, he got ahead and she was left behind. Then the man's horse neighed and said to the mare: 'Hurry up! How slow you are!' And the mare replied: 'It's all very well for you, you're carrying master alone, and I'm carrying three—the mistress, and her child in her, and I've got a foal inside me.' At that the man burst out laughing. His wife noticed, prodded the mare on and caught up with him. Then she asked him why he'd been laughing. He said: 'Oh, no particular reason, you know how it is.' That wasn't enough for her, and she went on at her husband to tell her why he'd been laughing. He began to dig his toes in: 'Get on with you, wife, God be with you, what's the matter with you? I don't know myself what it was.' But the more he resisted, the more she went on at him to tell her why he'd been laughing. In the end the man said to her: 'Lord, if I tell you, I shall die at once.' But she paid not the slightest attention to this, and went on at him again just the same, saying that he'd simply got to tell her. Meanwhile they'd reached home. Getting down from his horse, the man at once ordered a coffin to be made and put in front of the house when it was ready. Then he said to his wife: 'There you are! Now I shall lie in that coffin and tell you why I was laughing. But as soon as I've told you, I'll die straight away.' So he laid down in the coffin, and took one last look around him. Just then the old mastiff came along from the fields and sat down at his head and began to cry. The man noticed and said to his wife: 'Bring a bit of bread and give it to the dog.' The woman brought a bit of bread and threw it down in front of the dog, but the dog wouldn't even look at it. A cock came up and started pecking at the bread, and the dog said to him: 'You wretched greedy thing! All you think of is food, and there's the master going to die.' The cock replied: 'Well, he'd better get on with it, if he's such a fool. I've got a hundred wives myself, and whenever I find a grain of corn I call them all up;

when they come along, I just swallow it, and if one of them starts to get angry, I go at her with my beak. And this master isn't man enough to keep one woman quiet.'

Now when the man heard this, he got up from his coffin and took a stick and called his wife into the room. 'Come in, wife, and I'll tell you.' Then he went at her properly with the stick. 'There you are, wife! There you are.' And so the woman calmed down, and never again did she ask him to tell her why he'd been laughing.

APPENDIX B

THE SLAVONIC AND SERB ALPHABETS

THE old Slavonic alphabet contained at least 45 letters, a number of which were obviously unnecessary in the Serbian language as it had evolved by the second half of the eighteenth century. Slavonic-Serbian, the modified form of old Slavonic encouraged by the Serbian Orthodox authorities of the time, still contained 40 letters, including some that were clearly unnecessary for current Serbian speech and some of which the usefulness could be strongly disputed. In the former category were the letters familiar in Russian, ы and ъ (the hard sign); the latter included the following letters: ѣ ('ye' as in 'yet'), я ('ya'), ю ('you'), й and i (used to soften vowels following them) and ь (the 'soft sign' used to soften consonants).

In general, Serbian consonants are hard unless otherwise indicated, though the Serbian short o corresponds to the Russian hard ı ('Beograd' for 'Belgrad'); in Serbian also the Russian soft sign in the verbal infinitive is expressed by an extra terminal vowel (говорити for говорить).

Vuk was by no means the first to evolve the principle of a strictly phonetic alphabet, or to apply the principle to Slavonic-Serbian orthography. The Slovene Blaž Kumerdej stated in a grammar of 1779 (which was not printed at the time): 'Any sound heard in our language should not have to define it more than one sign, one letter. It does not suit our language that a single letter should be written that is not pronounced.'

Kopitar adopted this principle in his Slovene grammar (1808), and Sava Mrkalj first attempted to apply it to Serbian orthography. His alphabet (1810) consisted of 26 letters as follows (the cursive form is given in each case below the capital letter):

А Б В Г Д Е Ж З И [I] К Л М Н О П Р С Т У Ф
а б в г д е ж з и [i] к л м н о п р с т у ф
Х Ц Ч Ш [Ь]
х ц ч ш [ь]

Vuk's final alphabet is based on this version, with the omission of the letter bracketed, and of the soft sign ь. He arrived at his final 28 letters by a number of stages. In his first *Song-book* (1814), he retained, in addition to Mrkalj's letters, ѣ, я, and ю, and used the softened Т (ть) for the sound 'ch' (as in 'Chalk'). After his talks with Luka Milovanov

at Buda (1814) he altogether discarded, theoretically at least (he was still cautious in practice), ѣ, я, and ю, substituting э, ia, iy; for the sounds ня ('nya') and ля ('lya') he wrote нѣа and лѣа. He began to discuss at this stage the substitution of the new compound letters which he finally adopted, љ, њ, and ћ, for лѣа, нѣа, and тѣ; and he contemplated another new letter дь in substitute for дь, for the sound 'dj' ('gi' in 'giraffe').
This brought Vuk very close to the near-final stage of his alphabet. For two or three years, however, he hesitated. In his letters of 1815-18, even to Kopitar, he continued to use ю, я, ы, й and even ѳ ('th' as in 'thing'). In his second *Song-book* (1815) he reverted to ѣ. Vuk was subject at this time to the influence both of the Archimandrite Mušicki, and of some Serb *émigré* leaders then living in the Austrian Empire; these all discouraged him from appearing to break the orthographical links with Russia and to Latinize the Serbian alphabet. It was Kopitar who urged him constantly to trust his own judgement, and in particular to introduce 'j' as a vowel-softener; although Kopitar did not approve whole-heartedly of Vuk's new signs љ, њ, and ћ.

Vuk first applied his phonetic principles consistently to the Serbian alphabet in the first edition of his *Dictionary*, 1818. Here he finally omitted й, i, and ь from Markalj's alphabet, included 'j' and his new letters љ, њ and ћ, and added two new letters to express a softer and a harder 'dj' sound, ђ ('gi' as in 'giraff') and џ ('J' as in 'James'). The letters х ('ch' as in 'loch') and ф ('f' as in 'father'), together with the hard sign, were shown at the end of the table of letters with which he concluded the preface to the first edition of his *Dictionary*, accompanied by a note explaining that they could hardly be found in genuine Serbian words. Many years afterwards, as a result of his travels in Dalmatia and Montenegro, he accorded them full orthographical rights in the second edition of his Dictionary (1852). Vuk's final alphabet, which has become that of the Cyrillic or Serbian version of the Serbo-Croat language, thus ran as follows (the cursive form is given beneath the capital letters):

А Б В Г Д Ђ Е Ж З И Ј К Л Љ М Н Њ О П Р С Т
а б в г д ђ е ж з и ј к л љ м н њ о п р с т
Ћ У Џ Ч Џ Ш Х Ф
ћ у џ ч џ ш х ф

APPENDIX C

FORMS OF THE SOUTHERN SLAVONIC LANGUAGE

THE Southern Slavonic (*južno*slovenski) languages fall into two groups. From the first or Eastern group the Old Slavonic or Church Slavonic (staroslovenski) language developed, and, somewhat later, Macedonian and Bulgarian. The second or Western group includes the South Slav (*jugo*slovenski) languages, Serbo-Croat and Slovenian (slovenački).

Little need be said here about the first group, except that Old Slavonic, as used in Serbia, was subject to a number of changes at least from the twelfth to the eighteenth century. In the twelfth century it was, as a literary language, considerably adapted to the forms then current in Serbia (the 'Serbian recension'); and only in the eighteenth century was it re-adapted for ecclesiastical and literary use to more traditional 'Russian-Slavonic' forms. The educational mission sent by the Holy Synod of Moscow to Karlovci, 1727-37 (see p. 48, n. 1) did much to re-establish the prestige of a Russianized form of Slavonic as the literary language *par excellence* among the Serbs of the Austrian Empire. Thus in one form or another Church Slavonic was the literary language of Serbia until well into the eighteenth century; whereas in Croatian and Dalmatian literature there had been a breakthrough to popular language in the fifteenth and sixteenth centuries.

Within the second main group (Western or South Slav), there were three main sub-groups:

(*a*) *štokavski*, the dialect of Slavonia (east Croatia), Bosnia, Hercegovina, and much of Serbia (so called because of the form of the relative neuter and interrogative pronoun, 'that' or 'what?'—'što').
(*b*) *kajkavski*, the dialect of Kranjska and north-west Croatia ('kaj' for 'što').
(*c*) *čakavski*, the dialect of the lands immediately to the east of the above, and also of Istria and Dalmatia ('ča' for 'što').

Within sub-group (*a*) (*štokavski*), there were again three dialects:

(i) *ikavski* ('mliko': milk).
(ii) *ekavski* ('mleko').
(iii) *jekavski* or *ijekavski* ('mljeko' or 'mlijeko').

These could not, and cannot, be allotted to fixed geographical districts, though now by and large *ekavski* is spoken in Serbia and *jekavski* in Bosnia, Hercegovina, and Croatia.

Vuk favoured the *jekavski* form of *štokavski*, as the dialect of central Hercegovina, where in his view the purest popular language had been spoken, and as the dialect in which he had heard the best versions of the traditional 'popular songs' collected by him.

APPENDIX D

REVIEW BY JAKOB GRIMM OF BOOK III OF VUK'S LEIPZIG COLLECTION OF SERB 'POPULAR SONGS', 1823

(*Göttingsche Gelehrte Anzeigen, nos. 177–8, 5 November 1823*)

[This is an almost complete translation of Jakob Grimm's review, subsequently reprinted by Vuk as part of his own introduction to Book I of his Leipzig collection, published in 1824. Short extracts from Grimm's review are given in Chapter XI, § 5. A translation of the greater part of Vuk's own introduction is given in Appendix E.]

THE reviewer . . . wants to report without delay on an undertaking begun without any noise (that is the way in which good and fruitful things usually begin), which will in time make the whole of educated Europe take notice and as a start will inevitably have beneficial effects for the editor's native land.

These Serbian popular songs are not the result of laborious research in old manuscripts, but have all been recorded from the living voice of the people; perhaps they have never been written down before, and in this sense they are not old, but they are likely to have a long life. Some of them . . . celebrate deeds which happened not so much as 20 years ago; and one cannot detect that those concerned with the older and less definitely historical events of popular songs are any different in style and manner. The Serbian popular songs can hardly be compared directly with what we regard as German folk-songs. The following differences can be observed. German folk-songs show the crudity of form usual in popular dialects; in their content there are artificialities and gaps which can easily be explained when we consider how long it is since the subjects represented have been eliminated from the environment of educated people. The Serbian popular songs on the other hand are couched in pure and noble language, while the narrative is full, clear, and without confusion from beginning to end. In the Serbian territories there are no crude vulgarities of popular expression, at least not in the blatant forms common here in Germany. [Grimm's own note: Degenerate and mixed forms occur perhaps only in towns, where Turks, Germans, and other foreigners live, or the clergy try to impose their obsolescent church language; in the country everyone speaks purely.] The editor could take down everything direct from the mouth of the singer, without altering or filling out the words or the metre. Such alterations completely spoil even imperfect popular songs; they are like patches of fine cloth which will not match the coarser texture. We should not be surprised by the absence of the coarse and common elements in the Serbian language; a thousand years ago and less, things were the same in Germany. Just as now in Serbia there is no divergence between the poor peasant and the respectable man in purity of language, and just as the men of Hercegovina keep to their native way of speech, so with us formerly. The men of Franconia, Saxony, etc., each thought the speech of their native land the best, but master and men everywhere spoke the dialects alike. The history of our language shows that the process of education was confined to a few dialects only until in the end one literary language was left alone in the field, while regional dialects lost their importance and sank into vulgarity and obscurity. Probably as soon as Serbia attains culture, one way of speech will prevail over others, and then the age of those epic songs will be over—that is of their continued live existence; they will continue to be prized and admired as precious relics of antiquity.

The pictorial introductions of many of the songs are incomparable. For example, when the theme is the wooing of a maiden, the song begins:

> From the time when the world was fashioned,
> Never did so fair a flower blossom,
> As the flower which so fairly blossomed
> In Udbina, by the Turkish border.

Or the theme is to be a bloody battle, and the introduction runs:

> Two black ravens flew, two coal-black ravens,
> From high Cer and over Čokešina,
> And their beaks unto the eyes were bloody,
> And their claws were bloody to the knee-joint.

The birds alight at the house of one who fell in battle, are questioned by the wife, and tell her in detail of the events which they saw.

Even more poetic is the beginning of the following ballad:[1]

> The moon speaks hard words to the Day-star:
> 'Where have you passed the time, star, o Day-star,
> Where have you passed, where have you lost your time,
> Lost your time for three livelong days?'

---

[1] The reference is to the song 'How the Jakšić brothers shared' (see Appendix A, No. 2).

> The Day-star to the moon makes answer:
> 'Where have I passed, where have I lost my time?
> All over the white town, over Belgrade,
> Where I looked and saw a mighty wonder.'

What a fine thought, that two stars far above the world should talk to each other about the fate of individual men, and out of interest vary their course! The whole moving and morally cautionary tale is then put into the mouth of the star.

Another characteristic feature of these Serbian poems. They introduce the subject-matter in the most vivid way, by putting questions about similar subjects and giving them negative answers, until they introduce the proper one. Unforgettable is the lament of Hasan Aga which has been paraphrased by Goethe[1] and which in the original begins:

> What shines white there on the green mountain?
> Is it snow, or swans that shine there?
> Were it snow, it would long have melted,
> Were it swans, they would long have flown.
> Neither snow is it nor swans shining,
> But the tents of the Lord Hasan Aga.

So lively is the picture that one fairly sees the ranks of the tents in the distance.

There is a similar introduction on p. 215:

> What cries out aloud up in Banjan?
> Is it a fairy, is it a snake in anger?
> No, a fairy would be flying higher,
> And a snake would hide beneath the rock.
> T'is no fairy, t'is no snake in anger,
> T'is the voice of Perović Batriću
> In the hands of Osman Čorović.

Thus from the first line the reader has a most striking picture of the danger which encompasses the hero of the song.

Longer passages, which there is no space to quote here, would show that the tenderness and restraint displayed in these typical words and pictures characterize the contents of the individual songs. Bravery and bold spirit, loyalty, the power over friend and foe of a noble disposition, strange adventures and fortunate wooing—this is their subject-matter. In No. 3 ['How the Jakšić brothers shared'] there is a gripping picture of the value of harmony between brothers. In a fit of passion, one brother has determined to have the other poisoned. His falcon has its wing broken by a magic duck, while he is out hunting; how goes it, my grey

---

[1] See Chapter XII, § 2, and Appendix A, No. 1.

falcon, he cries, without your one wing? The bird replies: Without my one wing, I am as brother without his brother. Struck by these words, the hunter rushes home so impetuously that his horse tumbles at the last bridge and breaks a leg. The falcon and horse that are thus destroyed were significantly the cause of the brothers' quarrel. Readers of the 'Edda' will inevitably be reminded by these words of Erp's touching comparison between the help given by brother to brother and that given to us by hand or foot. So close are the themes of all primitive poetry.

There is a noble portrait in No. 29 of Knez Ivan giving compassion and tears, riches and land to ransom the Serbs from Turkish captivity; blessings on Ivan's soul; none recognized what he had done, neither did any thank him, nor did any praise his deed; yet Ivan wants praise from no one, since Christ the King will reward him, when he comes to the Kingdom of eternal truth.[1]

The Serbian songs provide much-needed and substantial material for the study of epic poetry, which has hitherto been all too one-sided. The second part of Vuk's collection is bound to be of outstanding importance, since it will give us the older songs (the subject-matter of which is more mythical) and is likely to surprise us with many stories hitherto unknown: the first part is reserved for 'women's songs', which could be described as mainly lyrical, and are written in various metres. Even those who in general have no feeling for the simplicity of these compositions, and who are inclined not to rate them so high as we do, can hardly withhold their applause, if they know any of the current Slav languages, from the purity and musical quality of the Serb tongue. The book will reveal to them a wealth of genuine Slav words, forms, and expressions, which have been unknown or forgotten. The Russian can read himself into the language without difficulty, the Ukrainian even more easily, the Czech and Pole will probably find it more difficult. . . .

---

[1] The song to which Grimm here alludes was one of those collected by Vuk from Philip Višnjić, under the title *Knez Ivan Knežević*. Vuk wrote a short sketch of Knez Ivan's life, published in Davidović's *Zabavnik* ('Entertainer'), Vienna, 1820. It ends as follows: 'Till 1813 he lived quite well in the Mačva, but in 1816 I heard that he had moved to the village of Grabovac above Zemun, and had one horse and some hacks, with which he earned bread for himself and his family. Perhaps he is still living there in this way. . . . Thus then has fortune long borne hard on Ivan Knežević, as on many honest and notable men in this world. These last years in the Srem he has been poorer than he ever was in his own district, and God knows how he lives now. But Christ the Lord, when he starts to reward every man according to his deeds, will pay him too for all the good that he did, and reward him for all his troubles in this world; and the Serbian people, so long as it speaks the Serb language, will sing his name and remember him with all honour and thankfulness.'

Germans who wish to study a Slav language can be recommended the Serb above all others, because of its clarity, beauty, and (this can be added as the result of Herr Vuk's labours) because of the charm of its historic literature. The principal aid to reading continues to be Vuk's dictionary. His grammar is written only in Serb; a German translation must be, and we hope soon will be, undertaken.

APPENDIX E

VUK'S INTRODUCTION TO BOOK I OF HIS 'LEIPZIG COLLECTION' OF SERB 'POPULAR SONGS', 1824

[VUK's introduction is the fullest, if not the last, statement of his views on the classification, local origin, composition, circulation, age, subject-matter, number, and metre of Serbian heroic songs. The first part of it was a reprint of Jakob Grimm's review, translated at Appendix D. The following translation of the rest is not complete, but I have indicated in brackets the nature of any substantial passage that is omitted. Some passages have already been quoted in the main text.]

All the songs printed in the first small book at Vienna in 1814 I brought to Vienna in my head (except the one about the noble wife of Hasan Aga, which I said at the time was taken from Fortis's *Journey in Dalmatia*), and there I wrote down all I could remember. Thus certain of them were written down and printed with errors (some resulting from ignorance, some from the desire to correct the language by the general standards of our literary men of the time). These I have now corrected, according to the correct renderings which I have heard from various men and women singers. The six heroic songs from the first collection I have left out altogether for the time being, since up till now I have not happened on any singer who could give me a correct and complete version. [Vuk's note giving examples of incorrect versions is omitted.] Thus too I have for the present omitted the song about the noble wife of Hasan Aga until I could hear it somewhere from a borderman[1] or Dalmatian. The songs which were afterwards printed in the second small book of 1815, and all these subsequent ones, I have noted from the lips of men and women singers.

All our popular songs can be divided into heroic songs, sung to the *gusle*, and women's songs, which are sung not only by women and girls, but also by men, particularly young men, and most often by two people in unison. Women's songs are sung by one or two people simply for the singers' entertainment, but heroic songs are mostly sung to be heard by others; so in the singing of women's songs more regard is paid to the singing than to the song itself, and in the singing of heroic

---

[1] i.e. a *graničar*, or man from the military border district between Croatia and Bosnia.

songs more to the song. Today heroic songs are sung most often and with most interest in Bosnia, Hercegovina, Montenegro, and the southern mountainous parts of Serbia. In these regions even down to to day almost every house has its *gusle* and also particularly every shepherd's hut. It would be hard to find a man who does not play the *gusle*, and a good many women and girls too can do so. In the lower parts of Serbia (near the Sava and the Danube), *gusle* are less often found in the houses, but I still think that one could be found in each village (particularly on the left bank of the Morava). In the Srem, and also in the Bačka and Banat, only blind men today have *gusle* (and even they have to learn to play them—many of them do not sing songs, but simply prayers to a *gusle* accompaniment), while others are much ashamed to hang up a 'blind man's *gusle*' in their houses. [Vuk's note on an honourable exception in Buda is omitted.] So in these districts heroic (or, as they are called there, 'blind men's') songs are sung by no one but blind men, and in the Bačka by occasional women (who sing without the *gusle*). From this it is easy to see why heroic songs are sung worse in the Srem, Bačka, and Banat than in Serbia, and in Serbia worse near the Sava and Danube than further inland, especially in Bosnia and Hercegovina. Again, to the west of the Srem, the further you go through Slavonia to Croatia and Dalmatia, the more generally popular you will find heroic songs to be.

As regards women's songs, I think that today most are to be found in the nearer and lower districts (where there are less of the heroic) and in the towns of Bosnia; for just as in the lower districts people are softer, so in the higher regions even the women (except for those in the towns) are fiercer and think more of heroic deeds than of love. Perhaps too this results from the fact that in the nearer and lower parts, particularly in the Srem, Bačka, and Banat, as in the Bosnian towns, the women and girls lead a more social life. In the towns of the Srem, Bačka, and Banat, indeed, even the women's popular songs are no longer sung, but rather some kind of new ones composed by learned people and students and apprentices.

Certain songs are so much on the border between women's and heroic that it is very hard to decide where to put them. [Vuk's examples are omitted.] Such songs may resemble the heroic rather than the women's type, but it would be hard to hear them sung to the *gusle*, even by women, and because of their length they would hardly be sung like women's songs (i.e. unaccompanied), but rather simply recited.

It is clear that heroic songs are still composed today, and I think therefore that it is not superfluous to say something about their composition. So far as I have been able to find out, heroic songs are sung mainly by people of middle or advanced age. In the districts mentioned, where heroic songs are still most often sung, there will not be anyone who does not know a number of songs (if not completely, at least in part), and there will be some who know more than fifty, perhaps even up to a hundred. Now anyone who knows fifty different songs, if he has any gift for it, will easily be able to compose a new one. Besides this it should be realized that in these regions the peasants have not so many worries or needs as people in Christian countries, but live much as in those times which the poets call the Golden Age. In Tršić there was a man who right up to old age composed many comic songs, of which I know none in full, but will give here some fragments. [Vuk quotes here a number of examples, including that summarized and partially translated in Chapter II, § 3.]

I have only included these examples in order to make it easier to understand how our heroic songs took shape (and still do so). Just as old and young men with a turn for comedy compose comic songs, so others compose historical songs about battles and other important events. It cannot be found out exactly who sang any song for the first time, and this is not really surprising in the case even of the latest (much less of the older) songs, since they are of popular origin. It is surprising however that among the people no one regards the composition of a new song as involving any special skill or renown; not only will no one take credit for it, but everyone denies responsibility (even the true composer) and says that he heard it from someone else. This applies to the latest songs, of which it is known that they cannot have been transmitted but must have taken shape here and now about something which happened only a few days ago; when the subject-matter and the song are only as much as a year old, or the song concerns some far-off happening (even if it only took place yesterday), no one bothers about its origin. Women's songs are not often composed nowadays, except occasionally when the girls sing to the boys and the boys to the girls. . . .

The different versions current of single songs clearly shows that all songs did not immediately (in their first beginnings) take the shape that they have now, but some individual began and composed something as best he could, and then, as it went from mouth to mouth, the song would grow and become finer—or in some cases get shorter and worse; for just as one man will talk better and more clearly than another, so too they will differ in singing or reciting songs. In Book II of this collection two songs are printed about 'the foundling Simeon' . . . and 'how Marko Kraljević recognized his father's sword' . . . and in Book III two about the 'Wedding of Stojan Janković', and similarly a number of songs could be found for almost every subject. Possibly some of these songs about the same subject may have been originally composed in different ways by different people, but in most cases (and especially where the difference is small) various singers have adapted them (a single original) to their own several ways, as still happens today. Thus any reader can realize why certain songs . . . resemble each other, and are different from other songs which also resemble each other. . . .

Although there are enough people who know many songs, it is still hard to find anyone who remembers them well and clearly. In this respect Tešan Podrugović (God rest his soul) was the first and best of all whom I have found and heard these ten years past. . . . He was an excellent player of the *gusle*, but could not or would not sing at all, but recited songs as from a book. For the collector of songs, such people are the best, since they pay particular attention to the order and the sense, while singers (particularly those who are no more than singers) in many cases sing without thinking of the sense, and can only sing one line after another and cannot recite (I have had my troubles with such people).[1]

Heroic songs are circulated mainly by blind men, travellers, and *hajduks*. The blind men go begging from house to house right round the country. In front of every house they sing a song, and then ask for something to be given to them; when something is offered, they will sing more. On holidays they go to the monasteries and churches for the services and sing the whole day long. Again when a traveller arrives at a house for lodging, it is usual to ask him to sing to the *gusle*, so that travellers sing and listen in the evenings. Then the *hajduks* in winter . . . drink and sing to the *gusle* all night, mainly songs about *hajduks*.[2]

When a song is brought from Hercegovina to the lower part of the country where people do not speak the dialect of Hercegovina, they sing in their own dialect,[3] for example 'devojka', 'deva' . . . etc., leaving out the letters 'ij' in many words where they are needful for the scansion, for example 'lijepo' (for 'lepo') . . . etc. The men of Hercegovina would certainly do the same in the case of songs that were brought to them from the low country. Thus it is hard to mark and classify the women's songs[4] by their original dialect; I have simply printed them as I heard and copied each one. The women's songs marked with a 'T', I heard and copied down at Kragujevac from certain Turkish gypsy girls from

---

[1] See Chapter VII, § 2, for another description by Vuk of Tešan Podrugović's excellence in this respect, and Chapter X, § 6, for his description of the difficulties of taking down songs from Starac Milija, who could only sing them.

[2] This passage has already been quoted in Chapter II, § 3.

[3] The dialect of Hercegovina was *ijekavski*, that of 'lower' Serbia (and Eastern Serbia) *ekavski*. See Appendix C.

[4] Vuk omitted a stage of his own argument. The normal lines of the 'women's songs' were much shorter than the trochaic pentameter of the 'heroic songs'. The metre thus often made it impossible to use the *ijekavski* ('lijepo') rather than the *ekavski* form ('lepo').

Sarajevo, just as they are sung there by Serbian women of the Moslem faith.

[A paragraph on the peculiarities of dialect in these particular songs is omitted.]

As regards the age of our songs, I would say that some of the women's songs are older than any of the heroic. Of these latter, few date from before Kosovo and none from before the Nemanja dynasty,[1] while among the women's songs some may be a thousand years old, for example, some of the 'princesses'' and 'rain-makers'' songs. I think that the Serbs had traditional heroic songs before Kosovo, but the changes of that time had such a strong effect on the people that they forgot practically everything before it, and it was only [of events] from that point that they began again to make tales and songs.

[Vuk mentions two pre-Kosovo songs that he had heard in unsatisfactory versions, and a number of songs about the Nemanja dynasty in Kačić's *Agreeable discourse*, which were, in his opinion, clearly later compositions.]

The majority of heroic songs today are from the sixteenth and seventeenth centuries, and concern the heroes and pirates of the coast, who took refuge from Bosnia and Hercegovina in the coastal district under Venetian protection, and from there formed warrior companies, like the *hajduks*, and defended the Venetian borders against the Turks.... Such songs are also sung by Serbs of Moslem faith in Bosnia, but in their versions their own people usually win and enslave or entice Christian women and girls.

If all our heroic songs were collected, there would certainly be five times as many as are collected here, if not more. Only from what I have heard about (and not been able to collect) at least two books could be made as large as this third volume.[2]

[Vuk then describes at some length the song of the wedding of the King of Buda, 'mainly for the sake of my kind reviewer' (Grimm), how he had heard it from two sources at Kragujevac, and the differences—fairly small—between the two versions.]

Perhaps it may be useful to mention here that in the case of certain songs I heard fragments only as a child, and, for all my searching and questioning since then, no one has been able to recite them to me in full—but only the fragments which I knew, and the rest is told as a tale. [Vuk gives an example, quoting verses of a song and interspersing them with prose narrative.]

Of such fragments of various songs one could collect a whole book full.

---

[1] The Nemanja dynasty reigned from 1168 to 1371.
[2] The third volume of the Leipzig collection contained 35 poems, and ran to 396 pages.

APPENDIX E

Of recent songs from the year 1815[1] (and especially about the battles at Požarevac and Dublje) there are many more and much better than the fragments given here at the end of Book III, but so far I have not been able to collect them.

I think it now time to talk about the rules of our popular songs. This is not the place to speak at length about them. I shall only make a beginning and note as shortly as possible what I have found out up to now (with no particular intention and rather by the way) in transcribing and printing the songs. If I have made mistakes, I hope that our poets will freely pardon me and correct them.

All our heroic poems have ten syllables (in a line) or five trochaic feet, with a pause (caesura) after the second foot, for example:

$$- \cup - \cup \quad - \cup - \cup - \cup$$
Podizhe se / Crnojevic Ivo

In fact in many lines normal speech would give a long syllable instead of a short and vice versa, thus:

$$\cup - \cup \cup \quad - - \cup \cup - \cup$$
I ponese / tri tovara blaga
$$\cup - - \cup \quad - \cup \cup - \cup \cup$$
Ja kad tako / svadbu uredise

This is the way the lines would be spoken, and this is how they are read or recited, but when they are sung, all the feet are made into trochees:

$$- \cup - \cup \quad - \cup - \cup \quad - \cup$$
I ponese tri tovara blaga, etc.

[The rest of the introduction is devoted to a detailed analysis of the metres of the women's songs. These are considerably more complicated; I have not attempted to translate any such songs in the text or Appendices of this book, and have therefore omitted Vuk's analysis as of purely specialist interest.]

[1] This sentence of Vuk's was designed to soften the wrath of Miloš Obrenović (see Chapter XI, pp. 180–1).

APPENDIX F

VUK'S WRITINGS ON MONTENEGRO

IN 1834, Vuk published in a German perodical *Ausland* a descriptive article, 'A view of Montenegro', designed primarily to spread Njegoš's fame abroad and to counter the idea (publicized, for example, in Brockhaus's encyclopaedia) that Montenegro was nothing but a brigand area. Here Vuk dwelt on the history of Montenegro's continuous resistance against Turkish attacks and oppression, and on the heroic example thus set to other European countries. He reserved for a later and fuller work his full comments on, for example, the clan system in Montenegro and the primitive conditions at Cetinje.

Vuk's major work on Montenegro was published in 1837, in the German language, *Montenegro und die Montenegriner, ein Beitrag zur Kenntniss der europäischen Türkei und des serbischen Volkes*, J. G. Cotta, Stuttgart and Tübingen. The original Serb text was discovered over a hundred years afterward in the Bogišić library at Caftat (Vuk's daughter, Mina, had sold it among other papers after his death to his friend Baltazar Bogišić), and published in *Izdanje novog pokolenja*, and *Prilozi*, xx, nos. 3–4, Belgrade, 1953 and 1954). See *Kovčežić*, ii, p. 105, article by N. S. Martinović.

Montenegro und die Montenegriner contained a full and frank account of a society even more primitive than that of early nineteenth-century Serbia. The ruder aspects of it were distasteful to Vuk himself, who did not relish the exhibition of the heads of decapitated Turks in Cetinje. His work contains detailed sections on the geography and history of Montenegro, on its relationship with neighbouring countries, on the clans, the various means of livelihood practised, the monasteries and churches and the education of the monks and priests. The last, most detailed, and most important section is devoted to manners and customs, including particularly marriage and funeral customs. Vuk here sets out comparatively systematically the sort of description which is to be found under scattered individual entries in his *Dictionary* (indeed he adapts and repeats a number of such entries).

Montenegro had considerable success in attracting the attention of the Austrian and German public to the affairs of the Principality, in spite or perhaps because of the frankness with which Vuk described its political system. There was at the time of Vuk's visits to Montenegro still no effective central government; total anarchy was tempered mainly by the blood feuds of the clans, which acted as some kind of deterrent to crime. Vuk paid tribute to the efforts of the former and contemporary Prince Bishops to abolish the custom of feuding (he particularly admired Peter Petrović Njegoš's attempt to reconcile the clans), but thought that they could only bear fruit later; in 1837 there were insufficient funds to set up the forces needed to enforce government from the centre. Vuk's description of clan warfare was written in a spirit far removed from that of Njegoš's own heroic vision as expressed in his poems: 'This war between neighbours is conducted exclusively for the sake of killing and looting.... In each company there are normally from ten to twenty men, whose object is to kill one of their enemies or to seize or steal something.'

Some details of Vuk's work proved to be rather strong meat for the more patriotic among literate Montenegrins. In particular the description of the Senate House, with one door for Senators and another for donkeys, aroused some ill feeling. Njegoš himself is said to have been annoyed by this (though any resentment which he felt was certainly not lasting), and one of his suite is reported to have rounded on Vuk: 'No one would have known about the Prince's donkey, and now, for your benefit, the whole of Europe knows. Hadn't you anything better and more sensible to write about than that donkey?'

BIBLIOGRAPHY

1

THE standard life of Vuk Karadžić, *Život i rad Vuka Stefanovića Karadžića* ('Life and work of Vuk Stefanović Karadžić'), is that of Ljubomir Stojanović, published in 1924. It is an extremely long, full, and valuable work, and contains extensive quotations from Vuk's correspondence and other original material. It is however at best not an easy book to use, and it has long been out of print.

A new biography, *Vuk Stefanović Karadžić*, was published (Nolit, Belgrade) in 1964, the centenary year of Vuk's death; this is by Professor Miodrag Popović of Belgrade University. It is full, but not so massive as that of Stojanović; it is intended for a wider public and contains many generalized descriptions of Vuk's environment. References have been deliberately excluded from it. A substantial book on Vuk's relations with the Croats has recently been published—*Vuk i Hrvati* ('Vuk and the Croats') by Viktor Novak, Naučno Delo, Belgrade, 1967—but I have been unable to study this in full.

I do not know of any modern biographies in other European languages.

2

A new edition of Vuk's works is being published by Prosveta, Belgrade, and at the time of writing (spring 1968) three volumes have appeared, the *First* and *Second Song-books* of 1814–15, the *Dictionary* of 1818, and the *Proverbs* of 1836. The complete edition will run to about thirty volumes, and should be definitive; the editors have access to the large collection of Vuk's manuscript remains preserved at the Serbian Academy of Science and Art.

It will be particularly valuable to have a new and full edition of Vuk's correspondence. The seven volumes, published between 1907 and 1913, are out of print. There will also be a new edition of all Vuk's collections of 'popular songs' with his own introductions and notes (see 3 (iii) below). The full edition of Vuk's collections (12 volumes, 1932–6) has for some time been out of print; but there are in the meantime a number of full anthologies of the 'popular songs', and I have found very useful *Antologija Narodnih Pesama* ('Anthology of popular songs'), ed. Vojislav Djurić, Srpska Književna Zadruga, 1965.

3

I have relied much on other anthologies of Vuk's works published in recent years (largely on the centenary of his death), covering various aspects of his work and often overlapping each other. These are more likely to be obtainable by the interested reader, though No. (i) is out of print:

(i) *Selected Historical and Critical Writings and Letters*, 3 vols., with introduction and notes by Djuro Gavela (Director of the Vuk and Dositej Museum, Belgrade). Srpska Književnost, Belgrade, 1962.

(ii) *Vuk Karadžić o Srpskoj narodnoj poeziji* ('Vuk Karadžić on Serbian Popular Poetry'), edited by Borivoje Marinković, Prosveta, Belgrade, 1964. This is a full collection of Vuk's introductions and notes to his various editions of 'popular songs', together with items relevant to the songs from his critical and miscellaneous writings, including his letters.

(iii) *Susreti s Vukom* ('Meetings with Vuk'), edited by Golub Dobrašinović and Borivoje Marinković, Matica Srpska, 1964. A collection of references to and reminiscences about Vuk by those who met him, particularly in his later years.

(iv) *Raskovnik: Proza iz Rečnika* ('The Magic Herb: prose from the Dictionary'), edited by Radomir Konstantinović, Prosveta, Belgrade, 1964. An anthology of anecdotes and descriptive passages from the two editions of Vuk's *Dictionary* and some of his other writings.

(v) *Životi Srpskih Vojvoda* ('Lives of the Serb Leaders'), edited by Golub Dobrašinović, 'Branko Djonović', Belgrade, 1963. A collection of Vuk's short biographies of contemporary heroes, singers, and traditional figures.

(vi) *Vuk Stefanović Karadžić*, selected works, Narodna Knjiga, 1964. A comprehensive one-volume anthology, edited for schools by Golub Dobrašinović, with introduction and a full table of important dates in Vuk's life.

(vii) *Vukovi Zapisi* ('Vuk's Writings'), edited by Vojislav Djurić, Srpska Književna Zadruga, Belgrade, 1964. Another sizeable anthology, including many of the best-known 'popular songs'.

4

A great deal of valuable material on detailed aspects of Vuk's life and work is contained in the annual collection of articles and notes issued by the Vuk and Dositej Museum, Belgrade, under the title *Kovčežić* ('Treasure Chest'). This covers also the life and work of Dositej Obradović. So far (April, 1968) seven volumes have been issued, 1958–66. There are also many valuable contributions on Vuk in the *Prilozi za Književnost, jezik, istoriju i folklor* ('Contributions on literature,

BIBLIOGRAPHY

language, history, and folklore'), published annually in Belgrade. I have mentioned a number of such articles in the notes on this book, under references to *Kovčežić*, or *Prilozi*.

5

On political history, I have made much use of Vladimir Stojančević, *Miloš Obrenović i njegovo doba* ('Miloš Obrenović and His Age'), Prosveta, Belgrade, 1966, which contains a useful bibliography; and, for the history of the Serbian Revolution, 1804–13, of Dr. Miroslav Djordjević, *Politička Istorija Srbije XIX i XX Veka* ('Political History of Serbia in the 19th and 20th Centuries'), I, Prosveta, Belgrade, 1956. For economic history, Danica Milić, *Trgovina Srbije, 1815–1839* ('Serbian Trade, 1815–1839'), Nolit, Belgrade, 1959, is useful.

On the general social background, Georges Castellan's *La Vie quotidienne en Serbie au seuil de l'indépendance, 1815–39*, Hachette, 1967 (in the series *La Vie quotidienne*) is invaluable to those who cannot read Serb (and very useful to those who do—unfortunately I have not been able to profit fully from it). It contains a detailed bibliography and quotes at length from the main French and German travel-books covering Serbia at this period, Ami Boué, *La Turquie d'Europe*, 2 vols., Paris, 1840, and Otto von Pirch, *Reisen in Serbien in Spätherbst 1829*, 2 vols., Berlin, 1830.

For the cultural and literary background of the Serb community in Austria-Hungary, I have found extremely valuable two works of Jovan Skerlić, *Srpska Književnost u XVIII Veku* ('Serbian Literature in the 18th Century'), Belgrade, 1923 (this covers a much wider field than its title indicates), and *Istorija nove srpske Književnosti* ('History of Modern Serbian Literature'), Belgrade, 1914, reprinted 1967.

On the general development of Ottoman rule in Europe, I have consulted particularly Bernard Lewis, *The Emergence of Modern Turkey*, London, 1961; Wayne J. Vučinić, *The Ottoman Empire: its Record and Legacy*, Van Nostrand, New York, 1965; and articles by Wayne S. Vučinić, Stanford Shaw, and Trojan Stojanović in *Slavic Review*, December 1962.

For an Austrian point of view on the period of Vuk's life, I have studied Hugo Hantsch, *Geschichte Oesterreichs, II: 1614–1918*, Verlag Styria, 1962; and Hermann Wendel, *Der Kampf der Südslawen um Freiheit und Einheit*, Frankfurt am Main, 1925. C. A. Macartney's *The Habsburg Empire 1790–1918*, Weidenfeld and Nicolson, 1969, unfortunately appeared only when this book was at the printer.

Among English secondary sources, H. W. V. Temperley's *History of Serbia*, G. Bell, London, 1919, remains invaluable.

Other books consulted on more specific aspects of Vuk's varied activities are listed at appropriate points in the notes to this book, and the titles are not repeated here.

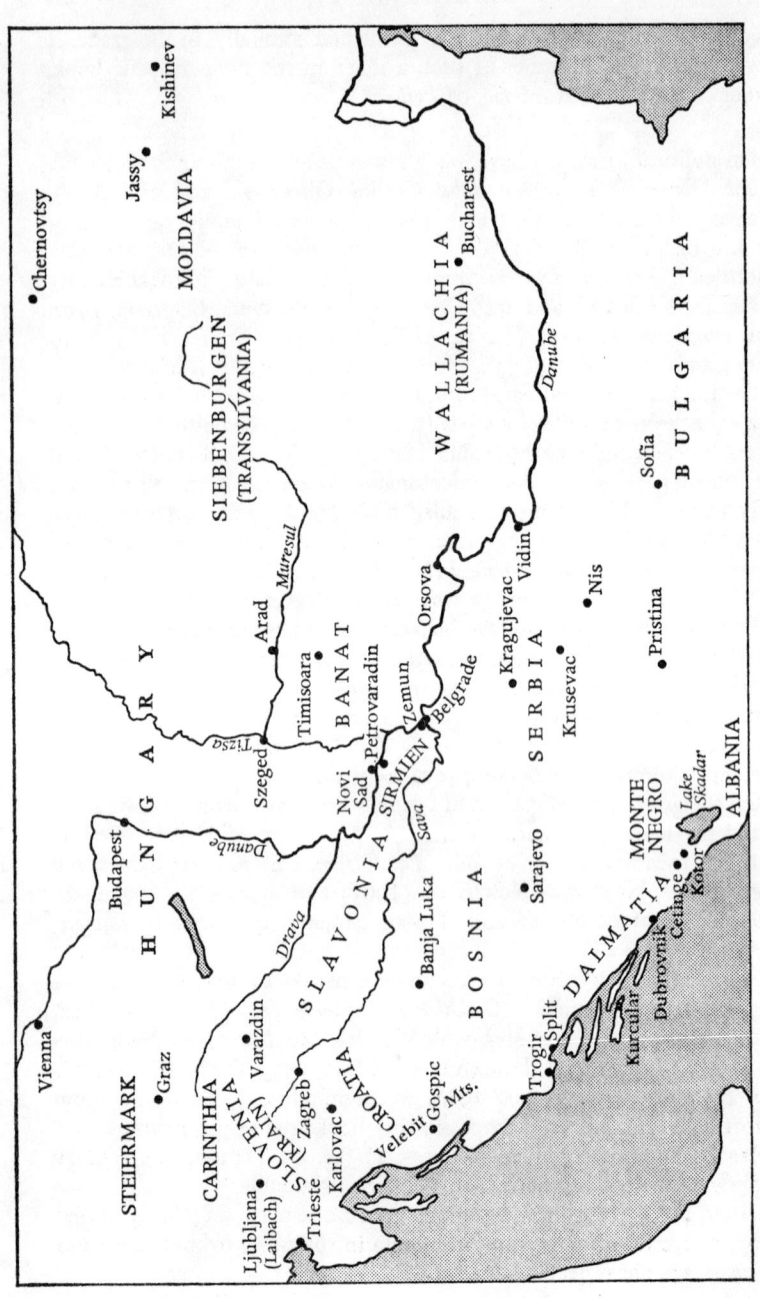

MAP 1. Serbia and adjacent districts or countries

MAP 2. Serbia

INDEX

Abdulina Buna (revolt of Abdula, 1821), 168.
Adelung, F., 85, 99, 104, 117, 136–7, 140–1, 173–4, 182, 208–9, 220, 229.
Agatangelos, Metropolitan of Belgrade, 160.
Akerman, Convention of (1826), 221, 224.
Alexander I, Emperor of Russia, 58–9, 142, 144–5, 176, 179, 218.
Ali Pasha of Janina, 168.
'Amidja' (Paštrmac), 234–6, 243, 264.
Atanacković, P., 302.

Bakunin, M. A., 310.
Barthélémy, Abbé de, *Voyage du jeune Anacharsis en Grèce* (1795), 84.
Beethoven, L. van, 194.
Bell–Lancaster educational system, 157.
Bellegarde, Eugénie-Lucie-Adelaide de, 80.
Bentham, Jeremy, 204.
Bible Society of London, 7, 133, 137–8, 205, 237, 239, 274, 325–6, 329–30, 332.
Bible Society of St. Petersburg, 7, 133–4, 136–8, 141, 143–5, 148–50, 159, 182, 215, 325.
Bodzhansky, O. M., 297.
Bogišić, B., 401.
Bowring, J., 202–7.
Brahms, J., 200.
Branković, Dj., 139.
Brentano, K. von, 196.
Brlić, I., 300.
Bucharest, Treaty of (1812), 71–2, 75, 88, 146, 210, 221.
Byron, Lord, 194, 204.

Čarapić, Dj., 223, 251, 267.
Čarnojević, A., Patriarch of Serbia, 12, 92.
Catherine, Empress of Russia, 176.
Chesterfield, Lord, 52.
Chulkov, M., 191.

Church Slavonic, see under Serbian language.
Code Napoléon, 236, 279.
Čolakovic, F., 222.
Corvinus, Matthias, King of Hungary, 132.
Crnobarac, D., 342.
Čurčija, Dj., 41–3, 239.
Curzon, R., *Monasteries in the Levant*, 22.

Dahijas, 37–8, 40.
Daničič, Dj., 307, 312, 323, 328, 330–1, 337, 342.
Danilo, Prince of Montenegro, 341, 345.
Danilov, K., 147, 191.
Davidović, D., 65, 79, 84, 87, 99, 111, 118, 120, 123, 137, 139, 151, 154, 226, 239, 272, 393.
Demelić family, 166–7, 220.
Denis, Michel, 193.
Derzhavin, G. R., 304.
Diebitsch, Field-Marshal Baron I., 39.
Djakova Buna (students revolt, 1825), see Popović, Miloje.
Djordjević, Marko, 163, 209–10, 237.
Dmitriev, I. I., 140, 142.
Dobrnjac, P., 72, 74–5, 146, 161.
Dobrovski, Abbé J., 81–2, 84, 123, 136, 138, 150–1, 172.
Dolgoruki, Prince D. L., 279.
Draškovic, Count J., 300.

Eckermann, J. P., 199.
Emanuel, General Dj. A., 220.
Erasmus, 272.
Ero's Communion, Serbian popular tale, 124, 380.
Ero from the other world, Serbian popular tale, 165, 380–2.

Fallersleben, H. von, 81.
Fauriel, Claude, 197, 201, 204.
Fénélon, Abbé F., *Télémaque*, 52, 69, 79, 126.

INDEX

Ferdinand I, Emperor of Austria, 190.
Fesl, Abbé, 229.
Fonblanque, T. de G. de, 343.
Fortis, A., *Voyage in Dalmatia* (1774), 192–3, 200, 202, 361, 373, 395.
Franz, Emperor of Austria, 120–1, 176.
Frušić, D., 65, 79, 84–7, 99, 119, 151, 155, 174–5, 182, 216, 273, 276.

Gagović, A., 37.
Gaj, L., 296, 299–301, 308–10, 313.
Garašanin, I., 345–6.
Gavrilović, J., 282.
Gerhard, W., 199, 202.
German, M., 167, 170, 208–12, 220–1, 225.
Goethe, J. W. von, 5, 77, 177–9, 182, 188, 192–3, 195, 200, 361, 364, 366.
Golitsyn, Prince A. N., 144–5.
Golovkin, Count Y., 120, 170, 212, 215.
Grimm, Jakob, 5, 8, 77, 87, 95, 112–13, 139, 165, 170, 177–8, 182, 185–9, 195–200, 207, 213, 217–18, 220, 222, 244, 274, 321, 335, 338, 351, 359, 364, 366, 395.
— Review of *Serbian popular Songs, Book III*, Leipzig, 1823, 185–6, 388–94.
Grujić, Jevrem, 345–6.

Hadji Stoilo, Panta, 237, 240, 253, 268–9.
Hadjić-Svetić, J., 167, 224, 244, 279–82, 291, 303, 305–7, 311, 340.
Hanka, V., 172.
Harte, B., *Dracula*, 22.
Harvey, F., Bishop of Londonderry, 193.
Hasan Pasha, Vizir of Serbia, 37.
Hasanaginica ('Song of the wife of Hasan Aga'), 193–6, 198, 203, 361–3, 392, 395.
Haxthausen, Baron W. von, 196–7.
Haydn, F. J., 194.
Herder, J. G., 2, 65, 78, 85, 90, 95, 193–4, 200.
Herodotus, 84.
Hetaireia, 116, 160–1, 168, 223.
Hildebrand, Lay of, 196.
Hilferding, A., 344.
Hodges, D. J., 279.

Homer, 8, 184, 192, 195.
Hoppe, W., 291.
How the Jaksić brothers shared, Serbian heroic song, 178, 198, 364–6, 391–3.
Hütten, U. von, 129.

Ilić, S., 275.
Illyria, Kingdom of (1815), 80, 200, 299.
Illyrian Court Chancellery, Vienna, 47.
— movement, 7–8, 294–301, 308–9, 313.
— provinces (1809), 80.
Isailović, D., 241, 263.

Jakob, T. A. L. von ('Talvj'), 197–200, 203, 206.
Janissaries, 34–7, 57.
Janković, P., 303.
Jassy, Treaty of (1792), 58.
Jefferson, T., 81.
Jelačić, Baron J., 309–11.
'Jelovkin', *see* Golovkin.
Johnson, S., 52.
Joseph II, Emperor of Austria, 47–8, 52, 102, 176.
Jovanović, A., 292–3.
— S., Archimandrite of Tronoša, 17–18.
Jugović, I., 54–6, 100–1.

Kachenovski, M. I., 140–1.
Kačić-Miošić, A., 90–1, 95, 191, 193, 373, 399.
Kalaidovich, K. F., 140.
Kamenica, Battle of (1809), 71.
Kamenski, General N. M., 67.
Kapper, S., 200, 334–6.
Karadjordje, leader of the Serbian revolt, 2, 4, 28, 38–43, 53–60, 65, 67–76, 79, 86–7, 97, 111, 115–16, 134–5, 143, 146, 156, 160, 167, 182, 197, 199, 209, 211, 225–6, 229, 252, 255, 267, 277, 286–8, 344, 355, 378.
Karadjordjević, Alexander, Prince of Serbia, 229, 285–7, 290, 302, 309, 332, 343, 345.
Karadžić, Anna (*née* Kraus, wife of Vuk), 86, 116, 122–3, 148–9, 154, 163, 175–6, 243, 247–8, 334–8.
— Dimitrije (son of Vuk), 334.

INDEX 411

— Jegda (mother of Vuk), 11, 26.
— Joksim (grandfather of Vuk), 23-4.
— Mina (daughter of Vuk), 334-8, 348-50.
— Obrad (cousin of Vuk), 107.
— Sava (son of Vuk), 163, 334, 338.
— Stefan (father of Vuk), 11-12, 15, 19-20, 43-4, 77, 106.
— Toma (uncle of Vuk), 23-4.
— Vuk Stefanović, survey of life and work, 1-10; early years, education and country background, 11-27; participation in Serb revolt (1804), 40-4; further education at Karlovci (1805-6), 45-6, 53; in Belgrade (1806-8), 53-6, 61; illness at Tršić, 61-2; cure and intellectual stimulus in Buda (1810), 63-6; administrative work in Serbia, service with Hajduk Veljko (1810-13), 66-78; settles in Vienna, meets Kopitar and starts literary career (1813-14), 79, 86-90; introduction to first book of popular songs (1814), 90-7; visit to Buda and work on *Grammar* (1814), 98; views on Serbian language and alphabet, 103-6, 125-6, 151-2; visits Srem and collects popular songs (1815), 106; visit to Serbia (1816), 114-17; work on *Dictionary* (1816-18), 117-26; marriage (1818), 122-3; literary quarrel with Vidaković (1814-18), 126-9; journey to Russia (1819), 131-49; plans translation of New Testament, 132-4, 136-8, 182; relations with Count Rumyantsev, 132, 136-8, 140-1; literary work in Vienna (1819-20), 150-4; in Serbia, at Miloš Obrenović's court (1820-1), 155-63; return to Vienna (1821), difficulties with censorship, and further trip to Miloš's court (1822), 163-71; in Germany (1823-4), 172-89; meetings with Grimm and Goethe, 177-9; correspondence with Miloš about popular songs, etc., 180-2; historical work, including *Life of Miloš*, in Vienna (1824-8), 208-29; visit to Miloš in Serbia (1827), 231-2; collaboration with Ranke on *The Serbian Revolution* (1827-8), 226-9; administrative work in Serbia (1828-31), 230-43; relations with Miloš, 231-6; Chief Magistrate of Belgrade, 240-3; breaks with Miloš (1831-2), 243-53; *Letter to Miloš Obrenović* (a political manifesto, 1832), 253-68; returns to Vienna (1832), 272; meeting with Njegoš and journey to Montenegro (1834), 273-5; receives pension from Miloš (1835), 276-7; controversy with 'constitutionalist' Hadžić (1837-9), 278-80, 286-8; loses pension after Miloš's abdication (1839), 282; support from Obrenović family and travels with Mihail Obrenović (1844), 282-6, 289-90; restoration of Serbian pension (1844), 290-2; connection with 'Illyrian' movement (1834-50), 294-301, 308-13; relations with visiting Russian scholars (1841), 295-7; linguistic debates in Serbia (1842-7), 301-8; editor of popular songs and stories, 314-23; translator of New Testament, 323-4; history and publication of translation of New Testament (1847), 325-30; revision of *Dictionary* (1852), 330-3; family life in Vienna (1845-59), 334-9; foreign awards, 338-9; travels in Serbia (1850-63), 339-42; diplomatic missions for Mihail Obrenović (1860-3), 343-8; return to Vienna and death (1864), 348; estimate of work and character, 349-59.
WORKS:
First *Song-book* (Vienna, 1814), 90-7, 177, 191.
Second *Song-book* (Vienna, 1815), 111.
First *Song-book* (enlarged edition, Leipzig, 1823), 173, 182-3, 186, 317, 395-400.
Second *Song-book* (enlarged edition, Leipzig, 1823), 173, 182-3.
Third *Song-book* (Leipzig, 1823), 164, 173-5, 182, 185-8.
Fourth *Song-book* (Vienna, 1841), 283, 314.
Serbian grammar (1815), 99-101, 105-6, 109, 117, 124, 178, 186-7, 198.
Dictionary (1818), 9, 11, 15, 20-2, 114-30, 135, 139-40, 166, 177-8, 184, 186-7, 216-17, 238, 306, 328, 373, 376, 380, 387.

Karadžić, Vuk Stefanović:
WORKS (*cont.*):
  Dictionary (Second edition, 1852), 330–3.
  Description of Monasteries of Serbia (1821), 162.
  Letter-book (1824), 219, 359.
  Day-star (Calendar, from 1825), 15, 212–15, 219, 229, 231.
  History of Contemporary Serbia (1828), 164, 167, 208–12, 219–26, 229.
  The first year of the war against the Dahijas (1828), 37.
  Lives of the Serbian Marshals (1829), 18, 166.
  Letter to Miloš Obrenović (1832, published 1843), 252–68.
  Proverbs (1836), 109, 275, 289.
  Montenegro and the Montenegrins (1837), 275, 294–5, 401–2.
  Translation of New Testament (1847), 7, 109–10, 132–3, 150–1, 157–60, 182, 215, 237–9, 274–5, 312, 323–30.
  Serbian popular tales (1850), 108–9, 165, 321–3, 378–85.
  Specimens of the Slavonic–Serbian language (1857), 342.
  The Governing Council of Serbia in Karadjordje's time (1859), 146, 344.
  Life and customs of the Serb people (1867), 15, 373.
Karamzin, N. M., 136, 140–3, 156.
Karapandza, S., 69, 108, 116.
Karl VI, Emperor of Austria, 46.
Kerr, L., 340.
Khičanin, S., 331.
Kiselev, General P. D., 279.
Klopstock, F. G., 50, 193.
Knezević, I., 393.
Knjazhević, D., 295.
Kobilić, see Obilić.
Kollar, J., 299, 338.
Kopitar, B. (Jernej), relations with Vuk, 2–4, 10; early life, 79–81; Austro–Slav policy in Vienna, 81–3; relations with Austrian Serbs, 83–5; ideas on 'national language', 85–6; first meeting with Vuk (1813), 86–90; inspired Vuk's Serbian grammar, 98–100, 105–6; literary plans for Vuk, 108–10, 112; work with Vuk on *Dictionary* (1818), 114, 116–18, 124–5, 127, 129, 131; contact with London Bible Society (1819), 133, 134–7, 147–8, 150, 155, 157–8; defends Vuk, as censor, against Orthodox Church (1822), 164–5; 166–7, 170, 172, 174; correspondence with Vuk in Germany (1823), 175–9; defence of Vuk to Vienna police (1824), 183–5, 186–7, 191, 195–7, 204–5, 215, 217; helps to secure Vuk's Russian pension (1826), 218–19, 222, 224–5, 227, 230, 232, 241, 243, 246, 248, 250, 258, 269–70, 272, 274, 286; last years and death (1844), 297–9, 301, 317–18, 329, 332, 341, 344, 349, 351–2, 357–8, 386–7.
Köppen, P. I., 140–1, 149, 218–19, 224.
Koraes, A., 81–2, 98, 217.
Kosovo, battle of (1386), 24, 190, 193, 331, 399.
Kossuth, L., 311.
Kotzebue, A. F. F., 241.
Kraus, Anna, see Karadžić.
Krylov, I., 304.
Kukuljević-Sakcinski, I., 312.
Kumerdej, B., 386.
Kutchuk Kainardji, Treaty of (1774), 58.

Laibach (Ljubljana), Congress of (1821), 161, 164.
Lamartine, A. de, 201.
Leeves, Revd. H. D., 237.
Leontije, Metropolitan of Serbia, 60.
Leopold I, Emperor of Austria, 46.
Leopold II, Emperor of Austria, 34, 47, 118.
Lessing, G., 52.
Lieven, Baron V. K., 290.
Ljubibratić, see Magaraševic.
Loewe, Carl, 200.
Lomonosov, M. V., 304.
Lubomirski, Y. L., 310.
Lucian, 84.
Luther, Martin, 129, 150.

Macpherson, James, 192.
Magaraševic, Dj., 153, 213, 279.
Majevski, V., 135.
Malinovski, A. F., 138, 140.

INDEX

Maria Pavlovna, Grand Duchess of Weimar, 179, 182.
— Theresia, Empress of Austria, 46.
Marko Kraljević, hero of Serbian popular songs, 108, 320, 340, 374–5, 397.
Marmont, Marshal, 83.
Masaryk, T., 172.
Matica Srpska (literary society), 213, 279–80, 302, 329.
Mažuranić, I., 296, 312.
Mehitarists (Armenian monks in Vienna), 118, 215, 274, 326.
Mérimée, P., 8, 201–3.
Metternich, Prince C. von, 10, 164, 166, 168, 185, 245, 247, 270.
Miklošić, F., 312.
Milija, Starac (singer), 168–70, 189, 316, 319, 398.
'Miloje Djak', see under Popović.
Milovanov, L., 65, 70, 273, 280, 386.
Milovanović, M., 56, 74, 99–100, 265–6.
Milutinović, S., 66–7, 69, 199, 223, 273, 280.
Mirecki, F., 200.
Mirko, Vojvoda of Montenegro, 346.
Molar, P., 225.
Montagu, Lady M. Wortley, 35.
Mrazović, A., 100.
Mrkalj, S., 65–6, 70, 85, 104–5, 386–7.
Mula, Pasha of Vidin, 68–71.
Müller, Chancellor F. von, 199.
Murad, Sultan, 190.
Mušicki, Archimandrite L., 50, 84, 90–3, 96, 106, 109–10, 112, 114, 116, 119, 122–3, 125, 128, 132–3, 139, 148–9, 152–4, 213, 215–16, 221, 316, 387.
Mustapha, Pasha of Belgrade, 35–8, 40, 56, 68.

Nadezhdin, N. I., 295–7.
Napoleon I, Emperor of France, 1, 57–9, 71, 80, 83, 105, 144, 200, 244, 266.
Nenadović, J., 40–3, 53, 55, 115, 225.
— M., 19, 38, 310.
Nesselrode, Count K. V., 170–1, 182, 210.
Nestorovic, U., 84.

Nibelungenlied, 295, 299.
Nicolas I, Emperor of Russia, 4, 218, 220, 244, 248, 279, 299, 312, 338.
— Prince of Montenegro, 345.
Njegoš, Petar I, Prince Bishop of Montenegro, 37, 150.
— Petar Petrovic II, Prince Bishop of Montenegro, 273–6, 290, 294, 307, 326, 341, 401–2.
Nodier, C., 200, 203.
Novikov, N., 191.

Obilić, M., hero of Serbian popular songs, 74, 190, 193, 373–4.
Obradović, Dositej, 47, 50–3, 61, 64, 77, 80, 84–5, 88, 102–3, 351.
Obrenović, Christofor (nephew of Miloš), 167, 209, 226.
— Jevrem (brother of Miloš), 255, 278, 280, 282.
— Ljubica (wife of Miloš), 240, 255, 284.
— Mihail (son of Miloš, Prince of Serbia), 5, 282, 284–6, 290, 293, 302, 314, 321, 330, 343–6, 359.
— Milan (elder son of Miloš), 263, 280.
— Miloš, Prince of Serbia, 2, 4–5, 7, 10, 68, 107; early life and leadership of Takovo revolt (1815), 115, 118–19, 146; Vuk at his court (1820–1), 155–61; reaction to Greek revolt (1821), 161–2, 163–6; interest in Vuk's History of Serbia (1822), 167–8; gift of money to Vuk (1823), 169–71, 174, 176; annoyance with Vuk's writings (1824), 180–3, 185, 187–9; attitude to Vuk's historical work (1825–7), 208–12, 219–20; receives rank of hereditary Prince, 221; encourages Vuk's new biography of himself (1827–8), 222–7, 229; motives for employing Vuk (1829–32), 230–1; relations with Vuk as official at Kragujevac (1829–30), 232–8; achieves autonomy for Serbia (1830), 239; relations with Vuk as Chief Magistrate of Belgrade (1830–2), 240–3; urges Vuk to return there (1832), 243–7; break with Vuk, and description of his rule in Vuk's letter to him (1832), 249–71, 273; grants

Obrenović, Miloš (*cont.*):
 pension to Vuk (1836), 276–8; growing opposition, and expulsion from Serbia (1836–9), 278–82; political intrigues from Vienna (1839–43), 282–6, 287–93, 309–10, 316, 329, 340; returns to power and dies (1859–60), 343–4, 350, 356–8, 378, 400.
— Petrija (daughter of Miloš), 167.
Ognev, F. S. (fiancé of Mina Karadžić), 336–8, 340.
Orphelin, Z. S., 84, 102, 212.
Orthodox Church, role among the Austrian Serbs, 46–9.
Ossian, 85, 184, 192–3, 200.

Palacki, F., 338.
Paštrmac, see 'Amidja'.
Pazvan Oglu, of Vidin, 36–7, 57, 68, 168.
Percy, Revd. T., *Reliques of Ancient Poetry*, 192–3, 195, 317, 320.
Peter the Great, Emperor of Russia, 104.
Petrović, V., 342, 347.
Philike Hetaireia, see *Hetaireia*.
Pinkerton, Revd. R., 133, 136, 138.
Plutarch, 84.
Podrugović, T. (singer of heroic songs), 107–8, 315, 319, 321, 374, 398.
Pogodin, M. P., 295–6, 341.
Pope, A., 52.
Popović, Miloje, 264, 267.
— Professor Miodrag, 321, 403.
— Vasa, 169, 180, 182, 233, 238, 243–6, 262, 340.
Popovski, A., 242–3.
Pressburg, Treaty of (1805), 80.
Pushkin, A. S., 8, 135, 143–4, 202–3, 304.

Radičevic, B., 307–9, 337–8, 342.
Radojković, M., 254, 257.
Rajačić, J., Metropolitan of the Srem province, 309, 311, 326–7, 329.
Rajović, T., 235, 241–2, 268–9.
Ranke, H. von, 228.
Ranke, L. von, 5, 9, 77, 205, 227–30, 263, 273–4, 282, 286, 290, 298, 332, 340, 357, 359.
— *The Serbian Revolution*, 5, 13, 43, 227–9, 290.
Rask, Professor R. C., 140.
Razumovski, Count A. K., 120.
Richardson, S., 52.
Rodofinikin, 60.
Rousseau, J. J., 49, 52, 193, 200.
Rumyantsev, Count N. P., 132, 136, 138, 140–1, 146, 148–9, 162, 170, 173–4, 182, 213, 218, 259, 290.

Sacy, S. de, 133.
Šafarik, J. P., 80, 204–5, 217, 241, 263, 304, 325, 328, 338.
Savić, J., 15, 43, 54, 60, 63, 67, 70, 75.
Scott, Sir W., 9, 194.
Sedlnicki, Count J., 164, 245, 247–8, 270.
Selim II, Sultan of Turkey, 35.
— III, Sultan of Turkey, 34–6, 57–8, 71.
Serbia, under Ottoman rule: villages, 13–14; group households (Zadruge), 14–15; monasteries, 16–17; schooling, 18–19; role of Orthodox Church, 20–1; folk-customs, 21–2; oral traditions and poetry, 22–7; land-ownership, 28–30; local government, 31; brigandage (Hajduks), 32–4.
— revolt against the Turks (1804–5), 28–39.
Serbian, language in 18th and early 19th century, 64–6, 81–8, 98–105, 301–8, 386–9.
— popular songs, 23–7, 314–21, 361–73, 390–400; see also under *Hasanaginica*, *How the Jakšić brothers shared*, Karadžić, V. S., Kopitar, Milija, Podrugovic, *The building of Skadar*, and Višnjić.
— popular tales, 22–3, 108–9, 321–3, 378–85.
Serbo-Croat, language 300–1; Vienna Agreement (1850), 312–13; Novi Sad Agreement (1954), 313, 386–9.
Shishkov, Admiral A. S., 136, 140, 143, 145–6, 157, 218–19, 221, 276, 278, 296.
Simić, A., 268–9.
Sistovo, Treaty of (1791), 34.
Slav Congress, Prague (1848), 8, 310–11.

INDEX

Slavonic-Serbian, *see* Serbian, language in 18th century.
Sobolovski, S. A., 202.
Socrates, 55.
Solarić, P., 84, 126.
Solon, 55, 84.
Sreznevski, I. I., 11, 15, 21, 46, 62, 66, 86–8, 100, 114, 287, 297, 301.
Stael, Madame de, 200.
Stanisavljević, Marija ot, 63.
Stanišić, P., 287, 339.
Stejić, J., 233–6, 249–51, 283.
Stojanović, L., 100, 403.
Stojković, A., 131–2, 215, 237, 239, 250, 325, 329.
Stojković, M., 72, 74–5, 161, 262.
Strange, J., 193.
Stratimirovic, S., Metropolitan of Karlovci, 45, 49–50, 77, 83–5, 91, 102–4, 116–18, 121, 125, 129–30, 134, 138, 143, 150–2, 154, 164–5, 180, 184–5, 213, 215, 217, 220, 237–8, 246, 248–50, 274–5, 311, 326, 329.
Strauss, D., 332.
Stroganov, Count G. A., 146.
Strossmayer, Bishop J. J., 331.
Studenica, Monastery of, 16, 232, 236.
Stulić, J., 121.
Suvorov, M. T., 48, 101–2.
Swift, J., 52.
Symonds, J., 193.
Szyrma, K., 303.

Takovo, revolt of (1815), 107, 115, 180.
'Talvj', *see* Jakob, T. A. L., von.
Tatishchev, D. P., 248.
Tekelija, S., 73, 90, 134, 302, 306.
Teodorović, M., 74.
Teodosija, Knez, 39.
The building of Skadar, Serbian heroic song, 188, 198–9, 366–72.
Themistocles, 55.
Thomson, G., 194.
Tilsit, Treaty of (1807), 58.
Tirka, M., 119–20, 137, 166, 216.
Tirka, T., 69, 119, 121–2, 137, 166, 183.
Tirol, D., 175, 183, 196, 214.

Tkalac, I., 298–9, 337–8.
Todorovic, L., 159–60, 168, 211, 234, 237.
Todorović, R., 62.
Toleranz-patent (1781), 47.
Trongśa, Monastery of, 16–19, 23, 26, 29.
Trśic, birthplace of Vuk Karadzić, 11–12, 14, 26–7, 29, 286, 339–40.
Turgenev, A. I., 38, 136, 140, 142–3, 296.

Urošević, M., 246–7.
— S., 267.

Vater, Professor, J. S., 172, 179, 182, 186.
Veljko, Hajduk, 9, 68–9, 72–6, 78, 214, 226, 239, 355.
Vidaković, M., 93, 126–30, 351.
Vienna, Treaty of (1809), 80.
Višnjić, P., 41, 110–11, 393.
Vodnik, B., 83.
Voltaire, F. M. Arouet de, 49.
Vrčević, V., 341.
Vrhovać, Bishop M., 85.
Vučić, P. T., 284–5, 290–1, 307, 343.
Vujica, 74.
Vukomanović, A., husband of Mina Karadžić, 338.
— J., son of above, 338.
Vuković, A., 163.

Watson, –, alleged English historian, 73.
Wellington, Duke of, 73.
Wieland, C. M., 153.
Windischgraetz, Prince A. von, 310.
Wolf, C., 52.
Wolf, F. A., 95, 195.

Ypsilanti, Prince A., 161.
— — C., 36, 74.

Zhukovsky, V. A., 140, 142–3.
Živković, Savka, 69, 77, 79, 87, 90, 110.
— Stefan, 69, 77, 79, 87, 90, 108, 116, 215, 237.
Zois, Baron, 80.

Duncan Wilson, a distinguished classical scholar of Balliol College, Oxford, joined the British Diplomatic Service in 1946. He was twice posted to Yugoslavia. During his first tour (1951-53) he applied himself to learning Serbo-Croatian and absorbing as much of the indigenous history and culture as time permitted. He and his wife travelled widely — they were especially fond of walking in the mountains and visiting the monasteries and historic sites of the country in the company of Yugoslav friends.

Thus when Sir Duncan returned to Belgrade as British Ambassador (1964-1968), he did so as a man well-versed in the language and culture of Yugoslavia. The year 1964 marked the centenary of the death of Vuk Stefanović Karadžić, the pioneering folklorist and linguist who codified the modern Serbo-Croatian language. Sir Duncan immersed himself with enthusiasm in the literature that had been assembled to mark the occasion. Fascinated by the period, and particularly by Vuk himself, Sir Duncan decided that the tale should be retold in English. The resulting book has been widely acclaimed (especially in Yugoslavia) as a brilliant exposition of the emergent Serbia in the first half of the nineteenth century.

On leaving Belgrade, Sir Duncan was appointed British Ambassador to the Soviet Union (1968-71). He then became Master of Corpus Christi College, Cambridge, (1971-1980). He died in 1983. His other publications include *Tito's Yugoslavia* (1979).